Taiwan's Presidential Politics

Published in cooperation with the
East-West Center

TAIWAN IN THE MODERN WORLD

TAIWAN IN THE MODERN WORLD

Taiwan's Presidential Politics

Democratization and Cross-Strait Relations in the Twenty-first Century

Muthiah Alagappa
Editor

AN EAST GATE BOOK

M.E.Sharpe
Armonk, New York
London, England

An East Gate Book

Copyright © 2001 by East-West Center

Library of Congress Cataloging-in-Publication Data

Taiwan's presidential politics : democratization and cross-strait relations in the twenty-first
century / edited by Muthiah Alagappa.
    p. cm.— (Taiwan in the modern world)
Includes bibliographical references.
ISBN 0-7656-0833-2 (alk. paper); ISBN 0-7656-0834-0 (pbk.)
    1. Elections—Taiwan. 2. Democratization—Taiwan. 3. Taiwan—Politics and
government—1988- 4. Taiwan—Foreign relations—China. 5. China—Foreign
relations—Taiwan. I. Alagappa, Muthiah. II. Series.

JQ1538 .T355 2001
320.95124'9—dc21   2001049155

Printed in the United States of America

BM (c) 10 9 8 7 6 5 4 3 2 1
BM (p) 10 9 8 7 6 5 4 3 2 1

In memory of Michel Oksenberg,
good friend and colleague
who will be deeply missed

Contents

List of Tables and Figures

Tables

Figures

Preface

Much international attention was focused on the 18 March 2000 presidential election in Taiwan. A presidential election in another country the size of Taiwan would have barely registered on the radar screen of major powers like the United States, the People's Republic of China (PRC), and Japan. Taiwan is no ordinary country, however, and Chen Shui-bian, who won the election, was not a run-of-the-mill candidate. The election was perceived to have far-reaching consequences, not only for the future of democracy in Taiwan and more broadly in Asia, but for war and peace among the major powers.

A Japanese colony from 1895 to 1945, Taiwan was a frontline state during the Cold War as the Kuomintang (Nationalist) Party and Chinese Communist Party engaged in a conflict over who had the title to rule all of China. Now the identity, status, and relationship of Taiwan to the People's Republic of China are the subject of a bitter dispute between Taipei and Beijing. The Taiwan Strait conflict is perhaps the most acute contest in the Asia-Pacific region and indeed has the potential to embroil the PRC, the United States, and Japan in a major war. The nature, intensity, and prospects for settlement of the cross-strait conflict have been dramatically affected by the Taiwanization and democratization processes that have been under way for more than a decade. In addition to bringing about a change in the system of government, these two processes have nurtured ideas about Taiwan's identity and status that are unacceptable to the PRC.

The 2000 election came in the wake of a dramatic downturn in cross-strait relations precipitated by Taiwan President Lee Teng-hui's characterization of the Taiwan-PRC relationship as a "special state-to-state relationship" and Beijing's perception of the "two-state theory" as a violation of the "one China" principle. Viewing the election as a crucial test and opportunity to curtail the Taiwan independence movement, Beijing made a determined effort to prevent the election of Chen Shui-bian, the candidate of the pro-independence Democratic Progressive Party (DPP). Chen is a native Taiwanese and a longtime proponent of Taiwan's independence. The entire PRC political and military leadership went on the offensive, declaring that "a vote for Chen is a vote for war." They cautioned the Taiwanese people to choose wisely. The election attracted a good deal of attention in the United States, as well, because of Washington's commitment to Taiwan's security and concerns that the United States could be drawn into a cross-strait war. Because of its implications for peace and security in the Taiwan Strait and more broadly in the Asia-Pacific region, the election attracted the attention of Taiwan's neighbors as well.

While international attention turned on the implications for war and peace, domestic interest in the election centered on the concern to eliminate "black and gold" politics (money and mafia), deepen political reform, and consolidate democracy. Despite the impressive gains made since the lifting of martial law in 1987, the Kuomintang's (KMT) continued political domination was viewed as limiting the legitimacy of the new democratic political order and stifling further democratic development. The public was profoundly disenchanted with the transplantation of the authoritarian practices and political mobilization based on money politics and organized crime of the previous regime into the new democratic order. Hence, the 2000 presidential election was viewed as a historic opportunity to strengthen political reform, deepen democracy, and vest the new political order with broad-based legitimacy.

Democracy in Taiwan was also a focus of international attention. The ideals of democracy and human rights assumed greater significance in the post–Cold War foreign policy of the United States and the international community. The West viewed the 2000 election as a key indicator of democratization in Taiwan and indeed democracy in Asia. Democratization in Taiwan runs counter to the claim that democracy is incompatible with Chinese-Confucian values. If democracy succeeds in Taiwan, then it is presumed it will set an example for other Asian societies as well.

Thus, the March 2000 election was far from a routine election. Diverse goals and expectations—both domestic and international—were associated with it. The election's outcome could be consequential for the political future of Taiwan, for the future of democracy in Taiwan and Asia, and for war and peace among the major powers. This study investigates the domestic and international implications of two key outcomes of the election: the victory of Chen and the defeat of the KMT. Together these two outcomes signify the crossing of important thresholds both in the democratization of Taiwan and in the transformation of the cross-strait conflict. With respect to democratization, Chen's election is the first alternation of power in the highest political office in the land. Moreover, it is the culmination of the Taiwanization process that had been under way for more than a decade and brings to power a new generation of political leaders in Taiwan who have no connection to the Chinese civil war. The defeat of the KMT candidate and the election of Chen also engender greater confidence in the democratic competition for power and invests the postauthoritarian system with greater legitimacy. It becomes increasingly unthinkable that state power in Taiwan can be acquired by other than democratic means. With respect to cross-strait relations, Chen's election and his future "one China" policy further advance the transformation of the conflict that began in 1991. The dispute is no longer over who is the rightful ruler of China; today, it is over Taiwan's identity and status and its proper relationship with the PRC. Although independence was not the burning question in the campaign (and Chen soft-pedaled the issue to broaden his electoral base), the election of the only candidate not committed to eventual unification with the PRC indicates the distance that has been traveled on this matter in the last decade. While there is no overwhelming support for independence (or for unification), it has become more legitimate as an option. The key point is this: From the perspective of Taipei, the conflict is no longer rooted in the civil war and unification with the mainland is not a given. It is simply an option that can be negotiated taking into account the altered interests and self-image of the people on Taiwan. The transformation of the dispute makes conflict settlement even more difficult and perpetuates the impasse in cross-strait dialogue.

While the election of Chen is a major development, the causes underlying his election, the nature of his victory, and the challenge of governance he confronts limit the consequences for democratization and for cross-strait relations. Chen is a minority president; his party does not control the legislature. Unless he develops a working relationship with the KMT-dominated Legislative Yuan, political reform and deepening of democracy are not likely to make much headway. With respect to cross-strait relations, Chen does not have a mandate to act in a decisive manner. His ability to act has been further constrained by the opposition alliance against him and Beijing's refusal to deal with him.

The twenty-four scholars from Taiwan, the PRC, the United States, and Southeast Asia participating in this study met in a stimulating and productive workshop in Honolulu on 20–22 August 2000. The papers prepared by the contributors were rigorously reviewed in the workshop and then revised for this volume. I would like to thank all the authors for their contributions. Moreover, I would like to thank Richard Halloran, Harry Harding, Hidenori Ijiri, James Kelly, Denny Roy, Xu Shiquan, Godwin Chu, Kimie Hara, Charles Morrison, Marcus Noland, and Kate Zhou Xiao for their contributions in the workshop. All these scholars gave generously of their time and expertise. I would also like to acknowledge Yoshihide Soeya, Benjamin Self, and Sheila Smith for their assistance in reviewing the Japan chapter. Godwin Chu was a good collaborator.

The project was enormously rewarding. It enabled me to develop a much deeper understanding of a crucial issue in Asia-Pacific security, the political changes under way in Taiwan, and their significance for regional security and democratic development in Asia. The project also connected me to a new circle of scholars. I hope the reader will find the book useful and as stimulating to read as it has been for us to write.

Many people have helped in this undertaking. June Kuramoto ably organized the workshop, Ralph Carvalho handled the fiscal matters associated with the project, Yoshihisa Amae provided invaluable research assistance, Phyllis Tabusa assisted with the references, Lillian Shimoda provided efficient secretarial support and helped prepare the report on the project, and Don Yoder copyedited the penultimate draft of the manuscript. Special thanks are due to Ann Takayesu for word processing the entire manuscript and preparing it for publication.

Finally, I would like to express my deepest appreciation for my wife Kalyani. Her forbearance and support have been crucial in completing this book along with two others.

Muthiah Alagappa
1 May 2001

Taiwan's Presidential Politics

Introduction: Presidential Election, Democratization, and Cross-Strait Relations

Muthiah Alagappa

The people of Taiwan have completed a historic alternation of political parties in power. [The] first . . . in the history of the ROC, [it is] an epochal landmark for Chinese communities around the world. Taiwan has set a new model for the Asian experience of democracy. . . . Taiwan stands up . . . representing the self-confidence of the people and the dignity of the country, [and] symbolizing the quest for hope and the realization of dreams.
—ROC President Chen Shui-bian

Let me advise all these people in Taiwan. Do not just act on impulse at this juncture, which will decide the future course that China and Taiwan will follow. Otherwise . . . you will regret it very much and it will be too late to repent. The Chinese people are ready to shed blood to prevent Taiwan from breaking away. Whoever stands for one China will get our support.
—PRC Premier Zhu Rongji

This election clearly demonstrates the strength and vitality of Taiwan's democracy. . . . I believe the election provides a fresh opportunity for both sides to reach out and resolve their differences peacefully through dialogue. We will continue to conduct close unofficial ties with the people on Taiwan in accordance with the Taiwan Relations Act and our "one China" policy as embodied in the three communiqués with the People's Republic of China.
—U.S. President William Jefferson Clinton

In a dramatic development, Chen Shui-bian, the candidate of the opposition Democratic Progressive Party (DPP) and a longtime advocate of Taiwan's independence, emerged victorious in the presidential election on 18 March 2000. Characterized by observers as historic, a watershed, a peaceful revolution, and so forth, the election's outcome was remarkable for a number of reasons. It was only the second time in Chinese history that a president has been directly elected by the people. The first was in 1996 when Lee Teng-hui was elected president of the Republic of China (ROC). Even more significant, it was the first time in Chinese history that power at the highest level was transferred to an opposition candidate peacefully in a democratic fashion. The peaceful succession to the presidency by an opposition candidate is all the more remarkable in light of the fact that Chen only secured a plurality, 39.3 percent of the votes cast. James Soong, who ran as an independent candidate, came in a close second with 36.8 percent of the total votes. Despite the very close vote, James Soong conceded quickly and gracefully. There was no serious contestation of the election; and the military, which has been socialized to reject Taiwan independence and whose loyalty to a DPP-led government was in doubt, quickly affirmed allegiance to the president-elect and his government.[1]

Equally significant was the sound defeat suffered by Lien Chan, the candidate of the Kuomintang (KMT [Nationalist]) party. Despite the KMT's enormous financial resources and vast political machine, Lien Chan secured only 23 percent of the votes cast—16 points behind Chen. The wide margin of his defeat created great disarray within the KMT and raised concerns about the future of the party that had dominated Taiwan since 1949.[2] It also brought to an abrupt conclusion the era of the highly popular Lee Teng-hui, the first elected ROC president, and signaled the end of strongman rule.

Chen's victory, moreover, came in the wake of a series of threats from a PRC leadership that warned, implicitly and explicitly, that "a vote for Chen is a vote for war." Deeply upset with Lee's "splittist" policy, especially the "two-states formula" he advanced in July 1999, and concerned that a Chen victory would further strengthen the Taiwan independence movement, undermine the "one China" principle, and make unification even more difficult, the entire PRC leadership—Vice-Premier Qian Qichen, Premier Zhu Rongji, and President Jiang Zemin—warned that Beijing would not tolerate any move toward independence and cautioned the Taiwanese people to choose wisely. The PRC's white paper "The One China Principle and the Taiwan Issue" issued on 21 February 2000 added a new condition warning Taipei that indefinite delay in negotiations on unification would constitute grounds for Beijing to use force. The PRC military leadership was even more vociferous in trying to influence the outcome of Taiwan's presidential election.

While the concern to maintain stable cross-strait relations affected the positions of the presidential candidates, the PRC's effort to influence the outcome of the election did not have the desired effect. Indeed, it may have increased electoral support for Chen and James Soong. Moreover, while the cross-strait relationship was an important issue, it ceased to be a contentious topic among the three leading candidates by late 1999 when the campaign got under way in earnest. By this time the positions of all three leading candidates on cross-strait relations had converged, each trying to appear more moderate and flexible than the incumbent president. (See chapter 5.) Chen, however, was still the only candidate not formally committed to eventual unification with the mainland. The central issue in the election contest was political reform—especially the elimination of politics "black and gold" (mafia and money). Other domestic issues like constitutional reform, augmentation of the power of local government, protection of human rights, and strengthening the integrity of the judicial system were also important. In general, issues associated with political reform and deepening democracy were more crucial in deciding the outcome of the election. (See chapters 1 and 2.)

Many in and out of Taiwan viewed the 2000 presidential election as a crucial indicator of the ongoing consolidation of democracy in that country —a process that began with the formation of the opposition DPP in 1986 and the lifting of martial law in 1987. As democratic transition in Taiwan was an early manifestation of the spread of the third wave of democracy to Asia, its success was also deemed to have consequences for democratic development elsewhere in Asia, especially in Chinese-Confucian societies including the PRC. Indeed the fate of the KMT might suggest the future of the remaining one-party-dominant democracies in Asia. And given the prominence of democracy and human rights in American foreign policy and Washington's crucial role in the cross-strait conflict, the outcome of the 2000 election is of consequence not only for U.S.-Asia policy but for peace and security in the Asia-Pacific region.

Purpose and Themes

The significance of the 2000 presidential election, therefore, goes well beyond deciding the president of Taiwan for the next four years. As a key step in the Taiwanization and democratization process under way in Taiwan, the election and its outcome have far-reaching consequences for a wide range of domestic and international issues and players. The two key outcomes of the election, as noted, were the victory of the pro-independence opposition candidate and the defeat of the candidate of the KMT party, which had monopolized political power for five decades. This study investigates the consequences of these two outcomes for democratic development in Taiwan, for political change in the PRC, for political change in the one-party-dominant, quasi-democratic regimes in Southeast Asia, for cross-strait relations, and for American and Japanese policy.

Our central conclusion is that Chen's victory and the KMT's defeat mark the crossing of important thresholds both in Taiwan's democratization and in the transformation of the cross-strait conflict. With respect to democratization, victory by an opposition candidate in the competition for the highest political office in the land is a key development in the alternation of power at the national level. Chen's election is also the culmination of the Taiwanization process that had been under way for more than a decade and brings to power a new generation of political leaders in Taiwan who have no connection to the Chinese civil war.[3] The defeat of the KMT candidate and the election of Chen also engender greater confidence in the democratic competition for power and invest the postauthoritarian system with greater legitimacy. It becomes increasingly unthinkable that state power in Taiwan can be acquired by other than democratic means. With respect to cross-strait relations, Chen's victory, his native Taiwanese origin, and his future "one China" policy further solidify the transformation of the conflict that has been in progress since 1991. No longer is the dispute over the system of government and the rightful ruler of China; today it is primarily over the identity and status of Taiwan and its proper relationship with the PRC. Although independence was not the crux of the campaign (and Chen soft-pedaled the issue to broaden his electoral support), the election of the only candidate not committed to eventual unification with the PRC is indicative of the distance that has been traveled on this matter in the last decade. While there is no overwhelming support for independence (or for unification), it has become more legitimate as an option.[4] From the perspective of Taipei, the conflict is no longer rooted in the civil war and unification with the mainland is not a given. It is simply an option that can be negotiated. The transformation of the dispute makes conflict settlement even more difficult and perpetuates the impasse in cross-strait dialogue. Although Chen's election is an important development, the causes underlying his election, the nature of his victory, and the challenge of governance he confronts limit the consequences of his victory for democratization and for cross-strait relations. Chen is a minority president and his party does not control the legislature. Unless he develops a working relationship with the KMT-dominated Legislative Yuan, political reform and deepening of democracy are not likely to make much headway. On the issue of cross-strait relations, Chen does not have a mandate to act decisively. His power has been further constrained by the opposition alliance against him and Beijing's refusal to deal with him.

Although Chen's election is important in its own right, its significance can be better appreciated in the context of the broad political and economic processes at work in Taiwan—the approach taken here. This study advances seven themes: First, Chen's victory is historic, but its significance is limited by the fact that he won only by a plurality and the KMT continues to dominate the Legislative Yuan. Both these considerations constrain Chen's mandate and his ability to govern effectively. Contrary to the claims of Chen, the DPP, and many observers, Chen's victory constitutes only a partial alternation of power at the national level. A full alternation hinges on the DPP's ability to emerge as the majority party in the Legislative Yuan election scheduled for December 2001. Second, Chen's victory is another milestone in Taiwan's democratic development. Yet his limited mandate and the challenge of governance confronting him may constrain further democratic reform in the short term. Although democratic development in Taiwan has made impressive gains, in several ways it still cannot be considered consolidated. Third, the KMT's defeat can be viewed as part of a worldwide trend toward the gradual demise of the one-party-dominant political system. Political change in the PRC may not replicate that in Taiwan, but the KMT experience is relevant and offers several key lessons for the Chinese Communist Party (CCP) in managing political change. Similarly, the KMT experience suggests that continuation of one-party-dominant, quasi-democratic regimes in Singapore and Malaysia cannot be taken for granted. Although the People's Action Party's (PAP's) lock on political power in Singapore remains unchallenged, the dominant position of the United Malays National Organization (UMNO)-led Barisan Nasional in Malaysia has been substantially undermined. The continuation of one-party-dominant regimes in both these countries hinges on the satisfaction of stringent conditions that are difficult to satisfy indefinitely.

Fourth, Chen's election is a further step in the process of redefining the conflict between Taiwan and the PRC. Reflective of the different dynamics at work in Taiwan and the PRC, the election's outcome further increases the complexity of cross-strait relations, making resumption of the suspended cross-strait talks and a final settlement even more difficult. Fifth, the conflict is unlikely to be settled until the conflicting parties, particularly the PRC, come to terms with the transformed nature of the conflict and address the central identity questions that now inform the dispute (or until the PRC develops the military capability and political will to impose a settlement by force). An expansion of mutually beneficial cross-strait social and economic interactions may temper friction and improve the bilateral climate, but such interactions on their own are unlikely to resolve the political identity and status questions.

Sixth, the dynamics of Washington's interaction with Taipei and Beijing has been altered substantially by democratization in Taiwan, economic liberalization in the PRC, and the termination of the Cold War. Yet the fundamental goals of American policy remain intact. Although it is likely to continue to be a source of frustration to Beijing, to Taipei, and to some in the U.S. policy community, the policy of deterring the forceful absorption of Taiwan by the PRC as well as preventing Taiwan's independence still appears relatively sound. The zero-sum situation between Beijing and Taipei, however, makes the continuation of this policy particularly difficult. The policy could fail if either party steps beyond the current bounds. Washington might then be confronted with an even more undesirable situation. American interest is best served by fostering more amicable relations between Beijing and Taipei without appearing to confer unilateral advantage on either party. And seventh, the changing dynamics of the cross-strait conflict and the changing calculus of Japan's national security are straining the system that has governed Tokyo's Taiwan policy since 1972. Similarly, political changes in both countries and the departure of Lee Teng-hui have eroded the basis for the Japan–Taiwan bilateral relationship. A new basis for Tokyo's Taiwan policy and the bilateral relationship may be in the early stage of construction. These themes are elaborated in the following pages. We begin with a discussion of Chen's victory and its significance in the context of Taiwan's political system.

Chen's Victory: Historic but Limited Mandate

To ascertain the significance of the election's outcome, we must be clear on what was (and what was not) at stake in the election, the powers vested in the office of the presidency, and how that office relates to the other key institutions in the exercise of state power. The March 2000 election was for the office of the president only. The Legislative Yuan election is not due until December 2001. The four-year term of the 315 elected delegates to the National Assembly was due to expire on 20 May 2000, and the election for these positions should have been held concurrent with or soon after the presidential election. A series of constitutional amendments engineered by the KMT and the DPP (based on short-term political calculations) and passed in November 1999 by the KMT-dominated National Assembly, however, extended the term of the assembly's elected members by two years. The amendments also instituted a new system of proportional assignment of assembly seats to political parties, an arrangement that was to begin in June 2002. Because of the public uproar that ensued, the Council of Grand Justices (CGJ) was requested by the Legislative Yuan to rule on the legality of these controversial amendments.

In March 2000, barely a week after the presidential election, the CGJ ruled the constitutional amendments invalid—they breached fundamental principles of the Constitution—and instructed the elected members of the National Assembly to step down when their current terms expired. This ruling resulted in another constitutional amendment in April 2000 that curbs the power of the National Assembly. Although the assembly still has the power to vote on impeachment of the president and vice-president, on constitutional amendments, and on national boundary changes, the power of initiative on these issues was transferred to the Legislative Yuan. Further, the assembly ceases to be a standing body. It will convene only when a specific initiative on the issues under its purview is proposed by the Legislative Yuan. The amendment also freezes popular election to the National Assembly. Assembly seats in the future will be proportionally assigned to political parties. Thus the National Assembly has been downgraded to a "contingent deliberative body" that can convene only on the initiative of the Legislative Yuan.

This transformation leaves the office of the president and the Legislative Yuan as the two key institutions in the exercise of state political power at the national level. Popularly elected since 1996, the president is the head of state, represents the ROC in foreign relations, and commands the armed forces. The president has the power to conclude treaties, declare war and make peace, declare and revoke martial law (subject to confirmation by the Legislative Yuan), appoint and remove civil and military officials in accordance with the law, appoint the president and vice-president of the Judicial Yuan (with the consent of the Control Yuan), appoint and dismiss the premier (although it is not clear whether the president can dismiss the cabinet without the premier's concurrence), and establish a national security council with subsidiary organs as stipulated by law. The Legislative Yuan, comprising elected members who serve for a three-year term, is the highest legislative organ of the state. It has the power to decide on statutory and budgetary measures, on bills regarding martial law, declaration of war, conclusion of peace, and international treaties, and other important affairs of state.

The semipresidential political system in Taiwan resembles the French Fifth Republic in a number of ways, but without its comparable provisions for cohabitation and breaking deadlocks in the event of divided government. (See chapter 2.) Where such provisions do exist, often they entail the dismissal or resignation of a person or dissolution of an institution—making for intrigue, unpredictability, and tension between the president and the Legislative Yuan. The president, for example, can independently appoint the premier and his cabinet. Although such appointments do not require confirmation by the Legislative Yuan, the legislature can initiate a no-confidence motion if more than one-third of its total members desire. If more than half the total members vote for the no-confidence motion in an open ballot that must be taken within seventy-two hours of its initiation, the premier must resign. In response to the no-confidence motion, the president, on the recommendation of the premier, can dissolve the Legislative Yuan and call for a new election. Another point of tension issues from the lack of clarity over who has the power of initiative and which institution has priority in dealing with key matters like national security and cross-strait relations. Moreover, the Legislative Yuan has its own agenda. In the absence of assigned priority and executive veto power, the president and premier have no means to steer the legislative agenda or check the assertiveness of the Legislative Yuan. The executive/legislature relationship is further complicated by the manner in which differences over policies and bills are to be resolved—an arrangement that can result in frequent showdowns. If the Legislative Yuan does not concur with an important policy of the Executive Yuan, it may ask it to alter the policy. The premier, in turn, may ask the Legislative Yuan to reconsider its request. If two-thirds of the Legislative Yuan members present at the meeting uphold the original resolution, the premier is required to abide by the resolution or resign. The same procedure applies in the case of differences over bills passed by the Legislative Yuan.

A further point of potential tension and unpredictability in the executive/ legislature relationship—especially in the event of divided and fractious government—relates to the Legislative Yuan's power to initiate a recall or impeach the president and vice-president. A recall may be initiated upon the proposal of one-fourth and passed by two-thirds of the total members of the Legislative Yuan. The recall itself, however, hinges on public approval in a national referendum. More than half of the electorate must participate in the referendum, and of those participating more than 50 percent must support the recall. The Constitution does not specify the grounds for the initiation of a recall. Impeachment can be initiated on a proposal by more than one-half and passed by more than two-thirds of the total members of the Legislative Yuan, whereupon it is submitted to the National Assembly for consideration. Under this system, an assertive legislature dominated by an opposition party can significantly erode the power and effectiveness of a president, reducing him to a nominal head of state.

Although there were confrontational episodes, the tensions in Taiwan's political system did not come to a head during the Lee Teng-hui era because the KMT controlled all three institutions—the presidency, the Legislative Yuan, and the National Assembly. Moreover, Lee started off as a weak president but over the years—especially after his spectacular 1996 victory in the first popular election for the office—came to command enormous power and moral authority. Through deft maneuvering and deployment of this authority as well as the enormous financial resources and vast political machine commanded by the KMT, he could engineer coalitions to override opposition to his policies. Lee presided over a one-party-dominant democratizing country. In several respects his rule was a continuation of the strongman rule of Chiang Kai-shek and his son Chiang Ching-kuo.

Even if the KMT candidate had won the March 2000 election, this situation could not have continued. Lien Chan lacks Lee's charisma and popularity, and the KMT has been losing electoral support for well over a decade. The situation would be even worse if an opposition candidate won the election, for he would be confronted with a Legislative Yuan and National Assembly still dominated by the KMT. This is what transpired with the election of Chen. In July 2000, the DPP had only 66 seats in the 220-member Legislative Yuan, while the KMT had 114 and James Soong's People First Party had 17. The opposition-dominated Legislative Yuan has in fact severely limited Chen's power to govern. Beijing's "divide and rule" strategy and the willingness of Taiwan's opposition leaders to play along with that strategy has further isolated Chen and in some ways marginalized the presidency. The situation is made worse by the fact that Chen won only a plurality of the votes cast. As Larry Diamond observes in chapter 1, Chen's victory was due in large part to extraneous factors: the moral exhaustion of the KMT and the public disenchantment with that party; the splits within the KMT leading to the independent candidacy of the hugely popular grassroots politician James Soong; the last-minute revelation of the financial scandal affecting James Soong, which also hurt the KMT; Lee Teng-hui's determination to block James Soong; and Lee's ambivalent attitude toward Lien Chan. Collectively these factors created essentially a three-way contest that was advantageous to Chen and the DPP. It is unlikely that Chen would have won in a two-way contest.

The net effect of such considerations is that Chen's power is limited. He started his presidency from a very weak position that has been further sapped by the fact that the DPP, already a minority party in the Legislative Yuan, is internally divided—with Chen's own faction in a minority. Perhaps Chen, like Lee before him, may in time enhance his power and authority. Much will depend on his ability to forge a working relationship with the opposition parties to govern effectively and, in the long term, on the DPP's ability to emerge as the majority party in the Legislative Yuan. For the present, however, the significance of Chen's victory is limited both in terms of political power at the national level and in the mandate to govern. In a democratic setting, especially under the amended ROC constitution, the presidency is not necessarily the most powerful institution. A powerful opposition in control of the Legislative Yuan can substantially curtail a president's power and effectiveness. Thus, for a meaningful alternation of power at the top, it is not sufficient to win the presidency alone. A party must control both the presidency and the Legislative Yuan.

Democratization: Crossing a Threshold

Despite the limitations just noted, the election of Chen is a major step forward in the evolution of democracy in Taiwan. Since the lifting of martial law in 1987, Taiwan has witnessed several fundamental developments relating to political participation, protection of individual rights, freedom of association, freedom of the press, development of civil society, development of political society, institution of competitive politics for the acquisition of state power, accountability of elected and appointed officials in the exercise of state power, and redistribution of power in favor of democratically constituted institutions.

Democratic Development and Limitations

Political participation has been closely linked to the indigenization of Taiwan's politics. Since 1945, political power in Taiwan had been controlled by the mainlander Nationalists (KMT) who fled to Taiwan in 1949 upon their defeat by the communists in the Chinese civil war. The native Taiwanese, whose loyalty was considered suspect by mainlanders, were effectively excluded from positions of state power at the provincial and national levels. In turn, the Taiwanese viewed mainlander rule as a foreign imposition akin to colonial domination. This situation altered fundamentally with the onset of democratization and the restoration in 1987 of the constitutional rights of citizens that were initially suspended as an exigent measure to counter the threat of invasion from the mainland. Taiwanese political participation—already on the rise in the 1970s and 1980s at the local level and in the form of illegal opposition to the KMT at the national level through the *tangwai*—increased dramatically after the lifting of martial law.[5] Not only did the DPP grow as a native Taiwanese political party, but the KMT's composition and native Taiwanese participation in its power structure also underwent a dramatic transformation. The indigenization of the KMT was given a big boost with Chiang Ching-kuo's appointment of Lee Teng-hui, a native Taiwanese, as vice-president in 1984 and Lee's succession to the presidency in 1988. Under Lee, the KMT's Taiwanization accelerated. The percentage of native Taiwanese in the KMT's Central Standing Committee rose from under 20 percent in 1976 to about 60 percent in 1993, while membership in the Central Committee rose from just over 10 percent to about 70 percent in the same period.[6]

The termination of martial law and subsequent relaxation of state control of the media (press, radio, television) and the freedom to associate, combined with the legalization of opposition parties, contributed to the development of a vigorous civil society in Taiwan.[7] Although there still are a number of shortcomings, the legal system now guarantees and protects civil society. In the martial law era, when opposition political parties were illegal, the repressed civil society was the key avenue for political discourse and expression. Political dissidents acted through social movements that, after the lifting of martial law, openly questioned the policies and practices of the KMT government. The legalization of opposition political parties has not reduced the vibrancy and political role of civil society in Taiwan. Their contribution to the 1990 National Affairs Conference convened by President Lee is indicative of their post-martial-law role. As well, the development of independent media undermined the KMT's monopoly of communication and information. By providing an outlet for the views of opposition political leaders and leaders of civil society, the flourishing independent media stimulated the development of competitive politics. Beginning as a vehicle for staking a claim for the indigenous community against an alien regime, in time the civil society contributed to the liberalization and eventual transformation of the Leninist party-state political system. Civil society in Taiwan continues to advance the interests of individuals and social movements and act as a watchdog to prevent abuse of state power. Further, as observed by Thomas Gold, much of the political agenda is now "set by ideas in the media, think tanks, social movements, and autonomous organizations."[8] Political leaders seek to co-opt or latch onto popular ideas in civil society.

The development of political society and competitive politics has also come a long way since 1987. The birth of the DPP in 1986 and its formal legalization in 1989 broke the KMT's stranglehold on political power at the national level. Focusing initially on national identity and democratization—and subsequently on the issues of electoral reform and competition—the DPP and its alliance with the mainstream reform faction in the KMT under Lee Teng-hui contributed much to the development of competitive politics in Taiwan.[9] The ROC constitution was amended in 1991 to allow the direct election of the Legislative Yuan the following year. Constitutional amendments in 1994 eased the restrictions on eligibility for political candidacy and authorized the direct popular election of the president and vice-president. Taiwan's first direct election for these offices was held in 1996.

Seeking not to lose political ground to the DPP, the KMT, concurrent with the liberalization of national politics, began an internal transformation of the party. Although several vestiges of its earlier Leninist character remained and Lee made all important decisions, the party became more democratic in its structure and operation. The KMT's gradual transformation—including Taiwanization of the party—combined with growing dissatisfaction with Lee's pragmatic foreign policy and his intolerance of dissidents within the party (but his tolerance of DPP radicals) bred substantial struggle and division in the KMT. Following an unsuccessful attempt to topple Lee, the New KMT Alliance dominated by mainlanders split from the KMT to form the New Party (NP) in 1993. The number of parties has since increased. The Legislative Yuan in 2000 had representatives from the KMT, the DPP, the NP, the People's First Party (PFP), the Democratic Alliance, the Non-Party Alliance, the Taiwan Independence Party, and the New Nation Party. Candidates from five parties contested the 2000 presidential election.[10] Although the development of a strong political society and competitive politics in less than a decade was quite impressive, the KMT's continuing dominance (as observed by Yun-han Chu in chapter 2) "complicated the prospect for democratic consolidation."

The KMT initiated and supervised democratization process transplanted elements of authoritarianism into the democratic system.[11] The emergency powers of the president and the creation of a national security agency under his authority, for example, were transplants from the previous regime. Often constitutional amendments were designed to serve the short-term partisan interests of the KMT. Also, the KMT infected the new electoral politics with its customary mobilization practices rooted in organized crime and money politics. In general, the continuing dominance of the KMT with its vast financial assets (estimated in 1999 at US$3 billion) and political machine created an uneven playing field that hampered competitive politics. The public's disenchantment with the KMT-dominated system deprived the new democratic institutions of broad-based legitimacy. There was widespread perception that such shortcomings of the fledgling democratic system would never be addressed so long as the KMT was at the political helm. This feeling was reflected in the public's demand for political reform, especially the elimination of money and mafia-like politics, in the March 2000 election campaign.

Significance of Chen's Election

It is in this context that Chen's election is important. Had Lien Chan won, the public would have attributed his election to the "black and gold" politics associated with the KMT. Public skepticism of the system would have continued and might even have deepened. The one-party-dominant system would have become more entrenched and the DPP would have been viewed as a professional opposition party with little chance of ever wresting power at the national level. Continuation of the old ways would have suppressed competitive politics. But the win by a DPP candidate has broken the KMT's lock on state power at the national level. The peaceful transfer of presidential power to a candidate who campaigned on political reform and had little prospect of winning engenders confidence in democratic institutions and processes and legitimates them. Although this is the second direct election for the office of president, it is as significant as the first from the perspective of democratic development: the first transfer of power to an opposition candidate in the highest elected office in the land. It also helps to strengthen the tradition of free, fair, and open competition for the acquisition of state power. For all these reasons, Chen's election may be viewed as crossing an important threshold in Taiwan's democratic development.

Chen's election has generated high expectations for further political reform. As noted earlier, the decisive issues in the campaign were related to political reform and expansion of democracy; and Chen himself championed these issues. Further deepening of democracy means addressing several key issues: undertaking political and constitutional reform to remove the vestiges of authoritarianism, leveling the playing field and altering the rules to strengthen competitive politics, neutralizing the enormous advantages still enjoyed by the KMT (including regulation of party-owned businesses), eliminating money and mafia politics, overhauling the electoral system, augmenting the power of local government, strengthening the integrity of the judicial system, creating an independent human rights commission, and dealing with the unresolved question of national identity. The historic turnover of power in the presidency appears to be an opportune moment to push through such long-awaited reforms and consolidate democracy.

Political Reform and the Challenge of Governance

The key question is whether Chen can formulate and carry through a far-reaching reform program. In this regard, his performance has been disappointing. Chen's first year in office was marked by political showdowns (between the Executive Yuan and the Legislative Yuan, between political parties, and within the DPP itself), a dramatic economic slowdown, and scandals involving the president and vice-president. Chen faces many formidable challenges, chief among which is the challenge of governance. As noted earlier, if the president's party does not control the Legislative Yuan he has little power to influence the legislative agenda. An opposition-dominated legislature can embarrass the president and significantly erode his power, especially if he does not enjoy broad-based legitimacy. This has been the case with Chen. A difficult situation has been made worse by Chen's lack of experience, his inept handling of issues, and the division within the DPP. His handling of the controversial fourth nuclear plant issue, the political and constitutional crisis it created, and its eventual outcome illustrate this point and, more broadly, the challenge of governance confronting Chen.

After a long controversy, the construction of the fourth nuclear power plant was finally approved in March 1999 by the KMT government despite strong public opposition—especially from environmental groups objecting to nuclear power. Taiwan has had difficulty in disposing of nuclear waste, but it is also short of power. The KMT government had pushed the nuclear plant on the grounds that it was essential for Taiwan's economic development, whereas the DPP had traditionally been opposed to nuclear power. By the time of the March 2000 election, about 30 percent of the project had been completed at a cost of US$1.45 billion. Following Chen's victory, his cabinet decided to reevaluate the project. The proposed reevaluation was criticized both by the DPP legislators who wanted to abort the project and by outgoing KMT government officials who insisted on its continuation. DPP legislators proposed alternative sources of power, as well as measures to improve the efficiency of fuel distribution and use. KMT and PFP legislators, bitter from the defeat of their candidates in the presidential election, objected to such alternatives as the natural gas pipeline and insisted on construction of the nuclear power plant because of its impact on Taiwan's economic development and investment climate.

Differences over the fate of the project and Chen's inept handling of the issue led to the resignation of Premier Tang Fei and created a political gridlock between the Executive Yuan and the Legislative Yuan that threatened a constitutional crisis. Tang, a former general and defense minister in the Lee cabinet with close ties to the U.S. defense establishment, was chosen by Chen to lend credibility and an aura of national unity to his government. Differences between Tang and Chen over the nuclear plant and other issues as well as attacks on Tang from both flanks—the KMT/PFP coalition and DPP legislators over his decision to continue construction of the plant if the objections could be addressed—eventually led to Tang's resignation in October 2000, a severe jolt to the barely five-month-old Chen government.

Chen's inept handling of the issue was most evident in the announcement of the decision to cancel the project—an announcement by the new premier, Chang Chun-hsiung, that came barely an hour after the meeting between Chen and Lien Chan, leader of the KMT. Apparently a compromise was discussed at that meeting with Chen agreeing to give further thought to the matter.[12] The cancellation sparked a KMT/PFP coalition that challenged the legality of the presidential order to scrap the nuclear power plant and initiated a four-month-long political crisis that ended with Chen having to retract his order and authorize continuation of the project. In considering the legal challenge from the KMT/PFP coalition, the Council of Grand Justices ruled that as the presidential order was "a reversal of major national policy," the Executive Yuan had not followed due process of law in canceling the nuclear plant. The CGJ also called upon the Executive Yuan to follow the correct procedure as soon as possible and seek the Legislative Yuan's approval for the change in national policy. After listening to Chang's reasoning for the cancellation (as they were required to do by the GCJ ruling), on 31 January 2001 the Legislative Yuan passed a resolution ordering the Executive Yuan to resume construction of the plant.

Although Premier Chang initially claimed that the resolution was not binding on the Executive Yuan, soon it became clear that in the absence of a compromise between the two bodies, the matter would have to be resolved in accordance with the Constitution. The options here included the Legislative Yuan's adoption of either a binding resolution or a no-confidence motion leading to the premier's resignation, dissolution of the legislature, and a snap election. Ultimately, the Chen government capitulated under a "compromise agreement." It agreed to resume work on the plant and to retract its demand that the new legislature (to be elected in December 2001) should decide the project's budget. Its only gain was an agreement to negotiate an accord with the legislature on an energy bill before it is formally forwarded to the Legislative Yuan. This so-called compromise was opposed by the DPP caucus, which did not participate in the negotiations. Angry DPP supporters staged a protest outside the Executive Yuan when the cabinet ordered the resumption of construction of the nuclear power plant. They called for a public referendum to decide on the issue.

DPP supporters of political reform have also been disappointed with Chen's concessions to the conservative elements including the military. In the final makeup of his security team, for example, military officers retained all the top positions, especially in the National Security Agency and the Investigation Bureau. Human rights groups were particularly dissatisfied as military control of these agencies could block investigation of the past abuses of power against dissidents and opposition political leaders. Another disappointment was Chen's selection of Lee Teng-hui's son-in-law as chairman of the government-controlled TTV (Taiwan Television). These concessions to conservative elements could obstruct Chen's efforts to clean up mafia and money politics.

The challenge of governance facing Chen is indeed formidable. With the legislature controlled by the KMT, the bureaucracy still loyal to the KMT, and the PRC courting opposition leaders, Chen has become an isolated leader and ineffective. To govern he must develop a working relationship with the opposition parties, especially the KMT. Chen's initial reaction to his minority position was to eschew coalition with opposition parties and develop a government of national unity by tapping personnel from all parties. He was not successful in recruiting key personnel from across the political spectrum, however, and this endeavor ended with the resignation of Tang Fei. There is now little incentive for opposition political parties to form a coalition government as the Legislative Yuan election is approaching fast. The only option open to Chen is to work with the opposition on issues of common interest. This strategy implies that far-reaching reforms—especially those designed to level the playing field and boost competitive politics—are unlikely to make headway anytime soon. Chen could well cite the KMT's obstacles to political reform in order to make a strong case to the Taiwan people for a DPP-controlled Legislative Yuan. To avoid such an accusation, the KMT may want to cooperate on selected issues. If the KMT retains control of the Legislative Yuan after the December 2001 election, the record of the Chen presidency on political reform is likely to be minimal if not dismal. Chen's victory in the March 2000 election may well be a milestone in Taiwan's democratic development, but it has not significantly enhanced the prospects for further political reform.

Democratic Consolidation

Two related questions should be addressed here: Has democracy in Taiwan been consolidated? And has Chen's victory contributed to the consolidation of democracy in Taiwan? Much has been written about the meaning of democratic consolidation, what it entails, how to recognize it. As with any major concept in social science, there is no universal definition of the concept. Indeed, some analysts question its theoretical and practical relevance as well as its operationalization in terms of political institutionalization.[13] My purpose here is not to enter this debate, but to inquire whether democracy in Taiwan has taken sufficient root that its persistence is assured.

How do we ascertain that this has transpired? Here, the definition of democratic consolidation advanced by Linz and Stepan is useful.[14] They define democratic consolidation as a "political regime in which democracy as a complex set of institutions, rules, and patterned incentives and disincentives has become the only game in town." In this situation, no significant political group seeks to supplant the democratic regime or secede from the state. Even in the face of severe crisis, the overwhelming majority of the population is committed to finding solutions within the parameters of the democratic regime. And all players become habituated to resolving conflicts on the basis of established norms. Attempts to find solutions outside the democratic framework will not only fail, but be punished in accordance with the law. Linz and

Stepan contend that three minimal conditions—stateness, completion of democratic transition, and a democratic government in office—must be met before one can speak of democratic consolidation. By stateness they mean the domestic and international acceptance of the state's authority and identity. The second condition is the holding of free and contested elections and the elected government's inclusion in all significant domains. The third condition is that the incumbent government must function in accord with the constitution and the law of the land.

Before evaluating the consequences of the 2000 election for democratic development in Taiwan in terms of these criteria, it is useful to review earlier evaluations. The first direct election to the presidency in 1996 was the focal point of several assessments of democratic development in Taiwan. Arguing that substantial progress had been made in regime transformation, establishment of civilian control over the military, reform of the electoral system, institution of a competitive party system, popular election of the national legislature and the president, and the development of civil society, Hung-mao Tien calls the 1996 election "a symbol of the conclusive phase of democratic consolidation."[15] In his view, the developments culminating in the 1996 presidential election satisfy the two cardinal dimensions of the "procedural minimum" definition of democratic consolidation advanced by Robert Dahl.[16] Tien goes on, however, to say that "despite Taiwan's successful democratic transition" it cannot be considered consolidated until the national identity issue is resolved. Writing in the same volume, Thomas Gold says that Taiwan has become a "stable democracy."[17] After reviewing Taiwan's progress in five arenas—civil society, political society, rule of law, state apparatus, and economic society—Gold concludes that "democratic consolidation has occurred." But he cautions that this does not mean "the system is set in stone" and warns that the elite and the public must manage challenges confronting Taiwan through democratic institutions and procedures such that democracy becomes "the only game in town." Also writing in the same volume, Larry Diamond views the 1996 election as a victory for the democratic process. But he adds that further institutional reforms—to modernize political structures, alter the electoral system, control organized crime, and complete the extrication of the ruling party from state, society, and economy—are required. And even with such reforms Diamond argues, "consolidation cannot be clearly achieved until control of government passes smoothly to the political opposition through the electoral process."[18] Thus, the consensus after the 1996 election appears to have been that democratic transition was complete but not consolidation. Observers cited additional reforms that must be undertaken, as well as issues like national identity that must be resolved.

Have these reforms and issues been addressed since 1996? And does Chen's election advance democratic consolidation in any substantive manner? The answer to the first question would appear to be in the negative. As noted earlier, political and constitutional reform, leveling the playing field to strengthen competitive politics, eliminating money and mafia politics, and strengthening the judicial system were among the major issues in the March 2000 presidential campaign. These reforms are still outstanding and the prospect for their early enactment is slim. The issue of national identity, particularly the international dimension, remains unresolved and may in fact have been accentuated by Chen's victory. The election's outcome, however, has led to at least a partial alternation of power at the national level. If alternation of power is a crucial condition, as Diamond contends, then it is possible to argue that Chen's victory has made an important contribution. Full alternation, however, has yet to occur. In chapter 1, Diamond concludes that the "outcome of the 2000 presidential election was a momentous victory for democracy" and that the victory marks "for many people in Taiwan the true completion of the country's poignant and protracted transition from authoritarian rule to democracy." In other words, democratic transition is complete but consolidation is not.

With respect to the conditions stipulated by Linz and Stepan, Taiwan has completed democratic transition and has a democratically elected government that is committed much more than the preceding KMT governments to functioning within the law. However, it falls short on the condition of stateness. Although the state's authority and identity are no longer hotly contested in domestic politics, this is not the case internationally: The PRC disputes Taiwan's status as a sovereign political entity, and the bulk of the international community denies formal diplomatic recognition to Taipei. This shortfall is mitigated by the fact that the international community (less the PRC) treats Taiwan as a de facto sovereign state; and Western support for democratic development in Taiwan does enhance the state's international identity and authority. Taiwan's shortfall in stateness is peculiar. While it is unlikely to be resolved quickly, it is also unlikely to affect the consolidation of democracy. As exemplified by the modification of the "one country, two systems" formula to include a democratic system of government in Taiwan and other recent overtures, even Beijing, which contests the sovereign status of Taiwan, has come to accept that Taiwan's democratic development is here to stay. Thus, although there is still a shortfall in meeting the stateness condition, it is possible to argue that it is not a crucial setback for democratic consolidation. In any case, it is beyond the control of Taipei.

More significant from the perspective of democratic consolidation is whether democracy is the only game in town and whether the key players have internalized democratic norms and play by the rules of the game. Here there is still some doubt. In one sense, democracy is the only game in town. It is unthinkable that state power can be acquired except through elections. Any reversion to authoritarian rule or military intervention would be massively opposed by the polity. In any case, there is no group that seeks to supplant the democratic system. Yet the commitment of key players to adhere to the rules is still not deep-rooted. The opposition, for example, has still to accept its loss in the presidential election and play the role of a loyal opposition. Rather than wait for the next election, the KMT in alliance with the PFP seeks to exploit every constitutional and legal loophole and deploy its still significant residual power to render the executive ineffective and if possible to recall, impeach, or force the resignation of the duly elected president. Indeed, serious national interests and long-term goals seem to be absent in the international behavior of opposition leaders guided by short-term political calculations. Opposition leaders, for example, have been quite willing to align with Beijing in order to create an anti-Chen united front. For its part the executive, due largely to inexperience and ineptness, has not followed constitutionally sanctioned procedures; and segments of the DPP still believe in street politics to promote their political agenda. Democratic values and norms have yet to be fully imbibed by key players and several key reforms still are outstanding. Thus, democracy in Taiwan is well advanced and cannot be turned back, except at great cost, but it has not yet been consolidated.

Democracy in Asia: No Immediate Effect But Important Lessons

The outcome of Taiwan's March 2000 presidential election is not comparable to the 1986 people power revolution in the Philippines or the South Korean uprising of 1987 that ousted the military-backed authoritarian government or the lifting of martial law that initiated democratic transition in Taiwan in 1987. Apart from their domestic consequences, these watershed developments had an international demonstration effect in lending moral support to similar movements in Burma, the PRC, and several other Asian countries. Chen's victory had no such consequence. Nevertheless, the election's outcome—particularly the defeat of the KMT and its exit from the highest office after dominating politics for more than fifty years and presiding over Taiwan's political and economic miracles—offers important lessons for the PRC and the remaining one-party-dominant, quasi-democratic systems in the region. This does not mean that the Taiwan model will be replicated in these countries. Political change in each country, of course, will follow its own path. Even so, there are common dynamics that could well influence the direction if not the pace of change in these states.

Taiwan: Model for Political Change in the PRC?

At their inception the political systems in the PRC and Taiwan were similar in several respects. Both the CCP and the KMT shared "the same traditions of governance based on centuries of imperial rule, both were embedded in the same political culture, and both were initially organized as Leninist parties."[19] After retreating to Taiwan, the KMT—modeling itself on the victorious CCP—built a party-state system in which the party dominated all state institutions, including the military, and penetrated and controlled all levels and aspects of society through a cadre system and a network of party cells. Founded on the principle of democratic centralism and exercising complete monopoly over political power, the CCP and the KMT banned all political opposition inside and outside the party. Both parties had the goal of transforming their societies and reunifying the two political entities; but there were important differences. Unlike the CCP, building a communist state was not the goal of the KMT. At least in rhetoric, it was committed in the long term to building a democratic capitalist state. Although it banned organized opposition at the national level, the KMT did tolerate local opposition and competition. In the economic sphere, the KMT did not seek to build a command economy. The state in Taiwan did play a key role in the economy, but economic development was pursued in the context of the international market economy and there always was room for the private sector. Another important difference was the native Taiwanese perception of the KMT as an alien force. The internal political dynamic that issued from the drive to shake off mainland domination as well as the international isolation of Taipei in the 1990s were key forces in shaping political development in Taiwan. Such a dynamic was absent in the PRC.

   While the KMT modeled itself politically on the CCP in the early years, the chaos of the Cultural Revolution and the failure of the PRC's command economy led the CCP under Deng Xiaoping's leadership to pursue economic and intermittent political reforms that had a striking resemblance to those followed by the KMT in the early years.[20] Andrew Nathan claims that several of the economic policies pursued by the CCP in the post-Mao era—the "coastal development policy" announced in 1988, for example—were "explicitly modeled on Taiwan's experience." And the Chinese campaign to transform state-owned enterprises into joint-stock companies drew "some of its inspiration from the success of the Taiwan model." Chinese democrats arguing the case for political reform often cited the Taiwan experience—where the Chinese cultural heritage and a Leninist structure have not been a bar to democratization. The cultural and historical similarities noted earlier, the growing convergence in economic policy, and the limited political liberalization under way in the PRC have led some observers to believe that Taiwan may serve as a model for political change in the PRC and that cross-strait interaction may promote political liberalization and democratic transition on the mainland.

Bruce Dickson, however, argues that the CCP is unlikely to follow the KMT's lead in sponsoring political liberalization and democratic transition.[21] His basic argument is that the conservative nature of the elite and the greater totalitarian legacy make the CCP less responsive and less able to adapt to the changing environment. The thrust of the CCP's behavior over the last five decades has been to alter the environment through the use of coercion rather than liberalize in response to demands from below. Reform and liberalization, to the extent they have been pursued, have been deployed as an instrument of state policy at the initiative of the party leadership to serve its interest or as a consequence of a change in its goals and worldview. The balance of power within the CCP leadership, which has been prone to frequent division and conflict, has been persistently aligned against political reformers—leading to crackdowns on democracy advocates and their supporters. The CCP has uncompromisingly rejected alternative ideologies and demands from below—witness its reaction to popular protests in 1989 and the ongoing campaign to crush the Falungong movement. The many advantages still enjoyed by the CCP including monopoly over legitimate violence, according to Dickson, will allow it to survive without responding to internal and external demands. Further, the difficulty of managing an ideological shift would make it especially hard for the CCP to embark on political liberalization and democratization. Based on this analysis, Dickson concludes: "If democracy comes to China, it is more likely to be after the breakdown of the current regime and the creation of a new one, rather than the result of continuous regime change as occurred in Taiwan." He reiterates this theme in chapter 3 of this volume with the clarification that he is optimistic about the prospects for democracy in China, but pessimistic that the CCP will be the sponsor of such change.

For different reasons, CCP leaders, officials, and policy analysts are also skeptical about the relevance of the Taiwan experience for the PRC. In support of this contention, they note that the PRC and Taiwan differ greatly in legacy, condition, and size; that the Chinese leadership and especially the public have little knowledge of Taiwan's political dynamics; and that the rancorous behavior of Taiwanese politicians and more generally the island's tumultuous politics hold little attraction for the Chinese. General arguments are advanced by the PRC political elite against democracy as well: The Chinese people are not ready for democracy; large democracies have a poor record of promoting economic development and political stability; and the experience of the former Soviet Union, its successor Russia, and the former Eastern European states is decidedly negative.

Although the behavior of the CCP leadership thus far supports Dickson's contention, one can envisage a set of circumstances under which the CCP leadership, despite its current rhetoric, will have to undertake political liberalization. The ideological foundation of the CCP's title to rule has been severely compromised. The nationalism and economic performances that now underpin its claim to legitimacy are not a durable basis for the control of state power. Although the CCP still enjoys disproportionate material and institutional advantages and may have little interest in sharing power, the present system cannot endure for long without change. The incumbent CCP leadership does not have the same moral authority as Mao Zedong or Deng Xiaoping, and the authority of the next generation, due to gain power in 2002 and 2003, will be even weaker. They will not be able to suppress demands from below in the same ruthless manner as their predecessors. Moreover, further economic modernization and increasing international interaction and dependence on the global market economy as a consequence of membership in the World Trade Organization (WTO) will in due course alter the balance of power within the party leadership as well as between party, state, and society. A policy of unresponsive domination is likely to become untenable as an option. Indeed, it is not unthinkable that a new generation leadership, in the interest of survival, may embark on a process of liberalization under the label "democracy with Chinese characteristics." From the CCP's perspective, change initiated from within by the party leadership may appear less risky and therefore more attractive than change from below that could result in its ouster. Further, the absence of organized political and civil society in China makes political change from below, as in the Philippines and South Korea, highly improbable.

Regardless of how political change may come about, Taiwan's 2000 presidential election and more broadly its democratization (as noted by Dickson in chapter 3) offer several important lessons for the PRC. The first lesson: Democracy is not incompatible with Chinese culture or the Confucian tradition. Contrary to arguments insisting on cultural and developmental prerequisites, the Taiwan experience supports the view that democratic values can be nurtured and developed by the process of change itself. Although culture may be a given, it is not static.[22] Cultures evolve; and because cultures have several strands, there is no one-to-one correspondence between a specific culture and a specific political system. Often a culture can support more than one type of political system. The second lesson is that democracy does not necessarily lead to social and political disorder. By institutionalizing the rules and procedures for acquiring and exercising state power, democratic development has reduced political conflict in Taiwan considerably. There is a self-serving tendency to equate the fistfights and messiness of democratic government with political chaos. The chaos in Taiwan, to the extent that it exists, pales in comparison to the excesses of the Cultural Revolution and the political succession struggles in the PRC. China's real fear appears to be its own history of instability and the recent experience of the Soviet Union leading to its breakup and the continuing lack of stability in Russia.

The third lesson is that democracy is not incompatible with economic development. Over the last fifteen years Taiwan has done remarkably well under democratic government. Its current economic problems have little to do with democracy and are exacerbated by political leaders who sidestep the rules of the democratic game. The nondemocratic PRC and other nondemocratic countries face even more serious economic challenges. Fourth, as observed earlier, democracy builds moral authority and reduces the incidence of political conflict. It also enhances the state's international standing and moral authority. Despite its formal ostracization, democratic and economically developed Taiwan enjoys substantial international support. The PRC's international reputation, by contrast, while on the rise, suffers because of the authoritarian nature of its government. Although democracy itself does not enhance international standing, it adds a moral dimension that can be status-enhancing for a major power.

Finally, the experience of the KMT in Taiwan and the communist parties of Russia and Eastern Europe suggests that democratization does not mean the end of the line for the CCP, especially if it takes the initiative in liberalization. There is always the risk that the process may outrun the initiator, of course, but in time the risk of fighting a rearguard action may be even greater. The Taiwan experience demonstrates that while success in economic modernization is important, it cannot guarantee monopoly of political power. People are not just economic animals. They are also social and political beings. In time, political concerns must be addressed in their own right. They cannot be continually bought off by economic prosperity or suppressed by fear of authority. Fear of the uncertainty of democracy—that the CCP may lose control over who wins—and the CCP leadership's own self-interest may in the short term inhibit democratic development in the PRC. In the medium to long term, however, political liberalization and democratic transition may well be inevitable. This does not mean that the PRC will become a Western-style liberal democracy; but a more open political system that tolerates some competition and sharing of power is likely—and in this context the Taiwan experience may be relevant.

Relevance for Quasi-Democracies in Southeast Asia

The outcome of the March 2000 election—particularly the defeat of the KMT after dominating politics for nearly five decades—may also hold important lessons for the one-party-dominant, quasi-democratic regimes in Singapore and Malaysia. In Singapore the People's Action Party (PAP) has dominated the state and controlled political power since 1959. The Barisan Nasional (BN; National Front) and before that the Alliance Party have controlled political power in Malaya and then Malaysia since 1957. The PAP's total domination of Singapore parallels the KMT's domination of Taiwan in the early years. The PAP had a strong cadre system, but unlike the KMT it did not have a network of party cells in the various state institutions and did not penetrate and control society to the same degree as in Taiwan. The PAP has uncompromisingly rejected alternative ideologies and has been a leading proponent of Asian values and the one-party-dominant system in Asia. Although it has organized regular elections, the PAP tends to view them more as a referendum on its performance and a means of gauging public support than a genuine competition for state power. Opposition parties exist in Singapore but frequently under threat of persecution. Civil society has been tightly controlled. The space for political and civil society is severely circumscribed.

The domination of the Malaysian state by the UMNO is less absolute than that of the PAP in Singapore. Elections have been held regularly and a parliamentary form of government has functioned since 1957, except during the two-year emergency following the May 1969 race riots. Opposition parties have acquired political power at the state level in Malaysia through elections and are an important force in national politics as well. Civil society, however, has been kept on a short leash. Both countries have a plethora of security legislation that the governments can deploy at will to arrest and detain persons without trial for substantial periods. As in Taiwan under the KMT, the Malaysian and Singapore governments play a crucial role in economic development that has been pursued through the market economy system and export-led growth strategies. Indeed the PAP and the UMNO-led BN governments have presided over dramatic economic growth and improvement in the economic well-being of their people. There is a key difference, however: Singapore and Malaysia have multiethnic populations and do not confront the Taiwanese/mainlander divide or a serious external threat to their political survival. Singapore believed its survival was seriously threatened in the early years after its separation from Malaysia in 1965, but over the years this concern has receded (though not disappeared). Although Singapore has a multiethnic population, the Chinese segment constitutes 77 percent of its population and its leadership has at various times articulated a Confucian ideology and model for Singapore. Such parallels make comparison of the PAP and the UMNO-led BN with the KMT meaningful and the Taiwan experience relevant for Singapore and Malaysia—not as a source of contagion, but in terms of key lessons and as a basis for investigating the future of the dominant parties in these two countries.

Although the PAP has been in power for over three decades, the quasi-democratic political system in Singapore like that under the KMT in Taiwan has not acquired full legitimacy. The PAP's domination, its electoral districting policy, its suppression of opposition politics, and more generally its top-down "government knows best" authoritarian approach to governance is perceived to have stacked the deck against genuine competition for political power. This perception and a general disquiet about the PAP, the intensity of which has varied over time, deprives the PAP government and its political system of full legitimacy. In several ways, this disquiet recalls the public yearning for political reform in Taiwan before the March 2000 election—a demand stemming from the belief that democracy cannot be consolidated under KMT domination. Despite its phenomenal economic success and efficient government, the PAP has not been successful in articulating and gaining public acceptance of an ideological basis for its continued domination of the state.[23] Public skepticism in Singapore is much milder than in KMT-dominated Taiwan, however, and the associated legitimacy problem seems less acute for the PAP than for the KMT.

In chapter 4, Chua Beng Huat concludes that the Taiwan experience may have some relevance for Malaysia, but "is unlikely to have any impact or influence on the political development in Singapore." Several reasons can be advanced to explain the PAP's continued domination of Singapore.[24] Above all, it has performed well and adapted expeditiously to the changing international environment. Through regular elections and other mechanisms, the PAP has been able to assess its domestic political standing and respond to certain demands from below while continuing to justify a high level of state autonomy in the name of survival and future prosperity. Due to the farsightedness of Lee Kuan Yew, there has been an intergenerational transfer of power to an elite very much in the mold of the no-nonsense, action-oriented, first-generation leadership, but without a similar political base. Self-selection has ensured unity and continuity. The PAP has not suffered the internal division and conflict that have troubled the KMT, especially under Lee Teng-hui. In Taiwan such divisions led to the creation of new political parties and eventually a three-way contest for the presidency in March 2000. The PAP leadership has for the most part been free of corruption and has taken severe action against tainted leaders and officials. Money and mafia politics is not an issue in Singapore.

A good surveillance network, coupled with quick and strong suppression, has kept the political and civil society in line and allows little room for alternative ideas and organizations. The public's response has been one of resigned acceptance and periodic registration of dissent through protest votes in elections. Through good performance, minimal adaptation, and the inculcation of fear, the PAP has been able to continue its nearly total political domination of the island city-state. Revolution from below is unlikely; and elite-initiated change from above is likely to be more of the same in the vein of a "kinder and gentler" government that offers a limited opening of public space for "organized creativity and fun." Although dramatic change appears unlikely, the PAP's continued monopoly of political power hinges on meeting a set of strict contingents: able, honest, and united leadership that is renewed periodically; good performance; a relatively weak indigenous private sector; a middle class dependent on government employment; a controlled and decimated opposition; a civil society confined to a narrow spectrum of public space; and a politically docile population. Cracks in any one of these elements, especially in the leadership, could open up space for contestation of the PAP's lock on political power.

In contrast to Singapore, the political dominance of the UMNO-led Barisan Nasional in Malaysia appears to be weakening. The factors that underpinned UMNO's domination of the BN and the latter's control of political power—representation of Malay unity in pursuit of the goal of Malay dominance in a multiethnic society, a disunited opposition, a weak civil society, and sustained economic growth—have all come under challenge.[25] To protect Malay interests and rights thought to be seriously threatened by non-Malays, it was argued that Malay unity was a must and the Malay community had to unite behind UMNO. This claim struck a responsive chord among the Malays and was reinforced by the events leading to the May 1969 race riots. Malay political dominance has since become entrenched. No party can expect to capture political power without Malay leadership. And the economic position of Malays has improved dramatically. With Malay supremacy established, the struggle for power has increasingly hinged on intra-Malay as opposed to interethnic competition. Although intra-Malay political struggle was not absent (as manifested in Mahathir's challenge to Tunku Abdul Rahman's leadership of UMNO in 1969 and the 1976–1978 Harun Affair), the Mahathir-Razaleigh struggle for UMNO leadership in 1987 was a serious clash that led to the split of the party and the creation of UMNO Baru and Semangat 46. Even so, Semangat 46 was unsuccessful in challenging UMNO's dominant position.

The Mahathir-Anwar open split in 1997, the arrest of Anwar on charges of corruption and sodomy, his farcical trial and conviction, the creation of a new Partai Keadilan (Justice Party), its cooperation with the Partai Islam Malaysia (PAS) and the Democratic Action Party (DAP) to create the Barisan Alternatif (BA; Alternative Front) and a more vocal civil society, all appear to be posing a much greater challenge to UMNO than Semangat 46's alternative front. In large part, the challenge is directed at Mahathir (who has been in power since 1981) and his autocratic tendencies. While he has made important contributions to Malaysia's economic development, Mahathir has undercut the checks and balances in the political system and concentrated power in the executive. Cronyism and corruption, while not absent earlier, have become rampant under his rule—ironic for a man who started with a pledge to clean up government. His "un-Malay" treatment of Anwar has angered Malay supporters, even within UMNO, who increasingly view Mahathir as a liability. The BN's victory in the 1999 general election was due largely to non-Malay support. With Malay voters supporting the opposition and with Chinese voters, angered by Mahathir's playing the race card to shore up Malay support, holding back their support, the BN lost the crucial Lunas by-election contest in 2000. Although the BN has become weaker, the BA is still a marriage-of-convenience party united more by its opposition to Mahathir than by a common ideological platform. It is still unclear if the voters will trust the BA to govern. The chief beneficiary of recent developments has been the Islamic Party, which now holds the reins of power in two of Malaysia's states. If present conditions prevail, it looks set to increase its power and influence in several other states.

Like the KMT, however, Mahathir and UMNO are down but not out. Mahathir's unorthodox handling of the financial crisis earned him much credit in the eyes of Malaysians, though his privatization and government buyback schemes of failing *bumiputra* companies raised public ire and allegations of cronyism. Mahathir has always been able to bounce back, but this time around the odds against him appear to be greater. And UMNO, still with many strengths, may manage to retain power. But the dominant position of Mahathir and UMNO is no longer unassailable. Like so many other Asian leaders, Mahathir's failure to recognize when to bow out may irreparably tarnish his position and legacy. The challenges facing UMNO—autocratic ruler, split in the leadership, corruption and money politics, and the growing force of the opposition and civil society—are similar to those that led to the defeat of the KMT candidate in Taiwan's 2000 presidential election.

The continuation of one-party-dominant regimes is predicated on the satisfaction of a stringent set of conditions that may be impossible to perpetuate indefinitely. The record in Asia suggests the decline rather than the ascendance of one-party-dominant regimes. The one-party systems in Burma, South Korea, the Philippines, and Indonesia have all collapsed. Although the CCP continues to monopolize political power, it faces challenges of legitimacy that will compel it to adapt if it is to retain the title to rule. The Indian National Congress and Japan's Liberal Democratic Party, though more successful, have split several times and are now pale shadows of their former selves. The KMT, though still powerful, appears to be moving in the same direction. The one-party-dominant system in Malaysia is in trouble. Only the PAP's domination of Singapore appears to be holding.

Cross-Strait Relations: Conflict Transformation and Continued Impasse

Chen's election, his beliefs, and his policy orientation since the election further advance the transformation of the Taiwan Strait conflict that has been under way since 1991. The deep differences between Taipei and Beijing in their understanding of the conflict have created profound disagreement over the basis for a final settlement and more immediately over the basis for resumption of the cross-strait dialogue that was suspended in 1999.

Redefining the Conflict

The structure and dynamics of the cross-strait conflict have been fundamentally transformed from an unfinished civil war between two mainland parties over the title to rule China (including Taiwan) to a conflict over Taiwan's identity and status and its relationship to the PRC. The Taiwan Strait conflict has its origins in the Chinese civil war between the CCP and the KMT. Proclaiming the People's Republic of China in October 1949, the victorious CCP asserted the right to rule all of China including the "province" of Taiwan to which the KMT had fled and established a government in exile. The realization of this goal was thwarted by a change in American policy in the wake of the outbreak of the Korean War and the deployment of the Seventh Fleet to the Taiwan Strait in June 1950. Nevertheless, the PRC persisted with its goal of liberating Taiwan initially by force and subsequently, when the force option became unrealistic, through peaceful means. For its part the KMT, with American support in the context of the Cold War, not only consolidated its position in Taiwan but also did not retract the claim that its ROC government represented all of China. In opposing the communist government on the mainland, which it considered illegitimate, the KMT followed the policy of "no contact, no negotiation, no compromise." In this standoff phase, which lasted through the 1980s, both the CCP and the KMT were committed to the notion of a reunified China (including Taiwan) under a single authority. Their dispute was primarily over who would govern the country and secondarily over the political ideology of China.

Beginning in 1991, the conflict began to undergo fundamental changes. The central disputes ceased to be over the system of government and the title to rule. Instead they hinged on the identity and status of Taiwan, on whether Taiwan is part of China and should be unified with the mainland, and on the meaning of China and its political manifestation. Much of the transformation was due to political change in Taiwan—the rise of a distinct Taiwanese identity, the indigenization of politics, political liberalization, and democratic transition—and the island's growing economic prosperity. The rise of Taiwanese identity was rooted in the separate existence of the island of Formosa for much of the last hundred years and the resistance of the native Taiwanese (Han Chinese living on the island before the migration of the late 1940s) to suppression and domination by the "alien" mainlanders (Chinese who emigrated to Taiwan in the late 1940s and early 1950s and their offspring).[26] Viewing themselves as culturally and politically distinct from the mainlanders, the native Taiwanese political elite espoused Taiwanese nationalism, self-government, and an independent Taiwan state. The mainlanders, by contrast, particularly the old guard of the KMT and its supporters, were committed to Chinese nationalism and unification with the mainland. The clash over national identity manifested itself initially in the struggle for political power to determine who would govern Taiwan—the mainlanders or the native Taiwanese who constituted about 80 percent of the population—and subsequently in Taiwan's relationship with China.

The competing national identities, as observed by Alan Wachman, were inextricably linked to political liberalization and democratization on the island.[27] Resistance to the KMT's political dominance crystallized in the *tangwai* social movement that espoused the cause of the native Taiwanese and subsequently led to the creation of the native opposition party—the DPP. Recruitment of new leaders initially to replace the old guard that was passing from the scene, and subsequently to counter the rise of the Taiwan nationalist opposition, led to the Taiwanization of the KMT as well. By the late 1990s, native Taiwanese held many of the key positions in the elected branches of government, in the bureaucracy, and, to a lesser degree, in the military. Lee's ascension to the presidency, his subsequent election to the office by a wide margin in the country's first direct presidential election in 1996, the election of Chen in 2000, all indicate that native Taiwanese now play a key role in the government and politics of Taiwan. Taken together Taiwanization and democratization effectively buried the old KMT and its mainland policy, eliminating one of the two parties to the unfinished civil war and dramatically altering the self-image of Taiwan among the political elite and the public.

As they were not a party to the Chinese civil war, the new KMT under the leadership of Lee Teng-hui and the DPP espouse radically different visions of Taiwan's status and relationship with the mainland. Upon his ascension to power in 1988, Lee supported the KMT's goal of unification with the mainland. As he consolidated his position and wished to counter the growing appeal of the DPP, however, Lee's stance on the status of Taiwan and its relations with the mainland began to alter. Abolishing the temporary provisions that were in force during the national mobilization for the suppression of the communist rebellion, in April 1991 Lee effectively terminated the state of civil war. And the constitutional reforms enacted in 1991 prepared the ground for Lee's "one China, two political entities" formula. He now began to emphasize that the Taiwanese people had to control their own destiny and preserve their identity and dignity. With respect to relations with the mainland, he pursued a "Taiwan priority" China policy.[28] Seeking to clarify the Beijing/Taipei relationship, he declared that it was not one between a central and provincial government (that is, not a domestic matter), but a relationship between two equal political entities. The two sides may eventually unify, he said, but only when "freedom, democracy, and equal distribution of wealth" apply on both sides of the strait. In the context of growing pressure from the PRC and the United States to open political talks with Beijing, Lee subsequently defined the relationship in 1999 as a "special state-to-state relation."[29] This special relationship, he claimed, was based on the 1991 constitutional amendments that declared the two political entities equal and on the fact that the Republic of China has been a sovereign state since 1912. He further stated that although "one China" does not exist at present—because it is divided and ruled by two equal sovereign states—it is a possible option for the future when the two sides are unified under democratic conditions.

The DPP's position on the status of Taiwan and its relations with the mainland is rooted in its reading of a historical and cultural distinctiveness of the people on Taiwan and in the principle of national self-determination. It seeks to define Taiwan's identity and status apart from the Chinese civil war and the orthodoxy of the 1972 Shanghai communiqué.[30] At the time of its founding, the DPP pledged loyalty to the ROC constitution. While the party constitution stipulated that the future of Taiwan should be decided by all the people resident in Taiwan, it neither embraced independence nor rejected unification. But the party resolutions adopted since then—in 1988 (the 417 resolution), in 1990 (the 1007 resolution), and in 1991—clearly made "a sovereign, independent, and self-governing Republic of Taiwan" an integral part of the party constitution. The resolutions also specified that Taiwan does not belong to the PRC and the sovereignty of Taiwan excludes the mainland and Outer Mongolia. Chen and the DPP, however, claiming that Taiwan was already independent, soft-pedaled the independence option in the lead-up to the March 2000 election. Nondeclaration of independence has been linked to the nonuse of force by the PRC. Chen and the DPP made conciliatory statements on the relationship with the mainland. Yet the independence clause in the Constitution remains unaltered and Chen, while not opposed to considering a future "one China," has kept open the option of independence.

Though their positions were not identical and the Lee-led KMT had deep differences with the DPP, by the end of the 1990s, both the DPP and the KMT under Lee had come to view Taiwan as an independent state with its own identity, its own system of government, and a status equal to that of the PRC. The KMT effectively jettisoned its claim to represent all of China. Acknowledging the cultural affinity with the mainland and recognizing the threat of force from the PRC, Lee and the DPP were willing to consider unification and a future "one China" under democratic conditions, but unlike the old KMT and the CCP they were not wedded to these goals. The positions of the Lee-led KMT and the DPP diverged widely from that of the PRC, which was still rooted in the unfinished civil war.

Since its founding in 1949, the PRC has claimed that it is the only legal government of China, that Taiwan is a province of China, the liberation of Taiwan is an internal affair, and that American intervention created and has sustained the Taiwan issue, preventing the realization of the long-cherished goal of unifying China.[31] Beijing firmly opposes any activities that could lead to the creation of "one China, one Taiwan," "one China, two governments," "two Chinas," and an "independent Taiwan," or the claim that "the status of Taiwan remains to be determined."[32] Reunification of Taiwan with the mainland is considered critical by Beijing to end the "100 years of national humiliation" and to bring the Chinese civil war to a conclusion. Reunification is also considered critical to bolster the legitimacy of the CCP whose title to rule increasingly hinges on its nationalist credentials, to prevent separatism in Tibet and Xinjiang, to prevent U.S. hegemony in the Western Pacific area, and to regain the rightful international position of China in the Asia-Pacific.

The PRC's policy has evolved over the years. Following the return to power of Deng Xiaoping as supreme leader upon the termination of the Cultural Revolution, the normalization of Sino-American relations in 1979, and the changes that have occurred in Taiwan, the PRC, at least from the perspective of Beijing, made a radical change in policy. Dropping the goal of liberating Taiwan, Beijing advocated reunification on the basis of the "one country, two systems" (communism and capitalism) formula. While this formula and its subsequent elaboration including Jiang Zemin's Eight Point Proposal of 1995 offered several concessions (Taiwan would have its own political and economic system and its own military forces; talks between the two parties would be on an equal footing; Chinese do not attack Chinese), the core position remains unchanged.

There is only one China, Taiwan must reunify with the mainland, and

Beijing retains the right to use force in order to bring about unification. While Beijing is willing to delegate most of its internal sovereign authority to Taipei, it has stood firm on denying international sovereign status and space to Taiwan, which it continues to view in zero-sum terms. On the political (not ethnic) identity issue, Beijing has indicated some flexibility since the March 2000 election. Vice-Premier Qian Qichen, responsible for handling the cross-strait issue, has stated that one China does not have to mean the PRC or the ROC. Chen, however, has opposed this idea on the ground that internationally there would only be one China, which in effect would be the PRC. Acceptance of this formula means that Taiwan would lose its international identity and its fate would be sealed as part of one China. Although there is disagreement over strategy and tactics, the bulk of the Taiwan political elite and the public do not support unification (or formal independence).

Although Beijing believes it has gone a long way to accommodate "intransigent" Taipei, its concessions do not mean much to the Lee and Chen governments, for their views on the identity and status of Taiwan have altered dramatically. Because of Taipei and Beijing's different understandings of the conflict, a deep cleavage has developed over its settlement. For Taipei, unification is no longer the only option. Along with independence, it is one of several options. Unification might be a future goal, but the content and process through which it is to be achieved must be negotiated between Taipei and Beijing on an equal footing. Taipei's immediate concern is to consolidate its de facto independent identity and status, although it is not opposed to developing a special political relationship with Beijing. Much of this thinking is embodied in Chen's future "one China" policy. For Beijing, unification is a must. Given the return of Hong Kong and Macao and the perceived momentum toward Taiwan independence, there is growing impatience in Beijing. It rejects an independent status for Taiwan and the future "one China" proposition.

Democratization in Taiwan—and the absence of comparable political reform in the PRC—have accentuated the identity difference between the two states, making a settlement even more difficult. Taipei now links future unification to democratic development on the mainland. Weak political leadership on both sides implies that the far-reaching concessions required to move forward are unlikely to be forthcoming anytime soon. Frustrated with this situation, Beijing is increasing its reliance on the threat of force as an instrument of policy in its portfolio.

The asymmetry in understanding of the conflict and its settlement became especially acute with Lee's articulation of "special state-to-state relationship" in 1999 that has been dubbed by Beijing as the "two-state theory," leading to the suspension of the Koo-Wang cross-strait dialogue that had begun in 1993. Seeking to curtail the independence momentum in Taiwan and deeply distrustful of the DPP, Beijing tried to prevent a Chen victory in the March 2000 election. Despite the pressure from Beijing, Chen won the election resulting in the continuation of the impasse across the Taiwan Strait.

Continuing Impasse in Cross-Strait Dialogue

Concerned to demonstrate that he can manage relations with the mainland, aware of Beijing's deep distrust of him, and recognizing that the bulk of the Taiwan electorate supports the status quo, Chen has attempted to develop a new framework for cross-strait relations that transcends the independence/ unification dichotomy and Lee's "no-haste" policy. To facilitate this aim, at the outset of his presidency Chen tried to allay Beijing's fears by stating that if the PRC refrained from the force option, he would not declare independence, would not change the Republic of China appellation, would not inscribe the two-state theory into the Constitution, and would not abolish the National Unification Commission and the National Unification Guidelines. To promote better relations, he proposed bypassing the difficult issue of sovereignty and normalizing economic relations including accelerating the three links (direct trade, transport, and postal links) through the WTO framework.[33] But because of his belief that the Taiwanese people must have the right to self-determination, Chen has not abandoned the independence option. This option is also viewed as the ultimate deterrent and counterweight to the PRC's threat of force in cross-strait relations. Chen has therefore refused to accept the "one China" principle as the basis for resuming cross-strait dialogue. Nevertheless, expressing his determination to achieve peace, Chen, unlike his predecessor, has been much more open in seeking ways to enhance mutually beneficial relations with the mainland. To demonstrate his sincerity in improving cross-strait relations, Chen has proposed the new concept of the future "one China" with the goal of establishing a special political relationship between the ROC on Taiwan and the PRC. Although he initially rejected the 1992 understanding, Chen has acknowledged the positive consequences that followed the "spirit of 1992" and indicates that he may be prepared to accept the 1992 understanding as "one China, different interpretations."

Beijing has rejected Chen's overtures. Perceiving that Lee and Chen are seeking to entrench a new understanding of the conflict and create a new status quo, Beijing steadfastly insists that Chen must first accept the "one China" principle—as agreed to in the 1992 understanding. Acceptance of the "one China" principle is viewed as crucial to establish a firm baseline and prevent further steps toward Taiwan's independence. If Chen were to accept the "one China" principle, Beijing has indicated its willingness to negotiate all related issues on an equal footing and reiterated its willingness to allow some ambiguity on the issue of whether one China means the PRC. Nevertheless, Beijing appears to have concluded that Chen—given his personal beliefs and his delicate political situation—will not accept the "one China" principle. At the same time, in light of Chen's narrow mandate and the dire consequences that are likely to follow, Beijing also seems to have concluded that he will not push for formal independence. Based on this reading, Beijing's strategy, as observed by Qingguo Jia (see chapter 6), comprises the following elements: continue to advocate peaceful reunification on the basis of the "one China" principle; refuse to deal with Chen; form a united front with Taiwanese opposition parties and with Chen's opposition within the DPP to pressure him to accept the "one China" principle; foster dialogue with the legislative branch of the Taiwan government and with Taiwanese nongovernment organizations; increase military pressure on Taiwan by building up the People's Liberation Army's (PLA) military capability and tightening the conditions for its use of force; exert pressure on the United States to act in accord with the "one China" principle and limit its political, diplomatic, and military support (including arms sales) for Taiwan; and limit the international support and space for Taiwan.

The crux of the impasse is the "one China" principle and the 1992 understanding of it—viewed by Beijing as the baseline, but viewed by Taipei as the surrender of its de facto sovereign status even before beginning negotiations. The 1992 Hong Kong meeting to prepare for the 1993 Wang Daohan-Koo Cheng-fu talks bogged down over the meaning of "one China." To overcome this impasse, the Straits Exchange Foundation (SEF, the Taiwan body responsible for cross-strait talks) proposed that each side express its own interpretation. Its version was that "when the two sides are jointly striving to seek national unification, even though both sides insist on the 'one China' principle, they have different understandings regarding the meaning of 'one China.'" The ARATS (the mainland body responsible for cross-strait talks), after some delay accepted the SEF proposal to have separate interpretations. Its interpretation held that "both sides insist on the 'one China' principle and strive to seek national unification. During the course of discussing practical issues involving the two sides, they will not deal with the political meaning of 'one China.'" The SEF interpretation views the cross-strait talks as a means to discuss the unification issue, whereas the ARATS statement implies that unification is a given and that the focus of cross-strait talks will be on practical issues and not on the political meaning of "one China." This 1992 understanding (acceptance of the "one China" principle, but to maintain different interpretations regarding its meaning) served as the basis for the 1993 and subsequent cross-strait talks until their suspension by the PRC in 1999 in response to Lee's characterization of the existing PRC-Taiwan relationship as a "special state-to-state relationship."[34] Beijing viewed Lee's characterization as a violation of the "one China" principle.

Unless a way can be found around the "one China" issue, formal resumption of cross-strait dialogue is unlikely. The current standoff may well be acceptable to all parties, however, and continue as long as there is no fresh provocation. Chen's overtures have been criticized by segments from within the DPP as too hasty and unilateral without reciprocal concessions from the PRC; they have been denounced as ambiguous by opposition leaders who appear to accept or at least are not opposed to the "one China" principle. With little room to maneuver, Chen may have no option but to stay with his current ambiguous stance. As we shall see in the next section, Washington opposes the use of force to bring about a settlement of the conflict and would do its utmost to prevent situations that could precipitate a war in which it would inevitably become involved. A continuation of the status quo is in Washington's interest. Beijing, too, has an interest in the status quo, for its continuation addresses a key concern that Taipei might declare formal independence or amend the Constitution. An indefinite delay in commencing political talks aimed at unification may test Beijing's patience, but its options are not unlimited. Although it can build up its military capability and threaten the use of force, the cost of the invasion option is very high. It appears unlikely, then, that Beijing will resort to the use of force in the absence of a major provocation from Taipei. Even then, because of the many ugly consequences, it is unlikely that Beijing will choose the war option although it may seek to tighten the noose on Taiwan.

The unarticulated preference for the status quo is reflected in the easing of tension across the strait and the progress toward establishing the three mini-links (direct trade, transport, and postal links between Kinmen and Matsu islands, and the Xiamen and Mawei ports in the mainland Fujian province). While political talks have stalled, economic interaction across the strait has not been unduly affected. Beijing has warned Taiwan companies doing business in the PRC that they cannot make money in the mainland and support Taiwan independence. Until now, under Lee's no-haste policy, Taipei has attempted (without much success) to limit Taiwanese investment in the mainland. It is possible that both parties will come around to viewing economic interaction as a noncontroversial channel to promote mutually beneficial cross-strait relations in the hope that this will temper the political impasse and foster political cooperation in the long term. In chapter 7, Tain-Jy Chen and Cyrus Chu contend that economic interaction in the WTO framework offers a win/win strategy and argue the case for subordinating politics to economics in cross-strait relations. President Chen's WTO proposal suggests that

Taipei may now be ready for this approach. But in light of its "politics first" stance, it is not clear if Beijing is ready for it—yet.

Democratization and Cross-Strait Dialogue

By increasing the number of players and facilitating cross-strait tactical alignments, democratization in Taiwan has complicated cross-strait dialogue.[35] Until quite recently, the pace and direction of dialogue depended only on two parties: the KMT and the CCP. With Lee's departure from the presidency and the loss of the KMT's lock on political power, the field in Taiwan has been thrown wide open. Chen's narrow margin of victory and the KMT's continued domination of the Legislative Yuan make the situation even more complex. No institution or party in Taiwan has the mandate or the legal authority to manage cross-strait relations on its own. Chen's effort to make cross-strait relations the domain of the executive (the "government first" approach) has been opposed by the opposition parties which, with the support of Beijing, have attempted to set up a parliamentary task force on cross-strait relations to undercut Chen's authority. For its part, Beijing seeks to exploit the cleavages in Taiwan's democratic politics to advance its interests in collusion with parties and leaders opposed to Chen. While this strategy may serve the short-term interest of Beijing and the opposition parties, in the long term it may have the structural effect of reducing the autonomy of the negotiating parties and empowering other voices. With democratization, political leaders cannot act in contravention of the electorate's preferences. Leaders can no longer negotiate a settlement over the heads of the people. Public support is crucial, and for the moment the public supports the status quo.

Although there has been no comparable political reform in the PRC, the authority of the CCP leadership has eroded as well. Political leaders like Jiang Zemin, Zhu Rongji, and Li Peng (and their likely successors) do not command the same moral authority as Mao or Deng. Unlike their predecessors, they cannot make far-reaching concessions. In a situation where the leadership on both sides of the strait is weak, no radical change in positions appears likely.

Democratization has also garnered considerable international sympathy and support for Taiwan, particularly in the West. Any use of force against democratic Taiwan, especially if it is unprovoked, will almost certainly bring sharp international reaction in favor of Taiwan.

Other Players

Beijing has all along claimed that the Taiwan issue is a domestic matter and insists that it will brook no foreign interference. It also contends that American intervention and support for Taiwan have sustained the conflict and complicated its settlement. The United States has not characterized itself as a party to the conflict since 1972, however, and has eschewed a formal mediating role. Yet the dynamics of the conflict cannot be understood without reference to the United States. Without American support, Taiwan would find it extremely difficult to sustain its present situation. Moreover, the U.S. relations with the PRC have had a substantial, even crucial, impact on the cross-strait relationship. Thus, several observers including Yu-Shan Wu and Alan Wachman (see chapters 5 and 8 in this volume), locate the Taiwan issue in the context of the triangular relations among the United States, the PRC, and Taiwan and claim that the intensity of the Taiwan issue is directly correlated with the state of Sino-American relations. To contain the threat of Chinese communism during the Cold War, the United States supported the ROC government. Since 1971–1972, however, opting to align with Beijing in order to contain Moscow, Washington has normalized relations with the PRC. Although the United States continues to have a commitment to the security of Taiwan, this commitment is tempered by the strategic goal of developing good relations with the PRC. The imperatives of this strategic bilateral relationship have subordinated and complicated Taiwan's quest for security and an independent identity. Though not to the full satisfaction of all three parties, the triangular relationship was relatively stable in the 1980s. Such stability was undermined by two developments: the termination of the Cold War, which reduced the strategic importance of China, and the democratization of Taiwan, which conjoined Taiwan's domestic politics and cross-strait relations and made it more difficult to regulate Taipei's international behavior. Complicating the dynamics of the triangular relationship, these developments raised concerns about the continued viability of Washington's Taiwan policy. While acknowledging that democratization in Taiwan culminating in the election of Chen has indeed complicated U.S. interaction with Taiwan and the PRC and exacerbated the quandary for Washington, Wachman contends in chapter 8 that the United States has no better alternative to its post-1972 policy. And while democratization in Taiwan has indeed been consequential, he says, the election of Chen itself has not made much difference to U.S. policy.

Washington's Taiwan Policy: Increasing Quandary

Since 1972, U.S. policy on the Taiwan issue has been informed by the competing imperatives deriving from the three U.S.-PRC joint communiqués (signed in 1972, 1979, and 1982) and the Taiwan Relations Act (TRA) of 1979. As stated in the 1972 Shanghai communiqué, the United States acknowledges and does not challenge the Chinese position that there is only one China and that Taiwan is a part of China. However, its interpretation of "one China" differs from that of Beijing. Also, Washington is noncommittal about whether Taiwan is now or should become part of the PRC. Further, it insists that the conflict across the Taiwan Strait—including the status of Taiwan and its relationship to the mainland—should be settled through negotiations without resort to force. The TRA states that the decision to establish diplomatic relations with the PRC "rests upon the expectation that the future of Taiwan will be determined by peaceful means," and that any attempt to do so through other means including boycotts and embargoes would constitute "a threat to the peace and security of the Western Pacific area and of grave concern to the United States." Under the TRA, Washington is committed to protecting the security of Taiwan including its social and economic system and the human rights of the people on Taiwan. In pursuit of this commitment, Washington reserves the right to sell Taiwan arms of a defensive character in the amount that is necessary to "maintain a sufficient self-defense capability." What constitutes necessary and sufficient is to be determined by the president and the Congress. Arms sales to Taiwan have been a controversial issue in the U.S.-PRC relations. As stated in the 1982 joint communiqué, both countries have different positions on this issue. Reiterating that the question of Taiwan is its internal affairs, Beijing objected to the arms sale and retained the right to raise the issue in the post-normalization period. Washington stated that it does not plan to carry out a long-term policy of arms sales to Taiwan and that the sale level would not exceed that in the years immediately before normalization of relations. Further, Washington stated its intention to reduce gradually the sale of arms to Taiwan and to seek a final resolution of this controversial issue through the creation of conducive conditions by the efforts of the two governments (Washington and Beijing). While Beijing asserts that the United States has violated its 1982 commitment, Washington maintains that its action is a consequence of Beijing's military buildup against Taiwan.

Washington, however, has not supported Taiwan's independence lest such a move may provoke a war with China. Even President George W. Bush, who in April 2001 authorized a large arms sales package and stated the U.S. commitment to the security of Taiwan in the most unequivocal terms in recent years, made it clear that Washington will not support Taiwan independence as it goes against the "one China" policy.[36] The divergent U.S. goals—seeking good relations with the PRC, but discharging its commitment to the security of Taiwan; not opposing unification, but preventing the use of force; supporting Taiwan's democratization, but limiting self-determination and opposing independence—have all been reflected in the policy of strategic ambiguity that Washington has pursued since 1979.

Balancing the competing imperatives of U.S. policy, never easy, became even more difficult with democratization in Taiwan, economic liberalization in the PRC, and the termination of the Cold War. Democratization altered Taiwan's international image and the rationale for American support. Taiwan's democratic image—accentuated by the threat of absorption by the larger and still Leninist PRC—has increased international support for it, particularly in the West. Democratization has broadened and strengthened Taiwan's constituency in the United States and reduced the flexibility of the administration. Washington's commitment is no longer a pledge to support one Leninist state against another out of strategic considerations or moral obligation to the people on Taiwan; its commitment is now grounded in considerations of strategic stability and the promotion of the American ideals of liberty and freedom. Failure to prevent the absorption of a democratic "ally" by a Leninist state can be unduly damaging to the domestic and international credibility of the United States. In Taiwan, Washington now has a reputational interest at stake. Democratization in Taiwan has also made it difficult for Washington to control Taiwan's international conduct. The leadership in Taiwan does not necessarily control the China policy, and Washington cannot be seen to demand that a democratically elected leadership behave in a way that contravenes the wishes of the majority of its people. The population's assent in negotiating a settlement of the conflict is critical—duly acknowledged in President Clinton's remarks following Chen's election.

Promotion of democracy, however, is only one plank of American foreign policy. Washington's commitment to prevent the forceful absorption of democratic Taiwan has to be reconciled with its strategic and economic goals, which demand cordial relations with the PRC. Although termination of the Cold War has reduced the importance of the PRC as a counterweight to the Soviet Union, Beijing is still a key player in matters of peace and security in Asia. Cooperation with Beijing is essential in addressing regional security issues. Economic liberalization and the growing salience of its market have made the PRC an important economic partner, as well, creating a constituency for it in the United States, especially in the business community. For these reasons, and to avoid getting involved in a war with China, Washington has demarcated the limits of its support for Taiwan. While it opposes forceful absorption, it does not support Taiwan's independence. The American rationale for supporting Taiwan could broaden to include a strategic dimension if Washington begins to perceive Beijing as a strategic rival whose foreign policy goals are seriously at odds with its own. In that case, a divided China may become an attractive option. Support for Taiwan might then be viewed as a means of limiting the strategic goals, ambitions, and horizons of

Beijing. This, however, is not the case right now. The United States does not challenge the PRC's position that there is "one China," but it is silent on what this means and whether Taiwan is part of the PRC. These are matters to be resolved by the Chinese people. Washington's stated interest continues to be to prevent unification by force.

Thus although democratization in Taiwan, along with economic liberalization in the PRC and the end of the Cold War, have altered the dynamics of American interaction with Taiwan and the PRC, the fundamental goals of American policy remain intact. And the policy of deterring both the forceful absorption of Taiwan as well as Taiwan's independence still appears relatively sound, although it represents a continuing source of frustration to Beijing, to Taipei, and to some in the U.S. policy community. Beijing is becoming impatient with the "no unification, no independence" policy of the United States as it basically thwarts the goal of unifying China on its terms. Certain segments of the PRC policy community view it as a divide-and-rule policy to perpetuate American dominance in the region. Taipei views the policy as permanently limiting its self-determination option and denying it de jure international recognition. In the absence of agreement between them, both the PRC and Taiwan have attempted through all means available to them—diplomacy, trade, threats, blackmail—to shift the American position in their favor. But a shift in one direction or another exacerbates the concern of the third party. The Clinton's "Three Nos" statement (the United States will not support Taiwan independence; "two Chinas" or "one China, one Taiwan"; and Taiwan's membership in international organizations where statehood is required) was viewed by Beijing as indication of a shift in the American position toward its own. However, such a "reformulation" was perceived by Taipei as weakening its position. The Clinton "tilt" contributed to Lee's clarification of the Taiwan-PRC relationship as a "special state-to-state relationship" and led to Taipei's redoubled efforts to mobilize American public opinion and muster support in the U.S. Congress for its position. Similarly, the granting of a visa to President Lee to visit Cornell University in 1995 and the deployment of two aircraft carriers near the Taiwan Strait in the context of Chinese missile firings and Taiwan's first direct presidential election in 1995–1996 were perceived by Beijing as American actions to enhance Taiwan's independence option and thwart the PRC's goal of unifying China. The April 2001 statement by President Bush, which some of his advisers depict was necessary to correct President Clinton's pro-PRC tilt, is viewed by the PRC as undermining its interests.

The zero-sum situation between Beijing and Taipei makes the maintenance of American policy particularly difficult. The policy could fail if one of the two parties steps beyond the current bounds. Although unthinkable now, China could at some point resort to force or Taiwan could declare independence. Washington might then be confronted with an even more undesirable situation. American interest is best served by fostering more amicable relations between Beijing and Taipei without appearing to confer unilateral advantage to either party. Washington has attempted to defuse crisis situations by communicating with both parties and has tried to promote better cross-strait relations through informal means including the hosting of Track Two meetings involving PRC and Taiwan officials and scholars as well as visits by high-ranking ex-American diplomats to Taipei and Beijing. Formal mediation does not appear to be an option. Ultimately, the conflict would have to be settled though direct negotiations between Beijing and Taipei. Although Washington is the key outside player in the Taiwan dispute, the implications of democratic development in Taiwan are not limited to the United States alone. For a number of reasons—including its colonial history and the U.S.-Japan security treaty—democratic development in Taiwan has political and security consequences for Japan, as well, which is beginning to assume increasing responsibility in matters of peace and security in East Asia.

Japan: Toward a New Taiwan Policy?

Japan's relations with Taiwan have gone through three phases, and a fourth phase may be in the offing. During the first phase (1895–1945), Taiwan was a colony of Japan. In the second phase from the end of U.S. occupation of Japan in 1952 through 1972, Tokyo, recognizing the Republic of China as the legal government of China, engaged in full diplomatic relations with Taipei. Relations with the PRC during this phase were limited primarily to the economic arena. In the present third phase, which began in September 1972, Tokyo recognizes the PRC as the sole government of China and has conducted only nongovernmental working relations with Taiwan. Since 1972, Tokyo's Taiwan policy has been an offshoot of the 1972 PRC-Japan joint communiqué. According to this communiqué, Tokyo, unlike Washington, which has its own interpretation of "one China," "understands and respects" Beijing's position that there is only "one China," that Taiwan is an integral part of the PRC, and that the Taiwan issue is China's internal affair. Unlike the TRA, there is no legal basis for Japan-Taiwan relations. According primacy to relations with the PRC, Tokyo has limited its relations with Taipei to "low politics." Beijing has near veto power in the arena of "high politics."

The bland and perfunctory official Japanese reaction to Chen's election is very much conditioned by the 1972 system that still governs Japan's Taiwan policy. In chapter 9, however, Yoshihisa Amae argues that democratization in Taiwan, along with the changing calculus of national security in Japan, will make it increasingly difficult for Tokyo to confine its Taiwan policy within the parameters of the 1972 system. The democratic nature of the government in Taiwan and the many international ramifications of the conflict, Amae argues, challenge the key premise of the 1972 system that the Taiwan issue is an internal affair of China. Further, the fundamental differences between Beijing and Taipei in their understanding of the conflict not only make a settlement highly unlikely in the near future; they also make the relationship more tense and liable to lead to open conflict.

Such tension and conflict—given Japan's proximity to the Taiwan Strait and the strategic importance of the sea lanes through which much of Japan's vital energy imports must transit—would undoubtedly affect the security of Japan. They would also involve the United States and hence have serious ramifications for Japan. Under the terms of the revised guidelines for U.S.-Japan security cooperation, Tokyo would inevitably have to support the American effort in the Taiwan Strait. Concurrently, Tokyo's relations with Beijing have soured. Though official policy pronouncements have not altered, there is growing concern in important segments of the Japanese policy community about a China threat. At the same time, the public image of China in Japan turned negative after the 1989 Tiananmen massacre. The negative image became more pronounced after the 1998 visit of Jiang Zemin to Japan, and the image of Taiwan became more positive. In light of these developments, the 1972 system is no longer an adequate basis for Japan's Taiwan policy. A new foundation that takes account of Japan's security and economic interests, as well as Japan's relations with the United States and the PRC, must be developed. Despite pressure from the PRC, Japan's refusal to repeat Clinton's "Three Nos" reformulation of American policy, and to guarantee the exclusion of Taiwan from the application of the revised U.S.-Japan security guidelines, as well as the granting of a visa for former President Lee to visit Japan in April 2001, may well signal the beginning of a new phase in Japan's Taiwan policy.

Chen's election implies, as well, that the basis for the Japan-Taiwan bilateral relationship in the twenty-first century must be constructed anew. Since 1972 the bilateral relationship has been built on the basis of interparty (Liberal Democratic Party [LDP] and KMT) and interpersonal (Lee Teng-hui) relations. The LDP and the KMT are now pale reflections of their former selves and no longer have a lock on national power. The weakening of the LDP and democratization in Taiwan have introduced many divergent voices in both countries. Moreover, the ex-colonial and pro-Japanese generation exemplified by Lee is passing from the scene in Taiwan. Not only has the new generation a dramatically altered self-image and conception of its relations with the mainland, but it is not beholden to the traditional nostalgic basis for Taiwan's relations with Japan. Such considerations, combined with the growing positive image of Taiwan in Japan, suggest that Tokyo must develop a new basis for bilateral relations that accords with current realities. The election of Chen and the transformation of the cross-strait conflict, Amae contends, present Tokyo with an opportunity to begin building a new relationship with Taipei. This, however, will not be easy. Apart from incurring the displeasure of Beijing, Tokyo will have to enter into a sustained dialogue with Taipei to forge a common understanding with the new leadership. In typical Japanese fashion, the basis for a new bilateral relationship and a new Taiwan policy is likely to evolve gradually in an incremental manner.

From the foregoing discussion, it is evident that the outcome of the March 2000 presidential election—the victory of Chen Shu-bian and the defeat of the KMT—have important consequences not only for democratic development in Taiwan, but may also have significant lessons for political change in the PRC and the one-party-dominant, quasi-democratic regimes in Southeast Asia. The election of Chen and the defeat of the KMT further advance the transformation of the cross-strait dispute that has been under way since 1991, making a final settlement even more difficult. Chen's statements on Taiwan independence before he became president, his reluctance since then to fully subscribe to the one China principle, and Beijing's negative reaction to Chen have continued the impasse in cross-strait dialogue that began in 1999 with the suspension of the Koo-Wang talks. Democratization in Taiwan has also complicated U.S. policy and undermined the premise of Japan's Taiwan policy as well as the basis for Tokyo's bilateral relationship with Taipei. These issues are dealt with in greater detail in the chapters that follow.

Notes

1. This does not mean that the military subscribes to the goals of the DPP or that democratic civilian control of the military has been consolidated.

2. Strictly speaking, the KMT has ruled Taiwan since 1945 when Japan turned over control of the island to the Government of China which was then headed by the KMT.

3. Lee Teng-hui, also a native Taiwanese, won the first presidential election in 1996.

4. In a survey conducted in August 1999 for the Taiwan Mainland Affairs Council (MAC), only 13.8 percent and 16.3 percent of the respondents supported independence and unification with the mainland respectively. A far larger number, 39.6 percent, supported the status quo until the situation clears up; another 12.2 percent supported the status quo forever.

5. "*Tangwai*" literally means "outside the party." The *tangwai* movement was the vehicle for non-Kuomintang candidates to cooperate, circumvent government prohibitions, criticize government policy, and run for office until political parties were legalized in 1989. The DPP, formed in 1986, grew out of the *tangwai* movement.

6. Hung-mao Tien, "Taiwan's Transformation," in *Consolidating the Third Wave Democracies: Regional Challenges*, ed. Larry Diamond, Marc F. Plattner, Yun-han Chu, and Hung-mao Tien (Baltimore: Johns Hopkins University Press, 1997).

7. See Thomas B. Gold, "Taiwan: Still Defying the Odds," in Diamond et al., *Consolidating the Third Wave Democracies: Regional Challenges*.

8. Ibid., p. 174.

9. On the key developments in Taiwan's democratization see Tien, "Taiwan's Transformation."

10. This number includes James Soong's People First Party that was formed after the election.

11. On the reasons for the initiation of political liberalization see chapter 7 in Andrew J. Nathan, *China's Transition* (New York: Columbia University Press, 1997). For the method and process of democratization, see the collection of essays in Tun-jen Cheng and Stephen Haggard, *Political Change in Taiwan* (Boulder: Lynne Rienner, 1992), and Tun-jen Cheng and Chia-lung Lin, "Taiwan: A Long Decade of Democratic Transition," in *Driven by Growth*, ed. James Morley and Harold Crouch (Armonk, NY: M.E. Sharpe, 1999).

12. "Bitter Row as Rulers Scrap Nuclear Plant," *South China Morning Post* (Hong Kong), 28 October 2000. See also "Taiwan: Poll Finds 33 percent Support Decision to Halt Nuclear Power Plant," *BBC Monitoring Asia-Pacific-Political* (London), 29 October 2000.

13. See the theoretical and conceptual chapters in *Consolidating the Third Wave Democracies: Themes and Perspectives*, ed. Larry Diamond, Marc F. Plattner, Yun-han Chu, and Hung-mao Tien (Baltimore: Johns Hopkins University Press, 1997).

14. Juan J. Linz and Alfred Stepan, "Toward Consolidated Democracies," in Diamond et al., *Consolidating the Third Wave Democracies: Themes and Perspectives*.

15. Tien, "Taiwan's Transformation."

16. Robert A. Dahl, *Polyarchy: Participation and Opposition* (New Haven: Yale University Press, 1971).

17. Gold, "Taiwan: Still Defying the Odds."

18. Larry Diamond, "Introduction: In Search of Consolidation," in Diamond et al., *Consolidating the Third Wave Democracies: Themes and Perspectives*, p. xli.

19. Bruce Dickson, *Democratization in China and Taiwan: The Adaptability of Leninist Parties* (Oxford: Clarendon Press, 1997), p. 3.

20. Andrew J. Nathan, *China's Crisis: Dilemmas of Reform and Prospects for Democracy* (New York: Columbia University Press, 1990), p. 153.

21. Dickson, *Democratization in China and Taiwan*.

22. For an expanded discussion of this point see Muthiah Alagappa, "The Anatomy of Legitimacy," in *Political Legitimacy in Southeast Asia: The Quest for Moral Authority*, ed. Muthiah Alagappa (Stanford: Stanford University Press, 1995), pp. 17–18.

23. For amplification of this point, see Muthiah Alagappa, "Seeking a More Durable Basis of Authority," in Alagappa, *Political Legitimacy in Southeast Asia*.

24. For the PAP government's maintenance of legitimacy, see Chua Beng Huat (chapter 4 in this volume) and Khong Cho Oon, "Singapore: Political Legitimacy Through Managing Conformity," in Alagappa, *Political Legitimacy in Southeast Asia*.

25. For the political legitimacy of the UMNO-led Alliance and later BN government, see William Case, "Malaysia: Aspects and Audiences of Legitimacy," in Alagappa, *Political Legitimacy in Southeast Asia*.

26. The definitions of native Taiwanese and mainlander are those of Alan M.

Wachman. See his *Taiwan: National Identity and Democratization* (Armonk, NY: M.E. Sharpe, 1994), pp. 15–16.

27. Ibid.

28. See C.L. Chiou, "Democratizing Taiwan: The Impact on Taiwan-China Relations," in *Uncertain Future: Taiwan–Hong Kong–China Relations After Hong Kong's Return to Chinese Sovereignty*, ed. C.L. Chiou and Leong H. Liew (Brookfield, VT: Ashgate, 2000).

29. Hung-mao Tien, "Taiwan's Perspective on Cross-Strait Relations and U.S. Policy," *American Foreign Policy Interests* 21(6) (December 1999):13–19.

30. Julian Jengliang Kuo, "Taiwan's New Policy Toward Mainland China," *American Foreign Policy Interests* 22(6) (December 2000):32–35.

31. Xu Shiquan, "The One-China Principle: The Positions of the CCP, the KMT, and the DPP," *American Foreign Policy Interests* 22(6) (December 2000):22–31.

32. See the 1972 U.S.-PRC Joint Communiqué.

33. Kuo, "Taiwan's New Policy."

34. I would like to thank Godwin Chu for clarifying the 1992 understanding.

35. Writing in 1990, Nathan argued that political reform in Taiwan had undermined the key assumption of the CCP's policy that the KMT has the power, if it so desires, to settle the cross-strait conflict. For this and other consequences of democratization, see Andrew Nathan, "The Effects of Taiwan's Political Reform on Taiwan-Mainland Relations," in Nathan, *China's Crisis*.

36. David E. Sanger, "Bush Tells Beijing the U.S. Is Ready to Defend Taiwan," *New York Times*, 26 April 2001.

1

Anatomy of an Electoral Earthquake: How the KMT Lost and the DPP Won the 2000 Presidential Election

Larry Diamond

On 18 March 2000, Taiwan experienced an electoral earthquake. After half a century in power on Taiwan, and after eight decades of continuous rule at the peak of political control, the Kuomintang (KMT) lost power in a free and fair presidential election. The electoral shock came just four years after incumbent President Lee Teng-hui had been decisively reelected with an absolute majority in a four-way contest. In 2000, President Lee's vice-president and anointed successor, Lien Chan, faced only two serious challengers. Yet he finished third with 23 percent of the vote. Lien badly trailed both the challenger of the historic opposition party (the Democratic Progressive Party, DPP), Chen Shui-bian—who won with 39 percent after having been defeated barely a year before for reelection as Taipei's mayor—and the KMT breakaway candidate, the former governor of Taiwan province, James Soong (Table 1.1).

The March 2000 presidential election dealt a humiliating defeat to the KMT as a party and to Lien Chan personally. Although many KMT politicians privately feared defeat—because Soong's challenge deeply divided the party and Lien himself was a lackluster candidate—none anticipated its scale. And it was by no means clear that Chen Shui-bian and the DPP would come out on top. A few months in advance of the election, Soong—the most effective grassroots politician in Taiwan—appeared headed to a decisive victory.

It is possible to attribute the KMT's defeat to a factor beyond its control:

The author gratefully acknowledges the research assistance of Rosie Hsueh.

Table 1.1

1996 and 2000 Presidential Election Results (Percentage of total vote)

Parties and candidates	1996	2000
KMT		
Lee Teng-hui and Lien Chan (1996)	54.0	
Lien Chan and Vincent Siew (2000)		23.10
DPP		
Peng Ming-min and Hsieh Chang-ting (1996)	21.1	
Chen Shui-bian and Annette Lu (2000)		39.30
New Party		
Lin Yang-Kang and Hau Pei-tsun (1996)	14.9	
Li Ao and Elmer Fung (2000)		0.13
Independent (KMT Breakaway)		
Chen Li-an and Wang Ching-feng (1996)	10.0	
James Soong and Chang Chao-hsiung (2000)		36.80
Independent (DPP Breakaway)		
Hsu Hsin-liang and Josephine Chu (2000)		0.63

the international zeitgeist that has seen democracy and freedom expand in almost every region of the world during the past quarter-century. The people of Taiwan were eager for change, for some kind of electoral shift that would turn out of power the only ruling party they had ever known. While Taiwan was indisputably a democracy by 2000, democratic vigor was lacking in a system that had never seen the ruling party lose control of any branch of power at the national level: not the presidency, not the cabinet (the Executive Yuan), not the parliament (the Legislative Yuan), and not the constitution-amending body (the National Assembly). In a sense, the stakes were limited in March 2000. No seats in the Legislative Yuan or the National Assembly were being contested. Although the president is not constitutionally required to obtain parliamentary approval of his choice of premier, the system retains much of the character of a French-style semipresidential system. Yet since 1949 power in Taiwan has flowed mainly from the presidency on down, and there could be no doubt that this was indeed the pinnacle of the political system.

In comparative perspective, the decision of Taiwan's electorate to pass control of that pinnacle to the opposition party now seems less extraordinary than it did at the time. Just one day later, on 19 March, the Socialist Party in Senegal lost a presidential election for the first time in the country's forty years of independence. Two and a half months later, on 2 July, Mexico's Revolutionary Institutional Party (PRI) went down to a crushing defeat in that country's freest and fairest presidential election, ending the seventy-one-year reign of the longest-ruling party in the world. One-party hegemony, it seems, is going out of fashion. Even though Japan's Liberal Democratic Party quickly returned to power after a brief electoral setback during the 1990s, it has lost its towering political dominance. The Congress Party of India is now a shell of its former self. Every successor to the communist parties that once ruled under dictatorship has lost a free and fair presidential election, even if some have subsequently rebounded to power under a banner of reform. In this era of globalization and democratization, people want political choice and change. But this does not explain why the people of Taiwan voted for change at the moment they did, and why the agent of change they chose was Chen Shui-bian.

Two further factors complicate the puzzle. Taiwan's voters had already used the ballot box to bring about dramatic electoral change at the level of city and county governments in the historic elections of November 1997. But there was much greater risk associated with giving the untested DPP control of the presidency, and thus of foreign policy, the national security establishment, and cross-strait relations. It was therefore widely assumed that while the DPP might win power at the local level, and perhaps even govern well, the voters would not risk entrusting the national future to the DPP—at least, not for a long time to come. Moreover, economically the country was in quite good shape. It had managed to avoid getting dragged down in the East Asian financial crash of November 1997. It had maintained a stable currency and low inflation while recording economic growth in the range of 5 to 6 percent a year or higher. This was well below the peak years of Taiwan's "miracle" growth, but quite respectable for a country moving into industrial (and even postindustrial) maturity, particularly at a time when many economies in the region were in crisis. There were social problems and grievances, to be sure, but nothing on a scale that would forecast an electoral earthquake.

Why, then, did the 2000 presidential election produce such a stunning outcome? As we shall see, there were five principal reasons:

1. *The moral and political exhaustion of the KMT.* No political party can remain in power for half a century and not grow arrogant, complacent, and corrupt. Even with its steady, effective stewardship of the country's economy, the KMT had not kept up with the voters' desire for reform on a number of fronts. There was particularly deep concern about "black gold" politics: the power of organized crime and its penetration into party politics and electoral representative bodies, reflected in the shady character of many local KMT factional leaders; the incestuous links between wealthy corporate interests and the party-state; the gigantic volumes of cash that sloshed around the political system, buying votes and influence; and the inability of the judicial system to rein in these perversions of democracy. These factors and related

hangovers from the authoritarian era, particularly the intertwining of the ruling party and the state, generated a national aspiration for comprehensive political reform.

2. *The split within the KMT.* Previously the KMT had easily prevailed in single-seat elections, except when it was divided. Such divisions opened the way to traumatic upsets, most dramatically in the 1994 race for mayor of Taipei. The KMT's inability to reconcile with James Soong and keep him within the party dealt it a severe blow.

3. *The campaign and the issues.* Chen Shui-bian and his party ran a brilliant campaign focusing on issues favorable to him, particularly "black and gold," and neutralizing the issue that threatened him most, cross-strait relations. By leaking a scandal about his personal finances, the KMT brought down the high-flying James Soong, but in the process also underscored the urgent need for political reform that Chen Shui-bian was stressing. The perfectly timed public endorsement of Chen by Lee Yuan-tseh, Taiwan's most revered intellectual and moral leader, helped push Chen over the top.

4. *The personalities.* Lien Chan was respected for his quiet competence, administrative acumen, and discretion during a twenty-year career in government as minister of transport and communications, vice-premier, minister of foreign affairs, governor of Taiwan province, premier, and then vice-president. But he was a dull, diffident, cold campaigner whose personality and family wealth conveyed an image of arrogance and social distance. James Soong and Chen Shui-bian, by contrast, were moving, charismatic, indefatigable campaigners who loved crowds and took naturally to the rigors of electioneering. In the search for votes, whether in person, on the stump, or on TV, Lien Chan was simply no match for these two natural-born campaigners, the most personally popular politicians in Taiwan after Lee Teng-hui.

5. *Lee Teng-hui's ambivalence.* There is little evidence to support suspicions that Lee Teng-hui deliberately sabotaged his own nominee in order to promote the cause of Taiwan independence through the candidacy of Chen Shui-bian. President Lee's highest priority was to stop Soong, however, rather than to elect Lien. And in the process he made many strategic decisions, maneuvers, feints, and perhaps miscalculations that cost his candidate and his party dearly.

I develop these interpretations in the following pages. After tracing electoral trends in Taiwan, showing growing competitiveness but continued KMT dominance of national politics, I review the strategies of the three campaigns and show how they evolved over time. I then trace key campaign events at two key points—in the early months when the race took shape and in the frenetic final week when it was decided—and outline how the campaigns positioned themselves on the issues. In conclusion I summarize how and why Chen Shui-bian won this historic election.

The Electoral Background

The 2000 presidential election was only the second direct presidential election in Taiwan's history. The first, in 1996, completed the Republic of China's long, artful decade of peaceful, incremental democratization. But it also confirmed, for the first time in a truly democratic presidential election, the KMT's continuing domination of the political system. In 1996, the incumbent president Lee Teng-hui shattered the opposition by winning 54 percent of the vote despite the presence of two strong independents, who had bolted from the KMT, as well as the DPP candidate, Peng Ming-min, a longtime advocate of Taiwan independence, who mustered only 21 percent of the vote while running a weak second (Table 1.1).

Although there had been electoral competition—in the sense of having multiple candidates for office—since the 1950s, organized electoral competition did not emerge in Taiwan until the 1970s when a small group of politicians who called themselves *tangwai* ("outside the party" or "non-Kuomintang") began to criticize the ruling party publicly and challenge it in local elections.[1] Even then the system was not open and democratic. The transition to democracy did not begin until the *tangwai* took the bold step in September 1986 of transforming themselves into a political party, the DPP. Although this was a violation of the law, President Chiang Ching-kuo chose to tolerate this historic step and followed in July 1987 by lifting martial law. These milestones had important implications for the triennial vote for parliament, the Legislative Yuan (LY). Shortly after the *tangwai* declared themselves a party, in the 1986 LY election their vote share increased from 19 to almost 25 percent. By 1989, with the momentum of democratization gathering under the recently installed Lee Teng-hui (who took office with the death of Chiang Ching-kuo in January 1988), the DPP vote share had increased to almost 30 percent. Overall the opposition share of the LY vote more than doubled between 1980 and 1995: from 13 percent to 33 percent. It slipped back in 1998 to just under 30 percent. With the vote of two small new electoral blocs sympathetic to the DPP, the Taiwan Independence Party and the New Nation Alliance, the overall pro-DPP vote seemed to hold at about a third of the electorate (Table 1.2). The DPP's share of LY seats declined from 33 percent to 30 percent, however, while the KMT's share increased from about 52 percent to 55 percent.

The slippage in the vote for its own LY candidates and its failure to break beyond its one-third ceiling on the national vote were not the biggest elec-

Table 1.2

Legislative Yuan Elections: 1980–1998 (Percentage of popular vote for political party or bloc)

Year	KMT	Tangwai/ DPP	Independents/ others	New Party	Taiwan Independence Party and New Nation Alliance
1980	71.7	13.0	15.3		
1983	69.4	18.9	11.7		
1986	66.7	24.6	8.7		
1989	59.2	29.9	10.9		
1992	52.5	30.8	16.7		
1995	46.1	33.2	7.8	13.0	
1998	46.4	29.6	13.9	7.1	3.1

Sources: Hung-mao Tien, "Elections and Taiwan's Democratic Development," in *Taiwan's Electoral Politics and Democratic Transition: Riding the Third Wave*, ed. Hung-mao Tien (Armonk, NY: M.E. Sharpe, 1996), fig. 1.1, p. 16; Hung-mao Tien, "Taiwan's Transformation," in *Consolidating the Third Wave Democracies: Regional Challenges*, ed. Larry Diamond, Marc F. Plattner, Yun-han Chu, and Hung-mao Tien (Baltimore: Johns Hopkins University Press, 1997), fig. 6, p. 151; and Linda Chao and Ramon H. Myers, *The First Chinese Democracy: Political Life in the Republic of China on Taiwan* (Baltimore: Johns Hopkins University Press, 1998), table 14, p. 284.

toral disappointments for the DPP in 1998. Its highest public officeholder, Chen Shui-bian, was defeated for reelection as mayor of Taipei despite wide praise for his performance (with job approval ratings hovering around 70 percent). Chen lost to a highly popular and appealing mainlander candidate for the KMT, former Justice Minister Ma Ying-jeou, in a two-way race where the latter was able to unite his political and ethnic base. This strategy proved sufficient in a city where mainlanders account for about 30 percent of the electorate.[2] Still Chen garnered two more percentage points than in 1994 (when he won a three-way race), and the DPP managed to capture the position of mayor of Kaohsiung, Taiwan's second-largest city, when Frank Hsieh defeated a nationally prominent KMT incumbent.

Even when Chen was defeated for reelection as mayor, many were speculating that he might soon be a formidable candidate for president of Taiwan, where mainlanders constitute only about half the proportion (15 percent) they represent in Taipei. As these analysts noted at the time, it is somewhat misleading to compare the single-seat contest for the presidency with the elections for the Legislative Yuan, because the latter are conducted mostly in multiseat constituencies under the complicated system of the single non-

Table 1.3

Total Percentage of Votes for KMT and DPP in County Magistrate and City Mayor Elections: 1985–1997

Year	KMT	DPP/ *Tangwai*
1985	60.9	13.5
1989	56.1	30.1
1993	47.5	41.0
1997	41.0	43.0

Source: Hung-mao Tien, "Elections and Taiwan's Democratic Development," in *Taiwan's Electoral Politics and Democratic Transition: Riding the Third Wave*, ed. Hung-mao Tien (Armonk, NY: M.E. Sharpe, 1996), fig. 1.2, p. 17.

transferable vote (SNTV). These elections turn heavily on candidate personalities, factional rivalries, and strategic considerations (for example, not nominating too many candidates for any one district). Looking at the trend in the other single-seat races, for county magistrates and city mayors, the DPP's national prospects appeared more hopeful. After winning the city of Taipei in 1994, the DPP captured twelve of the twenty-three other city and country governments on 27 November 1997.[3] For the first time in a national election, the DPP won a plurality of the total vote: 43 percent to 41 percent for the KMT, which won only eight city and country executive positions (three of them sparsely populated island jurisdictions) after having controlled seventeen. With control of Taipei as well, this gave the DPP executive power in local governments containing more than 70 percent of Taiwan's population.

The 1997 elections continued a decade-long trend of steady decline in the KMT's vote for city and county executives (Table 1.3). At the national level, however, there was much greater risk associated with political change, and arguably less reason for it. The DPP had never won more than a third of the vote in a national election. Thus most observers figured that the DPP had a ceiling of roughly 35 percent on its potential vote in the 2000 presidential election—and, moreover, that a DPP victory was possible only if the KMT split and the other 65 percent of the vote were fairly evenly divided between two strong contenders.

Campaign Strategy

A vitally important dimension of the election campaign concerned the electoral strategy of each campaign. In a tight, three-cornered race, anything was possible. Each campaign struggled mightily to avoid falling behind clearly into third place. Each knew that such a fate would induce many of its follow-ers to "dump" it in favor of the least offensive other alternative, in order to defeat the most feared candidate. In particular, Chen Shui-bian feared that if he fell behind his supporters might dump him for Lien Chan, in order to stop James Soong. Lien Chan felt that if he fell behind his supporters might dump him to stop either Chen or Soong. Initially, Soong was so far ahead in the polls that he seemed assured of victory if he could project a moderate pos-ture, but he also feared that if he fell behind his supporters would dump him and back Lien Chan in order to stop the "pro-independence" candidate, Chen Shui-bian. Each campaign knew that the race might be won with less than 40 percent of the vote. Both the KMT candidate, Lien, and the KMT renegade, Soong, knew full well that the only way the KMT could be beaten was if the two candidates split the party's natural majority support fairly evenly. Yet each held on till the end and proved powerless to prevent the electoral disas-ter that was foreseeable months in advance of the election.

Lien's Campaign Strategy

By the summer of 1999, the race for the 2000 presidential election campaign was a three-way contest between the ruling-party candidate, Vice-President Lien Chan, the ruling-party defector, James Soong, and the opposition party candidate, Chen Shui-bian. A few key events shaped the contours and even-tual outcome of the 2000 election. None was more important than Soong's entry into the race as an independent candidate. For Lien's campaign, this was a severe blow. Strategists in both the KMT party bureaucracy and the Lien campaign knew that when the party was united in single-seat contests, it had historically prevailed with ease, even in the more fully democratic contests of the 1990s. But when the party was divided, it was vulnerable. Never was this more clearly demonstrated than in the successive contests for mayor of Taipei in 1994 and 1998. When the KMT split in 1994 and the New Party put forward a dynamic candidate against a dull KMT incumbent, the DPP challenger, Chen Shui-bian, won an intense three-way race with less than 40 percent of the vote. Four years later, when the KMT won back New Party voters (and thus created a two-person contest) by nominating the popular mainlander Ma Ying-jeou, it won comfortably.

For the Lien camp in late 1998 and the first half of 1999, the paramount strategic aim was to duplicate the Taipei race of 1998, not 1994. Reflecting back after the election, some Lien advisers believe the race was really lost on 16 July 1999 when Soong declared his candidacy. Until then, their key goal had been to dissuade Soong from running. Their best means for doing so was to offer him the vice-presidential nomination. Another possibility was to offer him the post of premier, but for Soong the mere promise of the premiership would not have been credible. There was speculation that Soong might be dissuaded from running if he were made premier immediately—with a public announcement that he would remain in the job if Lien Chan won. Many Lien supporters and other pragmatists within the KMT wanted to bring Lien and Soong together into a "dream ticket." But there was no getting past the intractable opposition of the KMT chairman, President Lee Teng-hui.

Stopping Soong's ascent had become one of the overriding political missions of Lee Teng-hui. Why President Lee became so alienated from his former political lieutenant and KMT secretary-general is not entirely clear, but at least three factors played a role. First, Soong was the first mainlander to build a truly national political following since Lee Teng-hui had "Taiwanized" the KMT and the entire political system. During his four years as governor of Taiwan province (1994–1998), Soong worked brilliantly to develop his own political power base by cultivating direct ties to grassroots constituencies and cementing patron/client bonds with local bosses. As a result of his political genius and effective administration, Governor Soong's soaring political popularity had become second only to President Lee's— and his job approval ratings were actually higher than the president's. By the mid-1990s, Lee had become an imperious political leader who brooked no rivals; he may well have been jealous of his former lieutenant's blooming romance with the public. Soong, a shrewd, charismatic politician who had built up the KMT's local roots over two decades in the party organization, was becoming a political threat.[4]

Second, Soong harbored views on cross-strait relations that Lee Teng-hui distrusted. In fact, Soong's views on dealing with mainland China were in the pragmatic center of Taiwan's political spectrum. Essentially he favored preserving the political status quo—but the status quo of the early 1990s, not the status quo as Lee Teng-hui was seeking to redefine it by extending the rhetoric and symbols of Taiwan's separate national identity. Soong's opposition to President Lee's 1999 declaration of a "special state-to-state relationship" between Taiwan and the mainland, his resistance to Lee's other adventurous initiatives, and his emphasis on renewing the political dialogue with Beijing were seen by President Lee as threatening to reverse his own historic course.

These first two factors were aggravated by policy and political differences that emerged between the president and the governor after Lee Teng-hui's reelection in 1996. Soong objected to the accumulating fiscal burden that the central government was placing on the provincial government through a series of unfunded mandates and programs, particularly the National Health Insurance Plan (implemented in March 1995) and a monthly subsidy to senior farmers. Without adequate central government funding, he worried, these mandated programs would (and in fact did) swell the provincial government's budget deficits. His protests, however, were "interpreted by some in the central government as direct challenges, even threats, to their position and authority."[5] This was especially the case with Soong's opposition to the constitutional reform plan, formulated in late 1996 in collaboration between Lee Teng-hui's KMT and the DPP, to "freeze" the provincial government. The plan, which would terminate direct election of the Taiwan provincial governor and phase out most of the provincial government's functions, was justified as a means of streamlining government and saving money. City and country governments would be raised in status and the intermediate layer between them and the center could be largely eliminated. The New Party, however, saw this as yet another step in Lee Teng-hui's master plan to transform the Republic of China into a Republic of Taiwan, at least in everything but name. For Soong, publicly, this amendment would shut down a level of government that was delivering services and development to the people of Taiwan province (most of the country except for Taipei and Kaohsiung). Privately Soong saw the initiative as a calculated attempt to rob him of his political base and platform and thereby "prevent his popularity as the provincial governor from turning into the foundation of support for seeking higher office."[6] Although Soong did not carry his opposition into all-out public confrontation—by joining with the New Party to block passage of the constitutional amendment in the National Assembly—Lee Teng-hui took umbrage at Soong's refusal to go along from the start, viewing it as confirmation of Soong's ambition and untrustworthiness. The deepening rift "completely shattered the basis of trust and respect of this once 'father and son' relationship."[7]

For these and perhaps other reasons, Lee Teng-hui resolved to obstruct James Soong's path to the presidency by blocking his ascent on the political ladder to the point where he would lead the executive administration (as premier) or be in a position (as vice-president) to move up to the presidency. When Soong resolved to buck Lee's will and fight for the presidency directly, preventing Soong's victory in 2000 became the aging president's most impassioned goal. During the final weeks of the campaign, Lee Teng-hui spent most of his political energy and rhetorical fire attacking Soong rather than Chen Shui-bian, joining the drumbeat of KMT efforts to destroy Soong's image as a reformer. Lee's denunciation of Soong was unsparing:

> As a result of Soong's leaving the party, the "black gold" politics within the KMT has almost been cleaned up. The KMT is too clean to keep that kind of garbage-eating fish alive; therefore, [Soong's camp] quit the KMT in an effort to establish a so-called "non-partisan" politics.

It was horrible to witness that Soong had spent around NT$500 billion during his tenure as Provincial Governor for over five years. Because of that, now it will cost [the public] three months of wages to repay the debt.[8]

The president's unwillingness to denounce Chen Shui-bian in equally harsh terms—and the parade of endorsements of Chen by Lee's associates—fed countless rumors that President Lee gave up on Lien Chan and secretly encouraged his friends while gently signaling the public to back Chen over Soong. The evidence for this theory is sketchy and the reality is likely more complicated. Judging from his conduct during the campaign and the personal relationship that developed between former President Lee and President Chen since the 20 May inauguration, it is possible to infer that President Lee secretly wished the election of Chen, who shares Lee's commitment to Taiwan's separate identity much more than Soong or even Lien. To bolster this conspiracy theory, some analysts (including a number of deeply embittered KMT members) suggest that leading business and public figures who have been close to President Lee (such as Evergreen Chairman Chang Yung-fa and above all the president of the Academia Sinica, Lee Yuan-tseh) would not have come out to bless Chen's campaign in the final two weeks without some signal of approval from President Lee. Yet several of these prominent endorsers have indicated that there was no coordination or communication in advance with President Lee, and at least one insists he hid his plans from Lee for fear the president would try to talk him out of it. One senior figure in Lien Chan's campaign confided that during the final weeks of the campaign, President Lee rejected many hard-hitting drafts of speeches endorsing Lien and attacking Chen Shui-bian in favor of much milder language. Without much success, the Lien campaign urged President Lee to attack Chen vigorously and appeal to Lee's own following to dump Chen for Lien. For at least some Lien partisans, President Lee's support appeared lukewarm. For many Soong supporters (and not a few KMT loyalists), President Lee's insistence on promoting a successor so lacking in personal charisma was itself proof of his secret intention to sabotage his own party.[9]

In fact, President Lee did work for, campaign for, and appeal for his hand-picked successor, Lien Chan. In the campaign's closing days, he repeatedly sought to dispel the rumors he was secretly backing Chen. On 11 March (the day after Lee Yuan-tseh first offered his support to Chen), President Lee traveled to southern Taiwan to campaign for Lien. Acknowledging the rumors of a secret "abandon and save" campaign, Lee appealed to a gathering of KMT officials in Pingtung county "to avoid this kind of trap. Such a groundless rumor was meant to make us lose our confidence."[10] On 13 March, President Lee sharply criticized Chen to a visiting group of businesspeople:

"What experience does he have to make party rotation? No expertise, only fabrication. How can a person like this run the country?"[11] On 14 March, he flatly denied he supported Chen, and he urged voters to support Lien to avoid a war across the Taiwan Strait.[12] Again on 15 March, he explicitly sought to stamp out speculation that he was secretly supporting Chen, calling on voters not to "listen to rumors" or be "deceived by campaign tricks." "The more votes Lien gets, the more secure the country will be," he said.[13] To one of the KMT's largest rallies, in Kaohsiung on 12 March, President Lee declared: "Chen's National Policy Advisory Committee is absolutely not working."[14] And to a Lien rally in Taipei county on 16 March, two nights before the election, Lee urged voters to "dump Soong to save Lien" while taking another swipe at Chen: "Some immature DPP people said they would like to visit China and communicate with them. It's definitely a joke."[15]

In the final week or so, the president may have hedged his bet by not objecting when key friends in the business community revealed their intent to support Chen and by declining to turn his fire unreservedly on Chen. The most plausible interpretation is that Lee's obsession with stopping Soong pushed him in two directions: On the one hand, he sincerely wanted Lien Chan to win; on the other, he did not want to risk a Soong victory. Internal estimates by the KMT indicated that if Lee gave his all-out support to Lien, denouncing Chen as thoroughly as Soong, it could add five percentage points to Lien's vote. But in pulling down Chen, Lee risked helping to elect Soong rather than Lien. A week before the election, leading analysts doubted that Lee would "take the risk and lash out at Chen." Their skepticism proved correct.[16]

In the harm he did to his own party in 2000, Lee Teng-hui was guilty not so much of duplicity as myopia, arrogance, and stubborn pride. President Lee believed that his personal popularity could carry over to his vice-president. He felt that if Lien could draw close in the polls in the final few weeks, his own reverent base of support among native Taiwanese and the vaunted KMT political machine would combine to deliver at least a narrow victory.

If President Lee had been confronted with the certain knowledge that his own nominee could not be elected, there is little doubt he would strongly have preferred Chen over Soong. Some in the Lien campaign concede they knew by the final week of the campaign, after Lee Yuan-tseh endorsed Chen, that Lien was headed toward defeat. This knowledge derived both from private polling data and from field reports telling of campaign rallies lacking in attendance and enthusiasm as well as local bosses who were not mobilizing as they had in the past. Perhaps some party stalwarts were deluded by a number of rigged polls the KMT commissioned in a disinformation campaign to show Lien tied or in the lead, and thereby hold onto local factional leaders who might defect to Soong or sit on their hands. Countless public opinion polls were conducted toward the end of the campaign, however, and they circulated widely even though their results could not (by law) be reported in the final ten days. Even some independent polls were showing, up to the final few days of the campaign, a very tight race: Lien may have been trailing slightly, but three in ten voters were undecided (or at least undeclared) and anything could happen. Two days before the election, a CTN TV poll showed the three candidates tied with about 23 percent each. A *United Daily News* poll showed the race too close to call, with each candidate between 21 and 23 percent.[17] Taiwan-based equity fund managers, who have a big stake in predicting political developments, expected a Lien victory.[18] So too did many independent academic experts in Taiwan, who believed the KMT machine would pull out a narrow victory for Lien. And opinion polls had long shown a large plurality of the public expecting Lien to win.

There remains the question of why Lien Chan did not try to bring Soong onto his ticket even if it meant breaking with Lee Teng-hui. After all, a Lien–Soong ticket, reunifying the KMT, could not have been defeated by Chen Shui-bian, even if a miffed President Lee had sat on his hands. During the first half of 1999, however, another prospect privately haunted both Lien and Soong. They feared that Lee Teng-hui would seek to extend his presidential term as part of a constitutional reform to synchronize the timing of legislative and presidential elections. With the next Legislative Yuan election not due until December 2001, an extension of the presidential term (possibly, by some accounts, to January 2003) would have crippled Lien's political future. Lien dared not defy Lee Teng-hui while there was still a chance that Lee would seek to remain in the presidency. By the time public opposition had crystallized against that prospect, in mid-1999, Soong had become committed to running and announced in short order.

Even after Lien was nominated, his campaign had little choice but to rely on Lee Teng-hui to help put it over the top. In two senses, Lien Chan seemed in an enviable position. He was the incumbent vice-president of a long-ruling party with an outstanding record of economic prosperity and stability— even as much of the region was falling into economic crisis. And on the key issue of cross-strait relations, Lien held the center position while his opponents leaned toward the ends of the spectrum (Taiwan independence or accommodation with Beijing). But given Lien's weakness and unpopularity as a candidate, it was a very vulnerable center. Each of the campaigns understood from the very beginning the volatility of a three-person race and its intrinsic tendency to find a bipolar equilibrium. The nightmare for the Lien campaign was that if he did not remain competitive, his support would implode in a rush to prevent one of two alternative nightmares: for the tradi-

Table 1.4

Selected Public Opinion Poll Results

Date of poll	TVBS			United Daily News			DPP		
	C	L	S	C	L	S	C	L	S
3/2/99	20.1	10.8	54.0						
7/17/99				21	14	40			
11/15–11/18/99	21	19	32	19	20	33	25.3	15.3	32.0
12/5–12/9/99	23	21	34				23.7	19.4	30.4
12/27–12/30/99	25	22	26	22	19	25	28.9	23.1	26.0
1/21–1/27/00	24	23	29	22	23	27	28.3	22.9	25.0
2/11–2/13/00	24	23	22	22	26	24	28.4	22.8	24.4
2/26–3/4/00	24	24	27	24	20	24	25.8	22.0	24.7
3/5–3/11/00				22	27	26	26.2	23.0	23.9
3/12–3/17/00							27.6	21.2	24.9

Note: C signifies Chen Shui-bian; L, Lien Chan; and S, James Soong.

tional KMT voters, a victory of the "dangerous, pro-independence" Chen; for the moderate Taiwanese voters whom Lee Teng-hui had solidified behind the KMT, a victory for the mainlander "capitulationist," James Soong. To hold onto and expand the latter constituency in particular, Lien needed the president's vigorous support. To hold onto traditional KMT voters and win back many defectors, the Lien campaign had to find a way to puncture James Soong's soaring balloon.

As the presidential election race headed into autumn, Soong held a commanding lead. From March 1999 through September, in fact, Soong led handily in every major public opinion poll. In many polls, his support was twice Lien Chan's and almost twice Chen Shui-bian's. The day after he declared his candidacy on 16 July 1999, a *United Daily News* poll gave him 40 percent—to just 14 percent for Lien Chan and 21 percent for Chen. A *China Times* poll conducted ten days before had found very similar results. By October and November the race had narrowed somewhat, but Soong was still so far ahead that he seemed almost certain to win unless something dramatic happened to shake up the race. By mid-November, Soong was holding steady with around a third of the electorate openly supporting him. Lien and Chen were each winning about a fifth of the electorate or slightly more. These polling results published by two of the leading Chinese-language newspapers (the *China Times* and the *United Daily News*), known for their anti-independence or pro-unification editorial orientations, were essentially identical to those reported by the independent, all-news cable-television station, TVBS, and to those being obtained by the DPP in its own internal polling (Table 1.4).

The KMT believed for some time that they had a perfect instrument to burst Soong's balloon: a scandal about Soong's personal finances that would paint a contrast between his image as a selfless, caring governor dedicated to the public welfare and a private reality of embezzling party funds for his own enrichment. On 9 December 1999, KMT legislator Yang Jih-hsiung alleged in a news conference that James Soong's son, Soong Cheng-yuan, had bank accounts with large cash balances and demanded that Soong explain where they came from. The revelation of the scandal concerning Soong's personal and family finances was carefully timed to knock Soong out of the leading position in the polls before he became invincible, or before Lien became unelectable. In fact, Lien's campaign hoped that the scandal would vault the vice-president into a lead of five percentage points over Soong—a margin sufficient to trigger a dynamic of "dump Soong for Lien" in order to stop Chen.[19] The effect of the scandal was not what Lien, his campaign, and the KMT were hoping for, however.

The scandal leveled the race, but it did not invert it in the way Lien's campaign had hoped. Soong fell from a third of the vote to a quarter. By January, after Soong had bumbled through successive, contradictory press conferences on the matter, the race was very tight. But not only had Lien failed to gain the five-percentage-point lead over Soong his campaign had sought from the scandal, he was still trailing both Soong and Chen in most public opinion polls. The primary beneficiary of Soong's misfortune was not Lien but Chen Shui-bian, who in most polls gained between three and six percentage points during the month of December when Soong was reeling. This was likely due to the nature of the scandal: alleging that Soong had misappropriated KMT *party* money. Soong himself claimed the mysterious funds in his relatives' accounts were put there at the direction of President Lee for "party tasks" in the early 1990s (when the president was consolidating his control of the party with Soong's help). The inference many voters drew—that political corruption was more a KMT problem than a James Soong problem—played very nicely into the hands of the Chen campaign, which had made cleaning up a rotten political system its most prominent issue. It has been widely speculated that the KMT had still more to reveal about Soong, but backed off in the face of Soong's threat to reveal damaging information of his own and in the wake of Chen's alarming rise in the polls.[20] This was Lien's dilemma of a three-cornered race: After December, it was never clear whom he had to fear more, Chen or Soong. As a result, his campaign was never able to focus on knocking off one of his two competitors in order to climb out of third place.

In a tardy effort to respond to mounting public concern about the role of money in Taiwan's politics (stimulated by the Soong scandal as well as Chen's campaign), Lien announced on 2 January a plan to place the KMT's vast assets into a trust. The idea was to separate the party from direct control of its gargantuan business empire, estimated in the range of US$6–8 billion (which generates an annual income of $400 million for the party). But on the issue of political reform as well, Lien Chan was caught between conflicting imperatives. On the one hand, in the face of two vigorous, articulate challengers running hard against the KMT and the status quo, Lien needed to break cleanly with the politics of the past and commit to real political reform. On the other hand, trailing in the polls and lacking the personal appeal of his two rivals, Lien, by nature a cautious man, would not risk giving up the party's fortune or alienating (or even failing to utilize) the local bosses who had been delivering blocs of votes to the KMT. Many of these bosses and vote brokers had bad reputations as a result of criminal records and links to organized crime. Not surprisingly, Lien leaned heavily on this black network and never elaborated on his vague plan to place the party assets in trust. In what came to be widely viewed as the greatest blunder of his campaign, Lien appeared on stage at a Pingtung rally several weeks before the election with two of the most notorious "black gold" personalities, Luo Fu-chu and Wu Tse-yuan. This embrace of the two most powerful gangsters in politics (both members of parliament) helped prompt Lee Yuan-tseh to endorse Chen Shui-bian, which in turn swayed a crucial segment of the electorate to Chen.[21]

Having failed to deal a knockout punch to Soong in December, the KMT could only fall back on the very foundations of its political domination that the DPP had been inveighing against since the start of the campaign: "black and gold" mixed with a strong dose of fear. As in previous election campaigns (though not by so lopsided a margin), the KMT heavily outspent its opposition. Vast sums were expended not only on television and other advertising but also on campaign management and rallies and, in the final two weeks, on the distribution of funds to the KMT "organization"—the vast network of local bosses, brokers, retainers, and operatives that was riddled with shady records, corrupt contracts, and ties to organized crime.[22] The "organization," however, failed to deliver. Many of these bosses simply pocketed the large sums they were given to distribute as expressions of "gratitude" to individual voters.

Here again the Lien campaign faced dilemmas. It relied heavily on the KMT machine to deliver, but that machine was paralyzed in 2000 by the split between Lien and Soong. Having built and served this machine in key positions over two decades, Soong had already turned some of its cogs and wheels to his own purpose. Many of the local bosses who had reliably produced for the KMT in previous elections used KMT money to reward Soong supporters in 2000; according to a Taiwanese saying, they had the "skin of

Lien but the bone of Soong." Other bosses remained neutral, not wanting to antagonize either Lien or Soong supporters and not fearing postelection punishment from a ruling party that seemed likely to lose. Precisely because they were closest to the voters, these bosses perceived the lack of public enthusiasm for Lien's candidacy and the pointlessness of going all out in what appeared to be a losing cause. The incentive to mobilize local networks was also weaker because this presidential election (unlike 1996) was not coupled with a National Assembly election and hence lacked the connection to local-level races in which local factions would have a more immediate stake.

The fear factor failed as well. The KMT and the Lien campaign constantly and often crudely envisioned a national security crisis if Chen Shui-bian was elected president. Against a background of martial music and soldiers marching to war, KMT television ads in the final week of the campaign warned that 85 percent of men in their twenties would be sent to the battlefield in short order if Chen was elected.[23] A KMT newspaper advertisement showed "a man in army fatigues, his face hidden by a black gas mask, staring into a wall of flames. The figure represent[ed] Taiwan in the aftermath of a victory by Mr. Chen."[24] Lien himself cautioned that if Chen was elected, young men would have to trade in their "A-bian" knitted caps (a famous trademark of the campaign) for bulletproof helmets. The KMT alleged that China was already testing Taiwan's resolve with military maneuvers in the Taiwan Strait. Top military officers in Taiwan, however, downplayed the danger while remaining steadfastly neutral in the campaign. And Chen Shui-bian himself countered the fear campaign with a steady, disciplined adherence to a centrist line on cross-strait relations, a strong commitment to national defense, and a snappy TV advertisement showing his son (who was due to enter the military the next year) in an olive green T-shirt doing military-style, one-armed push-ups.[25] Noting that he was the only candidate with a draft-age son who would have to fight if China attacked Taiwan, Chen stressed that he was not going to do anything rash to jeopardize his life or others: "As a father, I understand the fear of parents who don't want to put their children into danger."[26]

Nor could Lien make effective use of Lee Teng-hui in the end. It was not only President Lee's reluctance to attack Chen Shui-bian that hurt. It was Lien's own ambivalence about where he stood in relation to Lee. As the campaign wore on, Lien sought to distance himself from Lee's more adventurous policies on Taiwan identity and relations with the mainland—an effort to win back Soong's mainlander constituency. Speaking to members of various "hometown associations" from Chinese provinces on 6 March, Lien emphasized his birth on the mainland (in Shaanxi province), his family's longtime involvement with China and Chinese culture, and the "historic missions" the KMT had undertaken.[27] But mainlanders remained suspicious of his connection to President Lee. And the more he ran to the right of Lee on Taiwan identity, the less prospect he had of winning over Lee Teng-hui's pro-Taiwan constituency.[28]

In the end, nothing worked for Lien Chan. His campaign entered its final two weeks hoping that money, the party machine, fear, and Lee Teng-hui would put him over the top. None of the four delivered many votes. If many campaign and party officials expected that Lien would lose, few anticipated the debacle that occurred. As one of Lien's top campaign officials reflected: "We were astounded that we lost by so much. We couldn't believe it."[29]

Soong's Campaign Strategy

James Soong entered the long campaign in July 2000 with formidable advantages and disadvantages. When he announced his independent candidacy he was by far the most popular candidate in the race. During his five-plus years as governor of Taiwan province, he had built a reputation as a tireless, efficient, hands-on administrator who cared about the people, listened to their concerns, and delivered what they needed. This earned him unheard-of levels of job approval from the public—consistently over 80 percent. With one eye to his political future, he toured the island constantly as governor, inspecting damage from natural disasters, delivering relief, attending funerals and weddings, hearing complaints, launching development projects, and distributing government largesse. According to one of his top aides, Raymond Wu, "In order to fully comprehend people's hardships and difficulties in life, he had visited each of the 309 cities and towns in the province more than three times while in office."[30] Four years of perpetual contact with the grassroots of Taiwan's politics and society had made him the most popular politician in Taiwan after Lee Teng-hui—an amazing political feat for a mainlander. His performance and persona as governor gave him a base of support that cut across the traditional divides of party and ethnicity. Even among native Taiwanese and DPP supporters, Soong won considerable respect and even admiration. He had also cultivated a substantial following among local bosses who had long supported the KMT but might now be prepared to back his insurgent challenge. With degrees from University of Berkeley and Georgetown University, he was keenly knowledgeable about the United States and the world and was respected in international circles. By his own estimation and that of many observers in Taiwan and beyond, James Soong was ready to be president.

Yet Soong was deeply conflicted about making an independent bid for the presidency. In fact, he pondered the momentous decision for something like a year. If he left the KMT, he would be a candidate without a party behind him and no access to the KMT's mammoth financial assets, which now would be turned against him. No one understood better than Soong, the former KMT secretary-general, the financial expenses involved in the care and feeding of a national political machine. As long as he was governor, he could use the resources of the provincial government to provide the jobs, services, development projects, and contracts necessary to construct a political machine loyal to him personally. But after his term ended, on 19 December 1998, he faced more than a year in the political wilderness with no official platform or staff, no political power, and no patronage to maintain his machine.

Sentiment and party loyalty also held Soong back. He had been a lifelong member of the KMT and had risen to its highest ranks. He worried that an independent campaign would be risky not only for him personally but also for the country. Soong was no less aware than the KMT that Chen Shuibian's only hope of victory was a three-way race that split the KMT.

For all these reasons, Soong tested the political waters discreetly, pondered, and wavered throughout 1998 and early 1999 even while he went about enhancing his political base. His clear preference was to take control of the KMT and democratize it. His ceaseless travels around the country had made him keenly aware of the widespread discontent with the domestic political situation, "particularly the increasingly rampant corruption and illegitimate government and business ties."[31] Soong challenged the party to hold a democratic primary election of its membership to determine the presidential nominee. Had the party agreed to this reform, he would have committed to respect its outcome and support the victor. But Soong himself would likely have won a democratic party primary election. Knowing this, both Lien Chan and President Lee insisted that the party use its indirect method of selection by the 2,000 delegates to the party's fifteenth national congress.

When Soong returned to Taiwan on 2 March 1999, from a nearly three-month hiatus in the United States, a TVBS poll gave him a staggering lead in a hypothetical three-way race: 54 percent for Soong to 20 percent for Chen and 11 percent for Lien. Yet he was still far from fully committed to running. He explored ways of healing his rift with the KMT leadership, but his hopes "were quickly dashed when he was not able to meet President Lee to possibly reconcile differences, and fellow KMT Central Standing Committee members routinely shunned him in its weekly meetings."[32]

In the end, Soong decided to run for several reasons. First, he was convinced he was the best candidate. Second, he was deeply concerned about the deterioration in cross-strait relations and sincerely believed his pragmatic approach could fashion a new political consensus in Taiwan that would repair the damage, which was to become a major theme of his campaign. Third, as the polls were showing, he had an excellent chance to win. And fourth, he realized through his constant contact with the grassroots that the voters were disaffected and the KMT machine was in disarray. Probably Soong, at age fifty-seven, also saw his presidential ambitions ending if Lien won and served two full terms as president.

Once he had declared, Soong's strategy was to derail Lien Chan and present himself as the only alternative to the risky, immature candidacy of Chen Shui-bian. In the terminology of the 2000 campaign, he had to persuade traditional KMT voters to "dump Lien for Soong to stop Chen." To do this, he stressed the need for political change—for reforming the KMT because it had grown out of touch with the voters. At the same time, he had to blunt the likely KMT effort to paint him as a "capitulationist" who would accommodate Taiwan too readily to the PRC's demands. For those voters undecided between Lien and Soong, he would make the political system more responsive but maintain a tough, pragmatic course in cross-strait relations. For those undecided between Chen and Soong, he stressed the dangers of a Chen presidency for Taiwan's security. At the same time, he embraced the ethnic center by proposing in August a "New Taiwanism" that recognized a future in Taiwan for all regardless of ethnicity or political affiliation. In every respect, Soong sought to capture the political center. He would bring political reform, but not radically convulse the system. He did not favor reunification with China in the near future, but he pledged immediate steps to resume the political dialogue with the mainland if elected while avoiding the provocations of the Lee Teng-hui era.

These broad contours of strategy, along with his political assets and achievements, would have carried James Soong to a decisive victory in the 2000 presidential election had it not been for "the revelations of the Soong family's mysterious accounts at the Chung Hsing Bills Finance Corporation and property in California and the spiraling amounts that Soong was accused of bilking from the party—amounting at one time to over NT$1 billion, but later revised downward to NT$360 million." By portraying himself "as the victim of the KMT's own shady culture," Soong generated some electoral sympathy and a backlash against the KMT.[33] But among key swing voters, especially younger voters, Soong's inability to offer a consistent and convincing explanation for how he came upon such wealth badly dented his image as a dedicated public servant committed to political reform. The KMT's revelations were perfectly timed. One high-ranking Soong campaign official reflected: "Had our campaign gone on through January without [the scandal], by the time of the Chinese New Year [in February] Soong would have been able to just name his premier because so many KMT members would have defected to him."[34] A top DPP campaign strategist concurs: "If there had been no financial scandal, then definitely Soong was going to win, and by a large margin, perhaps with 45 percent of the vote."[35]

Heightening the damaging effect of the scandal was an acute political quandary. To deliver the vote in the less urban areas of central and southern Taiwan, Soong had to rely on the same kinds of corrupt bosses and underworld figures that had soured the public on the KMT. But to fend off the surging campaign of Chen Shui-bian, he had to maintain his own image as a political reformer who would clean up the very type of politics he was having to rely on in many localities. It speaks volumes about Soong's popularity and political skill—and Taiwan voters' cynicism about their political system ("they all do it")—that he was able to recover to the point where he came within three percentage points of winning the presidency.

Chen Shui-bian's Strategy

When, in December 1998, Chen Shui-bian was defeated for reelection as Taipei mayor, many wondered whether he would still contest the coming presidential race. Although he took off three months to travel and reflect, there was not much doubt within Chen's camp or outside it that he would seek the presidency. Despite his election defeat, his term as mayor of Taipei was generally acknowledged to have been a success. The city was cleaner (literally and figuratively) than when he assumed office. The traffic flowed better, and the government worked better and was more responsive to citizen concerns. Not unlike James Soong—and in the most important jurisdiction after the central and provincial governments—Chen established the image of a tough, tireless, effective administrator. His defeat was owing to the large concentration of mainlander voters in Taipei, but this would not be the case in the country as a whole. With his roots in Tainan and his historic support for democratization and Taiwan independence, Chen was actually stronger in the south of the island. Moreover, no other DPP candidate had the remotest chance of victory in 2000. Chen and his advisers felt from the beginning that he had to run for president. His supporters expected it. Even if his chance of victory was not great, it was a chance, and he felt a historical imperative.

In contrast to his two main opponents, Chen faced the delicate task of keeping the election a three-way race. Soong and Lien each hoped to knock off the other and present himself as the only candidate who could stop Chen. If either had succeeded in this "dump-save" logic, Chen would have been outvoted in a two-way race much like the 1998 Taipei mayor's race. Thus, Chen's campaign had to modulate its criticisms carefully so that both Lien and Soong remained viable to the end. No scenario more worried the Chen campaign in the final weeks than the possibility that Lien and Soong would cut a deal to join forces and defeat Chen.[36]

Essentially Chen Shui-bian's campaign strategy was to neutralize the issue on which he was most vulnerable—cross-strait relations—by moving toward the center (a "middle way"), while playing up the issue on which he and the DPP had the greatest natural advantage: political reform. Even before he formally announced his candidacy on 28 May 1999, Chen Shui-bian was publicly stating that cross-strait relations would not be the focus of his campaign. Repeatedly he said there was no need to declare independence because Taiwan is already an independent and sovereign state. Underscoring the moderate image he was giving his campaign, he promised not to change the name of the country, not to hold a referendum on independence (despite the call for it in his party's platform), and not to write Lee Teng-hui's description of cross-strait relations as a "special state to state" relationship into the Constitution. "It is unwise and impractical to endanger the security of the people over symbolic issues," his position paper soothingly declared. Rather, he would "promote the normalization of relations across the strait" and a variety of mechanisms for dialogue and interaction. Chen repeatedly declared his eagerness to visit China after the election and his openness "to talks on any subject, on the condition that interaction is equal and peaceful."[37] At the same time, he pledged not to cut the defense budget or reduce welfare benefits for military veterans or their dependents.

Chen's campaign team knew that its best chance to win was to make the election a referendum on "black and gold" and democratization. If the leading issues were cleaning up crime and corruption and effecting a true rotation of power at the center, neither Lien Chan nor even James Soong could compete with Chen. For the sizable body of Taiwanese voters who were fed up with "black gold" politics and hungered for reform, Chen had to demonstrate that he was a more credible and committed reformer than Soong, who had spent his whole political life building up the KMT machine. The Chen campaign tried hard to remind voters that Soong helped to foster "black gold" politics and that many of his current supporters were still implicated in it. Persuading voters to "dump Soong for Chen" was seeming a formidable challenge, however, until the KMT did Chen the enormous favor of muddying Soong's reformist image with the revelation of financial scandal. Chen worked relentlessly to link Soong and Lien equally to "black gold" politics. "Those who are standing beside Lien Chan and James Soong are gangsters and corrupt officials like Lo Fu-Chu, Yen Ching-piao, Wu Tze-yuan, and Kuo Ting-tsai," Chen declared in the campaign's closing days.[38]

Chen's campaign believed its competition with Lien, by contrast, was to gain the support of those who opposed reunification under any circumstance and wanted to assert Taiwan's identity. Chen had to walk a fine line between suggesting that Lien was not tough enough to deal with China and not appearing so tough himself as to summon popular fears that he would be reckless. The key target population here was the Lee Teng-hui backers. Appealing for their support, Chen proposed on 9 March that Lee could become a global "peace and human rights envoy for Taiwan" if Chen were elected. While Chen sought to project a greater willingness than President Lee to do business with the mainland (above all to establish the "three direct links") and distanced himself from some of Lee's more provocative measures, his pro-independence history made him, for many Lee admirers, a more credible choice to carry on the incumbent president's campaign for Taiwan's separate identity.

The choice of issues merged well with Chen's electoral strategy. As the campaign geared up in July 1999, with Soong far ahead in the polls, Chen focused on staying in the second spot. For Chen the potential disaster was falling into third place. If he became stuck there for any length of time, his supporters might dump him for Lien in order to stop Soong. On the other hand, Soong's formal entry into the race also raised the serious possibility that Chen could win in a three-cornered contest.

Chen Shui-bian's presidential campaign, more than any other in 2000, was driven by continuous public opinion polling and sophisticated analysis of the results. In August and September 1999, detailed issue polls showed that a majority of voters supported the DPP position against the involvement of criminal gangs and conglomerates in politics and its demand for the rotation in power of ruling parties. But these polls also showed consistently that the electorate had severe doubts about Chen's ability to manage cross-strait relations. More than 30 percent of the public thought Lien Chan was best able to handle relations with China; 25 to 30 percent chose Soong; only 5 to 7 percent picked Chen. Such findings persuaded Chen that he had to avoid a hard-line, pro-independence position on cross-strait relations and embrace a pragmatic, moderate stance. Polling influenced other campaign positions as well. In January 2000, the *United Evening News* denounced a small mention in a Chen campaign white paper on economic policy suggesting the possibility of a new capital gains tax; when the campaign's polls showed a drop of three percentage points in his support, he abandoned the proposal.[39]

The Chen Shui-bian campaign began its polling fully a year in advance of the election. In every early poll it conducted, Soong was leading by ten to twelve points or more. Chen's campaign had to find some way of closing this gap, and many different factors were tested. None proved as potent as the endorsement of a single individual, Lee Yuan-tseh. The only Taiwanese scholar to win a Nobel Prize (as a professor of chemistry in the United States) and the most famous academic in a society that reveres scholarly achievement, Lee Yuan-tseh was the preeminent moral voice outside of Taiwan's party politics. A week before the Soong scandal erupted, a top-secret DPP poll indicated that if this Lee endorsed Chen, Chen would go from trailing badly to leading by two points. Independent polls also showed Chen's vote rising by as much as seven percentage points if Lee openly endorsed Chen.

It is not clear when Lee Yuan-tseh first decided to help Chen or was first approached about doing so. But conversations between Lee and Chen (and between Lee and other political figures) had been going on for months.[40] It appears that for some time in advance of the election, Dr. Lee had indicated his intention to help Chen in the race. What was uncertain was the timing of that help and the method he would use. Lee had been increasingly outspoken in condemning crime and corruption and appealing for political reform. In a 5 March speech covered widely in the mass media, Lee warned of a growing polarization between two forces in Taiwan's society: One was the idealism that had generated NT$23 billion in relief for the 21 September earthquake; the other was "the local factions and gangsters" that "have been all the more active in the devastated region" trying to capture the reconstruction spending. This resurgence of "the old evil forces" had given the cause of political reform an urgency that he had "never felt so intensely . . . until this year." In a thinly veiled slap at the KMT, Lee declared: "Replacing the 10,000-year party with another party is the direction our democratic politics should take."[41] The timing of Dr. Lee's endorsement of Chen—on 10 March, one week before the voting—was a strategic calculation by Chen's campaign to maximize his electoral momentum. The campaign had laid elaborate plans to attract a million people in the final week to three huge rallies in Taichung, Kaohsiung, and finally Taipei. Everything was building toward a crescendo of rising public support.

Lee Yuan-tseh's endorsement reinforced several themes of Chen Shui-bian's campaign. First, it affirmed Chen's determination to fight "black gold" elements and clean up Taiwan's politics; it also distinguished Chen from Soong as the only candidate with the moral commitment and clean background to wage this fight successfully. Second, along with the endorsements of other leaders in business and government (including Acer Computer chairman Stan Shih and former National Security Council official Chen Pi-chao), it blunted the opposing campaigns' efforts to paint Chen as a dangerous radical who would plunge Taiwan into conflict with the mainland, wrecking Taiwan's security and prosperity. Lee Yuan-tseh's endorsement, crowning a parade of endorsements, reassured wavering voters that Chen could govern responsibly. Third, Dr. Lee's endorsement, along with those of other public leaders who had advised or befriended Lee Teng-hui, strengthened Chen's bid for the Lee Teng-hui voters.

The Long Campaign: The Beginning and the End

The campaign began in one sense with James Soong's return to Taiwan on 2 March 1999 after an extended, low-profile stay in the United States following his departure from the governorship in December. Attempting to put at least a public face of reconciliation on their dispute, President Lee offered Soong a position in mid-May as a senior presidential adviser. When Soong rejected the powerless post, the KMT denounced his rejection as "impudent," deepening the rift. And when, on 26 June, Soong publicly ruled out running on the same presidential ticket as Lien Chan, the die appeared to be cast. Some KMT leaders continued to call on their party to do whatever necessary to form a Lien–Soong ticket, but on 16 July Soong finally announced his independent candidacy. At this point, his 40 percent standing in a *United Daily News* poll was twice that of his nearest rival, Chen Shui-bian.

July 1999 was also the month that Lee Teng-hui defined Taiwan's "special state-to-state relationship" with China. The DPP leaped to support this declaration while the New Party warned that Lee appeared bent on provoking war with China. Soong said Lee's position would bring unnecessary trouble upon the people of Taiwan, even though it expressed the determination of Chinese people of all races and political affiliations not to be ruled by Beijing.

On 31 July, Lien Chan formally announced that he would seek the KMT nomination for president in 2000, pledging to promote political reform and economic development while easing hostilities with China. At this point he trailed Soong in the polls by anywhere from twelve to seventeen points, and his support had inched up only slightly; but a plurality expected Lien to win.

The early part of September was dominated by the Lien and Soong campaigns trading accusations of money politics. Top KMT officials, including Lien and President Lee, charged that Soong was trying to buy the presidency: Taiwan would go downhill like the Philippines if Soong, who purchased his popularity with provincial government money, were elected.

On 21 September, a violent earthquake shook Taiwan and caused tremendous property damage in the center of the island. The tragedy offered Lien Chan an opportunity to exert leadership and shake off the image of a rich man distant from the people. The opportunity was not seized, however. By the beginning of October, he still trailed Soong badly in the polls.

The final week of the campaign was also its most momentous. It began with Lee Yuan-tseh's endorsement of Chen Shui-bian on 10 March. Although he did not explicitly tell the electorate to vote for Chen, his embrace was unmistakable. Calling the DPP candidate "a proper national leader," he promised to join Chen's National Policy Advisory Committee if Chen were elected:

"I admire Chen for his determination to carry out all kinds of reforms and to eradicate 'black gold' politics. I will help Chen to govern our country if he is elected." Emphasizing the moral urgency of the choice, he added: "I am worried about the future direction of our country, after seeing so many gangsters campaigning for our candidates."[42] Three days later he dramatized his endorsement by announcing his resignation from the presidency of the Academia Sinica in order to head Chen's National Policy Advisory Committee and work more intensively for social reform. Underscoring the two motivations for his endorsement—"to eradicate 'black gold' and to ease cross-strait relations"—Lee noted a "Taiwan-loving force" that was working "to halt Taiwan from degenerating; to improve the quality of our democracy." As if this were not drama enough, he said: "This is the most important decision in my life."[43]

Lee's endorsement was the jewel in a crown of distinguished personalities Chen Shui-bian was recruiting to join his planned advisory committee. Others who promised to join included Nita Ing, chair of Taiwan's High-Speed Railway Corp., Chang Yung-fa, founder of the Evergreen corporate conglomerate, Stan Shih, CEO of Acer Computer, Hsu Wen-lung, president of Chi Mei Corp., Chen Pi-Chao, who had just resigned as one of Lee Teng-hui's national security advisers, and presidential adviser and sociologist Hsiao Hsin-huang. By the time of his monumental rally in Kaohsiung on Sunday night, 12 March, Chen had announced a host of other prominent persons who, in agreeing to serve, had blessed his presidential quest. The list included three university presidents, Kao Chi-ming, president of I-Mei Food Co., Lin Chung-hsiung, chairman of E Sun Bank, and Lin Hsin-yi, vice-chairman of China Motor Corp.[44] While collectively these names did not approach in their electoral impact the weight of Lee Yuan-tseh alone, they enhanced Chen Shui-bian's stature, credibility, political momentum, and appeal to the floating Lee Teng-hui supporters.

Just as Lee Yuan-tseh was affirming his endorsement of Chen on 13 March, Taiwan's stock market dived 6.6 percent (a record for a single day). The plunge was "apparently sparked by fears of a KMT defeat in the presidential election but mired by speculation that the KMT willed it to happen."[45] Chen accused the KMT (one of the country's biggest institutional investors) of manipulating the stock market to scare voters away from supporting him; Soong said the fall was a sign the public had lost confidence in the KMT. Lien struck back by renewing one of his principal themes: Chen Shui-bian was "endangering national stability and development." This followed by only a few days the warning of Council for Economic Planning and Development Chairman Chiang Pin-kung that the stock market could fall to "below 100" (from its level of over 9,000) if a "certain person" were elected.[46]

On 15 March, just three days before the election, Chinese Premier Zhu Rongji went before the television cameras in Beijing to warn the people of Taiwan not to elect "the wrong candidate." Wagging his finger threateningly, he declared: "Let me advise all these people in Taiwan: do not just act on impulse at this juncture, which will decide the future course that China and Taiwan will follow. Otherwise I'm afraid that you won't get another opportunity to regret." The Chinese people, he said, "are ready to shed blood" to prevent Taiwan from breaking away. But "whoever stands for 'one China' will get our support."[47] Zhu's warning was particularly ominous coming on the heels of a PRC white paper the previous month threatening military action against Taiwan if it stalled indefinitely on reunification talks—capping a rising drumbeat of warnings and threats from the mainland.[48]

Chen Shui-bian and James Soong were both emphatic in rejecting Chinese pressure. "Taiwan won't be scared by the threats of force and won't reunify with China under the 'one country, two systems' formula," Chen declared. Implying the mainstream character of his position, he cleverly added: "According to China's logic [demanding the 'one country, two systems' formula], the only candidate they could accept is Li Ao [the New Party nominee, who went on to win 0.13 percent of the vote]. Who would vote for him?" Speaking that night before a huge crowd at the Chiang Kai-shek memorial in Taipei, Soong delivered one of the most memorable speeches of the campaign. "We do not fear negotiation," he declared, "but we will never negotiate out of fear." Soong roared to the crowd, "What do you want? Intimidation?" And the crowd roared back, "No!" "Peace?" he questioned; "Yes!" "Democracy?" And again the crowd roared back "Yes!" "This is the voice of Taiwan," Soong declared. Lien Chan's response was more ambiguous. Emphasizing Taiwan's sovereignty and independence, Lien pronounced: "The election is our business." Yet he could not resist using the PRC's latest verbal bullying to play again on the public's fear by reminding voters that "China's premier Zhu said just this afternoon that the path of Taiwan independence would only lead to bloodshed." Referring to Chen, he stated: "Some people here are too naïve" to think they could negotiate with China while representing supporters of Taiwan independence.[49] This attack reflected the overriding strategy of his campaign in its final days: to persuade voters that the choice was between Chen and Lien and convince them that Chen's victory would threaten war and economic turmoil.

Many analysts judged that Zhu's warning, in the words of New Party leader Hau Lung-pin, "triggered voters' negative emotions" and thereby stimulated support for Chen.[50] "Lien tried to exploit China's threat to his own advantage, unwittingly showing that he could not stand up to China. That obviously backfired," said Joseph Wu of National Chengchi University.[51] It is impossible to gauge the precise impact of Zhu's intervention and the candidates' responses. But in the DPP's internal tracking polls, Lien's support declined by almost two percentage points in the final week while Soong and Chen each gained a point to a point and a half (Table 1.4). A *United Daily News* poll found more dramatic hemorrhage in Lien's vote during the final week: 12 percent of his supporters had decided to vote for Chen and 5 percent for Soong, dwarfing the defections away from Chen and Soong.[52]

The final week of the campaign also witnessed a string of extraordinary rallies, particularly by the DPP. The KMT's rallies were flat, short on enthusiasm, and (judging by the thousands and thousands of undistributed flags, posters, and boxed meals) well short of the numbers expected, despite the huge investment in buses and paid organization to produce a packed house. Soong's rallies in the end also fell somewhat short of the numbers hoped for, though his supporters were passionate in their enthusiasm for him. Chen, by contrast, had both numbers and passion, and they mounted dramatically in the final week as his victory became increasingly plausible. An estimated 300,000 people attended his exquisitely orchestrated rally in Kaohsiung on Sunday night, 12 March (perhaps three times the number that attended Lien Chan's rally across town). The Kaohsiung rally was repeated in Taipei on the final night of the campaign. With perhaps 100,000 people jammed to a crushing presence inside the Taipei soccer stadium and as many on the streets outside, watching on big screens and parading jubilantly, the rally took on the feeling of a rock concert. On the enormous stage unfolded an hours-long procession of musicians, performers, marchers, and politicians (many of them former political prisoners), as well as teachers, doctors, lawyers, and others symbolizing Chen's breadth of support. Finally, at 11 P.M., in the mesmerizing glare of colored lights, fireworks, and a sea of sparklers lit by the crowd, Chen Shui-bian and his running mate, Annette Lu, emerged onto the stage and bowed, over and over, to the audience while the orchestra played Beethoven's Ninth Symphony. One should not underestimate the stimulus to DPP voter turnout generated by the outpouring of enthusiasm in these final, spectacular campaign rallies.

Campaign Issues

Many journalists, scholars, and ordinary voters in Taiwan decried what they saw to be the low tone of the 2000 campaign: the negative advertising, the hyperbolic rhetoric, the heavy tendency toward ethnic voting, the threats of economic chaos or war if a certain candidate were elected. Such failings are regrettable, but they are not uncommon in a (developing) democracy.

In one sense, Taiwan's 2000 presidential election campaign was most noteworthy for the issues that were absent. In the evolution of the advanced industrial democracies, three divisive issues beyond region, ethnicity, and personality have helped to structure the vote and the party system. During the nineteenth century and for much of the twentieth, these issues revolved, first, around class and status—the conflict between economic growth and distribution, between haves and have-nots, between business and labor— and, second, around the relationship between church and state and a host of social issues relating to personal matters such as marriage, divorce, and abortion. Recently these two lines of cleavage have been supplemented by and at times partially displaced by a third line having to do with what are called "postmaterialist" issues: protecting the environment, improving the quality of urban life, raising the status of women and historically marginalized groups, and so on.

Although each of the three major candidates released interesting and at times thoughtful position papers on some of these other issues, they weighed little in the campaign. Instead the campaign was dominated by two issues: cross-strait relations and political reform. The most striking aspect of the discourse over cross-strait relations in the campaign's final weeks was not the drumbeat of blunt threats and intimidation from mainland China; nor was it the crude playing to fear and anxiety by parties and politicians within Taiwan, especially the KMT. Rather, it was the dramatic convergence of all three candidates toward a common stance of moderation on the cross-strait issue, and the shift of the spectrum toward a new center position more accommodating toward China than that of Lee Teng-hui.

Each of the three main candidates pledged to explore opening up new direct links and expanding trade with the mainland. (Soong also tried to paint Lien as a captive of President Lee's "go slow, be patient" policy, which had cost Taiwan industries access to new and wider markets on the mainland.) Each expressed a desire to negotiate directly and on fresh terms with the PRC leadership. None emphatically endorsed Lee Teng-hui's declaration of a special "state-to-state" relationship. Indeed, not only did Chen Shui-bian promise not to declare independence or hold a referendum on the issue, he even pledged not to write the "state-to-state" relationship into the Constitution and downplayed Lee's initiative. Few people, even a year before, would have thought the historically pro-independence DPP could hold together in the campaign behind a stance on cross-strait relations in many ways more moderate than Lee Teng-hui's.

In terms of domestic policy, there was also convergence on social and economic issues. Each candidate responded to pent-up expectations for greater provision of social welfare. Lien Chan promised the elderly increased subsidies for health care and a long-awaited national pension program; to the young he appealed with a NT$100 billion program to subsidize loans for first-time home buyers. Chen Shui-bian countered with specific (and no less expensive) social programs including a NT$3,000 monthly pension for senior citizens as part of his "333 family welfare program." Chen and Soong promised to implement labor's demand to shorten the workweek to forty hours by 2002; Lien said it would be done by 2004.

But the dominant issue of the campaign was political reform—in essence, democracy itself. Chen and Soong both cast themselves as democratic reformers who would break up the encrusted power and privilege of the KMT and end the fifty-year embrace between party and state. Each targeted his campaign on public discontent with the character of government and the quality of democracy, pledging to crack down on crime, corruption, and insider dealings. Determined not to surrender the sacred ground of political reform, Vice-President Lien Chan vowed to place the gargantuan business empire of the KMT in trust and take new initiatives to attack vote buying and organized crime.

Undecided voters had to determine which of the three candidates was most credible in staking claim to the centrist, "median voter" position on cross-strait relations—a prudent embrace of the status quo while searching for new points of engagement and dialogue with the mainland—and which one was most credible in his claim to embody the national resolve for vigorous political reform. Many undecided voters were no doubt conflicted, because the candidate they most trusted on cross-strait relations might not be the one most likely to cleanse the political system. Yet differences on these issues narrowed dramatically during the campaign. If many partisan activists felt frustrated by the blurring of differences, if many intellectuals and voters felt disdainful of the coarse tone of the campaign, there was also a silver lining in the political convergence: the possibility in the next administration of historic breakthroughs on these two issues that most affect the future of democracy in Taiwan.

How and Why Chen Won

Few observers anticipated the fact or scale of Chen Shui-bian's election victory. Although he was far from capturing a majority, he did not win by a mere sliver. His 39.3 percent of the ballot bettered Soong by more than 300,000 votes and more than two full percentage points, and it exceeded the KMT's support by a stunning 2 million votes.

The political geography of Chen's victory revealed the ethnic and regional cleavages of Taiwan politics. Chen's main support came from the eight counties and cities of southern Taiwan, where Taiwan identity is strongest. In this region he received almost 48 percent of the ballot and amassed a huge, 848,000-vote lead over Soong (though only in his native Tainan county did he win an absolute majority) (Table 1.5). Chen lost the remaining jurisdictions of the country by half a million votes. Soong ran especially well (winning 46 percent of the vote) in the Taoyuan-Hsinchu-Miaoli region, which "has a large concentration of mainlanders, especially ex-servicemen and their families, as well as Hakka voters." DPP strength among Hakka voters was eroded by the defection of its former chairman, Hsu Hsin-liang (a Hakka), who ran as an independent against Chen. Although Hsu won only 0.6 percent of the vote, his attacks on Chen probably pulled away many more Hakka voters from Chen and may have reinforced the feeling "that the DPP has been a party for the Hokkien-speaking majority, to the exclusion of Hakka interests." Soong also won absolute majorities in the less populated east—composed disproportionately of mainlanders and aborigines (a constituency he had cultivated assiduously as governor)—and in the outlying islands with their sizable military communities.[53]

This interpretation of the electoral map coincides with what the DPP's internal polling identified as the demographic base of each candidate. By this analysis, 60 to 65 percent of mainlanders (including almost all New Party supporters) voted for Soong, 20 to 25 percent for Lien, and only about 10 percent for Chen. Half of all Taiwanese (Hokkien-speaking) voters supported Chen, 30 percent supported Lien, and 20 percent supported Soong. Hakka voters, the DPP polls estimated, split their votes 35 to 40 percent for Soong and about 30 percent for each of the other two candidates. Lien performed poorly among younger voters (under forty), winning only about 20 percent of this group while Chen may have captured 45 percent and Soong 35 percent. With the momentum generated by the endorsement of Lee Yuan-tseh, the Zhu Rongji intervention, and his thrilling final campaign rallies, Chen held onto almost all voters who identified with the DPP (winning back in the final two weeks many who had considered straying to Soong or Lien). In addition, the DPP estimates he attracted about a quarter of all KMT identifiers—an unprecedented achievement for the DPP in a national election.[54] If, as seems likely, most of these voters were Lee Teng-hui loyalists who dumped Lien for Chen to stop Soong, then Chen's campaign achieved one of its primary goals and this provided the margin of victory.

In sum, then, there are several reasons why Chen won. After half a century, the country was ready and indeed eager for rotation in power. There was widespread disgust with corruption, with organized crime, and with the KMT's inability to crack down on these corrosive forces. The rift between Lee Teng-hui and James Soong, and Lee's determination to bury Soong politically, generated a powerful independent candidacy that ate deeply into

Table 1.5

2000 Presidential Election Results by District (Percentage of vote won)

City or county	Chen Shui-bian	Lien Chan	James Soong
Taipei City	37.6	21.9	39.8
Taipei County	36.7	22.4	40.3
Keelung City	30.8	21.5	47.1
Taoyuan County	31.7	22.1	43.8
Hsinchu County	24.8	20.7	51.6
Hsinchu City	33.8	22.4	42.8
Miaoli County	26.8	22.2	49.6
Ilan County	47.0	19.5	33.0
Taichung County	36.5	24.7	38.1
Taichung City	36.9	21.2	41.4
Nantou County	34.5	18.2	46.9
Hualien County	21.4	19.3	58.8
Changhua County	40.1	25.7	33.7
Yunlin County	47.0	24.8	27.7
Chiayi County	49.5	23.1	27.0
Chiayi City	47.0	23.2	29.3
Tainan City	46.1	25.9	27.5
Tainan County	53.8	24.7	21.1
Kaohsiung City	45.8	24.0	29.8
Kaohsiung County	47.1	23.9	28.4
Taitung County	23.2	23.7	52.8
Pingtung County	42.3	27.7	25.5
Penghu County	36.8	23.2	39.6
Kinmen County	3.1	14.5	81.8
Lienchiang County	1.8	24.4	73.3

Source: China Post, 19 March 2000, p. 2.

the KMT's base of support. The split within the KMT made it possible for Chen to win even though his own pollsters and managers figured he could not capture more than 40 percent of the vote. The scandal surrounding Soong's family finances was a huge stroke of fortune for the Chen campaign that dragged Soong down from his lofty heights while further darkening the image of the KMT. Chen and his forces ran a brilliant, disciplined campaign that kept "on message" with political reform while adhering to a moderate line on cross-strait relations. Meanwhile, the KMT was saddled with a decent but dull candidate who lacked any popular base of his own and never ignited the enthusiasm of the electorate.

This may explain why Chen was able to mount a vigorous challenge for the presidency, but it does not fully explain why he surged to victory in the final two weeks of the campaign. Both independent analysts and Chen's own strategists believe the endorsement of Lee Yuan-tseh may well have provided the margin of victory, swinging 3 to 5 percent of the electorate or more to Chen. Beyond symbolizing moral integrity and reform, Dr. Lee also epitomized a political identity that was heavily Taiwanized but not clearly associated with the DPP.[55] Probably only Lee Teng-hui himself carried more influence with this crucially important constituency, which Chen Shui-bian had to carry in order to win. The massive, movingly staged DPP rallies and the parade of endorsements in the campaign's final week heightened Chen's political momentum and credibility, prompting many potential Lien voters to dump him for Chen (while a smaller number defected to Soong in order to stop Chen).

Finally, Chinese Premier Zhu Rongji's belligerent warning to the people of Taiwan not to vote for Chen Shui-bian backfired. Combined with Lien's clumsy response, the PRC's intervention shot new holes in Lien's sinking ship and reinforced the gathering sense that Chen was headed toward victory. A leading pollster for Chen estimates that Premier Zhu's warning may have cost Lien Chan several percentage points of the vote, with perhaps 2 or 3 percent of the electorate defecting to Soong and 3 or 4 percent to Chen. Those who worried that Taiwan had better heed China's warning and avoid provocative acts opted for Soong, not Lien. Those who were angered by China's verbal aggression and wanted a leader who would stand up to China voted this time for Chen, as they had voted for Lee Teng-hui in 1996. If the net gain for Chen was one or two percentage points, it was not decisive. But in a close race it was one of the factors that provided Chen with a modest margin of victory over Soong.

The outcome of the 2000 presidential election was a momentous victory for democracy. As James Soong stressed after the election, three-quarters of the electorate voted for political reform. If that is something of an exaggeration (not every vote against the KMT was a vote for reform), the election was a referendum on the country's "black gold" politics and a conscious decision to turn the ruling party out of power and purge the system at least to some extent. Nearly two in five voters supported a party that had been legalized barely a decade ago—a party that the PRC bluntly warned the electorate to shun and, moreover, that the KMT had extravagantly portrayed as the harbinger of economic and military calamity if it won the presidency. Yet when Chen Shui-bian was announced the winner, within three hours of the close of the polls the losers graciously acknowledged defeat and the military reaffirmed its loyalty to the constitutional process.

As the stunning results poured in on the night of 18 March, huge crowds gathered outside the DPP's campaign headquarters, aware that history was being made, jubilant at the mounting signs of victory for their beloved party and candidate. Music played, banners waved, campaigners spoke, lights glared, cameras whirled, supporters cheered and cried, as more and more people flowed in from every direction for one final rally: a celebration. By 8 P.M., with all the votes counted and the DPP victory proclaimed, the party introduced its winning ticket to a throng of national and international press that had crammed into the narrow ground floor of the headquarters. Crowded onto the podium were Chen Shui-bian, who, as a prosperous young maritime lawyer twenty years ago, had plunged into oppositional politics as one of the lead defense attorneys in the Kaohsiung Incident and later served several months in prison himself; Chen's wife, Wu Shu-jen, who was paralyzed from the waist down in 1985 after she was run over by a truck in what is widely believed to have been an assault by forces associated with the authoritarian regime; Chen's running mate, Annette Lu, the founder of the women's movement in Taiwan, who spent five and a half years in prison after her conviction in the Kaohsiung Incident; the DPP chairman, Lin Yi-shung, who, in the darkest days of the struggle against dictatorship, had lost his twin daughters and his wife in a murderous attack on his home that many believed to be the work of the dirtiest elements in the KMT regime; along with a host of other DPP politicians who had made great personal sacrifices in the long struggle for democratization. These were the people that the electorate of Taiwan was now entrusting with the leadership and security of their nation. This was the party and the movement that had just defeated the richest and one of the longest-ruling electoral parties in the world. Their victory marked for many people in Taiwan the true completion of the country's poignant and protracted transition from authoritarian rule to democracy.

Postscript: The Implications for Democratic Consolidation

One crucial test of an electoral democracy is the ability of the electorate to turn the ruling party out of power in a free and fair election. This test was passed decisively in Taiwan's March 2000 presidential election. But a robust electoral democracy is not necessarily a stable and consolidated one. Although the 2000 election was a major milestone in the development of what Linda Chao and Ramon Myers have called "the first Chinese democracy," it introduced a whole new set of problems. As became apparent over the course of President Chen Shui-bian's first year in office, Chen and the DPP were not fully prepared to lead the country. After decades of exclusion from governmental power at the center, problems of inexperience were inevitable. As Yun-han Chu observes in chapter 2, however, the more serious problem was Chen's unwillingness to recognize the weakness of his position as a "triple minority" president—and thus his inability to forge a viable strategy for governing based on a realistic formula for sharing power.

With his party holding barely a third of the seats in parliament and the Constitution providing for only "semipresidential" government (at most), Chen needed to find a way to enlarge his political base in order to forge a working majority in the Legislative Yuan. His initial strategy for doing so was to choose the former military chief of staff and outgoing defense minister in the KMT government, Tang Fei, as his new premier. But the gesture was never accepted by the KMT as real power sharing—and in any case Chen was never willing to grant Tang the authority to function effectively as premier. A brilliant and widely admired soldier-statesman, Tang bristled at having to rebuff repeated speculation that he was a mere figurehead. When he finally resigned—the impending decision to cancel construction of the fourth nuclear power plant was probably the final straw—Chen was left with a painful choice. At this point he either had to narrow his base further, with the appointment of a DPP premier, or reach out to one or both of the opposition parties at the price of appointing a premier from the KMT or PFP and thus losing control of the Executive Yuan. He chose the former course. The unilateral decision on 27 October 2000 to cancel the fourth nuclear power plant enraged the opposition, paralyzed government, and briefly provoked calls to impeach Chen or recall him from office. In the wake of this politically disastrous announcement, forging a broader, more viable base for governing Taiwan would have required a much more substantial surrender of executive power than would have been necessary at the beginning of Chen's presidential term when his approval ratings approached 80 percent.

Nor did the opposition parties distinguish themselves. While the KMT festered in the bitterness of its defeat, the PFP, looking toward the Legislative Yuan election in December 2001, maneuvered to harass the new government and present itself as the principal alternative to the DPP. Members of the new cabinet, even Premier Tang Fei himself, were subjected to humiliating, painfully long, and often pointless questioning during parliamentary interpellation sessions. Political retribution was visited in the form of cuts in administrative budgets. In perhaps the lowest moment, some KMT figures, on a visit to mainland China, reportedly advised the PRC authorities not to deal with Chen but to wait until they themselves had returned to power.

Democracy is consolidated when all political actors play by the rules of the democratic game and fully expect that their competitors will do so as well. Consolidation requires not only normative commitment to democracy, but compliance with the formal (legal and constitutional) and informal rules and restraints of democracy on the part of all political leaders, parties, and organizations, as well as the broad bulk of the mass public.[56] To be sure, the historic alternation in power that occurred with the inauguration of Chen Shui-bian on 20 May 2000 brought certain steps toward consolidation. As

Yun-han Chu observes in chapter 2, no one in the military or the state bureaucracy challenged Chen's authority as president. The alternation of ruling
parties occurred peacefully and even gracefully. The defeated parties accepted
their defeat and looked to the political and governmental arenas, not to the
streets, to recoup their losses. All this was healthy.

Democratic consolidation is often a protracted process, however. And
completing this process requires more than demonstrating that the political
opposition can become the ruling party without a collapse of the system. The
historic opposition must now demonstrate that it can govern effectively.
Progress toward consolidation requires good performance both economically
and politically. And the two are linked. Taiwan's economic slump beginning
in 2000 has been driven partly by a decline in investor confidence and worries over political instability. As well, there is concern about the stalemate in
cross-strait relations. As this book was being completed, the Chen government backed down from its decision to cancel the fourth nuclear power plant
and agreed to allow this one last nuclear plant to go forward. This move may
signal a broader readiness for political compromise and coalition building.
Yet as a new ruling party the DPP faces a sharp dilemma. Good political
performance means delivering on Chen Shui-bian's pledge during the 2000
campaign to crack down vigorously on "black and gold" elements. Vigorous
prosecution of gangsters and corrupt officials associated with the opposition
parties (as well as the DPP) could well heighten tension and mistrust between parties. If democracy in Taiwan is to be consolidated, not just the DPP
but the KMT and the PFP as well must demonstrate that they are ready for a
new era of politics insulated from corruption, vote buying, and organized
crime. And the KMT must accept the end of its historic penetration and control of various interest groups. Strengthening constitutionalism and the rule
of law is an essential, though not sufficient, condition for consolidating democracy in Taiwan.

Taiwan's democracy has made impressive strides over the past decade.
Today no one can question its authenticity and vigor. In some respects, the
mutual restraints and expectations of democratic practice are becoming internalized and institutionalized. But the mass public remains ambivalent in
its attitudes toward democracy,[57] and the political system has yet to find a
mode for operating Taiwan's semipresidential system effectively in the absence of a legislative majority for the ruling (presidential) party. Constitutional change to resolve the contradictory features of this system (toward a
more purely parliamentary or purely presidential) system would be helpful
but is very unlikely. The burden for democratic consolidation rests heavily
with the politicians—most of all Chen Shui-bian and his two defeated presidential opponents, who now lead the opposition parties. Their ability to rise

above immediate partisan and personal interests, to deepen democracy and reach accommodations, will determine whether Taiwan's democracy moves forward to consolidation in the coming years or stands still.

Notes

1. On the emergence of this political opposition in Taiwan see Linda Chao and Ramon Myers, *The First Chinese Democracy: Political Life in the Republic of China on Taiwan* (Baltimore: Johns Hopkins University Press, 1998), chap. 4. On Taiwan's transition to democracy see, in addition to Chao and Myers, Hung-mao Tien, *The Great Transition: Political and Social Change in the Republic of China* (Stanford, CA: Hoover Institution Press, 1989), and Yun-han Chu, *Crafting Democracy in Taiwan* (Taipei: Institute for National Policy Research, 1992).

2. Yun-han Chu and Larry Diamond, "Taiwan's 1998 Elections: Implications for Democratic Consolidation," *Asian Survey* 34(5) (September/October 1999):808–822.

3. As the only two municipalities not under the jurisdiction of Taiwan province, Taipei and Kaohsiung have been under a different electoral calendar than the other cities and countries, but all these posts are now directly elected for four-year terms.

4. It is also possible that Soong was becoming too openly ambitious. Jason Hu, Lien Chan's campaign manager and a high-ranking figure in the KMT, told a foreign reporter that the rift between Lee and Soong began in 1996 when Soong privately asked Lee to appoint him premier and was rebuffed. Soong denies this. See Erik Eckholm, "3 Taiwan Contenders All Urge Reform," *New York Times*, 26 February 2000, p. 7.

5. Raymond R. Wu, "Almost a Revolution: An Insider Perspective on Taiwan's Presidential Election in 2000" (paper presented to a conference of the Center for Strategic and International Studies, Washington, D.C., 28–30 March 2000), p. 4.

6. Ibid., p. 5.

7. Ibid.

8. Lauren Chen, "Lee Denies Plan to Abandon Lien in Favor of Chen," *Taipei Times*, 12 March 2000, p. 1.

9. This was not the first time that Lee Teng-hui had been accused of sabotaging his own party's candidate. Many New Party supporters and KMT traditionalists believe that Lee secretly dumped his party's candidate for mayor of Taipei in 1994, the incumbent Huang Tai-chou, and redirected support to Chen Shui-bian in an effort to stop the popular (mainlander) New Party candidate, Jaw Shao-kong.

10. Chen, "Lee Denies Plan," p. 1.

11. "Lee Stresses Morality Issues," *Taipei News*, 14 March 2000, p. 3.

12. "Lee Flatly Denies Supporting Chen in Presidential Race," *China Post*, 15 March 2000, p. 20.

13. Lawrence Liu, "President Tries to Dispel Talk He Secretly Backs DPP's Chen," *Taiwan News*, 16 March 2000, p. 1.

14. Chiu Yu-tzu and Jou Ying-cheng, "Lien Chan Hits the Stage with Lee," *Taipei Times*, 13 March 2000, p. 3.

15. Chiu Yu-tzu and Jou Ying-cheng, "President Calls on Electorate to Dump James Soong to Save Lien Chan," *Taipei Times*, 17 March 2000, p. 2.

16. Lin Chia-lung, "Taiwan's Presidential Election and Its Political Future," *Taipei Times*, 10 March 2000, p. 13.

17. These election-eve poll results were given to me by a high-ranking official of one of the campaigns.

18. In a survey of fifty-three equity fund managers based in Taiwan, Bloomberg News found that 57 percent expected Lien to win, 28 percent expected Soong to win, and 13 percent expected Chen to win. See "Market See Lien Victory," *Taipei Times*, 8 March 2000, p. 17.

19. Confidential postelection interview with an official from the Lien campaign. Another high-ranking official in Lien Chan's campaign gave a somewhat different account. He claims that by December the Lien campaign's goal was to draw at least even with James Soong in the polls in the expectation that the party's grassroots organization and membership would then carry it to victory on 18 March.

20. In reaction to President Lee's withering assaults on him, James Soong publicly warned on 6 March that he would start pulling skeletons out of the KMT closet if Lee did not relent. "I have always had the greatest respect for President Lee, but if they keep pushing me I may tell everyone about the tasks Lee handed me when I was the KMT's secretary-general. I'm afraid this will hurt the KMT and the country." See *China Post*, 7 March 2000, p. 20.

21. The Lien campaign was not helped by its response to Lee Yuan-tseh's condemnation of presidential candidates consorting with gangsters, a charge leveled during his press conference endorsing Chen Shui-bian on 10 March. Lien campaign spokesman Alex Tsai lamely declared: "We welcome whomever comes to our campaign rallies. We cannot ask them to produce a certificate proving they are law-abiding people." See *Taipei Times*, 11 March 2000, p. 1.

22. On 12 March 2000, the *New York Times* reported that the KMT had set aside more than US$60 million to "get out the vote." Although this sum seems high, even for the KMT, political insiders spoke of huge amounts being pumped into the KMT organization in the final two weeks, and there were numerous stories of attempted vote buying by the KMT. See "Vote-Buying Accusations Fly as KMT Denies N.Y. Times Report," *China Post*, 14 March 2000, p. 20.

23. "Vote for Lien, Avoid War; Campaign Staff Trumpet," *Taipei Times*, 10 March 2000, p. 1.

24. "China Turns Up the Heat, But Taiwan Candidate Loves Being Hated," *International Herald Tribune*, 10 March 2000, p. 7.

25. The ad campaign, which was also carried in the newspapers, noted that while Chen Chih-chung was entering the army the next year, neither the two sons of Lien Chan nor the sons of James Soong had to report for military service. The ad campaign coincided with a verbal assault contrasting Chen's commitment to Taiwan with that of his principal opponents. "All of Chen's friends, relatives, and teachers are in Taiwan," said Luo Wen-chia, one of Chen's closest and most quoted campaign managers. "Chen is not like the other presidential candidates who have money to send their kids overseas or let their own children grow up as Americans." See *China Post*, 8 March 2000, p. 1.

26. "China Turns Up the Heat," p. 7.

27. "Lien's Mainlander Achilles Heel," *Taipei Times*, 7 March 2000, p. 3.

28. Lin, "Taiwan's Presidential Election."

29. Confidential postelection interview with the author, 4 July 2000. Luo Wen-chia compared the KMT's electoral defeat in 2000 to its loss of the mainland to the communists in 1947: "At that time, the KMT had the best military equipment, the biggest organization, and lots of money, but it was very disorganized. Its generals did

not engage in battle. It had no common ideology or common faith." Interview with the author, 7 July 2000.

30. Wu, "Almost a Revolution," p. 2.

31. Ibid., p. 6.

32. Ibid.

33. Both quotes are from Laurence Eyton, "Lee Era Fades, and Consensus with It," *Taipei Times*, 17 March 2000, p. 7.

34. Confidential interview, 6 July 2000.

35. Confidential interview, 6 July 2000.

36. Just such a worry was attributed to the secretary-general of Chen's national campaign, Chiou I-jen, in a 15 March report. Whether this was good reporting or a leak to motivate Chen's supporters and generate sympathy is not clear. See "Chen Supporters Fear Soong, Lien Joining Forces," *Taipei Times*, 15 March 2000, p. 3. The concern may have been stimulated by a rumor that Soong had been offered the premiership in a Lien administration if he would drop out of the race. (Soong quickly shot that rumor down.)

37. Chen Shui-bian's Seven-Point Position on Cross-Strait Relations, 2 February 2000, Democratic Progressive Party.

38. Lin Chieh-yu, "Change History, Says Chen," *Taipei Times*, 12 March 2000, p. 1. These remarks, addressed to his final campaign rally in Taichung, were repeated often in the closing days of the campaign.

39. Confidential interview with a former Chen Shui-bian campaign official, 6 July 2000.

40. Initially, after Chen Shui-bian's mayoral defeat in 1998, Chen privately proposed to Lee Yuan-tseh that Lee run for president with Chen as his running mate. Later many DPP politicians dreamed that Lee Yuan-tseh would agree to serve as Chen's running mate. But to all these entreaties Lee gave the same answer he gave to suggestions shortly before and after the 2000 election that he serve as Chen's premier. Throughout Dr. Lee has insisted that he is not a politician. He is best equipped, he says, to contribute to public life in Taiwan from outside the formal arena of politics and government.

41. "Next Five Years Called Crucial for Taiwan," *Taiwan News*, 6 March 2000, pp. 1 and 3.

42. Lin Chieh-yu, "Chen's the Man, Says Lee," *Taipei Times*, 11 March 2000, p. 1.

43. Oliver Lin, "Lee Yuan-tseh Quits," *Taipei Times*, 14 March 2000, p. 1. As Lee Yuan-tseh's resignation as president of the Academia Sinica was never accepted by President Lee Teng-hui, Dr. Lee remains in the position.

44. Monique Chu, "Chen Rolls Out List of Big Names," *Taipei Times*, 13 March 2000, p. 3.

45. Anthony Lawrence, "TAIEX Tanks on Fears of KMT Loss," *Taipei Times*, 14 March 2000, p. 1.

46. Ibid.

47. William Ide, "Candidates Hit Back at Zhu Rongji," *Taipei Times*, 16 March 2000, p. 1; Paul Eckert, "China's Premier Threatens Taiwan," *Taiwan News*, 16 March 2000, p. 1.

48. On 4 March, PRC President Jiang Zemin reiterated the theme of the white paper: "If the Taiwan authorities refuse for an unlimited period to agree to a peaceful settlement of cross-straits reunification through negotiations, then the Chinese government will be forced to adopt all drastic measures possible." See *China Post*, 5

March 2000, p. 1. On 5 March, the People's Liberation Army accused a "prominent figure" in Taiwan of pushing for independence and said it had put its troops on alert in order to crush any such move. See *International Herald Tribune*, 10 March 2000, p. 7.

49. All these quotes are from Ide, "Candidates Hit Back."

50. Stephanie Low, "A-bian Wins—Just," *Taipei Times*, 19 March 2000, p. 17.

51. Irene Lin and Oliver Lin, "Analysts Begin to Fit Together the Pieces of Victory," *Taipei Times*, 19 March 2000, p. 19.

52. John Fuh-sheng Hsieh, "The 2000 Presidential Election and Its Implications for Taiwan's Domestic Politics" (unpublished paper, University of South Carolina, May 2000).

53. Bruce Jacobs, "Southern Strength Saved Chen, Elsewhere Soong Had the Edge," *Taipei Times*, 19 March 2000, pp. 17 and 19. Both quotations are from Jacobs.

54. Confidential interview, 6 July 2000.

55. Confidential interview with DPP campaign official, 6 July 2000.

56. Larry Diamond, *Developing Democracy: Toward Consolidation* (Baltimore: Johns Hopkins University Press, 1999), pp. 64–73.

57. See Yun-han Chu, Larry Diamond, and Doh Chull Shin, *Growth and Equivocation in Support for Democracy in Korea and Taiwan*, Studies in Public Policy 345 (Glasgow: Centre for the Study of Public Policy, University of Strathclyde, 2001).

2

Democratic Consolidation in the Post-KMT Era: The Challenge of Governance

Yun-han Chu

Chen Shui-bian's victory on 18 March 2000 was a historic event by any measure. It put an end to the Kuomintang's (KMT) fifty-five years of continuous rule over the island. It closed the epoch of one-party dominance and set forth a period of party realignment. It deflated Lee Teng-hui's charisma and brought his era to an abrupt and calamitous end. It triggered a generational turnover and pushed baby boomers to the forefront of governing responsibility. Most significantly, it urged the island's political system a major step toward the consolidation of democracy.[1]

From the perspective of democratic development, the power shift at the turn of the century was long overdue. Among the third-wave democracies, Taiwan's democratic transition has often been cited as a unique case: A quasi-Leninist party not only survived an authoritarian breakdown, but also capitalized on the crisis to its advantage.[2] From the late 1980s through the late 1990s, while the principle of popular accountability and open political contestation was being steadily legitimized and institutionalized, the KMT kept its political dominance largely intact through an impressive streak of electoral success.[3] The born-again KMT built a winning majority in much the same way as other dominant parties in advanced industrial democracies: on a rare combination of flexibility and rigidity along with a unique blend of

I thank Muthiah Alagappa, Larry Diamond, Michael Hsiao, and Yu-san Wu for their helpful comments and suggestions. I would like also to acknowledge the funding support of the National Science Council (NSC 89-2414-1-1-002-006), which enabled me to carry out the research for this study.

symbols and payoffs.[4] Although a partisan grip on the state apparatus was no longer the most decisive element, it remained an important ingredient of the KMT's electoral fortunes.

The political legacy of persistent hegemony by a former quasi-Leninist party has long complicated the prospect for democratic consolidation. Certain residual authoritarian elements were preserved and transplanted into the new regime. The incumbent-initiated constitutional change carried too many elements of unilateral imposition as well as short-term partisan calculation to give the new democratic institutions a broadly based legitimacy. The KMT's prevailing practice of electoral mobilization was transmitted into national politics. It infested electoral politics with organized crime and money politics and caused uneven development of the competitive party system from the very beginning. This legacy was also responsible for the ubiquitous presence of partisan politics in all organized sectors of the society. It compressed the sphere for public discourse, left too little space for an autonomous civil society, and made the creation of a nonpartisan mass media and a politically neutral civil service and military a daunting task. As a result, Taiwan's new democracy suffered from many lingering defects and newly developed weaknesses. None of them was deemed tractable so long as the KMT remained in power.

From the perspective of democratic governance, the Democratic Progressive Party (DPP) has come to power probably before its time. Chen Shui-bian did not deliver a convincing electoral victory. The DPP still lacks the necessary power base in the Legislative Yuan to steer the national policy agenda. Indeed, it is even debatable whether the DPP is the "governing party" after Chen Shui-bian's inauguration on 20 May. The DPP, moreover, has an embarrassing shortage of qualified talents to fill all the policymaking posts and run the elaborate state bureaucracy. More fundamentally, the DPP has yet to complete its ideological transformation to represent the mainstream view of society. In terms of its mentality, organizational ability, and administrative experience, the DPP is not fully prepared to take over. The challenge of governing responsibility is so formidable that it might hamper Chen Shui-bian's capacity to implement his reform agenda and could possibly dilute the significance of this historic turnover of power. At the same time, it is premature to write off the KMT. Much like the Liberal Democratic Party (LDP) in Japan after the 1993 debacle, the KMT is down but not out. Despite being in opposition, the KMT is still blessed with abundant resources and political talent, as well as administrative experience, which the DPP lacks. As the majority party in the Legislative Yuan, with over half of the seats, it has the strength to dominate the policymaking process and counterbalance the power of Chen's administration.

The Legacy of One-Party Dominance

To fully appreciate what Chen Shui-bian's victory may mean for Taiwan's democratic development, we must frame the year 2000 presidential race in the proper context. Despite all the progress achieved on his watch, toward the end of Lee Teng-hui's political tenure Taiwan's new political system still faced a series of daunting challenges as the new democracy had been slogging toward consolidation.

When the presidential campaign started to pick up steam in the fall of 1999, the country was actually in the midst of a constitutional crisis that had the potential to cast the very meaning of the election in doubt. On 4 September 1999, the KMT-dominated National Assembly passed a series of hotly contested constitutional changes to extend their own terms by more than two years and add five months to the current legislative term.[5] Under another amendment, future elections for the National Assembly would be canceled. Starting in June 2002, National Assembly deputies would be assigned by political parties according to a proportional rule—based on their vote shares in the last parliamentary election. The DPP had struck a deal with the KMT on term extensions in exchange for the safe passage of the proportional representation system—which was promoted by some DPP leaders as a way to suppress vote buying as well as a necessary stepping-stone for the eventual abolishment of the National Assembly.[6] DPP leaders defended the deal by arguing that term extension was a necessary evil because the incumbent deputies had to be "bribed" for adopting a proportional representation system that would prevent many of them from seeking reelection.

On the surface at least, Speaker Su Nan-cheng, a member of the KMT's central standing committee, appeared to be the driving force behind the successful passage of the controversial amendments. But most political pundits believed that Speaker Su would not have dared to engineer the damaging constitutional changes without a tacit endorsement by President Lee. It was widely held that Lee Teng-hui favored the latest constitutional amendments for a number of short-term political reasons. First, a concurrent election for president and National Assembly on 18 March 2000 might give James Soong—who had been governor of Taiwan province for six years and was much more closer to grassroot politicians than Lien Chan—the upper hand in soliciting help from KMT-affiliated local factions whose machines could piggyback the presidential campaign on the vote-mobilization activities for their National Assembly nominees. Second, it was an insurance policy against the prospect of a victory by James Soong, who had enjoyed a commanding lead in every poll thus far. Had James Soong ever been elected, the KMT could, with the DPP's cooperation, downgrade the future president into a nominal head of state by adopting additional constitutional amendments. Third, an extended National Assembly would give President Lee, who had pledged to stay on as chairman of the KMT until September 2001, the option to intervene in Taiwan's mainland policy as well as constitutional reform beyond 20 May 2000 when his official term expired. These expedient arrangements would enable him to wrap up his unfinished business including institutionalizing the controversial "special state-to-state" formula.

The public, however, was furious at the passage of these amendments. All three major candidates felt obligated to denounce the amendments and call for remedial measures. Lien Chan tried to distance himself from the unpopular actions by KMT deputies by pressing the party to take disciplinary action against the Speaker and certain National Assembly members. The passage of the amendments also touched off a heated debate among legal scholars over their constitutionality and the remedial measures that ought to be taken. To quell the popular uproar, some members of the Legislative Yuan formally requested the Council of Grand Justices to rule on the legality of the amendments—perhaps the most strenuous and potentially the most explosive case the council has ever had to deal with. On the one hand, the case under review is a clear breach of fundamental democratic principles. If the council fails to undertake remedial measures, the damage to the integrity and legitimacy of the Constitution will be beyond repair. On the other hand, in strictly legal terms it is not self-evident that the council has the authority to reject a constitutional amendment passed by the National Assembly. In fact, many National Assembly deputies not only questioned the council's authority in this matter but also threatened to punish the grand justices if the amendments were ruled invalid. On top of all these legal complications, the grand justices also had to take into account the fact that neither the KMT camp nor the DPP favored a timely ruling that would reinstate the concurrent National Assembly election and thus theoretically enhance James Soong's chances of winning. In the end, the Council of Grand Justices decided to wait out the presidential election.

This latest episode of constitutional tinkering was simply another revealing incident involving the island's politics of constitutional reform, which has been largely driven by unsavory hidden agendas and short-term political calculations at a particular juncture of the island's democratic transition. In the past, the KMT-initiated constitutional changes carried too many elements of unilateral imposition as well as short-term partisan calculation to give the new democratic institutions the broad-based legitimacy that a constitution of a consolidated democracy normally enjoys. Certain residual authoritarian elements were preserved under a largely KMT-initiated reform. Certain key elements in the abolished Temporary Articles, the hallmark of the old authoritarian rule, including the emergency powers of the president and the creation of a National Security Agency under the presidential office, were transplanted into the new amendments.

Furthermore, there is a dramatic lack of consensus over the nature and logic of the emerging constitutional order among the contending political forces.[7] After four phases of constitutional revision between 1990 and 1997, the Republic of China (ROC) Constitution was towed away from a parliamentarian system and shifted steadily closer to a semipresidential system akin to the French Fifth Republic. The emerging system differs from the French system, however, over some key designs. First, the French system requires the president to attain a majority mandate through the device of a runoff election if no candidate wins a majority on the first ballot. Under the ROC Constitution, the president is elected by plurality with no threshold of minimum electoral support. Second, the French system has built-in mechanisms to break a deadlock between the president and the assembly during a period of "cohabitation." Under the revised ROC Constitution, the president cannot dissolve the assembly on his own initiative. Instead, the president can dissolve the assembly only when the Legislative Yuan unseats the cabinet with a vote of no confidence. Third, the French system empowers the cabinet to steer the legislative agenda. Under the ROC Constitution, government bills enjoy no priority. The legislature controls its own agenda. Neither the president nor the premier possesses the constitutional weapon of "executive veto" to check legislative assertiveness. The cabinet can send back objectionable legislation and resolutions to parliament for reconsideration. But parliament has the final say if the same bill is passed again with an absolute majority—that is, half of the total seats plus one. The system's functioning may become wildly unpredictable when the majority party in parliament is different from the president's party or when no party has a parliamentary majority.

Moreover, the new amendments are vague on two important issues. First, it is unclear whether the new amendments empower the president to dismiss a sitting cabinet without the premier's own initiative, thereby changing the power relationship between the president and the premier in a fundamental way. Second, it is unclear whether the president enjoys preeminence in matters of national defense and foreign policy. With the introduction of the popular election for president, it becomes unrealistic to expect any future president, especially one with majority support, to exercise self-restraint in these two contested areas. This was not an issue under Lee Teng-hui because he could exercise control over the premier as well as the KMT caucus in parliament in his capacity as KMT chairman. The prospect of a power turnover after the year 2000 election had prompted many constitutional scholars to wonder how a non-KMT president could shape the cabinet and steer national policy without a power-sharing arrangement with the KMT that would most likely continue its majority control over the parliament until January 2002.

Also, it had been widely suspected that the prospect of a DPP victory might challenge the legitimacy of the constitutional order in a fundamental way. The DPP had long avowed to abolish the Constitution, which was viewed as a quintessential legal embodiment of the "one China" principle ever since the current constitution was originally adopted in 1947 when the Nationalist government still exercised effective governance over most of China. Instead, the DPP had persistently favored the adoption of a new constitution as a manifestation of the general will of the Taiwanese people. Although the DPP leaders had struck deals over constitutional amendments with the KMT during and after the National Development Conference,[8] these deals were considered by a great majority of DPP leaders as tactical moves rather than the final and lasting accord over constitutional arrangements. During the campaign, Chen Shui-bian tried to downplay concerns over his intention to carry out this long-standing platform; but a policy white paper on constitutional reform issued by his campaign headquarters still advocated the adoption of a new constitution, casting the country's constitutional future in great doubt.

Toward the end of Lee's tenure, therefore, the credibility, legitimacy, and integrity of the constitutional order were under severe strain. First, the next president might be drawn into a constitutional showdown between the Council of Grand Justices and the National Assembly. Second, the present constitutional arrangements were not designed for the prospect of a divided government—a likely outcome under the scenario of either Chen Shui-bian's or James Soong's victory. A political standoff between the president and the parliament would surely subject the credibility of the Constitution to a most rigorous test in terms of its guiding authority and institutional adequacy. Finally third, it seemed unlikely that any future president short of a majority mandate would be able to put a conclusive end to the constitutional conundrum and lay down a solid institutional foundation for Taiwan's new democracy. Most likely the next president would be facing a difficult choice between, on the one hand, strengthening the stability of the constitutional order through a rigorous observation of both the letter and spirit of the Constitution (thus self-limiting his capacity to steer the policy agenda) and, on the other, aggrandizing the office of the president still further through more constitutional tinkering (thus rendering the constitutional order in a perpetual flux).

Underdeveloped constitutionalism is not the only challenge facing Taiwan. The island's new political system is burdened with a host of other problems. First, the prospect of democratic consolidation in Taiwan is still clouded by quite a few holdover issues of democratic transition. As Hermann Giliomee reminds us, when a one-party dominant regime is a direct descendant of a party-state system, the properties of this new regime always call for close scrutiny.[9] The primary issue is the political neutrality of the military and security apparatus. This privileged branch of the state had long been a political instrument of the ruling party and was prominently presented in the KMT's formal power structure. From early on the KMT had installed a Soviet-style political commissar system to tighten its control over the military in terms of its political allegiance and ideological purity. Ranking military posts were disproportionately manned by mainlanders who invariably became loyal KMT members. Moreover, the security apparatus customarily conducted surveillance on the opposition and suspected threats to the KMT's top leaders without much consideration for due process. During Lee's tenure, in response to the opposition's demand for a "nationalization of the military," he took some cosmetic measures to ease the criticism. Instead of abolishing the party cells in the military, the KMT moved them underground and away from the barracks. And starting with the Fourteenth Party Congress, all high-ranking officers were taken off the delegation list and military generals on active duty were no longer nominated to the Central Standing Committee.[10] The military continued to discourage its officers from joining the DPP, however, and treated advocacy of Taiwan's independence as a threat to national security. Furthermore, under President Lee the military and security apparatus, in the name of presidential prerogative, continued to evade direct oversight by the members of the Legislative Yuan. Hence, there was always lingering doubt whether the military and security apparatus, as a highly politicized organ of the state, would ever voluntarily pledge its allegiance to a democratically elected non-KMT government—especially one carrying an unambiguous pro-independence credential. It was also hard to predict whether any future president would be able to resist the temptation of spying on his political enemies and policing domestic politics.

Another problematic legacy of the undisrupted dominance of a hegemonic party is an uneven development of the competitive party system. The prevailing structural as well as institutional constraints had limited the opposition from developing into a viable alternative to the KMT at the national level. From the very beginning the opposition parties had not enjoyed a level playing field with the KMT. The KMT benefited from its power of institution making, its privileged access to public-sector resources, its enormous organizational and financial might, and its coveted ownership of major electronic media.[11] The organizational expansion of the opposition parties was constrained by the very fact that the hegemonic party had already filled up most of the organizational space in the society and had locked in the support of key constituencies with both organizational and clientelist ties. For decades the KMT had been more than a political party in the normal sense. In the Taiwanese society, it has functioned as a "historical bloc" in the Gramscian sense.[12] It organized the society that it governed and structured the political arena in which it operated. As a result, the presence of partisan politics was ubiquitous throughout all organized sectors of the society. With the escalation of electoral competition, the organizational reach of partisan politics brought about a highly activated political society—which further compressed the sphere for public discourse.

The KMT's undisrupted hegemonic presence also aggravated the epidemic problem of "money politics" and "Mafia politics" and their troubling implications for the legitimacy of Taiwan's new democracy. During the authoritarian years, the adoption of a single nontransferable vote (SNTV) system and the co-optation of local factions were two important ingredients in the KMT's strategy for controlling the limited electoral process instituted at the local level. Most local factions relied on institutionalized vote-buying mechanisms to secure electoral outcomes. In return for their political loyalty, the economic premiums generated by local governments' procurement, zoning, and regulatory authority were distributed to the local factions, which typically had an economic stake in regional oligopolies such as public transport, credit unions, farm produce cartels, construction, public utilities, and certain illegal underground economic activities.[13] During the 1980s, confronted with an intensified electoral challenge from the opposition candidates and a steady decline in the effectiveness of the vote-buying practice, many local factions recruited gangsters and members of secret societies to safeguard their electoral strongholds. With the opening of electoral avenues, this pattern of structured corruption was quickly transmitted to the national representative bodies—a trend that was aggravated by a speedy indigenization of the KMT party's power structure. The old institutional firewall that had protected the party's central leadership from the infiltration of social forces via personal connections and lineage networks experienced a meltdown. Toward the end of the 1990s, the encroachment of "black and gold" politics had not only eroded popular trust in the new democratic institutions, but had also soured the island business environment. In fact, the popular discontent was so great that all major candidates in the year 2000 presidential campaign made "cracking down on black and gold politics" the number one domestic reform agenda. Even Lien Chan pledged to launch a war against "black and gold" politics. Most voters, however, did not believe this problem was tractable under continued KMT rule.

But it was the issue of national identity that remained the most unsettling factor for Taiwan's democratic consolidation. This issue, much like ethnic conflict, revolves around exclusive concepts of legitimacy and symbols of worth. Taiwan's national identity crisis must be distinguished, however, from the secessionist-oriented interethnic struggle that led to the disintegration of the Soviet Union and Yugoslavia. In Taiwan's internal debate the question is whether the island should pursue de jure (theoretical) independence or de facto (actual) territorial separation from the People's Republic of China (PRC).[14] Nonetheless, the dangers of internal political polarization and external intervention—inherent in any dispute over revision of territorial structure—are potentially there. Internally, the crisis evolved into a clash between two irreconcilable emotional claims about Taiwan's statehood and the national identity of the people of Taiwan. Externally, mirroring Taiwan's own internal conflict, a tug-of-war across the Taiwan Strait between two competing nation-building processes dragged on as the PRC attempted to impose its vision of nation building (the one-country two-system model) on Taiwan and vowed to use military means if necessary to stop the movement toward independence.

The internal conflict over national identity has died down considerably as Lee Teng-hui has been quite successful in harnessing the DPP's zeal for independence with a call for the formation of "a sense of shared destiny among the 21 million people" and a gradual retreat from the so-called "one China" principle. Even so, Taiwan's democratization has increased the possibility of external intervention. The growing aspiration for a separate Taiwanese identity among the people of Taiwan has fueled an ultranationalistic response from mainland China and provoked the communist regime to intensify its hostile reunification campaign—exemplified by the missile crises during the summer of 1995 and March 1996. At the same time, the threat of external intervention has placed an additional burden on the new democracy. The impulse to contain the political infiltration of the PRC has clashed with the values of political pluralism, minority rights, and due process. During the latest presidential election, supporters of Chen Shui-bian launched a negative campaign against James Soong, a mainlander, implicating him as a Beijing collaborator who might sell out Taiwan. These developments suggest that so long as the PRC stands ready to infiltrate Taiwan's domestic political process—and threatens to subvert, with the use of force if necessary, any democratically elected government that promotes Taiwan independence—Taiwan's new democracy remains vulnerable.

The Transition to Chen Shui-bian's Presidency

As it turned out, the resilience of Taiwan's new democracy has withstood the litmus test. The transfer of power from a KMT presidency to the DPP was quite peaceful, even though it has proceeded in the shadow of the PRC's military threat and worries about the resistance of the military and security establishment to a DPP takeover. Although Beijing was shaken by the news of Chen Shui-bian's victory, it chose to put Taiwan's new leader on political probation, despite the ultimatum issued by Chinese Premier Zhu Rongji on the eve of the election. An even more reassuring gesture came from Taiwan's mainlander-dominated military leadership. Two days after the election, General Tang Yao-min, Chief of the General Staff, publicly pledged allegiance to the new president.[15]

Chen Shui-bian did not overcome the two imminent obstacles to a peaceful transfer of power without some implicit political compromises, however. Hours after he was declared the winner, Chen extended his rhetorical olive branch to Beijing by expressing his willingness to negotiate with mainland China on the issues of direct links, direct commerce, investment, and military confidence-building measures. In his first exclusive interview with a foreign newspaper, Chen Shui-bian emphasized that peace and coexistence across the Taiwan Strait would be the "top priority" of his presidency—more important than such domestic concerns as the economy or fighting corruption. Taking a conciliatory posture toward Beijing's leadership, Chen even suggested that "the Democratic Progressive Party's mainstream agrees that Taiwan should be willing to discuss with Beijing the idea that Taiwan and the People's Republic are both part of 'one China.'"[16] In a subsequent interview with *Asahi Shimbun*, Chen indicated his hope that "the three links" would actually take place by the end of 2000 if Beijing were willing to respond positively to his peace overture and show its sincerity and goodwill.[17] To dispel any apprehension that his presidency might rupture cross-strait relations, in his inaugural address Chen pledged his "Four Nos": no to declaring independence, no to changing Taiwan's formal name from the Republic of China, no to enshrining "state-to-state" in the Constitution, and no to holding a referendum on formal independence. Notably he also said he would not abolish the National Reunification Council or the National Reunification Guidelines, both established by Lee Teng-hui in 1991. In fact, Chen made so many conciliatory overtures to Beijing that some of his DPP colleagues began to question whether he had made too many concessions too soon.

Chen took another bold move by appointing Tang Fei—the incumbent defense minister, former air force commander in chief, and former chief of the General Staff—as premier. Apparently Chen had hoped that Tang would provide a "stability card" to increase the public's and lawmakers' confidence in the new government. More important, he had hoped that the retired general's mainland and military background would bring the pro-reunification defense establishment under the control of the new government. Furthermore, he retained all the top officials of the military and security apparatus, in particular the head of the National Security Agency and the chief of the Investigation Bureau. In the final makeup of his national security team, all the senior positions went to the military establishment: the premier, the secretary-general of the National Security Council (Admiral Chuang Ming-yao), the defense minister (Admiral Wu Shih-wen), and the head of the National Security Agency (General Ting Yu-chou). While Chen was not pressured to make all these appointments, the prominence of top military officials in the new government nevertheless underscored the military's privileged status in the overall state apparatus and the new president's keen awareness of the need to pamper the military and security apparatus.

To discover the root cause for the smoothness of this power transition, we must poke beneath the surface and explore the path-dependent nature of Taiwan's regime transition. Chen's self-adjustment in political rhetoric during the campaign and his skillful political balancing act after the election did help. But this alone would have been insufficient without Lee Teng-hui's political, institutional, and ideological groundwork. It is no exaggeration to say that the reforms undertaken by President Lee made it possible for a peaceful power transfer from the KMT to a non-KMT power bloc. During Lee Teng-hui's long tenure, the island's political system had already withstood the test of an intraparty power alternation. It was a power shift, not from one political party to another, but from one ethnic (or more accurately subethnic) group to another. Nevertheless, the political restructuring and reorientation engineered by Lee Teng-hui was as monumental and radical as an interparty turnover of power.

During his tenure, Lee brought an end to mainlander's dominance in national politics. KMT old-timers were pushed out of the power center and substantially marginalized. The leadership stratum of the party and the state bureaucracy were thoroughly indigenized in terms of personnel and ideology. After the departure of Hau Bei-tsun in early 1993, the military and security apparatus, the last stronghold for the mainlander elite, was tamed and put under his personal control. To consolidate his civilian supremacy, Lee promoted native Taiwanese senior officers to the top command posts culminating in his decision to promote General Tang Yao-min as the first native Taiwanese chief of General Staff in 1998. The timing of General Tang's promotion turned out to be opportune for the historic shift of power.

More important, during Lee's tenure the principle of popular accountability and open political contestation was firmly legitimized and institutionalized while the electoral dominance of the KMT was kept largely intact. After the abolition of the Temporary Articles in May 1991 and three phases of KMT-directed constitutional revision in the early 1990s, most of the legal obstacles blocking the normal functioning of a representative democracy were removed one by one. The December 1992 Legislative Yuan election brought in a new parliament, wholly reelected by the people of Taiwan, and formally submitted the KMT's governing position to a democratic contest for the first time. The holding of the first popular presidential election formally subjected the apex of state power to the principle of democratic accountability. Since then, Taiwan's democratic transition has passed the point of no return. Today it would be unthinkable for any organized political force to turn back the political clock.

An equally significant development during his tenure was the transformation of the raison d'être of the state. The state was reengineered to foster the growth of Taiwanese identity and consolidate Taiwan's sovereignty both at home and in the international system. First the government-sponsored socialization mechanisms were gradually converted from a cultural agent of Chinese nationalism into an incubator of a "reimaged community" based on a new Taiwanese identity.[18] Lee also took measures to alleviate past grievances such as the 28 February Incident, restore the pride and self-respect of Taiwanese, and foster the growth of a sense of shared destiny among the 21 million people. Furthermore, Lee instilled a Taiwan-centered view into the management of the island's external relations and asserted a separate sovereign status for the ROC in the international community by launching a series of bold foreign policy initiatives. At home he introduced constitutional changes to redefine the compass of ROC sovereignty, as well as citizenship in full accord with the state's de facto territoriality.

At the close of the 1990s, popular aspirations for an independent Taiwanese statehood had become so crystallized and cohesive that the DPP's pro-independence platform was no longer considered radical. It took only a cosmetic adjustment in Chen Shui-bian's pro-independence stance to shift his candidacy, as well as the DPP, much closer to the new centrist position on this most salient issue. Finally, the fact that Lee had seemingly taken the strategy of "creeping independence" to its realistic limit—culminating in the announcement of his "special state-to-state" formula in July 1999—simply made Chen Shui-bian's soft-spoken maneuver on the cross-strait issue much more acceptable to the pro-independence fundamentalists. In a similar vein, Lee's daring moves—which were deemed so destabilizing by Washington and so provocative by Beijing—simply made Chen Shui-bian's professed pragmatism a lot more agreeable to Washington and tolerable to Beijing. In retrospect, then, Lee Teng-hui had essentially performed the function of a political bulldozer: clearing away all major political, institutional, and ideological obstacles to the possibility of a peaceful turnover of power at the end of his tenure.[19]

Prospects for Deepening Democratic Reform

The peaceful transfer of power from a KMT-controlled government to a DPP administration was a major democratic accomplishment in its own right. It established a new historical precedent and reinforced the popular belief in the legitimacy of the new democratic institutions. The turnover also ushered in a new era of democratic development and opened possibilities for the deepening of democratic reform—cracking down on "black and gold" politics, strengthening the fabric of civil society, and restructuring the party system.

Certainly a peaceful ending to the presidential contest cleared up the political obstacle to a timely resolution of the constitutional crisis. Barely a week after the election, the Council of Grand Justices ruled invalid the amendments passed by the National Assembly in September 1999 lengthening its term. By a vote of 14–2, the council ruled that September's amendments were full of flaws and constituted a clear breach of the fundamental principles of the Constitution. The council instructed that the assembly's 315 delegates should step down when their four-year terms came to an end on 20 May 2000. By then an election should be called to elect new deputies in accordance with the original provision of the Constitution.

The council's decision prompted the KMT and the DPP to engineer another round of constitutional amendments to block a National Assembly election just a few weeks after the presidential contest. The DPP opposed the election on the ground that it runs counter to its long-standing objective of abolishing the assembly as well as creating a unicameral parliament. At the same time, the two major parties (plus the New Party) worried that the election might inadvertently help James Soong to establish his new political party, the People First Party (PFP). The argument that the election might help Soong to sustain his electoral momentum was so powerful that the leaders of the two major parties were able to silence all dissenting voices and expedite the constitutional amendment package through the floor of National Assembly toward the end of April 2000.

The latest amendment package essentially rolls back all the power aggrandizement the National Assembly had bestowed upon itself during the 1990s, reverts the assembly back into a contingent deliberating body, and transfers many of its functions to the Legislative Yuan. Although the assembly retains the power to vote on the impeachment of the president or vice-president, on constitutional amendments, and on proposals to redraw national boundaries, it no longer has the power to initiate such changes itself. The right to formally propose such measures will, in the future, belong to the Legislative Yuan.[20] The assembly will cease to be a standing body; it will convene only when impeachment, constitutional reforms, or national boundary changes have been formally proposed. Moreover, the amendments freeze the holding of direct popular elections for the National Assembly. Future assemblies will be filled by a system of proportional representation.

Thus, in a totally unexpected way, the mercurial situation in the aftermath of the election compelled the deputies of the National Assembly to terminate their own political future and end a decade-long saga of constitutional tinkering. This latest round of constitutional changes was designed to deprive James Soong of a chance to convert his popularity into tangible political resources for his new political party; it also virtually closed off the possibility of future constitutional changes. As Liu Yi-teh, a leading DPP deputy, put it: "In the future the convening of the National Assembly should appear about as often as Halley's Comet."[21] Thus, despite all the flaws in the present Constitution, all political forces will have to learn how to live with it and abandon their habit of constitutional tinkering—not necessarily a bad thing for a new democracy where politicians became addicted to amending the Constitution while a concern for constitutional order and a respect for the guiding authority of the basic rules of the game have been in short supply.

Another positive development from the shift of power has been the meltdown of the corporatist arrangements that had chained many organized sectors to the state as well as the ruling party. Even before Chen Shui-bian was inaugurated, the KMT had lost control of some of the state-sanctioned organizations. A few weeks after the electoral debacle, for example, KMT-endorsed Huo Tsai-fong lost her bid to head the Chinese Federation of Labor. The KMT fought back by encouraging Huo to launch a new national labor organization, the National Association of Labor Unions, composed primarily of the labor unions based in export-processing zones. At the same time, the new government pledged to amend the Labor Union Law to remove the provision for singular representation. At a founding meeting for the Taiwan Confederation of Trade Unions (the organizational fixture of the independent labor movement), President-elect Chen Shui-bian promised to give the outlaw organization legal status.[22] This signaled the beginning of a new era for the development of democratic and autonomous labor unions.

The reelection of the leadership of the Chinese National Federation of Industry (CNFI) in July spelled the end of the KMT's stranglehold over business organizations as well. In this case, Lin Kun-tzong, a candidate favored by the KMT, handily won the position of chairman after his rival, Sun Tao-chun, allegedly backed by Chen Shui-bian, withdrew from the race at the last minute. But Lin's victory might simply mean that the future status of this top organization is in doubt. The CNFI might lose much of its governmental subsidies, its coveted status, and its privileged access to the policymaking process if Lin refuses to transform its partisan image. At the same time, the

CNFI might lose its status as an umbrella organization representing the entire manufacturing sector. Lin's victory also spelled a formal split of the CNFI. After he pulled out of the race, Sun announced his plan to form a rival organization that would give greater recognition to high-tech industries and the "new economy." These developments suggest that while partisan politics might stay, the KMT's monopoly over the organized interests has gone.

Chen's victory has raised popular expectations for a deepening of democratic reform in three critical areas: cracking down on money politics and gangster politics; protecting human rights; and removing the government's control over the electronic media. While it is too early to gauge Chen's progress on any of these fronts, developments thus far present a very mixed picture. Although the appointment of Chen Ding-nan, known for his integrity and tireless personality, as justice minister was widely applauded, Chen got off to a very bumpy start. His plan for an anticorruption task force was quickly scuttled by the ministry's Investigation Bureau as well as dissenting voices within the ministry itself. His proposal for recording all citizens' assets in a centralized computer system by ID number (similar to the ill-fated real-name reform implemented by South Korean President Kim Yung-san in his first year) was met with mixed reactions from human rights groups. These groups had been very encouraged by Chen Shui-bian's inauguration address in which he announced the new government's intention to set up a national human rights commission. But his decision to retain all the top officials of the intelligence apparatus, though perhaps a politically savvy move, did not resonate well with his human rights priority. This decision temporarily blocked any possibility for a probe into the security apparatus's past involvement in unlawful actions against dissidents and its illegal surveillance of political figures and opposition parties. More alarming, there are signs that President Chen Shui-bian has not ordered the security apparatus to cease its practice of unlawful political surveillance.[23]

Media watchdog organizations were disappointed by the appointment of Lai Kuo-chou, Lee Teng-hui's son-in-law, as chairman of the board of the government-controlled TTV.[24] This controversial appointment was widely conceived as politically motivated and a clear departure from Chen Shui-bian's campaign promise to turn TTV and CTS into public TV stations. This appointment also shed light on Chen Shui-bian's complicated liaison with the former president. Apparently Chen Shui-bian placed a premium on courting Lee Teng-hui's goodwill—perhaps out of the belief that Lee, with his residual influence over a number of KMT legislators, could prevent Lien Chan from forming an alliance with James Soong (the worst scenario for the new government as well as for Chen's reelection bid). This courtship, however, might obstruct his effort to crack down on "black and gold" politics because some of Lee's die-hard supporters in the legislature might turn out to be the worst offenders. It might also prevent his government from pursuing any cases that might implicate the former president. Certainly a renewed investigation into Navy Captain Yin Ching-feng's murder would signal the government's resolve to eradicate "black and gold" politics.[25] But Yin's case could conceivably implicate high-level officials in the previous government. At stake is not only the credibility of the new government but its very political survival.

The Challenge of Governing Responsibility

Before Chen Shui-bian can meet any of his campaign promises and pursue any of the reform agenda, he has to meet the challenge of governance first. When Chen appointed Tang Fei as premier and refused the KMT's demand for a party-to-party negotiation over a power-sharing scheme, he apparently overestimated the powers bestowed on the president by the Constitution as well as his chances of getting away with the political imperative for "cohabitation." Chen rejected proposals for forming a coalition government with either the KMT or James Soong's PFP. Instead, he established a "government of national unity" by drawing talents from different political backgrounds and negotiating with targeted cabinet members individually rather than on a party-to-party basis. For a short while Chen was receptive to a proposal by Shih Ming-teh (former DPP chairman) for forging a cross-party "majority coalition" in the Legislative Yuan to strengthen the DPP's influence over the legislature. But the proposal was dropped when DPP legislators split over which alliance would best benefit the DPP and Chen concluded that the KMT might never get its act together again after the humiliating defeat. As a gesture to elevate the office of the president above partisan politics, Chen resigned all party posts and vowed not to take part in the party's formal decision-making process. Just a few key advisers around him were involved in personnel decisions. Even leaders of the DPP's various factions felt they were not consulted during the government formation process. For a while Chen Shui-bian thought he could safely bypass brokering by political parties and run the government based on direct appeals to popular sentiment. After two months in office, he found himself steadily sinking into an economic and political crisis.

Chen Shui-bian came to the office with a poor understanding of what makes Taiwan's economy tick. His team erroneously believed that Taiwan's economic fundamentals were so sound that his government could simply leave the self-sustaining economy alone and attend to a progressive social agenda including the environment and social welfare. Thus, the new government canceled construction of the environmentally unfriendly Mei-nong Dam, proposed to reduce the workweek for laborers, promised pension checks to all elders above sixty-five, and vowed to reexamine the ongoing project of the fourth nuclear power plant. These priorities threw cold water on the business community, which did not anticipate that Chen Shui-bian's government would seriously implement his campaign platform. At the same time, the new government paid only scant attention to the multifaceted function the state used to perform. Little did his administration understand that behind Taiwan's booming and dynamic high-tech industry was a purposive and resourceful state that served, not only as a guiding element in a national effort to identify trajectories of technological diffusion and innovation, but as a catalyst motivating and enabling local firms to invest, upgrade, innovate, and internationalize.[26] Many high-tech executives found little substance in Chen Shui-bian's favorite slogan: "Developing Taiwan into a green silicon island." They got annoyed with the new government's announcement that in the future the government would tilt its emphatic support toward a struggling traditional industry and away from the booming high-tech sector. Less than two months after his inauguration, perceptions of a deteriorating business climate began to take hold and precipitated a long slide in Taiwan's stock market. Chen's government had bad luck as well with Taiwan's electronics makers who were increasingly feeling the pinch from slowing economic growth in the United States. The new government responded to the plummeting stock market with panic. Since the midsummer of 2000, the presidential office has instructed the Ministry of Finance to deploy all possible measures to prop up the stock market—cutting the allowable daily declines in individual stocks from 7 to 3.5 percent and pumping up to NT$300 billion from government-controlled provident funds (and later the National Stabilization Fund) into the stock market. Nevertheless, the stock market continued its slide, cutting the TAIEX (the broad-gauge composite index) almost by half in six months, pushing the composite index toward its lowest level since the March 1996 Chinese missile crisis, and inflicting government-controlled funds with huge losses.

The new government also inherited a fiscal crunch and an ailing financial sector. Over the last few years, the fiscal health of Taiwan's public sector had deteriorated rapidly after serial introduction of new entitlement programs. Reconstruction after the devastating earthquake of 1999 has virtually dried up the government's borrowing capacity under the Budget Law. Furthermore, Taiwan's banking sector never fully recovered from the financial crisis that hit East Asia in late 1997. Taiwan's sagging real estate sector and sluggish stock market simply compounded the problem as the banking sector was still saddled with nonperforming loans. Over the preceding two years, Premier Vincent Siew's cabinet held off a much needed banking restructuring by instructing the banks to roll over these bad loans with new ones. The KMT's electoral defeat hurt the banking sector, as well, because there was an implicit mechanism of coinsurance between the KMT and quite a few conglomerates whose creditworthiness was linked to their cozy relationship with the KMT leadership. Now the coinsurance schemes have faltered and the banks are saddled with loans that lack adequate collateral. As the banks became more cautious in their lending policy, the traditional manufacturing sector was squeezed between a credit crunch and rising labor costs as a result of the shortened workweek. News of an imminent banking crisis, factory closures, and rising unemployment began to hit the headlines in late September 2000. In November, the Directorate-General of Budget, Accounting, and Statistics canceled the release of a quarterly consumer confidence survey lest it have a depressing effect on the stock market and the economy. A month later, the Ministry of Economic Affairs held back a quarterly survey on Taiwan's economic outlook because it was "too bearish to tell the public."[27]

On the political front, too, the new government has lost its grip on the steering wheel. The "triple minority syndrome" surfaced sooner than anyone had expected. From the beginning, Chen's governing capacity was severely circumscribed by three facts: he was elected as a minority president; his party is a minority party in parliament; and his faction, the Justice Alliance, remains a minority force within the DPP. Moreover, the KMT regrouped much more quickly than political pundits had predicted. As soon as the KMT had restored its organizational coherence by electing Lien Chan as its leader, the former ruling party started to flex its political muscle as the majority party in parliament. The KMT caucus was determined to make the most of Chen's bounced checks—that is, the promises he had made during his presidential campaign but unable to deliver. President Chen Shui-bian had made a campaign promise, for example, to shorten the workweek from forty-eight hours to forty-four hours starting in 2001. Although the Executive Yuan proposed a bill to the legislature to put this promise into action, the government bill was declared dead on arrival. Instead, the KMT caucus decided to offer laborers a more generous deal. The caucus mobilized its members to shorten the maximum working time to eighty-four hours every two weeks. With the DPP holding less than one-third of the seats in parliament (see Table 2.1), the government's legislative proposals were repeatedly turned down or held up. Tang Fei gradually lost favor with the president as it became clear that the political value-added that the premier brought to the new government was evaporating rapidly. His cabinet had simply lost control of the legislative agenda.

After only four months in office, Tang Fei was forced to resign when he failed to work out a compromise between the president and the KMT-con-

Table 2.1

Distribution of Seats in Parliament

	Right after last parliamentary election (Dec. 1998)		After presidential inauguration (May 2000)	
	Seats	Ratio (%)	Seats	Ratio (%)
KMT	123	54.7	115	52.0
DPP	70	31.1	66	29.9
NP	11	4.9	10	4.5
PFP	—	—	17	7.7
Others	21	9.3	13	5.9
Total	225		221	

trolled parliament over the DPP's platform to scrap the ongoing construction of the fourth nuclear power plant. His departure set off a major political storm and seriously eroded the public's confidence in Chen Shui-bian's ability to govern. Then Chen stumbled into a political quagmire trying to outmaneuver parliament by pushing his new premier, Chang Chun-hsiung, a veteran DPP parliamentarian, to announce the decision to suspend construction without any warning signals and without parliament's formal consent. Chen's abrupt decision to suspend the nuclear power plan was a political disaster. The business community was stunned because it now seemed that Chen was not the pragmatic politician they had anticipated. Moreover, the decision inspired his two opponents, Lien Chan and James Soong, to mend their rivalry and form a united front that now controls an even more formidable voting bloc in parliament.[28] To retaliate against Chen's unilateral action, the two major opposition parties declared his decision reckless and unconstitutional, and vowed to take draconian actions: impeaching the president, perhaps, or introducing a motion to hold a recall election. The imminent political showdown further depressed the business community and sent the stock market into a nosedive. Signs of ineffective economic management sent shock waves through a business community that had got used to the frozen clarity of one-party dominance and now was confused by the unpredictability of "divided government." From this point on, Chen's political fortunes spiraled rapidly downward. In six months his approval rating slipped dramatically from a high of 77 percent in mid-June 2000 to 35 percent at the end of the year.[29]

Although everyone senses that a crisis of governance is in the making, there is no easy way out for Chen Shui-bian. For the president has no institutional lever to check the parliamentary majority. Unlike the French Fifth Republic, the president cannot dissolve the legislature (according to the ROC Constitution) unless it passes a vote of no confidence against a sitting cabinet. The KMT caucus apparently enjoys being the backseat driver for the moment and will not push for such a vote and risk an early election any time soon. Some DPP leaders reckon that Chen Shui-bian should have sought a coalition government when he took office. Now that he is in a much weaker position, it is simply too late to strike a reasonable deal with any opposition party.[30]

Political troubles at home have hampered Chen's ability to steer cross-strait relations onto a more stable course. In a search for new thinking and domestic consensus on cross-strait relations, Chen appointed a blue-ribbon cross-party task force; but both the KMT and PFP refused to take part. Instead, they pushed for their own platform demanding the reopening of the National Unification Council and a return to the 1992 cross-strait consensus on the "one China" principle. At the same time, Chen was under mounting pressure from the business community to reverse Lee Teng-hui's "go slow, be patient" policy and lift the longtime ban on the "three links"—direct trade, shipping, and airline connections—with mainland China. The "three-link" issue had been upheld by Lee Teng-hui as Taiwan's last trump card in winning political concessions from Beijing at the negotiating table. Ironically, now under a DPP government, the "three links" card is promoted by many business executives and opposition leaders as the only means in sight to rescue the sinking economy.

Witnessing a tidal wave of Taiwanese capital outflow seeking new market opportunities after China's World Trade Organization (WTO) entry, many DPP leaders have grudgingly concluded that the trend toward further economic integration with mainland China, despite its social and political ramifications, is inevitable. Watching President Chen being squeezed by political and economic forces toward accepting the PRC's terms for resumption of political talks, Beijing now deems the political situation across the strait much less threatening than it appeared right after the presidential election. Meanwhile the PRC continues to put military pressure on Taiwan through increased deployments while wooing opposition politicians from the island with warm treatment and Taiwanese businessmen with lucrative deals. The 18 March 2000 presidential election gave Chen a plurality of less than 40 percent, leaving Beijing to conclude that roughly 60 percent of Taiwan voters prefer a less confrontational stance toward the mainland. Based on this assumption, Beijing's leaders are awaiting a realignment of political forces on Taiwan either before or after the December 2001 election for the Legislative Yuan.

Shakeout in the Party System

Before Chen Shui-bian can introduce lasting changes for the better, he has to ensure that his party makes a handsome electoral gain at the next parliamen-

Table 2.2

Trend of Partisan Support: 1999–2000 (Percentage)

	Mid-Feb. 1999[a] NTU survey	6 Mar. 2000[b] TVBS poll	6 Apr. 2000[b] TVBS poll	27 Apr. 2000[a] Gallup poll	30 June 2000[b] TVBS poll	20 Dec. 2000[b] TVBS poll
KMT	29	25.9	14	9	10.2	11
DPP	23	22.1	27	23	34.9	25
PFP	—	—	18	15.1	18.1	21
NP	6	3.6	1	1		
Others		0.2	0.1			
Independent		42.1	40.4	41.9	26.8	32
	N = 1,213	N = 2,092	N = 1,115	N = 1,110	N = 1,058	N = 1,021

[a]Party identification.
[b]Closeness measure.

tary election. That prospect, however, looked very foggy indeed six months after he took office. The challenge facing the newly elected party chairman, Frank Hsieh, is ironic in that the DPP has both benefited and suffered from the meteoric rise of Chen Shui-bian. Chen's victory created a short-term bandwagon effect for his party, motivating more people, especially the young, to identify with the DPP. The level of partisan support—that is, the proportion of self-identified DPP supporters—escalated from about 22 percent of the electorate at the beginning of Chen's campaign to 34 percent after his inauguration, making the DPP the most popular party on the island. But the level of support has come down the same way it went up. Since the inauguration, Chen's governance problems and sagging popularity have brought the level of DPP support down to 25 percent by the end of 2000 (see Table 2.2). Most DPP leaders do not predict a substantial electoral gain in the next parliamentary election. Even under the best scenario, the DPP may become the largest party in parliament, but still will be about thirty seats short of a majority leaving the KMT and PFP together with a hefty majority control.

At the same time, the DPP is not immune from the generalization that a strong president tends to weaken the organizational strength of his own party. Ever since Chen's victory, voices within the DPP have proposed trimming the party's power by turning it into an "internally created party" and downgrading the chairman's coordinating role. After the euphoria of electoral triumph, the party, after being in opposition for so long, is facing an acute challenge of reorientation. This challenge manifested itself in the recent party congress, which was clouded by talk of vote buying and power grabbing and ended without any solid conclusion regarding its core values or future direction as a ruling party.

Complicating the DPP's problems has been the unexpected resilience of the former ruling party. As we have seen, the KMT is down but hardly out. The party's organizational integrity was seriously damaged by the power struggle between Lee Teng-hui and James Soong first and then by Lien Chan's humiliating defeat. Indeed a number of KMT legislators defected to James Soong's camp during and after the election (see Table 2.1). Moreover, the defeat touched off a backlash against Lee Teng-hui from the party's rank-and-file members, leading to his abrupt departure from the party chairmanship just weeks after the debacle. The KMT elected Lien Chan, the only consensual figure around, to head the party. Mourning over its electoral debacle, the party leadership was torn among three contending visions for the party's future. Lien Chan's supporters wanted to clean up the residual influence of Lee Teng-hui and consolidate Lien's power as soon as possible. James Soong's sympathizers insisted that the KMT has no future unless the party welcomes back Soong and regains the presidency with a reunited ticket four years down the road. Faithful followers of Lee Teng-hui were resolved to fight back if Lien Chan ever deviated from Lee's policy course or reached out to James Soong. As the party was left with no strong leadership and no clear sense of direction, the KMT's level of partisan support dropped more than half—down from about 29 percent at the beginning of the campaign to as low as 10 percent after the election—making the KMT the least popular among the three major parties for the moment.

Yet there are still a few things working in the KMT's favor. The Constitution's design almost guarantees KMT control of the legislative agenda before the next parlimentary elections, due in December 2001, as long as the party caucus sticks together. Moreover, a sense of crisis has prompted the party to undertake unprecedented organizational reform and open up the party chairmanship for direct popular election by all party members. Most significantly, it has turned over a new leaf and put an anti-"black and gold" clause into its party charter. Under this measure, members who are convicted or prosecuted for criminal offenses become ineligible for party positions as well as party nomination. Further, the KMT still enjoys a stalwart financial position. In fact, its financial might has enabled the party to retain talented former government officials through the creation of a new party think tank and to maintain its organizational links with many social groups by creating several grant-making mechanisms. Today it appears that the KMT has, temporarily at least, saved itself from further organizational breakdown. While the KMT is bound to lose its majority control in the next parliamentary election, its electoral strength remains formidable.

The next parliamentary election will be the first litmus test for the viability of James Soong's new party. Originally Soong had declined to form a new party despite demands from his supporters that he continue to lead the 4.6 million people who voted for him. Yet the prospect of upcoming elections for the National Assembly—his party's first chance to get its foot in the door to official power—left him with no choice. The drive to build up his new party was sabotaged, however, by the KMT and DPP's joint constitutional maneuver to abolish the National Assembly election. In the meantime, the PFP's hopes of attracting KMT politicians into its fold turned out to be overoptimistic, leaving the party with only seventeen seats (well under 10 percent) in the Legislative Yuan. The PFP appears to be in a good position to benefit from popular disenchantment with the discredited KMT as well as growing dissatisfaction with the DPP government. Based on recent surveys, the PFP is clearly the number one rival to the DPP in terms of popular support having inched toward about 21 percent of partisan support among the electorate only six months after its founding. The brightest prospect for the PFP lies in the forthcoming elections (in December 2001) for county and city magistrates, now the most powerful executive posts beneath the level of the central government.[31] In the presidential election of 2000 James Soong reaped the largest number of popular votes in fifteen counties and cities (out of a total of twenty-three). If Soong's popularity is transferable, the PFP will be in a better position to contest these crucial positions than the KMT, which suffered an electoral debacle at this level in 1997 (when its control of jurisdictions fell from seventeen to eight, three of them on sparsely populated islands).

Since the DPP is unlikely to produce a working majority in the reelected parliament on its own, the fate of its governing status will depend on whether it can prevent the KMT and PFP from forming a united front either before or after the December 2001 election. If the KMT's electoral strength turns out to be roughly equivalent to the DPP's after the next parliamentary election, the KMT will not be very interested in forming a grand coalition with the DPP. After the departure of Lee Teng-hui's underlings from the KMT's power nucleus, however, closer cooperation between the KMT and PFP becomes probable. If the degree of ideological affinity is the only factor, the possibility of a pan-KMT alliance—uniting the KMT, the PFP, and the New Party— looks a lot more promising than a DPP–PFP partnership. James Soong is not likely to choose to form a coalition government with Chen Shui-bian unless he is offered the premiership, a proposition seemingly out of the question from the DPP's perspective. Although some of Chen's top advisers are entertaining the possibility of splitting the KMT by joining forces with Lee Teng-hui's followers to create a "mainstream party," this is a very risky strategy. It would not only upset the DPP's own organizational integrity, but also prompt Lien Chan to seek a closer alliance with James Soong. The political future of Chen Shui-bian's government, therefore, still hangs in the balance.

By Way of Conclusion

From the perspective of democratic development, the shift of power at the turn of the century was long overdue. The resilience of Taiwan's new democracy has passed a long-anticipated litmus test. The peaceful transfer of power from the KMT-controlled government to a DPP-led administration is a major democratic accomplishment in its own right. It established a new historical precedent and reinforced the public's belief in the legitimacy of the new democratic institutions. Lee Teng-hui had essentially performed the function of a political bulldozer by removing all the major political, institutional, and ideological barriers to a peaceful turnover of power at the end of his tenure. Ironically, Lien Chan's humiliating defeat also deflated Lee Teng-hui's charisma and brought his era to an abrupt and calamitous end. At the same time, the peaceful ending of the presidential contest removed the political obstacle to a timely resolution of a pending constitutional crisis. In an unintended way, the political upset ended a decade-long saga of constitutional tinkering.

Nevertheless, the ongoing standoff between president and parliament subjects the credibility of Taiwan's Constitution to a most rigorous test both in terms of its guiding authority and its institutional adequacy. The current constitutional arrangements are not designed for the scenario of a divided government. Furthermore, there is a woeful lack of consensus over the nature and logic of the present constitutional order among the contending political forces. If Chen Shui-bian fails to secure a working majority in the reelected parliament, will he feel obligated to surrender the power of forming the cabinet to an opposing majority? Might he be loath to exercise his power to appoint the premier and risk a constitutional showdown with the opposition parties? There is no quick fix to these institutional shortcomings and ambiguities. Indeed, it is very unlikely that any future constitutional amendment proposals can enlist the support of the required three-quarters majority in parliament. Resolving the constitutional conundrum and laying a solid institutional foundation for Taiwan's new democracy, therefore, may become ever more elusive goals.

From the perspective of democratic governance, the DPP may have come to power before its time. The challenge of governing has turned out to be so formidable that it has diluted the significance of this historic rotation of power. Today the DPP government is torn between two polar expectations. On the one hand, the turnover of presidential power seems to present a historic opportunity to push through many long-awaited reforms: regulating party-owned business, suppressing vote buying by overhauling the electoral system, reducing levels of government and augmenting local government's powers and functions, strengthening the integrity and independence of the judicial system, and creating an independent human rights commission. None of these aims would have been possible under undisrupted KMT rule. Popular expectations were indeed very high. On the other hand, the challenge of governing as a minority has consumed much of the new government's energy and political capital, leaving Chen Shui-bian little space for tackling issues of democratic reform. Now with a gloomy economic outlook, an imminent crisis in local banking institutions, a bleeding stock market, and a weakened NT dollar, Taiwan's electorate suddenly has the economic bottom line to worry about.

Chen Shui-bian paid a high price for overestimating his chances of getting away with the imperative of "cohabitation." By the time he concluded he was unable to rule without a working majority in parliament, it was already too late to negotiate either a coalition government or a cross-party majority coalition in the legislature. Trapped in political gridlock, Chen has no choice but to wait out the current political turbulence and aim for attaining a substantial electoral gain for the DPP in the December 2001 parliamentary election or forming a new mainstream party through party realignment —or, preferably, some combination of the two. If he fails to deliver, he might end up, not just a one-term president, but a lame-duck and ineffective president as well.

Notes

1. For an extensive introduction to the concept of consolidation, see Juan Linz and Alfred Stepan, *Problems of Democratic Transition and Consolidation* (Baltimore: Johns Hopkins University Press, 1996), pp. 4–7.

2. The old KMT resembled Leninist regimes insofar as the symbiosis between party and state and the way the party-state organized and penetrated the society are concerned. For the quasi-Leninist features of the KMT, see Tun-jen Cheng, "Democratizing the Quasi-Leninist Regime in Taiwan," *World Politics* 42 (July 1989):471–499. I should point out, however, that on many important scores the KMT regime was quite different from the Leninist regimes of the former Soviet bloc. Unlike the communist regime, the KMT was long associated with the West; it had ample experience with private property rights, markets, and the rule of law; and it enjoyed the support of a distinctive development coalition. For a full treatment of the Leninist legacy in the Eastern European context, see *Liberalization and Leninist Legacies: Comparative Perspectives on Democratic Transitions*, ed. Beverley Crawford and Arend Lijphart (Berkeley: International and Area Studies, University of California, 1996).

3. Hung-mao Tien and Yun-han Chu, "Building Democracy in Taiwan," in *Contemporary Taiwan*, ed. David Shambaugh (New York: Oxford University Press, 1998).

4. Yun-han Chu, "A Born-Again Dominant Party? The Transformation of the Kuomintang and Taiwan's Regime Transition," in *The Awkward Embrace: One-Party Domination and Democracy*, ed. Hermann Giliomee and Charles Simkins (Capetown: Tafelberg, 1999).

5. A survey conducted by the *United Daily News* on the eve of passage indicated that more than 50 percent of respondents were against the National Assembly's extension of its current term.

6. Many DPP leaders told me they believed that popularly elected National Assembly deputies will never adopt self-terminating measures. On the contrary, they have every incentive to inflate the power of the National Assembly.

7. For the controversies over constitutional design see Yun-han Chu, "Consolidating Democracy in Taiwan: From *Guoshi* to *Guofa* Conference," in *Democratization in Taiwan: Implications for China*, ed. Hung-mao Tien and Steve Yui-sang Tsang (New York: St. Martin's Press, 1998).

8. In late December 1996, President Lee called a conference on national development that brought together government officials, academics, professionals, and representatives of the KMT, the DPP, and the independents to debate various proposals for constitutional reform. For the dynamics of the National Development Conference see Chu, "Consolidating Democracy in Taiwan."

9. On this point see Hermann Giliomee and Charles Simkins, "Introduction," in *The Awkward Embrace: One-Party Domination and Democracy*, ed. Hermann Giliomee and Charles Simkins (Capetown: Tafelberg, 1999).

10. Instead the military was represented by retired four-star generals such as Admiral Soong.

11. During the 1990s, the KMT-owned enterprises grew into one of the largest diversified business groups on the island. Through its Central Finance Committee (CFC), the party has either direct ownership or indirect investment in more than sixty-six companies—including nine companies listed on the Taiwan Stock Exchange and twenty-seven public companies. The book value of the party's stake in these thirty-six public companies alone was worth around NT$59.5 billion (US$2.4 billion) by the mid-1990s. Toward the end of 1990s, the KMT business empire was generating more than NT$7 billion of dividends a year.

12. For the concept "historical bloc" see Antonio Gramsci, *Selections from the Prison Notebooks of Antonio Gramsci*, translated by Q. Hoare and G. Nowell Smith (New York: International, 1971), pp. 136–137.

13. Joseph Bosco, "Taiwan Factions: Guanxi, Patronage and the State in Local Politics," in *The Other Taiwan: 1945 to the Present*, ed. Murray Rubinstein (Armonk, NY: M.E. Sharpe, 1994).

14. The Republic of China or Taiwan has existed as a de facto independent state since 1949 with the ROC government exercising sovereign rights on the island.

15. "The armed forces should therefore abide by the Constitution and be loyal to the leader of the country. I hereby announce on behalf of the armed forces that the military will be loyal to the new supreme commander of the country," he said.

16. *Los Angeles Times*, 22 March 2000.

17. *China Times Express*, 24 March 2000.

18. I adopt the expression "imagined community" from Benedict Anderson, *Imagined Communities*, rev. ed. (London and New York: Verso, 1991).

19. Here I intentionally skip the analysis on how his single-minded political campaign against James Soong divided the KMT and paved the way for Chen Shui-bian's victory. These developments are fully covered in chapter 1.

20. The parliament will take over other functions as well, such as confirmation of the nominees for the other three branches of government.

21. "Editorial: Don't Hold Your Breath," *Taipei Times*, 2 April 2000.

22. *China Times*, 2 May 2000.

23. Chen Shui-bian was evidently aware of the surveillance that the National Security Agency had placed on Frank Hsieh, the new DPP chairman, when he sent a private envoy to mainland China to negotiate a city-to-city exchange with Xia-men, a major harbor of Fujian province.

24. Although TTV is technically a privately run company, the government still holds 48 percent of its shares and is highly influential in selecting the board's leadership.

25. Yin was killed and his body dumped at sea off Ilan in 1993—apparently for his interference in naval procurement plans to purchase sixteen French *Lafayette* frigates worth US$4.8 billion as well as minesweepers from Germany. The case became a focus of cross-strait and international attention since an ex-mistress of former French foreign minister Roland Dumas admitted to having handled the kickbacks and revealed that some of the money had ended up with high-level officials in Taipei as well as Beijing. See *China Times*, 9 December 2000.

26. On the developmentalist dimension of the state see Yun-han Chu, "Re-engineering the Developmental State in an Age of Globalization: Taiwan in Defiance of Neoliberalism," in *Neoliberalism and Reform in East Asia*, ed. Meredith Woo-Cumings (Ithaca: Cornell University Press, forthcoming).

27. *Taipei Times*, 28 December 2000.

28. Accentuating the tactless political timing of the announcement was the fact that it came very shortly after President Chen held a high-profile meeting with Lien Chan. He had promised Lien that he would take into consideration Lien's strong opposition to any cancellation or postponement of construction on the power plant.

29. Based on the TVBS polls conducted on 6 March, 30 June, and 20 December 2000, respectively.

30. The KMT recently indicated that it is no longer interested in forming a coalition government. Instead, Lien Chan suggests that the majority party in parliament—the KMT—should form the government following the precedent of French-styled cohabitation.

31. The two special municipalities of Taipei and Kaohsiung, however, are elected on a different four-year cycle.

3

Taiwan's Democratization: What Lessons for China?

Bruce J. Dickson

Chen Shui-bian's election as president of Taiwan in March 2000 was clearly a nightmare scenario for Beijing. Despite his repeated claims of wanting to improve relations with Beijing, Chen was the only major candidate who was not formally committed to Taiwan's eventual unification with the mainland. Chen, along with the people of Taiwan and interested observers around the world, is now waiting to see how Beijing will respond to this turn of events. Much ink has been spilled already about the implications of Chen's administration for cross-strait relations.

The lessons of Taiwan's democratization for China's political system, and for the continued rule of the Chinese Communist Party (CCP), have not received nearly so much attention. But the prospects for further political reform in China, whether in the short or long term, have important implications for Taiwan's relationship with China. Chen's victory offers a mix of lessons, both positive and negative, for China's leaders and for Chinese society in general.

Let me be clear at the outset that I am optimistic about the prospects for democracy in China. In my book comparing democratization in China and Taiwan,[1] I concluded that the CCP was unlikely to be willing or able to broker the type of transition that the Kuomintang (KMT) initiated in Taiwan. Past decisions made by the CCP to repress demands for political change during the entire post-1949 period, coupled with the halting progress of political reform during the post-Mao period, do not give much hope that the

I would like to thank Muthiah Alagappa, Harry Harding, Jia Qingguo, and other participants at the conference for their useful suggestions on revising this chapter.

CCP will be the willing sponsor of democratization. This does not mean that democratization is unlikely in China—only that there is little evidence that the CCP will lead the transformation of China's political system and survive as the ruling party in a new democratic regime. On the basis of my book's argument, some readers have concluded that I am pessimistic about the prospects for China's democratization, not just the CCP's role in that process. The social and economic changes that are taking place provide good reasons to be optimistic about the prospects for democracy in China. Although social and economic change alone does not trigger democratization, it can provide a solid foundation for the consolidation of democracy once the transition from authoritarianism takes place. In understanding the dynamics of political change in China, we should be mindful of not just the general environmental factors that may facilitate the consolidation of democracy, but also the political calculations and choices that may trigger the transition.

In the end, democratization is a political process—the result of many decisions made by political leaders within the state as well as society. Taiwan's recent experience with democracy therefore offers important lessons about the feasibility and potential consequences of democracy in China.

Lesson 1: Democracy Creates Its Own Culture

Perhaps the greatest obstacle to China's democratization is the oft-repeated argument that Chinese culture is not compatible with democracy. Sun Yat-sen is probably the best-known exponent of the view that the Chinese are not ready for democracy and require an extended period of political tutelage before democracy is feasible in China. Recently, Zhu Rongji showed his lack of enthusiasm for the expansion of grassroots democracy by saying that the cultural level of the Chinese people, especially in the countryside, is not high enough to permit successful democratization. This is not only a self-serving argument made by China's leaders to maintain their authoritarian political system. It is a widely held belief in Chinese society as well. So long as people in China believe that their culture is not ready for democracy, they will be less likely to press for democratization or support those who do. Foreign scholars such as Samuel Huntington have argued similarly that China's Confucian traditions are incompatible with democracy.[2] This pessimistic attitude has placed a tremendous drag on the prospects for democratization in China.

Taiwan's democratization, however, reveals the fallacy of this argument. Democracy obviously can work in the Chinese political culture, because it is working in Taiwan. Taiwan is one of the best examples of the "transformation" path of democratization, a peaceful transition initiated by the ruling party. In fact, studies have shown that democratic values have grown as a consequence of the democratic transition—not just as a result of generational replacement, a slow process, but as the result of individuals turning away from traditional ways of thinking and adopting modern values more supportive of political democracy.[3] This finding shows that political culture is not immutable, indeed, it may be very malleable when the political environment undergoes fundamental change. Although the causal relationship between political culture and democracy is not well understood, Taiwan's case suggests that a democratic culture need not precede the democratization of the political system. Successful democratization may lay the groundwork for continued success by creating the political culture it needs to survive and flourish.

For many in China, however, the fact that democracy works in Taiwan is not proof that it can work in China. It is not just the skeptics who note that a tradition of democratic values is absent, or at best very weak, in China. Proponents of democracy in China also argue that the idea of democracy might be more attractive if historical precedents could be found in China, not just in the West or Taiwan.[4] To this end, much time and effort are spent looking for traditional beliefs and practices that might legitimate democratic government in contemporary China. This is a curious endeavor. It implies that democracy can only survive in the present if it existed in China's past. By this standard, few countries could ever become democratic because at some point, most countries lacked a democratic tradition. There is little doubt that certain values are conducive to successful democracy, but Taiwan's experience shows that a democratic culture may be the consequence of democratization and need not precede it. The search for democratic roots in China also suggests that democracy can be popularly acceptable only if there are hints of democratic values in China's antiquity, even if they have long been forgotten. This type of chauvinism remains a serious obstacle for China's democratic reformers and activists.

Lesson 2: Democracy Need Not Lead to Disorder

A second lesson for China from Taiwan's experience is that democratization does not necessarily lead to increased social and political turmoil. Taiwan's democratization shows that a country need not devolve into chaos once it abandons authoritarian controls over political participation. This is an important lesson for China's leaders, who have put the maintenance of political order at the top of their political agenda. In their own experience, they see that incidences of mass political participation have threatened China's stability. The Cultural Revolution, the Democracy Wall movement of 1978–

1979, student demonstrations in Shanghai and elsewhere in 1986–1987, the large-scale protests of 1989 in Tiananmen Square and other major cities—all seem to have convinced China's leaders that political participation is unpredictable and uncontrollable, a threat to the nation's stability, and therefore must be suppressed, even at a high cost.[5] The instability that accompanied democratization in the former Soviet Union—indeed the economic and political problems that still plague Russia—have reinforced their fears of democracy's threat to political stability.

The experiences of political protest in China and regime change in Russia continue to influence elite thinking on the potential impact of democratization in China. The experience of Taiwan, therefore, offers a useful counterexample. In Taiwan democratization has enhanced political stability. Although democratization led to an immediate and sharp increase in protest activities, especially on environmental and labor issues, these protests quickly subsided both in number and intensity.[6] In the early 1990s, the Democratic Progressive Party (DPP) abandoned street protests as an item in its repertoire, believing they had outlived their usefulness for raising public awareness of political injustice. With the continued democratization of the political system in the 1990s, the DPP recognized that other means of gaining concessions from the KMT were more effective. Members of the National Assembly and Legislative Yuan elected on the mainland in 1947 were finally forced to resign in 1990, and new elections to these bodies were held in 1991 and 1992, respectively. This made them legitimate forums for political debate and negotiation, and the DPP used them to good advantage. It also participated in the national conferences on major political issues in 1990 and 1996, helping shape the reform of the political system. In short, the consolidation of Taiwan's democracy moved the political contest out of the streets and into formal institutions.

Elite political conflict intensified after Chen Shui-bian assumed office, preventing him from gaining cooperation from the other parties to make progress on his reform agenda. But Chen's inability to govern effectively is qualitatively different from the social unrest that concerns the CCP's leaders. As Yun-han Chu shows in chapter 2, the current stalemate in Taiwan is due to a combination of the DPP's limited experience and talent and constitutional features that constrain the executive's ability to influence the legislative agenda. Chen and Lee Teng-hui before him did not have to demobilize an aroused populace engaging in widespread acts of political protest and civil disobedience, which is the main fear of China's leaders. Taiwan's experience with its democratic transition suggests that China's leaders will not necessarily have to confront political chaos once democratization begins. On the contrary, Taiwan's example shows that increasing the legitimacy of political institutions during the democratization process may diminish both the frequency and intensity of mass demonstrations and other forms of unconventional political participation.

Whether democratization threatens political order depends largely on the decisions made by political leaders. Russia may show the dangers inherent in the transition. But Taiwan's experience shows that skillful political leadership, both in the ruling party and in the opposition, can actually enhance political stability during the democratization process.

Lesson 3: Democracy Need Not Jeopardize Economic Growth

A third positive lesson concerns the impact of democratization on the economy. Many political leaders in China and other countries undergoing rapid economic growth believe there is a trade-off between democracy and economic growth.[7] A major concern is that democratization may raise pressures for higher wages and welfare spending, which in turn would reduce profitability and rates of growth. Moreover, there is a seemingly widespread popular belief that the violent end to demonstrations in Tiananmen Square in 1989 was necessary to provide the economic growth of the 1990s. This supposed trade-off between economic growth and democratization is apparently shared by many within both the state and the society in China.

Although the conventional wisdom holds that dictatorships grow faster than democracies, the empirical evidence is not so clear. An extensive comparative study by Przeworski and Limongi found that dictatorships do grow at a higher rate than democracies, but they suspect there was significant selection bias in the sample of dictatorships and democracies.[8] Dictatorships with poor economic performance were likely to fail and be replaced by democracies, while democracies with poor economic performance were likely to remain democracies. As a result, only dictatorships with relatively high growth rates remained in the sample, whereas the democratic sample included countries with low, average, and high growth rates.

In Taiwan's case, its rate of growth after democratization did decline a bit, but the regime change itself may not have been the decisive factor. After achieving extraordinarily high growth rates of 9.2 percent in the 1960s and 10.2 percent in the 1970s, Taiwan's growth slowed slightly to 8.1 percent in the 1980s and 6.2 percent in the 1990s. (See Table 3.1.) Compared to the economic performance of the other East Asian "Tigers," Taiwan has done better than Hong Kong, about the same as South Korea, and not as well as Singapore during the 1990s. (The other Tigers had growth rates of 4.4, 6.1, and 8.5 percent, respectively.) Taiwan has also outperformed the rest of the developing world as a whole. Most countries experienced declining growth

Table 3.1

Rates of Growth (GDP)(Percentage)

	1980–1989	1990–1998
Taiwan	8.1	6.2
China	10.1	11.2
All East Asia	8.0	7.9
Low- and middle-income countries	3.3	3.5
High-income countries	3.1	2.3

Sources: For Taiwan: *Taiwan Statistical Data Book*; for all others: *World Development Report* (Washington, D.C.: International Bank for Reconstruction and Development/World Bank, 2000), pp. 182–184.

rates during the 1990s, due to international economic influences, and Taiwan's trade-dependent economy was affected as well. But its performance remained exemplary, and it survived the Asian financial crisis better than most countries. Although it does face serious economic problems in the years ahead, these are unrelated to its democratization.[9] In fact, the hallmark of the "Taiwan miracle" was the government's ability to achieve growth with equity, so that democratization did not elicit policies aimed at raising living standards or income redistribution. Taiwan's economic modernization was not the key factor in its democratization (though it was clearly an important supporting factor),[10] nor has democratization itself led to economic decline. The lesson for China, and for other countries, is that democratization need not jeopardize economic growth. The trade-off between these two important goals is more perceived than real.

Taiwan's democratization was also followed by a rapid increase in government expenditures, especially on welfare programs, which typically reduce growth rates. Cheng and Schive describe how Taiwan's aging population, changes in the traditional family structure, and the growing income disparities have led to demands for new welfare programs and income transfers, such as subsidized health insurance and pensions.[11] Although support for these programs existed under the pre-1986 authoritarian regime in Taiwan, the democratic opening allowed them to gain greater public support during the 1990s. Increased welfare spending and other government expenditures have led to higher and higher budget deficits, which in turn may have led indirectly to reduced aggregate growth through higher interest rates that discourage new investment and capital formation. In short, some of the responsibility for Taiwan's slower economic growth during the 1990s was due to international factors and to the natural decline of growth after the explosive burst of earlier decades; but some of the slowdown can be traced to democratization.

The economic problems that Chen Shui-bian confronted upon taking office were considerable and complex. Some of the problems, especially the looming banking crisis, he inherited from the KMT, even though it is now his responsibility to address them properly. China's banking crisis, however, is already several orders of magnitude worse than Taiwan's. On this issue, China and Taiwan share a reluctance to make the political decisions necessary to alleviate the mess of excessive lending. Other problems were exacerbated by Chen's decisions. As Yun-han Chu describes in chapter 2, Chen and his advisers seem to have taken for granted the soundness of Taiwan's economy and undertook policies that he hoped would build popular support without sacrificing economic growth and business confidence. Instead, his early decisions sent the stock market into a steep decline and renewed doubts about the DPP's ability to manage Taiwan's economy. Chen's opponents fueled these doubts by blaming him for the problems cited in the *Economist* report and even calling for his impeachment because of the fall of the stock market (a particularly volatile index as stock markets go). The economic problems that Chen must handle are real and severe, but they are also in large part politically motivated. The current economic downturn is not the result of government policies to force higher wages and welfare spending. (The KMT pushed for an even shorter workweek than Chen wanted.) It is due, rather, to a combination of past decisions, slowed growth in the international economy, and current efforts by Chen's opposition to exaggerate the severity of the problems and Chen's own responsibility for them in order to undercut his popular support.

Lesson 4: Democracy Builds Moral Authority

A fourth lesson concerns political legitimacy. Democracy builds moral authority for elected governments both at home and abroad. During the consolidation of Taiwan's democracy, voters directly elected the president, mayors, and legislators at all levels. Despite recurring allegations of vote buying and other irregularities, these elections legitimized the winners. While incumbents may not be popular, their right to rule is not in question—in sharp contrast to the pre-1987 period when the KMT was widely seen as a foreign occupying force. Democratization led the KMT to reestablish the basis for its appeal to voters by emphasizing its contributions to Taiwan's development, abandoning its claim to be the legitimate government of all China, and downplaying the importance of reunification with the mainland as a short-term policy goal. Nationwide elections also made the DPP accept the legitimacy of political institutions. When the vast majority of seats in the National Assembly and Legislative Yuan were held by the "old bandits" who had been elected on the mainland but continued to serve decades later without having to stand for reelection, the DPP challenged their legitimacy by verbally and physically assaulting them. Once new elections were held for all the seats in these bodies—and as direct elections were held for the mayors of Taipei and Kaohsiung, the governor of Taiwan (a post later abolished with the consensus of both the KMT and DPP), and the president—the DPP relied more on public debate than on confrontation. The decline in political violence following democratization is an indirect measure of the increasing legitimacy of Taiwan's political institutions and their incumbent officials.

Democratization may also enhance a country's international prestige. International support for Taiwan has been maintained and even expanded in large part by its successful democratization. In this respect, Taiwan is both blessed and cursed by its proximity to China. A nation of its size elsewhere in the world would not attract the political attention that Taiwan does. Taiwan's democracy stands as a ready contrast to the still authoritarian regime in China. China's intentions toward Taiwan simultaneously threaten Taiwan's security and even survival, but they also attract international concern and at least implicit support. Domestic politics in the United States and to some degree in Japan might compel a military response if China decided to use force against Taiwan. The scenario of the People's Republic of China (PRC) forcibly occupying Taiwan, or coercing its surrender, is deeply troubling to many politicians in the United States and other countries. So long as Taiwan remains the only democracy in the cross-strait relationship, it will enjoy a measure of moral authority in the international arena that China will not.

However, if a democratic China pursued unification with Taiwan, international support for maintaining Taiwan's de facto independence might weaken. China's democratization might not convince the Taiwanese that unification is an attractive option; but without international support for the continuation of the status quo Taiwan's resistance to unification might not be tenable. Taiwan has stated repeatedly that it would willingly accept unification only if China democratized. This condition may be simply intended as a stalling tactic allowing Taiwan to buy more time to build support for the status quo. But if China truly democratized, Taiwan would have less moral high ground to stand on.

One of the goals of China's ambitious economic modernization effort is to obtain acceptance as a global power. Certainly it has begun playing a more prominent role in a variety of international organizations and regimes; but it is still stuck with the onus of resisting democratization. During his visit to China in 1998, President Bill Clinton stated his belief that China was on "the wrong side of history" for refusing to honor the political and human rights of all Chinese. Against the global trend of democratization during the past generation, China remains a conspicuous holdout. The tortuous democratization of the Soviet Union begun under Gorbachev led to an outpouring of international support—epitomized by the invitation to attend the G-7 meetings of advanced industrialized democracies—and Russia later became a formal member of this club. If China wants to be accepted as a global power, it may have to become democratic.

This is not a new notion, of course. Toward the end of the Qing dynasty, Yan Fu and Liang Qichao, two of China's most influential intellectuals, both noted that the most powerful countries at that time were also democratic. They concluded that China would need to adopt technology, ideas, and values from the West. This proposition has been a controversial point in China ever since, but it may be more true today than ever. For China to be accepted as a major player in the international system, and to be seen as asserting legitimate demands, it may have to become democratic. Put differently: So long as China remains nondemocratic, it may not be fully accepted as a legitimate actor by the other major players.

Lesson 5: The End of Communism Need Not Be the End of the Line

A final positive lesson is directly relevant to the future of China's elites. Taiwan's democratization—and that of formerly communist countries in Eastern Europe and the Soviet Union—shows that democratization is not necessarily the end of careers for leaders of authoritarian regimes. Those who lose elections can go on to other jobs, create foundations, or even get reelected in future elections. In the wake of the KMT's defeat in the March 2000 presidential election, a variety of foundations and policy and research institutes sprang up to give ousted party and government officials a place to work and to remain active on policy and political matters. Immediately after his crushing defeat, Lien Chan became chairman of the KMT and was put in charge of the commission overseeing party reform. More to the point, many former communist party officials in Eastern Europe were elected back into legislative and executive positions after the collapse of communist governments. In Lithuania and Romania, revamped and renamed communist parties once again became ruling parties, this time through the ballot box rather than revolution or installation by the Soviet Union. In Russia, Poland, and Hungary, communist parties remain influential opposition parties. These examples demonstrate that electoral defeat is not the end of political life for authoritarian rulers. Even after losing their monopoly on political power, Leninist parties and their leaders can survive and even thrive in a democratic setting.

In addition to these five positive lessons, Taiwan's democratization provides several other lessons that may be more disturbing, at least for China's leaders. These concern the inherent uncertainty of democracy, the fragility of the economy as the basis for a regime's legitimacy, and new forms of corruption tied to the electoral process.

Hard Lesson 1: Democracy Means Uncertainty

For China's leaders, one disturbing lesson concerns the uncertainty of democratic elections. The CCP seems uncomfortable with political processes when it cannot control the outcome. Democracy, however, is an inherently uncertain political process. According to Adam Przeworski: "The process of establishing a democracy is a process of institutionalizing uncertainty, of subjecting all interests to uncertainty."[12] This notion runs against the grain of a Leninist party like the CCP, which is designed to monitor and control all aspects of its environment, not to be subject to the whims of public opinion. Chen's victory in Taiwan is the most recent and, from the CCP's perspective, most vivid reminder that truly democratic elections are inherently uncertain. For advocates of political reform and democratization in the CCP, the transition of ruling parties in Taiwan may make it hard to convince skeptics in the CCP that elections will not sweep them out of power.

Although China has been experimenting with village-level elections for over a decade, party leaders have been reluctant to extend these elections to higher levels such as townships and counties.[13] The original rationale for village elections was based, not on the intrinsic benefits of democratic government, but on the possibility that these elections would replace ineffective village leaders with dynamic and entrepreneurial types and encourage the implementation of unpopular policies (such as family planning and taxation) in the countryside.[14] In recent years, although Jiang Zemin and other Chinese leaders have pledged to expand the scope of elections, they have so far made little progress. While there have been a few, and very quiet, experiments in certain rural townships and even urban areas in recent years, China's leaders have placed a greater priority on maintaining order, especially in the countryside, than on spreading democracy to higher levels of the political system.

The main obstacle to expanding elections is the fear that the wrong people will win. This has been a common theme in rural villages where township and county officials intervene in the election process to eliminate certain candidates or overturn the results if they do not meet with their approval. The extent of cadre interference is not known with certainty, but it is recognized as a widespread problem. As in many areas of policymaking in China, it is the attitude of local officials that seems to determine whether new political reforms will be enacted in a proper and timely way, even if they have been mandated by the central leadership.

Expanding democratic elections to higher levels of the political system would also seem to require the formation of opposition parties. In a village setting, where all the residents know everyone else, there is little need for political organizations because most political communication can be done face to face. Moreover, restrictions on the content and length of election campaigns reduce the need to have a political machine. But as competitive elections move to larger districts, where voters do not know the candidates by name or reputation and organization is needed to disseminate information and mobilize voters, political parties are indispensable for democratic elections. When Chinese officials and scholars are asked if competitive elections in townships or urban districts are possible without multiple parties, they typically say: "China already is a multiparty system." But they also acknowledge the folly of referring to the eight so-called democratic parties as the equivalent of true opposition parties. Although they recognize that competitive elections require multiple parties, they also recognize that the CCP jealously protects its monopoly on legitimate political organization. Without modification of this sacrosanct aspect of Leninism, the spread of democracy in China will be extremely difficult.

The gradual evolution of an organized opposition in Taiwan points up the country's sharp differences with China. Like the CCP, the KMT banned the formation of new parties before the democratization of Taiwan's political system. Unlike the CCP, however, the KMT tolerated participation by *tangwai* politicians in local and even national elections. In time the *tangwai* grew increasingly well organized, at least in the coordination of policy messages during election campaigns, and eventually formed the DPP in 1986.[15] There are several key points here: First, a political organization was allowed to exist even though the KMT tried to constrain its activities and access to the public and at times even tried to suppress it (as after the Kaohsiung demonstrations of 1979). Second, there was a channel for the political opposition to participate in (local elections and supplemental elections for the Legislative Yuan and National Assembly) so that political participation had a legitimate, if limited, outlet other than street protests and protracted social movements. Third, interest groups, especially those representing labor and environmental issues, used a combination of both legislative lobbying and street protests to influence policy and rally public support. In each of these areas, the KMT gradually allowed the expansion of organized political activity, creating a more inclusive polity that supported a peaceful democratic transition.

China has no equivalent of the *tangwai*. Democratic activists in various cities around China have tried to establish local chapters of the Chinese Democratic Party (CDP), but they have been systematically arrested and sentenced to lengthy prison terms of up to fourteen years. Moreover, without elections higher than the village level, efforts to create new parties such as the CDP will likely flounder because they do not have political activities they can effectively organize and coordinate. As noted earlier, elections above the village level will likely require new political parties in order to be meaningful. Moreover, new parties may need these higher-level elections in order to have a reason for being. Without legitimate channels for participation, such as those provided by regular elections, political parties will be limited to public demonstrations and private plotting. The CCP is committed to preventing both. Even public seminars and discussions of political topics have been periodically suppressed.

Political parties are not the only type of political organization needed for a stable democracy. In his list of the "procedural minimal" conditions for modern democracy, Robert Dahl includes the "right to form relatively independent associations or organizations, including independent political parties and interest groups."[16] As Philippe Schmitter and Terry Lynn Karl argue, both parties and interest groups are indispensable to democracy. Political parties channel political interests based on territorial constituencies, and their strength in the political system is based on their ability to generate votes. Interest groups are more important for representing functional interests and "have become the primary expression of civil society in most stable democracies."[17]

Although China has experienced an explosion of social organizations of all kinds, very few of them are able to act as true interest groups.[18] The "Regulations on the Registration and Management of Social Organizations," issued in draft form in 1989 and finalized in 1998, place sharp limits on the ability to form and operate organizations. Every organization must register with the government and be sponsored by a state organizational unit. The state's sponsoring unit is responsible for the organization's daily affairs, which may include providing officers and a budget. Social organizations have a representational monopoly, at least at their level. In a jurisdiction there can be only one organization for each profession, activity, or interest. When more than one exist, the state requires them to merge or disband.

At the same time, many social organizations, especially those representing business interests, have been able to develop good working relationships with local officials. Here again the attitude of local officials is essential. Indeed, research on social organizations of various kinds has found that the attitude of local officials is perhaps the primary factor in the growth and effectiveness of social organizations.[19] The support of local officials is uneven, however. It is strong in some communities and for some organizations, but it is not universal. Because this local official support is so unpredictable, it is no substitute for an institutionalized civil society—to which the Chinese government, like most authoritarian governments, remains opposed. The CCP has authorized the formation of civic associations to give it more flexible control over society, not to surrender its authority to them. Whether this strategy will be successful remains to be seen. But the CCP clearly intends to use these organizations for its own ends, not to grant them the autonomy to challenge the state.[20]

Hard Lesson 2: It Is Not Just the Economy, Stupid

The second negative lesson for China's leaders concerns the KMT's historic loss of power after governing Taiwan for over fifty years. During that time it compiled a record of economic and political development that has rightly been called the "Taiwan miracle." The KMT's success at implementing growth-oriented policies while narrowing the gap between rich and poor challenges the conventional wisdom that rapid growth and equity are not compatible goals for developing countries. Indeed, the KMT dramatically raised living standards and within roughly one generation transformed Taiwan's economy from a peripheral agricultural exporter into an industrial and technological power and a major player in the international trading system. On a parallel but separate track, it helped usher in the democratization of Taiwan's political system after a prolonged period of often brutal rule. It enlarged the scope of political opportunities for Taiwanese, as well, first within the KMT and later across the entire government and military.

The lesson for CCP leaders must be chilling: This remarkable record of economic and political development was still not enough to keep the KMT in power. Despite this undeniable record of prosperity, Taiwan's voters were ready to make a change—motivated by political issues such as corruption, the involvement of organized crime in politics, and the desire for policies that promote social justice. This may be an illustration of the emergence of postmaterialist values along with rising standards of living:[21] As people begin to take for granted that their material needs will be met, they become motivated by other concerns, primarily quality of life issues and political ideals. This thinking may be seen in voters' dissatisfaction with the domestic political status quo and an unresponsive KMT leadership that nominated the uninspiring Lien Chan as its presidential candidate, despite opinion polls showing he had very weak support. Whether the 2000 presidential election is seen as a referendum on the KMT's recent performance or on Lien's potential as president, the message was the same: The state of the economy does not guarantee the success of the incumbent party.

The CCP has been basing its legitimacy on its ability to achieve high rates of growth and improved standards of living. The fate of the KMT shows how hollow this strategy is. Taiwan has achieved levels of economic prosperity and democracy that are still decades away in China. Yet the KMT experienced a steady decay in the level of popular support (as measured by its share of the vote in elections over the past twenty or more years) and finally lost its ruling party status. Taiwan's democratization shows that the legitimacy of a ruling party cannot rest on economic growth alone. Not only does it make the ruling party vulnerable to inevitable economic downturns, but it overlooks the importance of noneconomic issues to the party's record in office. Improving standards of living in China will inevitably lead to demands for increased political participation, reduced state interference in the economy and society, and greater responsiveness of the state to social concerns. The CCP will have a difficult time postponing, much less surviving, a democratic transition if it stakes its claim on the economy alone.

Hard Lesson 3: Democracy Does Not Cure Corruption

The final negative lesson shows why the economy is not always the primary issue in determining electoral outcomes and, moreover, why Lien Chan lost and Chen Shui-bian won: Democratization itself does not cure corruption, though it can make it more visible and easier to address. During the authoritarian phase of the KMT's rule, corruption was certainly present in the development efforts of the regime. Local factions, most tied to the KMT, channeled construction and supply contracts to their supporters. This practice was central to the KMT's strategy for building public support for its policies and for incorporating local leaders into the party organization. But keeping this corruption within acceptable bounds (acceptable to KMT leaders, at least) was a top priority in the pre–Lee Teng-hui era. Chiang Ching-kuo in particular expected officials to set a high standard, and he periodically punished those who crossed the line.[22]

After the democratic transition, however, a new form of corruption emerged that was tied to the election process itself. Vote buying became more common and more costly. With increased competition from the DPP, the KMT had to give more financial benefits to local factions to keep their support and encourage their cooperation in mobilizing votes. The KMT was trapped in a dilemma: It needed the support of local factions to win elections, but the leaders of these factions were often notorious for links with organized crime and their own corruption. KMT members who ran without the party's endorsement had to raise huge sums of money for campaigns on their own. Moreover, many of the KMT's elected politicians had criminal records. A

Taipei Times article on 5 December 1999 cited a report by a former justice minister that about one-third of Taiwan's 800 elected officials had criminal backgrounds.[23] Public revulsion toward "black gold" was one of the keys to Chen's victory.

Democratization in Taiwan gave rise to a new form of corruption, therefore, and cleaning it up will be at the top of Chen's domestic policy agenda. But it has also tarnished the image of Taiwan's democracy by highlighting the close connection between elected officials and organized crime. China is already plagued with rampant corruption concerning its economy. The realization that democracy may compound its problems with a new type of corruption must be discomforting to advocates of democratization within China.

Prospects

The example of a ruling party—one that had been in office for over fifty years and was saddled with a reputation for corruption—being voted out of office captured the imagination of the Chinese who learned of Taiwan's recent presidential election. Informal (and certainly nonscientific) observations of Chinese scholars visiting the United States at the time of Taiwan's presidential election in 2000 revealed a high level of interest and a positive evaluation of the democratic process in Taiwan.[24] Many were intrigued by the election. They seemed to feel that if the people in Taiwan were able to vote for their leaders, the Chinese deserved the same opportunity. Although the election—and Taiwan's democratization more generally—does not seem to have created sympathy for Taiwan's perspective in the cross-strait relationship, it may have earned Taiwan some respect for showing a viable alternative to the present reality on the mainland.

Ironically, Chen's victory may reduce the support for political reform within the CCP leadership and delay meaningful democratization. Although Chinese society might be inspired by the example of Taiwan, China's leaders have been reminded that they have much to lose by initiating democratization before their popular support has a stronger foundation than simply economic growth. In such a context, the immediate risks of democratization may seem to outweigh its uncertain and future benefits, at least from the perspective of the state.[25] In the past, the CCP has chosen to maintain strict bounds on the political arena rather than gradually expand the opportunities for political participation as occurred in Taiwan. Rather than respond to the changing wants and needs of society, the CCP has generally opted to repress spontaneous demands for democratization or increased political reform. Throughout the post-Mao era, China's policy process has expanded to include a variety of new voices and groups, but only on nonpolitical issues and

only at the CCP's invitation. On matters of political reform and democratization, the CCP is determined to maintain the initiative and prevent non-CCP
actors from influencing the timing or content of the political reform agenda.
CCP leaders are well known to fear that democratization will lead to increased political participation that would prove to be destabilizing. Whether
warranted or not, this fear has shaped past calculations and actions. While
the CCP has instituted village elections and a variety of civic and professional organizations, the rationale for these innovations was not based on the
intrinsic merits of democracy; it was simply a means for the state to maintain
and improve its leadership over society.

The outcome of Taiwan's presidential election may be disheartening for
China's leaders with respect to the prospects for unification and their ability
to survive the democratization process once it begins; but it also suggests
that some of their fears may be unfounded. Democratization need not lead to
instability, economic stagnation, or the end of political careers for China's
current leaders. In my book cited at the beginning of this chapter,[26] I conclude that the CCP is unlikely to sponsor democratization and would be unlikely to survive if it tried. Past actions to limit and suppress political
participation have led to a backlog of grievances and a perception that the
CCP is incapable of reform and unwilling to compromise with legitimate
and reasonable calls for change. Under these circumstances, China is unlikely to experience a gradual and generally peaceful transition to democracy as occurred in Taiwan. Instead, when political change does come about,
it is likely to be sudden and possibly even tumultuous. Little has happened to
revise that earlier conclusion. While I remain pessimistic about the CCP's
willingness and ability to sponsor a democratic transition, I think that such a
transition is increasingly probable, although we cannot predict how or when.
Unlike the KMT in Taiwan, the CCP is unlikely to transform China's
political system. Instead, it is likely to be replaced as the consequence of
democratization.

Throughout the post-Mao period and up to the present, CCP leaders have
debated among themselves the proper kinds and pace of political reform:
What types of political reform are necessary to sustain economic reform?
What types might jeopardize party control? The debate is ongoing, and fear
of instability still seems to outweigh the perceived benefits of democratization. However, as Taiwan's example shows, it may not be necessary to post-
pone democracy in order to maintain growth and order. Taiwan's
democratization holds a variety of lessons for China. What conclusions will
ultimately be drawn by China's rulers, by democratic activists, and by society at large remains to be seen. Both the hopes and the fears of Chinese
democratization can be found in Taiwan's recent experience.

Notes

1. Bruce J. Dickson, *Democratization in China and Taiwan: The Adaptability of Leninist Parties* (Oxford: Oxford University Press, 1997).

2. Samuel P. Huntington, "The Clash of Civilizations?" *Foreign Affairs* 72(3) (Summer 1993):22–49.

3. William L. Parish and Charles Chi-hsiang Chang, "Political Values in Taiwan: Sources of Change and Constancy," in *Taiwan's Electoral Politics and Democratic Tradition: Riding the Third Wave*, ed. Hung-mao Tien (Armonk, NY: M.E. Sharpe, 1996), pp. 27–41.

4. This was a point emphasized by the Chinese scholars who participated in the conference at which the chapters in this book were originally presented.

5. Evidence for this assertion is vividly provided in the set of documents collected in Andrew Nathan and Perry Link, eds., *The Tiananmen Papers: The Chinese Leadership's Decision to Use Force against Their Own People—In Their Own Words* (New York: PublicAffairs, 2000).

6. Tun-jen Cheng and Chi Schive, "What Has Democratization Done to Taiwan's Economy?" *Chinese Political Science Review* (June 1997):1–24.

7. Samuel P. Huntington, "The Goals of Political Development," in *Understanding Political Development*, ed. Myron Weiner and Samuel P. Huntington (Boston: Little, Brown, 1987), pp. 3–32.

8. Adam Przeworski and Fernando Limongi, "Political Regimes and Economic Growth," in *Development and Underdevelopment: The Political Economy of Global Inequality*, ed. Mitchell Seligson and John Passe-Smith (Boulder: Lynne Rienner, 1998), pp. 395–405.

9. See the special report in the *Economist*, 11 November 2000.

10. Hung-mao Tien, "Transformation of an Authoritarian Party State: Taiwan's Development Experience," in *Political Change in Taiwan*, ed. Tun-jen Cheng and Stephan Haggard (Boulder: Lynne Rienner, 1992), pp. 33–55.

11. Cheng and Schive, "What Has Democratization Done?"

12. Adam Przeworski, "Some Problems in the Transition to Democracy," in *Transitions from Authoritarian Rule*, vol. 3: *Comparative Perspectives*, ed. Guillermo O'Donnell, Philippe C. Schmitter, and Laurence Whitehead (Baltimore: Johns Hopkins University Press, 1986), p. 58.

13. See Tianjian Shi, "Village Committee Elections in China: Institutionalist Tactics for Democracy," *World Politics* 51(3) (April 1999):385–412; Tyrene White, "Village Elections: Democracy from the Bottom Up?" *Current History* 97(1) (September 1998):263–267; and Lianjiang Li and Kevin J. O'Brien, "The Struggle over Village Elections," in *The Paradox of China's Post-Mao Reforms*, ed. Merle Goldman and Roderick MacFarquhar (Cambridge: Harvard University Press, 1999), pp. 129–144.

14. Daniel Kelliher, "The Chinese Debate over Village Self-Government," *China Journal* 37 (1997):63–86.

15. Dickson, *Democratization in China and Taiwan*; Shelley Rigger, *Politics in Taiwan: Voting for Democracy* (London: Routledge, 1999).

16. Robert Dahl, *Dilemmas of Pluralist Democracy* (New Haven: Yale University Press, 1982), p. 11.

17. Philippe Schmitter and Terry Lynn Karl, "What Democracy Is . . . and Is Not," *Journal of Democracy* 2(3) (Summer 1991):80.

18. Minxin Pei, "Chinese Civic Associations: An Empirical Analysis," *Modern China* 24(3) (July 1998):285–318; Tony Saich, "Negotiating the State: The Development of Social Organizations in China," *China Quarterly* 161 (March 2000):124–141.

19. Gordon White, Jude Howell, and Shang Xiaoyuan, *In Search of Civil Society: Market Reform and Social Change in Contemporary China* (Oxford: Oxford University Press, 1996); Jonathan Unger, "'Bridges': Private Business, the Chinese Government, and the Rise of New Associations," *China Quarterly* 147 (September 1996):795–819; Christopher Earle Nevitt, "Private Business Associations in China: Evidence of Civil Society or Local State Power?" *China Journal* 36 (July 1996):25–45; and Yijiang Ding, "Corporatism and Civil Society in China: An Overview of the Debate in Recent Years," *China Information* 12(4) (Spring 1998):44–67.

20. Bruce J. Dickson, "Cooptation and Corporatism in China: The Logic of Party Adaptation," *Political Science Quarterly* 116 (1) (Winter 2000–2001):517–540.

21. Ronald Inglehart, *Modernization and Postmodernization: Cultural, Economic, and Political Change in 43 Societies* (Princeton: Princeton University Press, 1997).

22. Dickson, *Democratization in China and Taiwan*, pp. 182–183.

23. Cited in Shelley Rigger, "The Democratic Progressive Party: Obstacles and Opportunities" in Bruce J. Dickson and Chien-min Chao, eds., *Democratic Consolidation in Taiwan: Assessing the Lee Teng-hui Legacy* (Armonk, NY: M. E. Sharpe, 2002).

24. This was true of visiting scholars at my university, and friends at other schools reported similar stories.

25. A similar point is made by O'Donnell and Schmitter about democratization in general: If hard-liners believe that democratization will threaten the political power and economic rewards they presently enjoy in an authoritarian system, they are unlikely to risk those benefits for the possibility of uncertain and intangible future benefits after a democratic transition. See Guillermo O'Donnell and Philippe C. Schmitter, *Transitions from Authoritarian Rule*, vol. 4: *Tentative Conclusions About Uncertain Democracies* (Baltimore: Johns Hopkins University Press, 1986), p. 16.

26. Dickson, *Democratization in China and Taiwan*.

4

Defeat of the KMT: Implications for One-Party Quasi-Democratic Regimes in Southeast Asia

Chua Beng Huat

One peculiar feature of post–World War II, postcolonial Asia is the emergence of single-party-dominant states—whether through popular elections, military coups, or the establishment of communist regimes. Among the popularly elected were the Indian National Congress, the Liberal Democratic Party (LDP) in Japan, the People's Action Party (PAP) in Singapore, and the Alliance Party (dominated by the United Malay National Organization, or UMNO) in Malaysia. The military or military-backed governments included Taiwan under the Kuomintang (KMT), the Philippines under Marcos, New Order Indonesia under Suharto, and Thailand under a string of successive generals. Communist Party regimes were established, after violent revolutionary wars, in the People's Republic of China, Vietnam, and Cambodia. Within a relatively short span of time, 1985 to 2000, most of these single-party-dominant states have unraveled for different reasons and have been replaced by multiparty political systems. Other than the communist regimes, the only single-party-dominant states remaining are the PAP in Singapore and the UMNO-dominated Barisan Nasional in Malaysia.

The most recent single-party-dominant state to be fully transformed into a multiparty state is Taiwan. In lifting martial law in 1987, the KMT changed an essentially Leninist state to a single-party-dominant democracy. With the election of a president from the former opposition party, the Democratic Progressive Party (DPP), the democratization of the Taiwanese polity is now complete, marked by the polity's maturity in managing the alternation of power. Taiwan can now be called a democratic state, not just "democratizing." The DPP's long struggle and ascent from the illegal fringe to the seat of elected presidency bears close analysis for demonstrative lessons for the two remaining single-party-dominant states in Southeast Asia.

Substantively, the history of a nation is unique unto itself. Analytically, however, there may be structural elements and processes that are broadly paralleled elsewhere. To the extent that the democratization of Taiwan is the history of the displacement of the KMT's single-party dominance, the structural configuration and processes of this displacement may be generalized in order to examine the potential for democratization in other single-party-dominant states. In comparing the Taiwanese instance with contemporary Malaysia and Singapore, we shall find that Taiwan's experience might be of relevance to Malaysia, but is unlikely to have any impact on the political development of Singapore for several reasons.

First, the ruling parties of Taiwan (the KMT) and Malaysia (UMNO) have been actively engaged in businesses in their national economies—leading to economic corruption among political elites and to money politics, which have fueled popular disaffection that feeds into public mobilization against the elites and the parties. In Singapore, it is the state and not the ruling party (the PAP) that directly owns many large corporations and enterprises, which are run by professional managers, either as state monopolies or as competitive enterprises. Singapore's politicians and civil servants are generally recognized as incorruptible. Second, the 1997 East Asian economic crisis precipitated a split in UMNO leadership that has had serious consequences for its dominance in Malaysian politics. It resulted, for example, in the breaking away of an important faction to form another party, the Parti Keadilan (Justice Party), which in turn collaborates with other political parties to constitute an oppositional coalition against UMNO. This pattern recalls both the formation of the DPP as a fragmented political party with a common enemy, the KMT, and the leadership split in the KMT during the 1999 presidential election in Taiwan. Such leadership fragmentation is unlikely to happen in the PAP, as leadership cohesion is generated by the very process of selection—each generation successively selecting the next, rather than free election by party members. Third, the opposition party or coalition in Taiwan and Malaysia has been able to gain the support of a mobilized civil society that shares the same anti–dominant party sentiments; in Singapore, by contrast, civil society remains largely underdeveloped, while the government continues to modify its policies to accommodate popular demands. This progressive liberalization of certain social and cultural spheres releases the pressure for structural political change. Finally, unlike the KMT and UMNO, which have introduced few innovations in the electoral system, the PAP has been using its power as the incumbent government to modify the electoral rules and processes that advantage it and, under normal circumstances, would almost guarantee its electoral victory.

The conjunction of political developments in Malaysia has already demonstrated its electoral effects—first in the significant loss of popular support and elected seats for UMNO in the 1999 general election and then in the defeat of UMNO's candidate in a November 2000 by-election in the home province of the long-governing prime minister, Mahathir Mohamad. While it would be premature to suggest that this is the thin end of the wedge leading to the displacement of UMNO from political dominance, it does raise the possibility of its eventuality. The rest of the chapter details these comparative developments.

Formation of a Taiwan "Nation"

After fifty years of Japanese colonization, Taiwan's return to China after World War II was initially anticipated by local Taiwanese with enthusiasm. This sentiment, however, took a drastic downward spiral almost immediately upon the arrival of the defeated and retreating KMT army. The possibility of a smooth political emplacement of the KMT regime, as the Republic of China (ROC), was permanently disrupted by what has come to be known as the 28 February Incident or the "228" Event.[1] On that day in 1947, the KMT army brutally put down a local uprising—an action that came to be etched deeply in Taiwanese collective memory as an instance of the slaughtering of "locals" by "mainlanders" or "*waisheng ren*" (people from outside the province). This event provided the historical, political, and discursive resource for the telling of a different history of Taiwan as opposed to the plausible history of continuity as part of the Chinese nation since the mid-seventeenth century under the Qing dynasty. Subsequently, local Taiwanese suffered a regime of "white terror" under the KMT's security apparatus, identified with the colonizing mainlanders, who constituted no more than 15 percent of the population. The terms "mainlanders" and "locals" thus became an ideological/identity/political divide providing one of the central discursive resources for the organization of opposition to the KMT and preventing the formation of a Taiwan "nation" so long as the "mainlanders" are in power.

The KMT attempted to erase the division by initiating a cultural industry to sinicize the Taiwanese—constructing "new foundations of social solidarity, spiritual consciousness, and ideological rationality" for the idea of a Chinese nation—but with ambiguous success.[2] Running concurrently, however, was the uninterrupted and interminable presence of a counterdiscourse of Taiwanese identity,[3] itself engendered partly by the KMT's sinization discourse.[4] This counterdiscourse materialized in the fight for the collective memory of the 228 Event. Immediately following the lifting of martial law, communities all over Taiwan began to clamor for construction of memorials to commemorate those who had perished in the incident. In 1993, Lee Teng-hui's government acknowledged the KMT's role in the incident and offered a formal apology to the people. A monument was built in Taipei, close to the presidential office, as a symbol of the "collective" tragedy in the history of Taiwan-as-a-nation rather than marking an ignominious event in the KMT's history as a colonizing outsider.[5] This was an act of distancing local Taiwanese history from a history of China, not a constituent element of the latter history. Meanwhile, the indigenization/Taiwanization of the KMT continued apace with changes in the ideological terrain.

With the steady consolidation of a "Taiwanese" identity, a Taiwan "nation" might be said to have already emerged by 1991. This Taiwan electorate could by then set aside, however temporarily, cross-strait issues and focus on domestic matters. Thus, by the early 1990s, the KMT and the DPP were in a sense just two political parties contesting to control a "national" parliament in a democracy and the election of the DPP's Chen Shui-bian in the 2000 presidential election was a "normal" democratic process of switching the ruling party. Three elements of this democratization process need to be fleshed out for comparative purposes.

First is the progressive expansion of electoral processes. To differentiate itself from the PRC, the KMT promised to establish constitutional democracy and had allowed for local elections at county and city levels since 1950.[6] These local elections provided opportunities, on the one hand, for the KMT to co-opt local leaders and, on the other, enabled local leaders to carve out their own political spaces and practices, including opportunities to contest the KMT. Competition, including those among KMT-sponsored candidates, had always been keen in these elections because getting elected was an assured path to wealth. For the electorate, apart from expanding the franchise, local elections served as arenas for education and practice in electoral politics, which voters took seriously; electoral turnout averaged 60 to 70 percent, sometimes reaching 80 percent.[7] In the 1970s, Taiwan's domestic political terrain was radically redefined. The U.S. recognition of the PRC in 1971 was followed by the PRC replacing Taiwan in the United Nations and subsequent abandonment of Taiwan by former allies. In the eyes of opposition forces, these setbacks in international diplomacy meant "there was no [longer] reason to place credence in the justification offered by the KMT for its continual domination of Taiwan,"[8] giving vent to explicit voices not only from Taiwan independentists, but also from democratically oriented mainlanders who were dissatisfied with the KMT's authoritarianism. Thus, after the 1970s, even if Taiwan as a nation was not yet ideologically articulated, the geographical Taiwan was the only political terrain for the KMT and its foes, lending logic to the first direct presidential election in 1996.

Second, economic development in the 1970s had spawned a new civil society that used "grievances about the serious social problems" to question "the mode of state control over civil society."[9] These problems included, among others, the consumer movement, environmental movement, women's movement, human rights movement, labor movement, and various social welfare movements.[10] Sharing one similar target—the state and its policies— and sharing similar sentiments of being victims of unfair exclusion at the hand of the state enabled the movements to form coalitions and alliances while maintaining a formal distance from all political parties, though understandably the DPP would express sympathy for the social causes. As Michael Hsiao points out, while the social movements had achieved certain successes in getting the KMT state to liberalize and become more responsive to social demands for change, such loosening up did not amount to democratization itself.[11] Democratization still required the institutionalization of political contest through political parties, elections, and alternation of the party in power.

Third is the rise of the DPP itself. The socially mobilized context provided impetus, encouragement, and confidence for those in the opposition to reconfigure their political position. The atmosphere emboldened non-KMT political leaders to exploit election opportunities, in the 1970s and 1980s, by coordinating their electioneering activities. Such loosely organized coordination for local elections in 1977 came to be labeled by the media as the "*tangwai*" (beyond political party)—a movement to mobilize masses for the democratization and independence of Taiwan.[12] Encouraged by the 1977 electoral achievements in the Taiwan Provincial Assembly, the coalition was formalized into the Tangwai Campaign Corps with the explicit aim of coordinating the campaigns for all non-KMT electoral candidates in all subsequent elections. Despite various repressive interventions,[13] this coalition declared itself, illegally, as the Democratic Progressive Party on the eve of the lifting of martial law. Its leaders then went on to capture the mayoral offices of different cities including Taipei and Kaohsiung. After losing a second term as mayor of Taipei, Chen himself went on to capture the presidential office, by a very slim margin, in a hard-fought election, aided by the split within the KMT itself. By then the Taiwanization and democratization of Taiwan politics were already far advanced. Chen's election instantiates this advanced development.

To summarize, then, the transformation of Taiwan—from a quasi-Leninist, military-backed regime, through a single-party-dominant state, to the current multiparty system of democratic politics—may be said to be the aggregated effect of several contextually and historically necessary elements. At the ideological level, particularly after the passing of the generation of leaders that came originally from the mainland, we note the emergence of a new "Taiwanese" identity (with or without the idea of "reunification") and, significantly, a KMT that is increasingly committed, if only by force of circumstances, to democratization of politics. At the level of political development we note three elements: for the opposition forces there was a common antagonist in the KMT, which was not only authoritarian but also constructed and identified as a "colonizing" force inherited from the past; there was a KMT that was fractionalized internally on the issue of reunification; and there was a strong civil society that was the precursor to political mobilization and the eventual coalescing of oppositional segments into a political party, the DPP. Drawing upon this set of contextually necessary elements, I want to explore the possibility of further democratization in Malaysia and Singapore and gauge the future of the dominant parties in these two countries.

Lessons for Malaysia and Singapore

Two aspects of the Taiwan situation can be recognized immediately in contemporary Malaysia and Singapore: In both countries, the development of civil society picked up speed in the closing years of the 1990s whereas political opposition of varying degrees has always been in place. An immediate difference, however, should also be noted: The British colonial legacy left both Malaysia and Singapore as postcolonial multiracial nations with three main races, namely Malays, Chinese, and Indians; thus race or ethnicity, in contrast to Taiwan, figures prominently in the respective polities. The effects of multiracialism on Malaysia and Singapore politics are differently configured. In Malaysia, the political dominance of Malays as the indigenous population is constitutionally entrenched and political parties are often organized along racial lines. In Singapore, by contrast, political parties are multiracial and no specific political privileges are granted to any particular group. These divergent stances toward multiracialism play a significant role in the political development of these two countries.

Malaysia[14]

Initially as the Federation of Malaya and since 1965 as Malaysia, the country has been governed, without interruption, by an alliance of three political parties, each organized along its own ethnic lines: the United Malay National Organization (UMNO), the Malaysia Chinese Association (MCA), and the Malaysia Indian Congress (MIC). Beside the alliance, there have been other ethnic parties, such as Parti Islam Se-Malaysia (PAS), which is a Malay Muslim party, and smaller multiracial parties such as the Democratic Action Party (DAP). The alliance was the political bargain brokered at the point of political independence from British colonial rule in the 1950s: The politically dominant position of Malays would be honored; the Chinese would continue to predominate in the domestic economy, as reflected in the appointment of a Chinese as the first minister of finance; and the Indians would be assured of a parliamentary presence, including representation in the cabinet. Racial divisions are therefore central to the political architecture of the alliance as the ruling coalition.

Many factors worked together to support the alliance's political dominance—not least the buoyant national economic growth throughout the 1960s,[15] which ironically rendered the racial division of economic and political power untenable. Emergent Malay demands for a greater share of the economic wealth, as well as the dissatisfaction of young Chinese with their political marginalization, came to a head in the 1969 general election. In this election the alliance lost, albeit marginally, its all-important two-thirds parliamentary majority precipitating one of the worst race riots in Malaysia because, as generally believed, the Malays feared displacement from political dominance in their own homeland. A state of emergency was immediately imposed.

In the aftermath of the riots and emergency rule, both the political and economic spheres were radically restructured. Politically, several smaller parties were invited to join the alliance, ostensibly in the interest of consolidating social peace, to constitute the National Front, or Barisan Nasional (BN). Since then BN has governed Malaysia, without any alternation of power at the national level, under the prime minister, Dr. Mahathir Mohamad. Meanwhile, UMNO progressively established itself as the dominant party and primary driving force in BN; elected members of the other parties were rewarded with junior political positions. While Chinese and Indians continue to be represented in cabinet positions, no Chinese has been appointed finance minister since the 1950s.

Economically, the Malay-dominated BN government instituted the New Economic Policy (NEP), a twenty-year plan (1970–1990) to redistribute wealth in favor of the Malays until they own 30 percent of the national wealth and in the process engender a Malay business class. The plan not only opened up opportunities for UMNO to enrich itself through proxy companies, but also created a political economy characterized by corruption and cronyism or, in the words of the UMNO government, "handouts" for the favored. (In this sense, the UMNO-dominated government recalls the KMT's position in Taiwan's economy.) Certain Malays were allocated undervalued shares of privatized state-owned companies. These shares could be purchased by borrowing money from the bank at special low interest rates; with the shares as collateral, one could then borrow more money for other investments, increasing the leverage for the borrowed money with each round. Privileged access to government contracts was given to Malay-owned companies. The NEP also trickled down to a broader base. Easy loan terms were also made available for small Malay businesses and generous scholarships, at home and abroad, were given to Malay youth. Not surprisingly, the NEP was popular with the Malays, adding depth to the legitimacy of UMNO among them.

The NEP, of course, was a very costly financial exercise. When oil and commodities prices, the backbone of Malaysia's economy, began to decline in the 1980s, the national budget could only be met through extensive domestic and foreign borrowing. Borrowing was relatively easy, because Malaysia was a good debtor, but debt expansion destabilized the national economy.[16] Weaknesses in the economy were exposed by the 1997 East Asian financial crisis, which in turn ripped away the veils that had masked disagreements among UMNO's leaders. Despite their public protestations otherwise, the most significant of these quarrels was the disagreement between the prime minister, Dr. Mahathir Mohamad, and the deputy prime minister, Anwar Ibrahim. The prime minister worked relentlessly to keep the IMF—with its one-remedy-fits-all financial strategy for saving troubled Asian economies—out of Malaysia. Instead, he preferred domestic strategies that Anwar Ibrahim allegedly opposed. These strategies—above all, stringent control of capital flow—eventually proved effective in pulling Malaysia out of the crisis, partially vindicating the prime minister against his critics. But high-profile bailouts of certain Malays selected for entrepreneurial leadership seriously tarnished the ideals behind the NEP, leaving it in disrepute and negating all the praise accorded to the program as well as the economic advances made by the Malay middle class.[17]

Differences between the two leaders were probably the primary cause of Anwar's removal from office and arrest on charges of corruption and sodomy. Throughout Anwar's dismissal, arrest, trial, and subsequent conviction, there were street demonstrations in Kuala Lumpur, the capital city of Malaysia, with calls for "Reformasi." Anwar was sentenced to a total of fifteen consecutive years in jail on the two charges. Combined with the five-year ban on political activity after his release, this sentence may spell the end of his political career. The detention and trial damaged the legitimacy of the Mahathir government and undermined the public's trust in government institutions, not least the police and the judiciary.

The jailing of Anwar provided the spur for mobilization of civil activists, particularly those working on human rights issues and political and media freedoms. With the advent of the Internet, Malaysian websites critical of the UMNO-fronted BN government mushroomed. The public's desire for alternative sources of information boosted the sales of non-mainstream papers; the PAS party newspaper, for example, began publishing twice a week due to popular demand. Ultimately the heightened activity brought together the political opposition and civil activists to establish a new multiracial party, the Parti Keadilan Nasional (National Justice Party), under the leadership of Anwar's wife, Wan Azizah Wan Ismail, and a long-time civil rights leader, Chandra Muzafar. Apart from its appeal to non-Malays, the Parti Keadilan also attracted Malays who were disenchanted with UMNO and wary of the fundamentalist Islamic party, PAS.

In the 1999 general elections, for the first time in Malaysia's political history, opposition parties—namely PAS, Keadilan, DAP, and Parti Rakyat Malaysia (Malaysian People's Party)—were able to set aside their differences and form a coalition, the Barisan Alternatif (BA), with a common focus of displacing BN from its two-third parliamentary majority and, more specifically, UMNO dominance. Although the coalition was to be disappointed in the overall results, there were many reasons for optimism. First, nine UMNO ministers and deputy ministers lost their seats and other key ministers were returned only by slim margins. Second, for the first time the total number of UMNO members in parliament is less than the total of its coalition partners. Third, PAS made significant gains in electing members of parliament, in addition to forming the government in two state assemblies, Kelatan and Trengganu, in peninsular Malaysia. Fourth, with little party machinery Parti Keadilan won five parliamentary seats and four state seats and was narrowly defeated in a few other constituencies. Fifth, BA was popular among Malays and Chinese in the urban areas around the Federal Territories in the state of Selangor. Sixth, in many of the constituencies UMNO candidates won with the significant increase of electoral support from Chinese voters. Finally, the greatest setback was suffered by UMNO, which saw its Malay support base halved, losing it to both PAS and Parti Keadilan. The split in the Malay community as a result of the Anwar affair was too obvious to be denied.[18]

The political structure in Malaysia in the late 1990s broadly resembled that of Taiwan under the KMT. Both UMNO and the KMT had amassed great wealth through their proxy companies and used the largesse of the state, undergirded by national economic growth, to gain legitimacy and popular support. In both instances, dissatisfaction with corrupt practices of the ruling regime engendered new social movements concerned with the environment, gender, human rights, the media, the consumer society, and an expansion of civil society. In Malaysia the economic and political crisis had speeded up the coalition of a restive civil society and opposition political parties with a common focus on a common enemy: the BN and UMNO. This situation is reminiscent of the coalition between civil activists and opposition elements in Taiwan, who had their common antagonist: the KMT. Politically, both coalitions were interested in displacing their respective regimes from power. The gelling of political opposition into the DPP in Taiwan was again paralleled in the formation of the Barisan Alternatif in Malaysia, though the BA is a much looser arrangement than the formation of a single party, even a fragmented one at that. It is here that the history of Taiwan's DPP may point a way for the development of political opposition in Malaysia.

The question is whether the DPP's trajectory might offer a viable future for the Barisan Alternatif. There are several obstacles in the path of BA. First, ironically, the BA's components are already organized as political parties with distinct histories and ideologies that are well recognized by the Malaysian electorate. PAS, for example, has always been an Islamic party with expressed desires of introducing Islamic law into the body social—if not the wholesale introduction of an Islamic state. DAP, by contrast, has always espoused multiracialism; and the Parti Rakyat has always been a "Malay" party with socialist aspirations. Apart from displacing BN and UMNO, these parties have their own agendas as opposed to the early composition of *tangwai* in Taiwan, where deep ideological differences were less pronounced, thus facilitating reorganization into a single party. In the present context in Malaysia, dissolution of ideological differences into a single but factional political party seems far-fetched. While a single opposition party might have encouraged democratization in Taiwan, it is not a sine qua non of democratization. In Malaysia, the displacement of BN and UMNO could result in a multiparty political arena that would facilitate alternation of power.

The first political task remains the displacement of BN and UMNO and the removal of single-party dominance. To do so, each component party of BA must be willing to suppress its own political agenda until the task is done. The central difficulty lies with PAS, the biggest party with the most explicitly Islamic agenda. Its presence in BA is both an advantage and a disadvantage. It is advantageous because without a central Malay/Muslim component, any challenge to UMNO, which has placed itself as the champion of Malay interests, would be a nonstarter. It is disadvantageous because the relative position of PAS vis-à-vis UMNO on Islam is commonly read by Malaysians as one of fundamentalism versus moderation, traditional versus modern. PAS's fundamentalist reputation alienates not only the non-Malays but also the urban Malay middle class, as reflected in the 1999 elections.

If BA is to succeed in unseating UMNO, PAS must tone down its desire for an Islamic Malaysia.[19] It must contest UMNO for the moderate political discursive space, project itself as reasonable about religion, win the hearts and minds of the Malay middle class, overcome the skepticism of the Chinese and Indian electorates, and gain the support of ideologically multiracial organizations and activists.[20] The 1999 general elections showed that PAS was prepared to relax its Islamic rhetoric and could in fact attract electoral support from urban, younger, and professionally trained Malays (some of whom even joined the party). These new members will have a moderating effect on its religious stance. Furthermore, young PAS leaders—citing the situation in Patani, southern Thailand, where the Malay-Muslim minority is struggling to maintain its own heritage and identity in the face of increasing absorption into Thai culture—have expressed greater understanding and sympathy for the Chinese and Indians who want to retain their own cultural identity. The moderation of religious ideology, sympathy for non-Malays, membership in BA—all are developments motivated by PAS's new ambition to break out of confinement in the northern peninsular states and attain national power; and for this it must expand its electoral base beyond the traditional Islamic votes.

The hurdles do not stop at the evolution of a moderate PAS, however. If PAS were to challenge UMNO for leadership of the Malay population, it would split the Malay vote, which would leave the outcome of elections uncertain and, as a consequence, place Chinese and Indian voters in the strategic position of deciding the outcome. In the 1999 elections, this was reflected in the swing of support of Chinese voters, who fear the rise of PAS, to UMNO—a swing that cost the multiracial DAP dearly. Occupying a strategic electoral position, the Chinese and the Indians will be able to extract political and economic concessions from the Malay parties. Consequently, it is a position that will not sit comfortably with the Malay electorate. Indeed, prior to the election a Chinese group called Suqiu (Malaysian Chinese Organizations Election Appeals Committee), headed by prominent members of various Chinese associations,[21] issued a long list of social and political changes for negotiation with the government. Furthermore, the MCA tried to obtain an additional cabinet position after having delivered the essential Chinese support that secured BN's overall victory in the 1999 elections. Both requests were rejected by Mahathir.

There are two likely outcomes to the scenario of two equally matched Malay political parties. First, if one uses the past as a guide, the conventional understanding is that the majority of the Malays will revert back to support UMNO after having vented their dissatisfaction with Mahathir's handling of the Anwar affair; in this case, UMNO's single-party dominance will continue. Evidence of this can be drawn from the case of Tengku Razaleigh Hamzah. After failing to unseat Mahathir for the party's top leadership,

Razaleigh left UMNO to form his own party, Semangat 46, ostensibly to rekindle the founding spirit of the original UMNO, which was formed in 1946. The party made little headway politically, however, and Razaleigh and his followers returned to UMNO in the late 1990s—just in time for the 1999 general election, in which he failed to accomplish his assigned task of regaining UMNO's control of the state of Kelantan.

The second and increasingly contemplated possibility is that the division in the Malay electorate may take root. This possibility receives much support from the way BA contested the 29 November 2000 by-election in Lunas, one of the constituencies in the state of Kedah, Prime Minister Mahathir's home state. In Lunas, a Parti Keadilan candidate ran against a BN candidate. There were some controversies within BA, however, regarding candidate selection. Allegedly a candidate proposed by the DAP was rejected by Keadilan on the grounds that he is an Indian, not a Malay. The allegation was denied by Keadilan, and the DAP, after some postelection deliberations, decided to remain in the BA coalition in the interest of maintaining a united front against UMNO and BN. The central issue for the by-election was defined by angry Chinese voters who took this occasion to vent their dissatisfaction against Mahathir's attack on the Chinese community immediately after the 1999 general elections, particularly his explicit reference to the Suqiu group as "communists" in his 2000 Malaysian National Day speech. Consequently, it was a foregone conclusion that Chinese in the constituency would vote for the Keadilan candidate. Despite the Chinese preference, the Malay voters did not close ranks as a group and support UMNO. Instead, the Keadilan candidate obtained more Malay votes than the UMNO candidate and won the election, indicating that Malay voters were exercising political preferences beyond any reductionist idea of "ethnic unity." An ideological shift appears to have taken place: Malay interests are no longer defined by UMNO at the center, relegating the other Malay parties to the political periphery.

Finally, after the by-election the UMNO leadership continued to attack one of the clauses in the Suqiu petition calling for abolition of the distinction between the indigenous, or "*bumiputra*" (son of the soil), and the nonindigenous citizen. UMNO tried to depict this as a challenge to Malay interests. First, the Peninsular Malay Students Federation was mobilized to issue its own list of demands on the government for the preservation of Malay special rights and interests. Then, the chief of UMNO youth challenged his counterpart in PAS to a national debate on the same issue. Moreover, Mahathir invited both PAS and Keadilan to a meeting to discuss the issue of "Malay unity." Although these strictures did not produce the effect sought by UMNO, Suqiu did withdraw its petition. The debate between the youth leaders was called off by the deputy prime minister and vice-president of UMNO,

Abdullah Badawi. This by all accounts saved the chief of UMNO youth from a potentially embarrassing situation. Mahathir's invitation was rejected outright by Keadilan. It maintained there was no split in the Malay electorate; rather, Malay voters were beginning to truly exercise their electoral voice in choosing between PAS, Keadilan, and UMNO. PAS accepted Mahathir's invitation, but insisted on changing the topic from the exclusive "Malay unity" to the inclusive "Malaysian unity." The prolonged negotiations over the constantly changing conditions for the meeting would suggest that the proposed meeting might never materialize. That the changes were introduced by PAS raises doubts about its willingness to participate in the proposed meeting; nevertheless, it had to stay engaged publicly and symbolically lest it be accused of being disinterested in the interests of the Malays, its main constituency of support.

Events after the 1999 general election and the Lunas by-election suggest that Malay votes may no longer be the monopoly of the two exclusive Malay parties, UMNO and PAS, or the Malay-predominant, multiracial Keadilan. This is itself a democratization of Malay politics and hence part of the democratization of Malaysian politics. Of course, the ethnic divides have not been erased and continue to exercise their effect on national politics. But given that Malays with their relatively higher birthrates have become the predominant population demographically, even though the Chinese and Indians hold strategic minority positions, Malays whether from UMNO or PAS will remain politically dominant and concessions to the strategic minorities can be readily contained thus reducing the possibility that the Malays may lose their special rights and interests in Malaysia. This, then, improves the BA's ability to cohere as a coalition of different political parties in the footsteps of BN. Hence, future political contests in Malaysia may well take the form of battles between two coalitions of parties and the alternation of power, signifying the achievement of political democratization, will be possible. Obviously, BA is in its earliest stages and the road ahead is long. One should take heed, however, that it took the DPP about thirty years to get to the Presidential Palace in Taipei.

One final note: Hitherto elections in Malaysia have been exercises in strategic racial politics rather than the ideals of democratic politics. To overcome the racial calculations that influence voting behavior is the ultimate challenge of Malaysia's political democratization.

Singapore

On the surface there are many similarities between Singapore and Taiwan: Both are island polities with an overseas Chinese population in demographic majority;[22] both are East Asia economic success stories; and until the election of the DPP president, both were single-party-dominant states. Indeed, when Chen Shui-bian was mayor of Taipei, he often expressed his admiration for Singapore's urban development. Despite these similarities, Taiwan's political democratization provides few lessons for Singapore, where the political space and political structure, in the hands of the PAP for the past forty years, are totally frozen and resistant to change.

And although they constitute more than 75 percent of the population, there are no political divisions among the ethnic Chinese as between Taiwanese and mainlanders. Furthermore, unlike the unyielding demand of Malay political dominance in Malaysia, Singapore is constitutionally a multiracial country. Reflecting the official multiracialism, for example, there are four official languages in Singapore: Malay, Mandarin, English, and Tamil. Though Malay is the national language, English is the primary language of government administration and all levels of education. The use of English neutralizes any "natural" advantages of the racial communities.[23]

As a multiracial society, Singapore's national interest is not synonymous with that of any of the racial communities. Formally and structurally, the Singapore state places itself above the racial communities and sees itself as the agency that maintains equality of treatment among them. In so doing, it secures a high level of relative autonomy to act vis-à-vis the communities. The rhetoric of multiracialism is doubly functional: First, it is often used to emphasize the divisions within the population—the better to provide reasons for state intervention into racial affairs and police racial group boundaries. Second, it is subordinated to a nationalist discourse that claims to transcend racial divisions by uniting the entire population in a nation-building project essential to the survival of the nation and hence all racial communities and individual citizens. Official multiracialism has thus enabled the PAP government to delineate a discursive and practical space for elaboration of a nation-building project, since separation and independence from Malaysia in 1965, through sustained efforts to build a national ideological consensus, the terms of which are constantly modified according to changing domestic political and economic conditions.[24] This policy stands in sharp contrast to the KMT's failed attempt to inscribe a concept of a Chinese nation in terms of both politics and national identity in Taiwan—an effort that resulted instead in deepening divisions between Taiwanese and mainlanders.

The nation-building rhetoric has been matched by Singapore's sustained economic growth over the past four decades, which has translated into broad improvement of the material life of all Singaporeans, the immediate effect of which is expansion of mass support and deepening of legitimacy for the PAP's continuity in government. Economic growth has, of course, engendered an expanding middle class. Given the path of Singapore's economic growth, driven by a combination of multinational enterprises and state-owned or linked enterprises—the middle class is composed overwhelmingly of wage-earning professionals. Without an independent economic base, the expanding middle class is generally supportive of the PAP government because its own fortune is tied to that of the government through the latter's successful economic policies. The prevailing sentiments are relative political apathy—though the populace is well informed about governmental and administrative decisions and action—and material contentment with a deep fear of falling out of the middle-class zone of assured employment and comfortable lifestyle.[25]

Taiwan's economic growth, by contrast, has been driven by indigenous enterprises and capital. Members of the business elite are often local Taiwanese who are opposed to the KMT's ideological emphasis on reunification. The middle class is relatively independent of the state and was often a victim of the repressive KMT's "white terror." The restive civil society of the 1970s was largely fuelled, in finance and in energy, by independent entrepreneurs and middle-class professionals. These elements were potentially available for mobilization by the DPP. No such financial and ideological resources are available to opposition political parties in Singapore, which have been enfeebled by the PAP's long string of repressive measures and legal maneuvers in the electoral processes.

With mass loyalty secured, the PAP government needs only to apply repressive measures very judiciously on narrowly targeted groups and people deemed subversive to the national interest. This has been done with great effect, in fact, it has generated long repressive shadows over would-be opposition groups and individuals.[26] It is within a space that is politically secured and demarcated by legal repressive measures that the PAP government has begun to liberalize the cultural sphere since the early 1990s. Consequently, the number of civil organizations has expanded and civil activities have intensified. Organizations are still required to seek registration with the Registrar of Society, however, which has the right to deny applications without providing a reason. The registrar is also empowered to threaten organizations with deregistration if they are deemed to have strayed from their declared purposes and constituencies. The right of association remains very restricted in Singapore. The right to public assembly is similarly constrained by the need to obtain permits from the Public Entertainment Licensing Unit, which is housed in the police department of the Ministry of Home Affairs. These restrictions severely curtail a social movement's ability to disrupt normal practices and normative discourse.[27] Instead, civil organizations tend to work themselves into the realm of "normal politics," operating within the government's agenda, as reformists.[28]

For an illustration of the differences in the politics of civil society, consider the process of urban planning. In Taiwan, civil activists have been able to organize themselves around such issues as municipal corruption, displacement of squatters, and the environment. In Singapore, by contrast, the government prides itself for being noncorrupt in a region where corruption is endemic; thus, corruption is a nonissue. As for squatter resettlement, instead of leaving the squatters homeless, as in some Taiwan instances, Singaporeans receive both financial compensation and housing that is superior to the shelters in question. As for the environment, Singapore is a well-planned (indeed excessively planned), well-maintained, green city-state with few pollution problems.[29] Nevertheless, the Singapore Nature Society is one of the most active civil organization. Its primary concern is to conserve what remains of the natural environment in the face of an expanding population and constant economic growth. Its primary grievance is to push government environmental agencies to meet their own standards of green space per capita. Beyond this, other grievances regarding the urban environment include the increased demand for conservation of heritage sites and the tendency of the government to engage foreign architects to design significant public projects. These are hardly explosive issues that can mobilize the population for political change. In Taiwan, by contrast, municipal politics formed a bridgehead for political change and the ultimate unseating of the KMT in the presidential office.

Perhaps the most dynamic cultural sphere in Singapore, since the early 1990s, is the arts. With rising education and economic affluence, there has been a rapid expansion of theater groups in Singapore that caters to the whole range of taste: from experimental theater to political-social commentary to mass entertainment musicals. More and more young Singaporeans are going to theater schools, music conservatories, and art and design schools. These activities are matched by the government's interest in engendering a "gracious society" and attracting foreign workers into the high end of the emerging global knowledge-based economy: finance and banking, the life sciences, and other high-technology sectors. Thus, a National Arts Council has been established. Significant sums of money—up to S$10 million annually—are dedicated to the encouragement of developing "culture" as part of urban development to feed the presumed demands and desires of the high-end globally mobile workforce who might be attracted to Singapore. Censorship has been relaxed significantly. Many theater groups with a sustained history of productions are given annual operating grants and exempted from submitting scripts to the censorship board, even though playwrights are increasingly explicit in their critical commentaries on local political and social conditions.

In sum, then, there has been a greater presence of civil society and a greater

liberalization of the cultural sphere, but no signs of further political democratization or any diminution of the PAP's determination to maintain political
dominance.[30] Indeed, the PAP government's ability to relax a rule when the
political cost is low and activities can be accommodated is crucial to the
continuance of its political power—a policy that releases the steam from
complaints, frustration, and alienation without allowing such negative sentiments to fester into political challenges.

In the terrain of electoral and parliamentary politics, the PAP has also
been rather innovative in both accommodating and constraining oppositional
tendencies. To accommodate the often explicitly expressed and widespread
desire for opposition voices in parliament, the PAP government has introduced two new sets of MPs: nonconstituency MPs and nominated MPs. The
nonconstituency MPs (NCMPs) are those who ran unsuccessfully in general
elections, but garnered the most votes among all the failed contestants. In
their desperation to be heard in parliament, prominent veteran opposition
party leaders, such as J.B. Jeyaratnam of the Workers Party, have gone back
on their initial rejection of this scheme and taken their place as NCMPs in
parliament. The nominated MPs (NMPs) are individuals—deemed to be of
independent mind and nominated by a few citizens or civil organizations—
who are inducted into government without standing for election in the first
place. Nomination and selection of NMPs has veered away from its original
intent of inducting independent-minded individuals to a policy of representation by sectors; for example, there is likely to be one woman NMP nominated by women's organizations, one unionist nominated by the National
Trades Union Congress, and a business member from the business community in each parliament. The number of nonconstituency MPs and nominated
MPs in each parliament is the decision of the elected government.

Moreover, the gerrymandered electoral boundaries have been radically
reorganized into "greater representative constituencies" in which four to six
electoral constituencies are grouped into a larger unit. Each contesting political party fields a team of candidates, and the team that garners the most
aggregate votes wins the entire slate of seats. While in principle this reorganization does not violate the axiom of one person, one vote, it nevertheless
confers advantages on the incumbent ruling party. Finally, municipal responsibilities have been transferred to elected MPs as managers of "town coun-
cils" that are responsible for maintenance of public housing estates, which
house more than 80 percent of the population—thus linking the exercise of
the vote to people's material life and discouraging them from voting against
PAP candidates who can draw more readily on government resources. Hence,
the ability of political parties to challenge the PAP in the electoral process
has been severely curtailed.

As there is little evidence of outside challenges to the PAP's stranglehold on state power, questions are often raised about the possibility of challenges coming from within the party. Might the party break up into different fractions that will challenge each other for political dominance, as in the case of the KMT just before losing the presidential election? The short answer is no. This is because the PAP has never been a party of internal factions, unlike the dominant political parties in former single-party-dominant states such as the KMT, the Indian National Congress, or the Liberal Democratic Party of Japan.

The PAP is a unitary organization with a highly centralized leadership structure and members who share a similar vision and ideology. This shared orientation is itself achieved by the very process of selection into the party hierarchy: While application for general membership is in principle open to everyone, candidates for election into parliament are selected by the induction of targeted individuals, who may or may not be party members, just before the elections. The backgrounds of these candidates are thoroughly investigated. Those who clear these checks are then put through a series of interviews with increasingly higher levels of party leadership as well as a series of psychological tests. Only those who survive all the processes are entered in elections. Furthermore, those selected are classified, from the time they enter politics, into ministerial material and generic backbenchers. The backbenchers seldom rise beyond the political office of parliamentary secretary, and only after long years of serving as an MP. In the normal process of party renewal, those who fail to "make the grade"—those whose competence in any area of an MP's work does not match the standard of performance set by the party—are asked to stand down to make way for "new blood." In a process maintained with such vigilance, the likelihood of party fragmentation is as good as zero. Disenchanted individuals do leave the party; but they do not join other parties or organize a new one, thus reducing the likelihood of competitive politics in the political sphere.

Clearly the economic, social, and political ingredients that coalesced over a thirty-year period culminating in the year 2000—the period that can be denoted as Taiwan's trajectory to democracy—are largely absent in Singapore. A *South China Morning Post* journalist once asked Lee Kuan Yew: "[What is the] impact of the DPP election on Singapore?" The senior minister answered categorically: "It has no impact on Singapore. Why should Taiwanese voting 40 percent for the DPP affect Singapore?"[31] If there is to be any democratization of the political sphere in Singapore involving serious multiparty contestations and alternation of power, something that is improbable for at least another decade, it is not likely to be substantive or structurally isomorphic with the trajectory of Taiwan.

Prospects

The history of the election of the DPP president, Chen Shui-bian, in Taiwan is the history of the democratization of Taiwan from a single-party-dominant or authoritarian state to a full multiparty democracy. It is within such a framework that one can ask how Taiwan's experience is germane for the future political development of the remaining single-party-dominant states: Malaysia and Singapore.

In the case of Malaysia, recent political developments during and after the East Asian financial crisis suggest that the dominant position of UMNO and therefore BN is weakening. The possibility of being challenged in the future by a coalition of political parties can no longer be ruled out, though admittedly its realization remains vague at present. This situation recalls the rise of the DPP and the displacement of the KMT. Here indeed the history of the DPP may offer some lessons for Malaysia's mobilized civil society and opposition forces. The formation of the DPP (with serious internal fragmentation and divisions that are part of its history) can serve as an object lesson, if not a model, for the alternative coalition, the Barisan Alternatif, which was formed initially in order to contest the 1999 general elections and perhaps displace the dominant party, UMNO—much like the early days of the DPP with its loose coalitions sharing a common aim of displacing the KMT from power. As we have seen, however, the substantive differences that separate the coalition partners in the Barisan Alternatif may be harder to overcome because of their differing party ideologies and issues of ethnicity and religion, specifically Islam—issues that were largely absent among the partners in the DPP's formation. Nevertheless, recent developments indicate that the constituent parties of BA are willing to set aside significant differences in the interest of unseating the long-governing Barisan Nasional and UMNO. Its eventual success or failure to do so is now a matter of historical contingence.

In the case of Singapore, however, the fault lines inhered in Taiwan's society and polity are completely absent. Although there are ethnic differences in Singapore, they are not politically divisive. The occasional instances of corruption will continue to be dealt with severely whenever discovered, in contrast to the conspicuous corruption and money politics of the KMT. The middle class in Singapore has no independent economic base, but is beholden to the economic policies of the PAP regime—in contrast to the Taiwanese middle class, which is independent of the KMT regime and therefore can be mobilized against it. The KMT under Lee Teng-hui was willing to democratize the political sphere as part of the strategy of secession from the PRC—whereas the PAP's determination to maintain its dominance remains undiminished, unrepentant, and unyielding through its continuous manipulation of the political system and the cultural sphere. In sum, then, as the likelihood of political democratization is virtually nonexistent in Singapore, no experience of democratization anywhere in the world is relevant to Singapore.

Notes

1. For eyewitness accounts of the reception of the KMT army in Taiwan and its political and psychological consequences, see Alan M. Wachman, *Taiwan: National Identity and Democratization* (Armonk, NY: M.E. Sharpe, 1994), pp. 94–98.

2. Allen Chun, "The Cultural Industry as National Enterprise: The Politics of Heritage in Contemporary Taiwan," in *From Beijing to Port Moresby: The Politics of Identity in Cultural Policies*, ed. Virginia R. Dominguez and David Y.H. Wu (Amsterdam: Gordon & Breach, 1998), p. 82. According to Chun there were three stages to the sinicization project: an era of cultural reunification, an era of cultural renaissance, and an era of cultural reconstruction. For a detailed discussion of Mandarin language policy and the competition between Mandarin and Taiwanese, see Wachman, *Taiwan*, pp. 107–110.

3. See David Y.H. Wu, "Invention of Taiwanese: A Second Look at Taiwan's Cultural Policy and National Identity," in Dominguez and Wu, *From Beijing to Port Moresby*, pp. 115–132.

4. See Allen Chun, "Rejoinder to Second Look," in Dominguez and Wu, *From Beijing to Port Moresby*, pp. 133–137.

5. Wu Jin Yong, "Nation-State Construction, Social Memory, and Monumental Space: The Construction of the 228 Monuments" (MA thesis, Graduate Institute of Building and Planning, National Taiwan University, 1994; in Chinese).

6. The cities of Taipei and Kaohsiung, however, did not have an elected mayor until the early 1990s.

7. Alexander Lu Ya-Li, "Political Opposition in Taiwan: The Development of the Democratic Progressive Party," in *Political Change in Taiwan*, ed. Tun-jen Cheng and Stephan Haggard (Boulder: Lynne Rienner, 1992), p. 159.

8. Wachman, *Taiwan*, p. 135.

9. Michael Hsiao Hsin-Huang, "The Rise of Social Movements and Civil Protests," in Cheng and Haggard, *Political Change in Taiwan*, p. 58.

10. For details on all these social movements, see Hsiao, "Rise of Social Movements," pp. 57–74.

11. Ibid., p. 71.

12. For a history of the formation of the DPP see Lu, "Political Opposition in Taiwan," pp. 121–146.

13. The most significant intervention during this period was the Kaohsiung Incident in 1979, when following a violent confrontation during a mass demonstration organized by the *tangwai*, under the auspices of its mass circulation magazine *Formosa*, more than a hundred *tangwai* leaders were arrested; see Lu, "Political Opposition in Taiwan," pp. 124–125.

14. In writing this section on Malaysia, I have benefited greatly from discussions with my colleagues James Jesudason and Syed Farid Alatas.

15. Several factors have been cited in the literature: internal social divisions, repressive measures of the state, the determination of the dominant party to dominate, ideological reshaping of the population's political consciousness to generate consensus, enfeeblement of opposition. For a detailed discussion of these factors regarding Malaysia, see James Jesudason, "The Resilience of One-Party Dominance in Malaysia and Singapore," in *The Awkward Embrace: One Party Domination and Democracy*, ed. Hermann Giliomee and Charles Simkins (Amsterdam: Harwood, 1999), pp. 127–172.

16. James Jesudason, *Ethnicity and the Economy: The State, Chinese Business, and Multinationals in Malaysia* (Kuala Lumpur: Oxford University Press, 1989), p. 122.

17. *Straits Times*, 14 January 2001.

18. Information on the 1999 election results was culled from the detailed account provided by John Funston, "Malaysia's Tenth Elections: Status Quo, Reformasi, or Islamization?" *Contemporary Southeast Asia* 22 (2000):23–59.

19. For a detailed discussion of the contest between UMNO and PAS for the Malay electoral ground, see Kamarulnizam Abdullah, "National Security and Malay Unity: The Issue of Radical Religious Elements in Malaysia," *Contemporary Southeast Asia* 21 (1999):261–282.

20. For details of the place of civil society in the Reformasi movement, see Meredith Weiss, "What Will Become of Reformasi? Ethnicity and Changing Political Norms in Malaysia," *Contemporary Southeast Asia* 21 (1999):424–450.

21. Member organizations of Suqiu: Chinese School Boards Association, Chinese Schoolteachers Association, Nanyang University Alumni Association, Taiwan Graduate Alumni Association, Federation of Hokkien Associations (and those of other dialects and locales), and the Selangor and Negri Sembilan Chinese Assembly Halls.

22. Furthermore, the majority of Chinese in Singapore are, like the Taiwanese, descendents from migrants from Fujian province. Hence, they speak the same Minnan or Hokkien language.

23. This policy does not eliminate class differences in facilities with the English language, however, which advantages the middle and upper classes.

24. For an analysis of multiracial discourse, see Chua Beng Huat, "Racial-Singaporeans: Absence After the Hyphen," in *Southeast Asian Identities: Culture and the Politics of Representation in Indonesia, Malaysia, Singapore, and Thailand*, ed. Joel Kahn (Singapore: Institute of Southeast Asian Studies, 1998), pp. 28–50. For details of the PAP's ideological trajectory from the 1950s to mid-1990, see Chua Beng Huat, *Communitarian Ideology and Democracy in Singapore* (London: Routledge, 1995).

25. For a discussion of middle-class sentiments in Singapore, see Chua Beng Huat and Tan Joo Ean, "Singapore: Where the Middle Class Sets the Standard," in *Culture and Privilege in Capitalist Asia*, ed. Michael Pinches (London: Routledge, 1999), pp. 137–148. See also Nirmala Purushotam, "Between Compliance and Resistance: Women and the Middle Class Way of Life in Singapore," in *Gender and Power in Affluent Asia*, ed. Krishna Sen and Maila Stivens (London: Routledge, 1998), pp. 127–146.

26. For a discussion of the repressive measures exercised across different social terrains, see Christopher Tremawan, *The Political Economy of Social Control in Singapore* (London: St. Martin's Press, 1994); for a biographical account by one who suffered direct suppression, see Francis T. Seow, *To Catch a Tartar: A Dissident in Lee Kuan Yew's Prison* (New Haven: Yale University Press, 1994).

27. The idea that a social movement's success depends on its ability to disrupt is suggested by Frances Fox Piven and Richard C. Cloward, *Poor People's Movements: Why They Succeed, How They Fail* (New York: Vintage, 1979).

28. See Garry Rodan, "State-Society Relations and Political Opposition in Singapore," in *Political Opposition in Industrializing Asia*, ed. Garry Rodan (London: Routledge, 1995), pp. 95–127.

29. For a detailed comparison of urban planning in Taipei and Singapore, see Chua Beng Huat, "Providing Public Spaces: Singapore and Taiwan" (paper presented at the Conference on Shaping a Common Future: Case Studies of Collective Goods, Collective Actions in East and Southeast Asia, Asia Research Centre, Murdoch University, Western Australia, 1999).

30. This was demonstrated in the 1997 general election. In the face of fierce competition in some electoral constituencies, the PAP threatened that if a constituency were to elect a non-PAP candidate, its public housing estates would not be upgraded by the housing authority. See Chua Beng Huat, "Public Housing Residents as Clients of the State," *Housing Studies* 15 (2000):45–60.

31. *Straits Times*, 24 August 2000.

5

Does Chen's Election Make Any Difference? Domestic and International Constraints on Taipei, Washington, and Beijing

Yu-Shan Wu

The election of Chen Shui-bian as the Republic of China's (ROC) tenth president in March 2000 ostensibly brought about great changes both in Taiwan and in cross-strait relations. Not only was political power transferred to the opposition peacefully for the first time in the ROC's history, but Taiwan and mainland China also began to face the stern possibility of Taiwan's independence. Chen's government, however, finds itself under strict domestic and international constraints. Internationally speaking, the United States has great stakes in the stability in the Taiwan Strait and finds itself deeply involved in the interaction between Taipei and Beijing. Here I apply the strategic triangle approach and the power-maximizing model to analyze cross-strait tensions in the context of Chen's election. As we shall see, the United States, mainland China, and Taiwan constitute a strategic triangle. This triangular structure puts specific constraints on the behavior of the three actors. Besides these external constraints, however, domestic factors bear on the policies of the political leaders in the three countries. In order to maximize political power, the leaders find it necessary to take specific actions toward the other two but mainly for domestic reasons. Thus, external factors (the strategic triangle) and domestic factors (power-maximizing calculations) take turns in determining policymakers' agendas, and shaping the interactions among the three actors on which peace and war in the region hinges.

Taiwan's presidential elections of 18 March 2000 have radically changed the ROC's political landscape. The Kuomintang (KMT) that had ruled the island country for more than half a century was dislodged from power and replaced by the opposition Democratic Progressive Party (DPP) led by its presidential candidate Chen Shui-bian. From the very beginning of the presidential campaign, the world cast its eyes on Chen's proclivity toward Taiwan independence and wondered about the impact of his possible election on cross-strait relations. The backdrop of such speculation is obviously the missile scare of 1995–1996 when Taiwan's first direct presidential election invited serious saber rattling across the Taiwan Strait in the form of the People's Liberation Army's (PLA) missile tests right off the island's two main ports and live military exercises in areas close to Taiwan. People worried that the tension built up in the strait since that confrontation might this time erupt into open armed conflict and drag the United States and Japan into a war with the People's Republic of China (PRC). A scenario of World War III was conjured up in the minds of pessimistic observers.

Developments since Chen Shui-bian's inauguration on 20 May 2000 seem to have dissipated this pessimism. As we shall see, however, Chen's election and the power transfer from the KMT to the DPP never posed any real danger to peace and stability in the Taiwan Strait and East Asia. This is the case because the three main actors in the Taiwan Strait—the United States, Taiwan, and mainland China—are conditioned by the strategic triangle and their domestic politics and hence would refrain from making provocative declarations or using force. The same reasoning, however, points to heightened tension in the strait and even serious conflict as the conditions for stability give way to factors that are more conflict-prone in the near future. This chapter integrates the strategic triangle approach and power-maximizing model to analyze the trilateral relations among Taipei, Beijing, and Washington. My purpose is not merely to analyze the interactions among the three players in the trilateral game, but also to develop general theoretical perspectives that can be applied to similar situations in other settings.

Theoretical Framework

Even a casual observer would not fail to notice the critical role the United States has been playing in cross-strait relations. Clearly, then, any analysis or prediction of future development in this area has to take the American factor into consideration. This is a typical case of a bilateral relation heavily affected by a third party. Because of the intensity of interactions among the three actors, Taipei, Washington, and Beijing, particularly since the end of the Cold War, one is witnessing the formation of a strategic triangle among these three players. However, before introducing the triangle concept to this analysis of cross-strait relations, I want to begin with some general theoretical observations and then develop the methodology of the chapter accordingly.

The relation between any two countries is determined by three groups of factors. The first group is the compatibility of their national goals. Security, economic, and ideological considerations play the key roles in determining whether their national goals are compatible. The second group of factors has to do with domestic politics. Often foreign policy is made with domestic political implications weighing heavily in the minds of the decision makers. A foreign policy may not make any sense internationally, but can be totally rational when domestic political competition is taken into consideration. The intensity of political competition and the vulnerability of the foreign policy elite are directly related to the policies they make. The third group of factors emanates from the influence of a third party to the bilateral relation. Again, a foreign policy that makes no sense in terms of bilateral relations may derive from the pressure of an important third party.

Empirically it is very difficult to separate these three sets of factors, as they usually operate simultaneously. Analytically, however, students of international relations must differentiate these three sets and their impact on the bilateral relation under study. For reasons of simplicity, let us call the three sets Group A (directly bilateral factors), Group B (domestic factors), and Group C (indirect or extended factors). In the literature of international relations, only Group A factors have been thoroughly analyzed; but to understand the dynamics of cross-strait relations, it is imperative to look into Group B and Group C factors, as well, which often outweigh Group A factors. In the following discussion, I concentrate first on Group C factors (concerning the third party) and develop a strategic triangle model. I then turn to the domestic arena and develop a power-maximizing model (domestic factors). After applying the two models to cross-strait relations, in the final analysis I integrate the strategic triangle and the power-maximization model and put Taiwan's postelection situation in this general framework.

The Strategic Triangle

The concept of the strategic triangle has been conventionally applied to the relationship between the United States, the Soviet Union, and the PRC.[1] But as Lowell Dittmer (a leading proponent of the notion) argues, this concept is applicable to any triangular relationship so long as three criteria are met: (1) it circumscribes the relationship among three rational, sovereign actors, (2) in which the bilateral relationship between two of them is contingent on their relationship with the third, and (3) national security is at stake. Clearly the Taipei–Washington–Beijing relationship satisfies these conditions. Also, following Dittmer's usage, one can identify this triangle as a "mini-triangle" compared with the "great strategic triangle" that denotes the relations between Washington, Moscow, and Beijing.[2]

Lowell Dittmer, Chi-cheng Lo, Tzong-Ho Bau, and I have developed various typologies for analyzing triangular relations. For Dittmer, the relation between any two triangular actors can be either positive (amity) or negative (enmity), resulting in four types of triangles: Ménage à trois (three positive relations), Romantic (two positive and one negative), Marriage (one positive and two negative), and Unit Veto (three negatives).[3] Lo follows Dittmer's analysis and postulates that when the number of negative relations in a strategic triangle is even, the result is a stable triangle. If the number of negative relations is odd, the structure is unbalanced and the triangle is unstable.[4] In the Washington–Taipei–Beijing triangle, the United States plays the role of a structural balancer.

I also adopt the basic concepts of Dittmer and differentiate six possible roles in the four types of triangles: "friend" in a Ménage à trois, "partner" and "outcast" in a Marriage, "pivot" and "wing" in a Romantic triangle, and "foe" in a Unit-Veto triangle (Figure 5.1).[5] Each of these six roles is then ranked in terms of the number of positive relations it has with the other two players and the nature of the relationship between the other two players. The greater the number of positive relations a triangular actor enjoys, the higher its rank. If two roles have the same number of positive relations, the nature of the other two's relationship determines the rank. A positive relation between the other two players means a lower rank for a triangular actor. Following this logic, the ranking of the six triangular roles is (from best to worst): pivot, friend, partner, wing, foe, and outcast. I also assert that strategic actors inherently seek to elevate their roles.

Bau elaborates on the triangular framework. He reranks my six roles and comes up with a somewhat different order (Table 5.1, page 160). For him, pivot remains the most desirable position, followed by friend and partner, then wing and enemy, and finally outcast. An outcast can elevate a role by turning one of its negative relations into positive (in this sense becoming a wing) or by sabotaging the other two's positive relation (thus becoming a foe). A wing can apply similar strategies to become a partner or a friend. So too can a foe become a partner. As for a friend or a partner, the only way to elevate its role is to seek the pivot's position.[6] Bau then applies this logic to the Taipei–Washington–Beijing triangle and comes up with six stages of development. For him, the original Marriage of the 1950s and 1960s was gradually replaced by a Romantic triangle. Then a Ménage à trois emerged as Taipei took steps to improve its relation with Beijing (1987–1994). The missile crisis of 1995–1996 is viewed as tilting Washington toward Taipei, thus bringing back a Marriage and reducing Beijing to an outcast. The latest rapproche-

Figure 5.1 **Strategic Triangles and Roles**

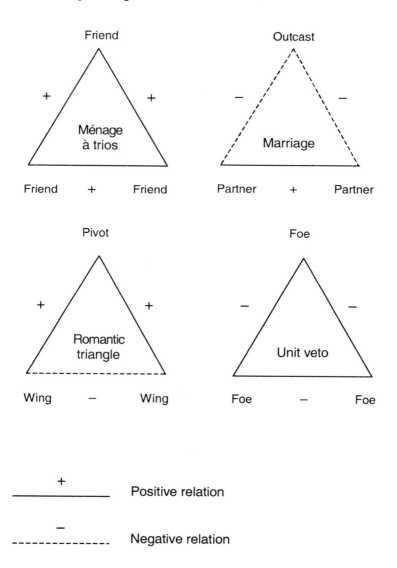

ment between Washington and Beijing and Koo Cheng-fu's (chairman of Taiwan's Straits Exchange Foundation) visit to the mainland suggest the triangle is again heading toward a Ménage à trois.[7]

I have applied a similar frame of analysis but come up with a different periodization. My "dual triangle" theme treats the Washington–Moscow–

Table 5.1

Ranking of Triangular Roles

Role	Number of positive relations	Relation between other two players	Rank (Wu)	Rank (Bau)
Pivot	2	Enmity	1	1
Friend	2	Amity	2	2
Partner	1	Enmity	3	2
Wing	1	Amity	4	3
Enemy	0	Enmity	5	3
Outcast	0	Amity	6	4

Sources: Yu-Shan Wu, "Exploring Dual Triangles: The Development of Taipei–Washington–Beijing Relations," p. 30; Bau Tzong-Ho, "Zhanlue sanjiao jiaose zhuanbian yu leixing bianhua fenxi—yi meiguo han taihai liangan sanjiao hudong weili," in *Zhengbian zhong de liang'an guanxi lilun* [Contending theories in the study of cross-strait relations], ed. Bau Tzong-Ho and Wu Yu-Shan (Taipei: Wu-nan, 1999), p. 345.

Beijing triangle as a "great strategic triangle" and the Washington–Taipei–Beijing triangle as a "mini-triangle." The configuration of the great triangle determines the policies of the actors in that game toward other actors, thus shaping the configuration of the mini-triangle (Table 5.2). Hence, Washington's need to seek partnership in Beijing predetermined the U.S. policy toward Taipei. Viewed in this light, the U.S. shift of diplomatic recognition from Beijing to Taipei is not construed as establishing a Romantic triangle, but a Marriage between Washington and Beijing, with Taipei reduced to an outcast. Nor is the cross-strait thaw since the late 1980s considered a decisive move toward genuine rapprochement. This means the Taipei–Beijing relation is still an enmity. The mini-triangle of the mid-1990s and Washington's intervention are proofs of the Romantic nature of the mini-triangle at this stage. In short, my characterization of the mini-triangle is more pessimistic concerning Taiwan's position and cross-strait relations.

The strategic triangle model serves at least two purposes: It provides a yardstick to evaluate a player's position in the triangle, and it asserts a general tendency in the players to elevate their roles (Bau and I) or for the system to equilibrate (Lo). Subjective intent notwithstanding, one finds many cases in which a triangular player's role was demoted, not elevated. This is the case, not only because domestic factors may come into play, but also because forces inherent in the triangle may bring about an undesirable outcome. This is the "derivative relation," a relation between triangular actors determined by the third party. There are three types of derivative relations. In Figure 5.2, derivative relation AC is based on two negative relations AB

Table 5.2

Evolution of Dual Triangles

	Great triangle	U.S.	PRC	USSR	Mini-triangle	U.S.	PRC	ROC
1950s	Marriage	Outcast	Junior partner	Senior partner	Marriage	Senior partner	Outcast	Junior partner
1960s	Unit veto	Foe	Foe	Foe	Marriage	Senior partner	Outcast	Junior partner
Early 1970s	Unit veto to romantic	Foe to pivot	Foe to wing	Foe to wing	Marriage to remarriage	Senior partner changing partner	Outcast to junior partner	Junior partner to outcast
Late 1970s	Marriage	Senior partner	Junior partner	Outcast	Marriage	Senior partner	Junior partner	Outcast
Early 1980s	Romantic	Wing	Pivot	Wing	Marriage	Senior partner	Junior partner	Outcast
Late 1980s	Ménage à trois	Friend	Friend	Friend	Marriage	Senior partner	Junior partner	Outcast
Post-Cold War	Collapse	N/A	N/A	N/A	Romantic	Pivot	Wing	Wing

Figure 5.2   **Derivative Relation Type I**

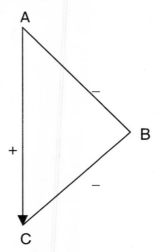

and BC. Here C is A's enemy's enemy. A natural tendency in A's attitude toward C is to develop an amity so that B as a threat can be contained. By the same token, C has a vested interest in developing a friendly relation with A in order to contain their common enemy B. The result may be a de facto or de jure alliance between A and C against B. This is derivative relation type I. In the great strategic triangle, one finds the Soviet expansion in the late 1970s acting as a major stimulus behind the quasi-alliance between Washington and Beijing. At that time, the common threat from the Soviet Union was so great that ideological differences between the United States and the PRC were overcome and the two countries ultimately established formal diplomatic relations—a perfect example of derivative relation I.

One may be influenced by one's friend to be nasty toward this friend's enemy. This is derivative relation II. As can be seen in Figure 5.3, A's hostility toward C derives from A's friendship with B and B's enmity with C (assuming there is no endogenous amity between A and C). The same logic does not apply to C's attitude toward A, however, as C does not face the same exogenous factors as A. The ROC's international isolation is a vivid example of derivative relation II. Usually, one finds no bilateral animosity between Taiwan and countries that do not recognize Taipei. Their nonrecognition derives from Beijing's objection to Taipei's independent position and their desire to keep good relations with the PRC. This is derivative relation II par excellence.

Derivative relation III, however, is not as predictable as type I or II. In type III, A is locked in enmity with B, but B has friendly relations with C.

Figure 5.3 **Derivative Relation Type II**

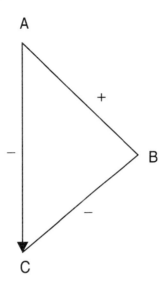

How is A going to deal with his enemy's friend? An intuitive response is repulsion, as C must appear unsavory to A. But if C is seen as manipulable, or important enough in its own right, A may court C in an effort to undermine the amity between B and C. In either case, the AC relation derives from AB and BC, just as in type I and II, but the exact mode of derivation depends on how A views C (Figure 5.4).

In sum, then, we find two forces shaping the behavior of players in a strategic triangle. One force is the innate drive in the triangular players to strive for an elevated role. The other force is the three types of derivative relations in which triangular players were induced, or pressured, into taking a specific attitude toward another player for the third party's sake. These two forces often conflict. Consider, for example, a partner in a Marriage triangle: Even though the elevation of role logic would induce it to improve relations with the outcast so that it may capture the pivot position, the type II derivative relation would suggest this partner keep its hostility toward the outcast. The logic of elevating one's role and the logic of derivative relations may reinforce each other under other circumstances. A partner in a Marriage triangle has an inherent interest in keeping an amity with the other partner following the elevation of role logic. Derivative relation I also suggests the partner should maintain friendship with the other partner, which is the first partner's enemy's enemy.

Figure 5.4   **Derivative Relation Type III**

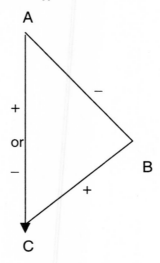

Derivative relations in a strategic triangle and the elevation of role logic conflict in the U.S. position in the Washington–Taipei–Beijing triangle. In the 1990s, one finds Taipei and Beijing doing their best to enlist American support on their side. While keeping formal diplomatic relations only with the PRC and showing tremendous interest in opening up the mainland Chinese market, the United States nevertheless continued its support of Taiwan's defense against a possible invasion by the mainland—to the extent of sending its carriers to the Taiwan Strait at the height of the missile crisis in 1996. Clearly, the United States has not tilted completely toward either Taipei or Beijing and must therefore be considered a pivot between the two wings of Taiwan and mainland China. As a pivot, however, the United States experiences cross-pressure from Taipei and Beijing. Following the elevation of role logic, the United States should keep good relations with both Taiwan and mainland China. Yet, derivative relation II dictates that the United States should keep away from Taipei, for Beijing's sake, and at the same time keep away from Beijing for Taipei's sake. This means Washington should maintain both amity and enmity with both wings. This is obviously mission impossible and goes a long way toward explaining the to-and-fro of Washington's position between the two Chinese antagonists, as shown in Figure 5.5 where Wa and Wb are the limits of Washington's two-way tilts.

I then developed the concept of "unintending pivot" to characterize the U.S. position between Taiwan and mainland China.[8] An unintending pivot falls into the pivot position not of its own volition. Usually it is a sated power

Figure 5.5   **Tilting of the Pivot in the Mini-Triangle**

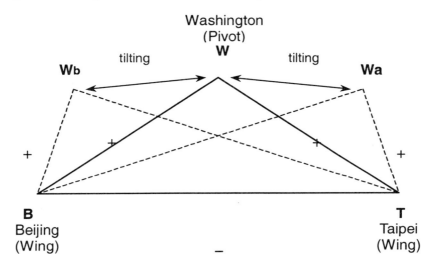

that does not aspire to attain the pivot's role in a Romantic triangle. It takes that role as a result of other players' actions. Unintending pivots do not have a firm commitment to their position and may swing to either wing and change the structure of the game from Romantic triangle to Marriage. The unintending pivot's inability to hold its role is a manifestation of the inherent instability of a Romantic triangle with a pivot subject to cross-pressure from the two opposing wings.

Since the Romantic triangle is inherently unstable and the role of the pivot is not always superior to all the other triangular roles, a recent trend in studying the Washington–Taipei–Beijing triangle emphasizes the desirability of developing a Ménage à trois. After all, the three "friends" in such a structure are not threatening one another. The benefit of playing the pivot and having the wings in a relationship of enmity to preclude their collaboration against oneself and to solicit concessions from them may not be enough to offset the cross-pressure from the wings to side with them. If the United States feels it is an unintending pivot, then the friend role is at least as desirable as pivot. The unintending pivot may then strive to improve relations between the wings so that it does not have to worry about being dragged into a war between them.

Another way of showing the inherent instability of the Romantic triangle is to calculate its aggregate payoff for actors. Following Bau, we give +1 to any amity any player enjoys and –1 to any enmity. Amity between the other

Table 5.3

Aggregate Payoffs of the Strategic Triangles

Strategic triangle	Player 1 payoff		Player 2 payoff		Player 3 payoff		Aggregate payoff	Rank
Ménage à trois	Friend:	+1	Friend:	+1	Friend:	+1	+3	1
Romantic	Pivot:	+3	Wing:	−1	Wing:	−1	+1	2
Marriage	Outcast:	−3	Partner:	+1	Partner:	+1	−1	3
Unit veto	Foe:	−1	Foe:	−1	Foe:	−1	−3	4

Source: Anthony Tu, "A Study of US–PRC–Taiwan Strategic Triangle During the Clinton Administration" (MA thesis prospectus, National Taiwan University, July 2000).

two players is a −1 for the player concerned; enmity between the other two is a +1. In this way we can determine the payoff of any given role. Calculating the aggregate payoff of a triangle by adding together the individual payoffs of the three actors in that triangle, we can come up with a system-level desirability of the triangle. The result is shown in Table 5.3.

From Table 5.3 we can see that a Ménage à trois is more stable than a Romantic triangle. As for the individual players, an unintending pivot is more interested in bringing about friendly relations between the wings, thus replacing the Romantic triangle with a Ménage à trois. The wings in a Romantic triangle also have a lot to win in a Ménage à trois. Thus, from a role elevation perspective, all the players would be better off in a Ménage à trois than in a Romantic triangle. From a systemic stability viewpoint, a Ménage à trois ranks highest (see Table 5.3). From a derivative relation perspective, if A befriends B and B befriends C, other things being equal, A is likely (but not certain) to extend friendship to C. At least there is no inherent force in a Ménage à trois to induce players to change the triangular structure because of derivative relation of whatever type.

Note that the great strategic triangle equilibrated in a Ménage à trois before it lost the Soviet Union as a triangular player (Figure 5.6). It can be postulated that there is an inherent tendency in a strategic triangle that brings all three actors to the conclusion through their interactions that a Ménage à trois is best for all of them. If this is the case, one can be optimistic concerning the Washington–Taipei–Beijing mini-triangle for it may also evolve toward a Ménage à trois. The elevation of role perspective, the derivative relations, and the aggregate payoff structure all point to the Ménage à trois as a desirable solution. It can be argued that Washington, as an unintending pivot, has already concluded that a Ménage à trois is preferable to a Romantic triangle and is throwing its influence on the two sides of the Taiwan Strait to bring about such an outcome.[9]

Figure 5.6   **Equilibrating Toward Ménage à trois**

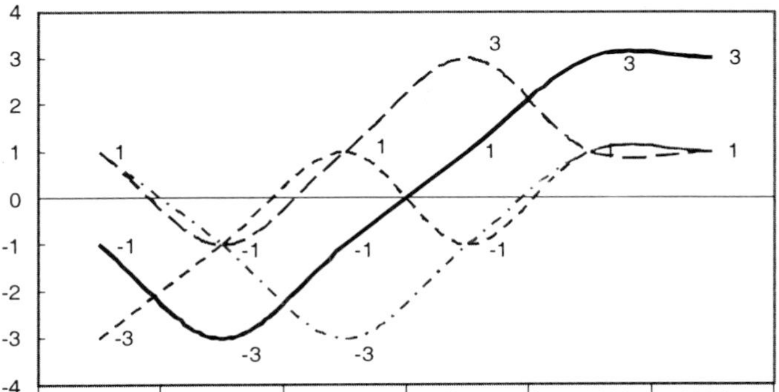

	1950s (Marriage)	1960s (Unit Veto)	1970s (Marriage)	Early 1980s (Romantic)	Late 1980s (Ménage à trois)	1990s (Ménage à trois)
—— Aggregate payoff	-1	-3	-1	1	3	3
- - - Washington	-3	-1	1	-1	1	1
- · - Moscow	1	-1	-3	-1	1	1
— — Beijing	1	-1	1	3	1	1

Source: Same as Table 5.3.

The strategic triangle framework is useful in pointing out the close inter-actions between Washington, Taipei, and Beijing and in devising the "rules of the game." The problem with this approach is its complete lack of consid-eration of domestic factors—especially the electoral cycles in the United States and Taiwan, which tend to reinforce each other through accidental synchronization (the coincidence of presidential elections in the two coun-tries). It is this drawback that the following approach is designed to address.

Power Maximization in Taiwan: Converging Toward the Center

It is only natural that political leaders should attempt to maximize their power and defend themselves against challenges from other power contenders. To preserve one's leadership position is arguably the primary goal of a political leader, whatever the political system. If this is an acceptable assumption, then foreign policymaking is never what it is claimed to be; that is, it is never geared completely to the international environment, but to a large extent is meant for domestic consumption. This means that a policy made ostensibly toward a foreign country may be mainly for attracting domestic voters or preempting opposing factions. These are the Group B factors mentioned earlier.

In the Washington–Taipei–Beijing triangle, the three players interact not only with their mutual and trilateral relations in mind, but also with the goal of the ruling elites to maximize their respective power. In this way, they are in two games simultaneously: One game is to maximize the national interest in the international environment; the other is to maximize the elites' power in the domestic environment.[10] Thus, the optimal strategy for an actor in the international game may well be suboptimal in the domestic game. The simultaneity of the two games makes it difficult to find a strategy that is satisfying to the actor on both fronts.[11]

Domestic constraints on the makers of foreign policy can take various forms. This chapter emphasizes the most obvious form: The ruling elite has an inherent interest in pursuing the kind of foreign policy that enhances its power in the domestic political system and also an inherent interest in evading policies that would undermine its power base domestically. In the case of the Washington–Taipei–Beijing triangle, we find Washington's China policy periodically affected by surges of idealism and Taiwan's mainland policy heavily constrained by electoral politics. For its part, the PRC's attitude toward Taiwan is closely linked with the self-perceived vulnerability of the communist ruling elite. In the case of the United States and Taiwan, presidential elections are central mechanisms through which domestic constraints on the policymakers reveal themselves. In the case of mainland China, the congresses of the Chinese Communist Party (CCP) have provided a battlefield for power struggles and thus set the schedule of periodic challenges to the incumbent ruling elite. In short: Democratic elections and party congresses in the three countries of the triangular game set the institutional background for the play of domestic constraints on the behavior of the actors toward one another.

Let us begin by taking a look at domestic politics in Taiwan and assessing its impact on Taiwan's mainland policy. There has emerged an unmistakable convergent pattern with respect to mainland policy among the major parties in Taiwan, even though their starting points are wide apart.[12] This convergence is based on a standard distribution of public preferences along the identity and interest axes. The distribution pattern of these preferences has a bearing on the parties' vote-maximizing strategies: Policy tends to shift toward the center. Thus democracy—which allows for divergent views—first disperses party positions and then—because of the dependence on public preferences—compels these positions to converge.

Up to the 2000 presidential elections, there have been three major political parties in Taiwan: the KMT, the DPP, and the New Party (NP).[13] After the presidential elections, James Soong who lost by a slight margin formed the People First Party (PFP), which takes a position close to the NP's stance but with a slight nativist tilt. The parties' mainland policies can be understood through their positions on two salient issues: unification versus independence (*tongdu wenti*) and security versus economic interest (*anquan yu jingji*).[14] While the identity issue is well known and has captured headlines worldwide, the interest issue is no less important and has exercised an increasingly greater impact on Taipei's attitude toward Beijing. Above all, the policy positions of the major political parties can be pinpointed only with reference to both issues.

We can use a spatial model to pinpoint the parties' positions in a two-dimensional space and delineate the movement of these positions over time. The parties' positions are determined through a careful reading of their official statements relating to the two issues. We can then explain the movement of their positions in terms of the normal distribution of public opinion on the two main issues relating to cross-strait relations. The distribution pattern is based on data gathered through a series of public opinion surveys conducted by the Mainland Affairs Council.

The parties' mainland policy positions can be pinpointed and their development traced on an integrated policy map.[15] This map is delineated on the horizontal axis by an identity spectrum and on the vertical by security and economic interest (Figure 5.7). There is a standard distribution of public preferences on both spectra. Those favoring a mixed identity (that is, those who consider themselves to be both Chinese and Taiwanese and favor neither rapid unification nor rapid independence) are the most numerous (Table 5.4, page 171) on the horizontal spectrum, as are those who place equal importance on both national security (including foreign relations) and cross-strait economic relations (Table 5.5, page 172) as shown on the vertical. This being the case, public preference is concentrated at the origin point where the two spectra meet. The vote-maximizing strategy shared by the political parties naturally induces them to move ideologically toward the point defined by the origin.[16]

It was democracy that brought about multiparty politics in Taiwan. Different parties developed different mainland policies based on their self-perception and ideological commitment. As noted in Figure 5.7, the old KMT position was in the lower-right region, emphasizing both unification and security. That position was challenged by the nativist political forces represented first by *tangwai* (literally outside the party) elements, then by the DPP. Originally the DPP's position was in the lower-left quadrant, emphasizing both independence and national security. Thus, even though the old DPP and the old KMT were diametrically opposite to each other on the unification-independence spectrum, it is clear they had no quarrel about the supremacy of security over economic interests.

The rapid economic exchanges between Taiwan and mainland China be-

Figure 5.7   **Converging Mainland Policies**

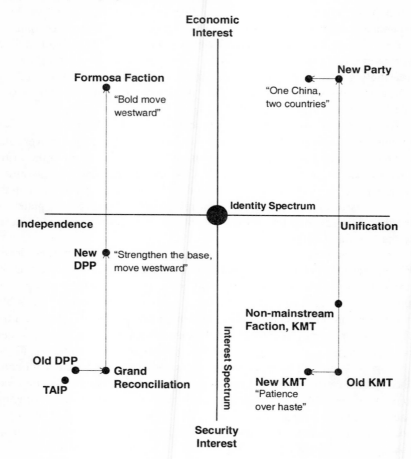

ginning in 1987 added the new dimension of security versus economic interests to the mainland policy considerations. The KMT's initial response to cross-strait business activities was characterized by caution and constraint. Party veterans, haunted by the bitter memory of losing the Chinese civil war, advised against investing too much in the mainland. The DPP had no qualms about accepting the legitimacy of the PRC as long as Beijing did not insist that Taiwan is an integral part of China. But when it became clear that the communist regime would never relinquish its claim on Taiwan, the DPP turned fiercely against the PRC—not because the party is staunchly anticommunist, but because it is against mainland China. Thus, both the old KMT and the old DPP were preoccupied with security, though for different reasons. This

Table 5.4

Public Opinion on National Identity (Percentage)

	Pro-unification		Middle positions		Pro-independence	
	Rapid unification	Status quo at present, unification in future	Status quo at present, future to be decided	Status quo at present and in future	Status quo at present, independence in future	Rapid independence
Sept. 1995	3.3	24.2	42.8	12.2	8.0	3.7
Nov. 1995	1.9	23.9	32.4	12.3	10.6	3.4
Feb. 1996	1.8	20.7	41.2	13.9	8.5	4.4
Mar. 1996	1.5	17.3	33.9	16.8	12.7	7.8
Aug. 1996	4.8	22.0	34.1	19.3	9.9	6.3
Feb. 1997	5.0	21.7	24.8	21.0	12.6	8.7
Aug. 1997	5.1	13.9	35.4	21.6	11.2	10.0
Sept. 1997	3.1	21.5	34.3	13.8	10.7	9.0
Nov. 1997	3.8	15.7	42.0	18.5	6.7	9.5
Apr. 1998	3.2	17.7	39.2	16.0	13.0	6.1
May 1998	3.9	17.2	36.6	16.0	11.6	6.7
July 1998	1.9	16.5	34.9	15.8	12.9	4.9
Aug. 1998	0.8	14.9	30.5	15.3	12.9	7.4
Sept. 1998	3.5	13.3	36.0	14.4	12.2	7.3
Oct. 1998	2.4	13.5	35.6	17.5	12.0	7.0
Mar. 1999	2.5	14.8	34.8	19.7	11.3	4.2
May 1999	2.4	14.1	30.8	19.4	13.6	4.6
Oct. 1999	1.6	14.9	36.6	15.6	17.0	4.6
Apr. 2000	2.7	16.2	30.2	21.1	14.6	3.9

Source: Mainland Affairs Council, *Zhonghuaminguo Taiwan diqu minzhong dui liang'an guanxi de kanfa* [Public opinion on cross-strait relations in the Taiwan district of the Republic of China], December 2000, p. 1.

Table 5.5

Public Opinion on National Interest (Percentage)

	Foreign relations more important than cross-strait relations	Foreign relations and cross-strait relations equally important	Cross-strait relations more important then foreign relations
Nov. 1995	28.2	16.2	18.8
Feb. 1996	29.3	43.7	14.1
Mar. 1996	29.5	41.2	17.9
Aug. 1996	35.3	38.3	23.0
Feb. 1997	38.6	37.3	17.9
Aug. 1997	30.8	43.8	22.5
Apr. 1998	26.4	49.1	15.3
May 1998	28.9	28.8	25.8
July 1998	29.0	23.6	25.6

Source: Mainland Affairs Council, *Zhonghuaminguo Taiwan diqu minzhong dui liang'an guanxi de kanfa* [Public opinion on cross-strait relations in the Taiwan district of the Republic of China], November 1998, p. 2.

means that no major party moved upward on the mainland policy map.

With the inauguration of Lee Teng-hui as president, the KMT began its tilt toward the center on the unification-independence axis, culminating in the "special state-to-state theory" of July 1999. The intraparty power struggle intensified, resulting ultimately in the departure of the New KMT Alliance from the party and the founding of the New Party. The NP then moved rapidly toward a position favoring economic interests (upward in Figure 5.7), positioning it as friendlier to the mainland. At the same time, the KMT non-mainstreamers found it difficult to leave the party and maintained its insistence on security concerns. Prime Minister Hau Pei-tsun had been a leading figure in the non-mainstream faction, but he was edged out in a showdown with President Lee in February 1993. Hau continued to champion the non-mainstream cause and became the running mate for Lin Yang-kang, another non-mainstreamer who challenged Lee in the 1996 presidential election. The Lin–Hau ticket garnered 14.5 percent of the popular vote compared to the 54 percent grasped by Lee and Lien Chan. Both Lin and Hau lost their posts as KMT vice-chairs for breaking party discipline by running on a separate ticket,[17] and the non-mainstream faction was further marginalized. After the presidential election failure, both Lin and Hau tilted decisively toward economic interests in mainland policy. Lin formed the Chinese Association for Promoting Cross-Strait Peace and Development (Zhonghua Taihai Liang'an Heping Fazhan Cujinhui), dedicated to abolishing the patience over haste policy (*jieji yongren*) and establishing links of the sort proposed by the mainland. It hoped that economic cooperation would minimize hostility from Beijing and reduce its threat to Taiwan,[18] a position almost identical to that of the NP.

The DPP began its move toward the origin point (Figure 5.7) after the 1995 parliamentary election. First Shih Ming-teh pushed the party away from its dogmatic insistence on Taiwan independence, moving the DPP's position to the right. Hsu Hsin-liang, chairman of the DPP and head of its Formosa faction, then advocated the "bold move westward" (dadan xijin) policy, which pushed the party upward on the policy map. The compromise reached at the DPP's China policy debate—labeled "strengthen the base and move west-ward" (qiangben jianjin)—lies between the old DPP position and that of Hsu Hsin-liang and the Formosa faction. The DPP has therefore moved right-ward and upward from its lower-left position, attracted by the weight of votes concentrated at the origin.

The NP began to show signs of change. Under the pressure of the upcom-ing parliamentary elections, a segment of the NP leadership advocated "one China, two countries" as the party's new formula on the identity question. On the map this is clearly a shift to the left. Since the NP's original position was in the upper-right region, this movement leftward fulfills the prediction that all political parties converge toward the point where the identity and interest spectra meet.

As we have seen, democracy is the driving force behind the mainland policies of Taiwan's various political parties. Ideological commitments and the initial need for support from the party faithful determined the initial po-sitions of the political parties mapped in Figure 5.7. Then, the need to maxi-mize electoral support and the concentration of public preferences at the center induced the three parties to adjust their mainland policy toward the middle ground—shown in Figure 5.7 as leftward moves by both the KMT and NP and upward/rightward moves by the DPP. This convergent pattern cannot be seen clearly without the analytical framework presented here. Based on this analysis, it is likely that vote-maximizing strategies will bring the parties even closer together provided that public preferences continue to clus-ter toward the center on the identity and interest spectra.[19]

The presidential elections present a picture that further attests to this theory of convergence toward the center. Since in the presidential race there was only one constituency, the converging pressure was strongest. For the DPP, the most urgent task was to present its presidential candidate Chen Shui-bian as a realistic and flexible leader who had the ability to manage cross-strait relations. Since Chen had shunned the 1998 China policy debate in which the DPP came up with the compromise formula of "strengthen the base, move westward," he was obliged to present a moderate posture toward the main-land to allay the fears of Taiwanese voters who equated the DPP's victory in the presidential elections to Taiwan's independence and war. Chen also had to profess his loyalty to the ROC in order to present himself as a serious contender in the presidential race. The DPP strategists felt this need for change keenly. As a result, the party passed a "Resolution on the Future of Taiwan" in May 1999 and for the first time grudgingly accepted the legitimacy of the ROC. Before that resolution was passed, the DPP's ostensible goal was to replace the ROC with a Republic of Taiwan, a new and independent nation, as stipulated in the party constitution. The change of tone evinced in the resolution was justified by claiming that Taiwan was already independent and thus there was no need to declare independence a second time.[20] The passing of the resolution was synchronized with the DPP's official nomination of Chen as the party's presidential candidate, which made the resolution's true intent crystal clear: to allay popular fears about the "revolutionary" nature of the DPP and present Chen with a moderate and realistic image.

In July, President Lee announced his "special state-to-state theory," which is almost identical with the DPP's long-held stance. This move by the KMT partially exempted Chen and the DPP from their negative image of being provocative toward the mainland. Now the KMT could no longer claim itself to be a force of stability as tension rapidly built up in the Taiwan Strait and the trust between Taipei and Washington was severely undermined. Enjoying the ideological triumph delivered by the "two-state theory," the DPP was nevertheless worried about deteriorating cross-strait relations and feared its lack of experience in handling crisis would jeopardize people's willingness to vote for Chen. The solution was to promote economic exchanges with the mainland by a proposal to modify the KMT's "patience over haste" policy. This was another major breakthrough. For even at the time of the May Plenum when the Resolution on the Future of Taiwan was passed, the DPP was still a staunch supporter of President Lee's conservative policy on cross-strait economic links. The need to present Chen as a moderate in the presidential campaign soon outweighed the insistence on Taiwan's security. In early November, Chen announced his proposal for direct sea links and a one-way air link, with profit sharing, with the mainland. For the first time, the DPP came up with practical steps to realize its "move westward" policy, and Chen's proposal went far ahead of what the KMT had proposed at the time in facilitating cross-strait exchanges. The DPP's white paper on "China Policy for the Twenty-first Century" of November further confirmed the new relaxed attitude toward communications and exchanges with mainland China.

In Figure 5.8 we find that the 1998 China policy debate in the DPP resulted in a compromise formula of "strengthen the base, move westward," but without any concrete policy to back it up. This is our starting point. The presidential elections and the need to show moderation brought about the 8

Figure 5.8 **Converging Presidential Candidates**

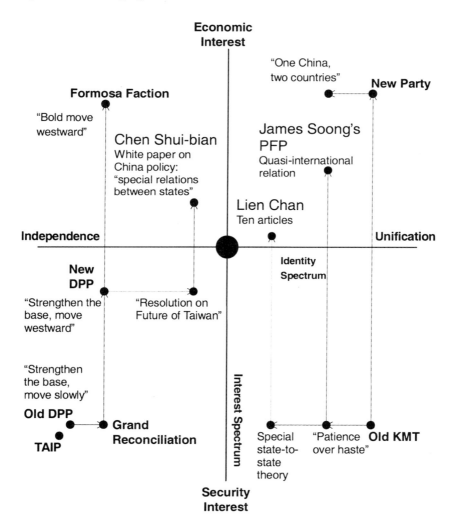

May Resolution on the Future of Taiwan, which moved the DPP's position a big step toward the center of the identity spectrum. The next major step was Chen's proposal for relaxation of the "patience over haste" policy. This is a move upward. Thus, we have Chen Shui-bian's position pinned on the map closer to the origin of the two axes than even the "strengthen the base, move westward" formula. The great impact of the presidential elections on the DPP's China policy is obvious.

The same convergent pattern is apparent with James Soong, the popular governor of Taiwan province. Soong's popularity brought him a solid political base outside the KMT and caused great anxiety in President Lee who had designated Vice-President Lien Chan as his successor. The competition between Lien and Soong would definitely hurt the KMT's chance to win the presidential elections and would benefit Chen Shui-bian. As it turned out, the serious conflict between Soong and Lien (with Lee standing in the background) and Soong's final decision to run on a separate ticket dashed any hope of a united pan-KMT camp against the DPP's onslaught. As an independent candidate, Soong nevertheless enjoyed the leading position in this three-way race until a financial scandal (*xingpiaoan*) broke out. Because Soong was the only mainlander among the three major presidential candidates, he was particularly vulnerable to accusations of betraying Taiwan's interest. As a result, Soong was extremely careful in his critique of the "two-state theory," questioning its decision-making process rather than its content.[21] He also came up with a mild proposal for relaxing regulations governing cross-strait exchanges. Soong's characterization of cross-strait relations was "quasi-international." With this careful maneuvering there was no doubt in Soong's supporters' minds that he occupied a more pro-unification and pro-exchange position than the other two leading candidates. Figure 5.8 pins Soong's position in the upper-right quadrant, closer to the NP's position than Lien or Chen. This accounts for the overwhelming support for Soong among the NP's followers.

Lien Chan's position on cross-strait relations was constrained by the fact that he was the handpicked successor to Lee Teng-hui and had to abide by the "two-state theory." But Lien was surrounded by a group of advisers who did not see eye to eye with Lee. Lien had long been advocating a "win-win" solution to cross-strait conflict. To take advantage of his moderate image in managing cross-strait relations, Lien proposed "ten articles" calling for a return to the guidelines for national unification that had been cast aside in the last years of Lee's reign. According to Lien's ten articles, Taipei would be willing to establish the three links and enter into official political dialogue geared toward unification with Beijing so long as there was goodwill from the mainland—the conditions set forth in the guidelines notwithstanding.[22] This proposal was a far cry from the "patience over haste" policy and shows that Lien's position is up in the upper-right quadrant.

If we examine the three presidential candidates' mainland policy position, we find all of them favoring a version of the "two-state" theory and all of them showing willingness to relax the "patience over haste" policy. The momentum for their convergence toward the center of the identity and interest spectra derived from the presidential elections and the perceived concentration of popular support for the middle-of-the-road policy.[23]

The domestic constraints on Taiwan's politicians work through their rational calculation to maximize votes. Because Taiwan's mainstream public opinion is located in the middle of the identity and interest spectra, presidential candidates rushed to the middle ground to capture votes. This is how domestic politics shapes Taiwan's mainland policy. But since the reason for moving to the middle ground is to win elections, the incentive for the politicians to stay in the same place after the elections must be reduced. One then would expect the original ideological stance of the parties to exercise greater influence on the politicians during the electoral intervals. For elections with multiple-seat constituencies, moreover, the incentive for converging toward the center is greatly reduced, for the candidates may then compete for the fundamentalist votes and diverge in their mainland policy positions. This, however, did not happen in Taiwan after the inauguration of Chen Shui-bian as the tenth president of the ROC on 20 May.

If we take a careful look at President Chen's statements after the elections of 18 March, we find he did his best to tone down the pro-Taiwan independence position he used to hold. Following the moderate line established in the Resolution on the Future of Taiwan and the white paper on the DPP's China policy, Chen declared in his inauguration speech that he would not declare independence, would not change the name of the ROC, would not insert the "two-state theory" in the Constitution, would not hold a referendum on independence, and would not abrogate the guidelines for national unification or abolish the National Unification Council—as long as mainland China does not use force against Taiwan. It is true that these disclaimers actually amount to "conditional independence"—a position held by the DPP before it adopted the Taiwan independence platform in 1991—and the new president is using independence as a deterrent against the PRC's use of force, thus putting Taiwan's independence on the national agenda for the first time. Even so, most people in Taiwan as well as international observers appreciated Chen's effort to stabilize the cross-strait situation and gave him due credit. They did so because there was widespread anxiety over Chen's possible move toward independence after his election. That he did not make such a move created a sense of relaxation that people attributed to Chen's self-constraint.

Chen's moderate line toward mainland China has survived the elections and the inauguration. He even came up with a version of the integration theory that proposes extensive economic exchanges across the Taiwan Strait prior to political integration. To reach a compromise with the KMT-led opposition, Chen endorsed the consensus reached by members of an advisory group headed by Lee Yuan-tseh, president of the Academia Sinica, that calls for responding to the mainland's "one China" principle with reference to the

ROC Constitution.[24] This gesture is meant to assure Beijing and the opposition that Chen has no intention of declaring Taiwan's independence. Finally, Chen directed the Mainland Affairs Council to institute the "three small links" between Kinmen, Matsu, and the mainland and thereby decriminalize the hitherto illegal trade between the two small offshore islands and the Chinese mainland. With all these goodwill gestures, however, Chen and his government are steadfast in refusing to exclude independence as an option for Taiwan's future. Thus, there is no acceptance of Beijing's "one China" principle. Here, we find a deadlock between the two sides of the strait.

Chen's consistently moderate line toward the mainland can be explained in three ways. First, Chen is still bound by the constitutional system and the balance of power in Taiwan's parliament, the Legislative Yuan. In 1997 the ROC formally adopted a semipresidential system in which both the president and parliament hold control over the government (the Executive Yuan). Since the president is a DPP member and the KMT still holds a majority in parliament (the DPP commands a mere third of the seats), the new government finds itself in a least enviable situation. Tang Fei, the defense minister of the outgoing KMT administration, was appointed by President Chen as prime minister without the consent of parliament in May 2000. Chang Chun-hsiung then replaced Tang in October because he had disagreed with President Chen over the fate of the fourth nuclear power plant. Although the president appointed Chang without any consultation with parliament, both Tang and Chang are responsible to a parliament dominated by the KMT majority. This constitutional stalemate—plus the fact that Chen got only 39 percent of the popular vote and beat James Soong by just a slight margin—makes Chen a minority president who cannot claim a mandate from the people to make dramatic constitutional changes toward Taiwan independence. Thus, even though Chen won the presidential elections, he is not in a position to suddenly switch back to his pro-independence stance of preelection days.

Second, Chen's cautious attitude can be explained in terms of the international environment. Here, the triangular considerations make their appearance. Chen is primarily concerned with how Washington views him and whether the United States would come to Taiwan's rescue if the mainland honored its military threat. After his election, his assurances about keeping the status quo were to a large extent meant to satisfy the United States. Washington's pressure on him, however, derives from the concern that any move toward Taiwan independence would put the United States in a truly difficult position: It would have to decide whether to protect a democratic Taiwan and check Beijing's expansion into the Pacific at the expense of an armed conflict with the PRC—a surging global power that has the potential to overtake the United States in two to four decades in terms of Gross Domestic Product (GDP). If the United States wants to keep good relations with the PRC, it has to constrain Chen's proclivity toward Taiwan's independence. This is derivative relation II. However, if the real intent of the United States is to safeguard democracy in East Asia and check the expansion of mainland China, then its real friend is Taiwan and armed hostilities in the Taiwan Strait would involve the United States on Taiwan's side. This also is derivative relation II. Since both derivative relations entail painful consequences of siding with one Chinese state against the other, the best choice for Washington is to prevent deterioration of the cross-strait relation. This means pressuring the new ROC president into endorsing the status quo and constraining his independence proclivity. The frequent visits by ex-officials of the United States and the numerous meetings between President Chen and the director of the American Institute in Taiwan, Raymond F. Burghardt, following Chen's election attest to the grave U.S. concern and the new regime's willingness to cooperate with the United States on cross-strait issues.

The third explanation of Chen's hewing to the moderate line after his inauguration is Taiwan's economic plight. Because of continuous political conflict, protracted stalemate over whether to continue building the fourth nuclear power plant, uncertainty surrounding cross-strait relations, the less-than-smooth landing of the American economy (particularly its high-tech industries to which Taiwan is tightly linked), and the continuous restructuring problems, Taiwan's economy experienced a dramatic downturn and the stock market lost 50 percent of its value. High growth and low inflation had always been the KMT's strongest appeal to the electorate. During the presidential elections, Chen took great pains to persuade people that the DPP had the ability to manage Taiwan's economy. Now with the economy taking a nosedive, Chen is forced to come up with liberal policies toward the mainland—the growth engine in the region. Any mismanagement of cross-strait relations would seriously hurt Taiwan's bruised economy; any step toward removing restrictions on cross-strait economic relations would be hailed by the market. If the DPP wants to expand its share of seats in the 2001 parliamentary elections, it has to boost the economy. Here, Beijing has the veto power, however, and will respond to Taiwan's overtures only if Chen is willing to soften his stance on the "one China" principle. This is the primary reason for Chen to stick to a moderate China policy and for Beijing to continue pouring cold water on Taiwan's overtures.

Power Maximization in the United States: Bouts of Idealism

A unique feature of American foreign policy is its strong idealism. This tradition was most clearly expressed in President Wilson's Fourteen Points and his ideal of the League of Nations. Wilsonian idealism competes tenaciously with realism in the making of American foreign policy.[25] It is rooted in the unique historical development of the American state, which takes high moral ground as its point of departure. This ideal was first nurtured and protected by the seas that separate the new nation from the Old World.[26] The growth of the country into a world superpower in the twentieth century further equipped it with the capacity to act on its ideological beliefs, even at the expense of great material interests, a luxury no other countries in the world can afford.

Nowhere is this dichotomy of idealism versus realism more pronounced than in America's China policy. For here the idealist's repugnance against a dictatorial communist regime clashes with the realist's need to deal effectively with a rising superpower in the East.[27] When idealism is strong, Washington takes a harsh look at Beijing's behavior and formulates its China policy accordingly. Since Taiwan is a kind of antithesis to mainland China—both before and after democratization at the turn of the decade—a critical view of the PRC easily translates into a sympathetic attitude toward Taiwan. But when realism is strong, Washington views the world through the prism of a Henry Kissinger and puts human rights and democratic aspirations on the back burner. With this perspective, the status of the PRC stands out and demands Washington's recognition. The domestic situation in the Chinese mainland is then said to have little to do with proper American policy toward it. Following this logic, Taiwan pales in its strategic and economic importance when compared with mainland China, and Washington's China policy swings to Beijing's side.

If America's position swings between Taipei and Beijing according to the balance between idealism and realism, what determines the relative strength of the two schools of thought? Since the 1980s a rule has been gradually established that synchronizes the balance of power between idealism and realism and America's electoral cycles. When a presidential election approaches, idealism runs high and the incumbent's realist China policy is subjected to criticism by his political opponents in Congress and in the press. In order to meet these criticisms, the incumbent president then takes some action to appease the idealists. If the incumbent wins (or his party's candidate wins), we should expect to see no great change in America's China policy. If he loses, the new president shifts to a hard-line policy toward Beijing and is a bit more friendly toward Taipei than his predecessor was. It does not take long before realism again reigns, however, and the new president changes course to reflect the country's business and security interests. In short: We should expect to see a rise of idealism and a downturn in Washington–Beijing relations when the American presidential election approaches. We should also expect an opposite development toward realism when the election is well over (and the next election is still far away). Elections force politicians to concentrate on domestic preferences, which always stress idealism. When relatively emancipated from electoral pressure, politicians are geared to international politics and realism creeps back.

We can easily substantiate this general observation. When President Carter swung to Beijing and dumped Taipei in 1979, he was vehemently attacked by the Republicans, led by their presidential candidate Ronald Reagan, whose campaign rhetoric included re-recognizing the ROC. After Reagan won the presidential election in 1980 there was high tension between Washington and Beijing, but the new president soon adapted to the international environment and changed course. The communiqué of 17 August 1982 set limits to future U.S. arms sales to Taiwan, and in 1984 President Reagan visited the PRC. The Republicans won the 1984 and 1988 presidential elections, so there was no significant change in Washington's China policy in these years. Even the most dramatic eruption of protests in China in 1989 did not bring about a reorientation of Washington's attitude toward Beijing.[28] In fact, the tenacity with which President Bush stuck to his friendship with Deng Xiaoping and his sending of a secret mission led by National Security Adviser Brent Scowcroft to Beijing to guarantee continuation of bilateral relations right after the crackdown demonstrates great policy consistence.[29] A major change in Washington's China policy occurred only when the next presidential election approached and the challenger Bill Clinton attacked Bush for kowtowing to Beijing's Tiananmen butchers. It was at this moment that Bush approved the sale to Taiwan of 150 F-16 fighters.

Clinton won the 1992 presidential election, and Sino-American friction ensued—just as when Reagan defeated the Democratic incumbent Jimmy Carter in 1980; and, like Reagan, Clinton swiftly adapted to the international environment and began to promote business relations with mainland China. Soon China's most-favored-nation status was delinked from human rights issues in 1994. But as the presidential election of 1996 approached, Clinton made a slight attempt to appease his congressional critics by approving the issuance of a visa to ROC President Lee Teng-hui so that he could accept an award from his alma mater Cornell. That move was made in the context of overwhelming congressional support for allowing President Lee to come in a private capacity. What happened next was totally unexpected from Washington's point of view. The PRC retaliated not only by cutting military ties and suspending many cooperation programs with the United States, it also sent missiles across the Taiwan Strait in a clear attempt to influence the ROC's first direct presidential election. The United States was forced to send in carrier combat groups to the Taiwan Strait, and Washington–Beijing relations sank to an all-time low.

If the presidential election of 1996 provided the background for a slight American tilt toward Taiwan, Clinton's winning the election proved instrumental in his launching a major campaign to reestablish close ties with mainland China.[30] The exchange of state visits by Clinton and Jiang Zemin in 1997 and 1998, the establishment of the "constructive strategic partnership,"[31] and Clinton's utterance of the "new Three Nos" all pointed in the direction of renewed amity between Washington and Beijing.[32] But as the 2000 presidential election drew near, new tensions arose in the United States between the candidates and Clinton's China policy came under severe attack. It was just like a replay of 1995, when euphoria was followed by sudden shocks and U.S.–PRC relations took a nosedive. In 1995 the catalyst was issuance of a visa to Lee. In 1999 it was the theater missile defense (TMD) and NATO's bombing of the PRC embassy in Belgrade that touched off the vicious cycle once again. Anti-American feelings surged in the PRC while the American side complained about China's abuse of human rights, the arrests of dissidents, the stealing of nuclear technologies, the illegal political contributions, the military threat to Taiwan, and other grievances. At the bottom of all these developments is the American electoral cycle. Zhu Rongji's visit to the United States in April 2000 and the huge concessions he offered was a bold countercyclical move, yet it failed to reverse the tide.[33] Taiwan benefited from the deterioration in Washington–Beijing relations as Congress, disregarding Beijing's fury, became more concerned with Taiwan's security.

It is apparent that during the campaign the Republican presidential candidate, George W. Bush, was much more critical of Clinton's "constructive strategic partnership" with Beijing than was his Democratic competitor, Al Gore, who had to defend his predecessor's line. This is a bit like Lien Chan's endorsement of Lee Teng-hui's "two-state theory" in Taiwan's presidential campaign earlier in the same year. After Bush was declared the winner, a major realistic shift of Bush's China policy was imminent. His intellectual mentor on foreign policy, National Security Adviser Condoleezza Rice, is famous for her realistic perspective and an unswerving pursuit of American interest.[34] Nor is idealistic proclivity to be found in Vice-President Dick Cheney or Secretary of State Colin Powell. In fact, in view of the limited idealistic surge in the Gore–Bush duel as well as the strong influence of former President George Bush on his son's China policy, the new president's turn to blatant realism will be made more readily than Clinton's shift in 1993–1994.

In sum, then, one finds that the U.S.–PRC relation goes up and down following the rhythm of American electoral cycles. The same can be said of Washington's relation with Taipei. Behind the fluctuations of these two relations is the waxing and waning of American idealism, which shapes the country's China policy. American politicians, quite like their Taiwan counterparts, are naturally concerned with the domestic implications of their foreign policies and are sensitive to the political pressure periodically brought to bear on them by elections. Their policies in the Washington–Taipei–Beijing triangle cannot be understood without reference to the domestic, power-maximizing calculations of the policymakers in the two countries.

Power Maximization in the PRC: Party Congresses

Political institutionalization in mainland China is comparatively lower than in the United States and Taiwan. Thus, the institutional and electoral constraint on Beijing's communist leadership is less obvious.[35] There is no strict constitutional structure that allocates power and regulates the behavior of political actors. Nor are there meaningful elections on the national level that prompt politicians to heed the mainstream public opinion. This does not mean, however, that the political leaders in the Forbidden City can decide on important issues whichever way they want. Different factions are competing for dominance in the Politburo, and bureaucracies are vying for power. Popular expectations are easy to whip up but hard to quell. In short, policymakers on the Chinese mainland face constraints that are less institutional and less electoral but real nevertheless.

The political system on the Chinese mainland is capable of producing paramount leaders, such as Mao Zedong and Deng Xiaoping, who were only minimally constrained by the institutions. The current CCP general secretary-cum-PRC president Jiang Zemin wields much less power, however, than his two predecessors. This means less discretion for Jiang in deciding on the mainland's Taiwan policy. Since nationalism is rising on the mainland and has become the main legitimating factor for the communist regime,[36] Beijing's basic attitude on the Taiwan issue is one of intransigent irredentism.[37] Under these circumstances, only paramount political leaders with indisputable authority can take a soft-line approach toward Taiwan.[38] Jiang is not in such a position, so his hands are tied. Beijing's last major concession toward Taiwan was Deng Xiaoping's bold initiative of "one country, two systems"— quite a liberal formula for a communist regime just emerging from its Maoist past.[39] This formula has still been the guiding principle for the mainland in handling the Taiwan issue. None of Jiang's proposals made in the 1990s went beyond "one country, two systems." This fact attests to the limits of Jiang's power. In sum, then, we find that the weaker the communist leader's grip on power, the more intransigent he is when dealing with Taiwan.

Jiang's power is periodically challenged. During the Dengist era, the CCP achieved a minimum degree of institutionalization by holding regular party congresses at five-year intervals. It is true that the outcome of the intraparty factional struggle is usually sealed before the party congress is held, and the congress only serves the function of ratifying the result of elite competition that took place beforehand. But with the regularly held party congresses, one can set a rough schedule of power struggles in the high echelons of the CCP. It is reasonable to expect challenges to the incumbent to rise when the party congress is approaching, and the political leader will be in a defensive mood when challenged. This generalization, applied to policymaking on the Taiwan issue, suggests greater maneuverability and possible concessions to Taiwan when the incumbent leader's power is secured between party congresses and great intransigence when the next congress is in the offing.

There is only one test of this general rule. The Fifteenth Party Congress of 1997 in which Jiang consolidated his power was the only congress held without a paramount leader. (Deng died in February of that year.) Jiang's status as successor to Deng was officially ratified at the Fourth Plenum of the Fourteenth Central Committee in 1994, when it was announced that "the transition from the Deng-centered second-generation collective leadership to the Jiang-centered third-generation collective leadership is completed."[40] Reflecting Jiang's newly acquired position, one witnessed his "eight-point proposal" (*Jiang ba dian*) in early 1995. Even though there was no breakthrough in the eight points that went beyond Deng's "one country, two systems," one nevertheless finds great tactical flexibility in this initiative.[41] Very soon Taiwan's Lee Teng-hui responded with his "six articles" (*Li liu tiao*) and there seemed to be an upward swing in cross-strait relations. Lee's Cornell visit obviously undermined the Jiang–Lee relationship, which we now know had been forged through secret meetings between the two sides.[42] Obviously Jiang did not prepare to respond to Lee's visit in the violent ways witnessed in July–August 1995 and March 1996 when he was first informed of Lee's decision to accept the invitation from his alma mater. The mainland's chief negotiator, Tang Shubei, came to Taipei in May to arrange for another Koo–Wang talk right in the aftermath of the announcement of Lee's visit. There was an abrupt turn of Beijing's response, however, and verbal attacks were soon accompanied by saber rattling. Missiles were launched near Taiwan right off the island's major ports. Clearly Jiang could not withstand the PLA's pressure to play tough.[43] The approaching Fifteenth Party Congress provided the hard-liners in the CCP a perfect occasion for pressuring Jiang into toeing their line.

After the smooth handover of Hong Kong and the successful Fifteenth Party Congress, Jiang secured a safe position and the CCP began sending signals to Taiwan for resuming cross-strait communications, which had been cut at the height of the 1995–1996 tensions. This step ultimately led to the Straits Exchange Foundation's delegation to the mainland in February 1988 and Koo's mainland visit in October. Certainly Beijing's change of attitude had a lot to do with China's confidence that the United States had shifted to their side with the exchange of state visits by President Clinton and Jiang Zemin in 1997 and 1998.[44] Yet the fact remains that Beijing's friendly overtures toward Taipei were aired right after Jiang Zemin had consolidated his power in a party congress. The power position of the communist leader and Beijing's Taiwan policy are obviously linked.

Power Maximization and Triangular Stability

Domestic factors play an extremely important role in shaping the policies of the United States, Taiwan, and mainland China toward each other. As we have seen, elections drive Taiwan's politicians to the middle ground in their mainland policies. Elections in the United States, by contrast, bring about surges of idealism and support for Taiwan, but realism and respect for Beijing's power between elections. In mainland China, party congresses set the stage for intraparty competition and reduce the maneuverability of the ruling elite in dealing with Taiwan. By integrating these three sets of domestic factors, we find that the best combination for the security of Taiwan is when both the United States and Taiwan are in electoral periods and mainland China is between party congresses. This was exactly the situation in 2000.

Domestic factors tell us there will be no serious crisis in the Taiwan Strait during and after Taiwan's presidential elections. This is the case because all of Taiwan's presidential candidates will show moderation and refrain from provoking Beijing in order to court the middle votes. In the United States, the fierce competition between Democrats and Republicans in the presidential campaign raises idealism to a height and stiffens the major candidates' policies toward Beijing. If the mainland again exercises its military muscle as in 1995–1996, without Taiwan's provocation, there is no doubt that the United States will respond in a decisive manner—an attitude fully reflected in Washington's response to Beijing's second white paper on the Taiwan issue announced in February 2000. This is the time when the United States was most sympathetic toward Taiwan; and because Washington and Taipei are closer to one another than they are to Beijing, the PRC has been showing considerable restraint since the proclamation of Lee Teng-hui's "two-state theory." Jiang Zemin can afford such a "moderate" attitude because his power is not being seriously challenged. As Taiwan's presidential campaign intensified in early 2000, the CCP's Sixteenth Party Congress was still twenty months away and a serious power struggle was only about to start. Jiang was relatively immune from the pressure of the hard-liners in the CCP—at least not beholden to them for their support in his power struggle with the challengers (Figure 5.9). Originally Taiwan's presidential elections of 18 March

2000 and Chen Shui-bian's inauguration on 20 May aroused a lot of concern, for it was feared that Chen might take provocative actions and prompt Beijing to resort to military means. An analysis of the configuration of domestic factors at the time, however, clearly shows that there is no crisis surrounding Taiwan's power transfer, for all three parties are interested in maintaining the status quo.

This pro–status quo configuration of domestic factors will not last long. As Figure 5.9 shows, all three actors may shift to the other end of the policy spectrum when their domestic political situation changes. In Taiwan, the Legislative Yuan elections scheduled for December 2001 would in all likelihood add to the DPP's seats in parliament and give a boost to the pro-Taiwan independence force. Because of the electoral system, the parliamentary election may not converge the candidates' mainland policies but may in fact diverge them, strengthening the pro-independence position. President Chen might also tilt in that direction. The current Chen–Chang system is in an extremely precarious situation and faces an overwhelming challenge from the KMT, which maintains a majority in the Legislative Yuan.[45] This situation will not last long. The DPP will gradually consolidate its grip on power, and Chen has been casting his eyes on the 2004 presidential elections— which he has a fairly good chance of winning. In short, Taiwan's pro-independence force is on the rise and will surge when the electoral constraints are weak. In the meantime, the U.S. presidential campaign has ended and the new president has been inaugurated. According to the pattern established in the past, the new president will soon become a realist, shedding his idealist rhetoric and shifting Washington's position toward Beijing. In mainland China, the CCP will find itself in an increasingly vehement power struggle and Jiang will have to adopt a harsh policy toward Taiwan as the Sixteenth Party Congress scheduled for 2002 approaches rapidly. The hard-liners in the party will attack his "softness" on the issue and blame him for the ineffectiveness of his previous friendly gestures sent across the strait. In short, beginning in mid-2001, the pro–status quo configuration of domestic factors in the triangle will begin to dissolve. Taiwan may become more provocative. The United States may lose its vigilance. And the PRC may turn hawkish. Although this forthcoming configuration is crisis-prone, it is as yet little detected and hence ill guarded against.

The Meaning of Chen's Election

As we have seen, the interactions in the security arena among Washington, Taipei, and Beijing form a strategic triangle and, moreover, a Ménage à trois is desirable from the perspectives of role elevation, derivative relation, and

Figure 5.9 **Domestic Factors and Strategic Triangle**

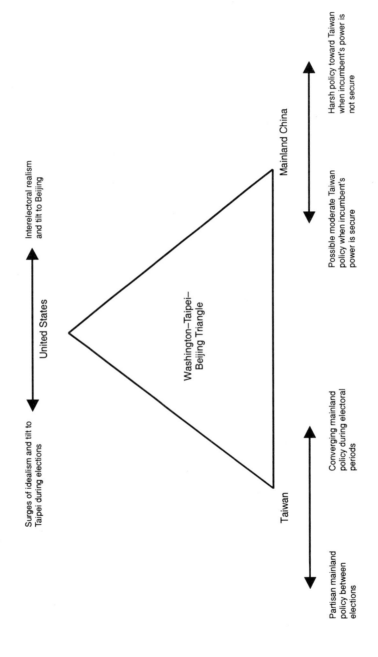

aggregate payoff. The United States is an unintending pivot between the two wings of mainland China and Taiwan, and American strategic thinking has developed toward stabilizing cross-strait relations and transforming the current romantic triangle to a Ménage à trois. But we also witness how domestic political constraints shape the behavior of the three triangular players. These constraints may be strong or weak depending on the mechanisms through which they are exercised. Presidential elections in the United States and in Taiwan bring pressure on the incumbents as well as on their challengers to conform to the mainstream public opinion. The CCP party congresses on the Chinese mainland act as a kind of functional equivalent to democratic elections in sensitizing the incumbent communist leaders to the Chinese nationalist feeling their rivals in the party can easily whip up against them. Elite power maximization is behind these phenomena. In this way, the power-maximization approach gives us a less sanguine perspective than the strategic triangle model. Certain configurations of domestic factors may lead to stability. Others are crisis-prone. From the power-maximizing, domestic perspective, there is no inherent tendency toward greater stability.

Strategic triangle and domestic power maximizing refer to two sets of factors (Group C and Group B) that compete for dominance in determining the security policies of Washington, Taipei, and Beijing toward one another. The primacy of the domestic game for political leaders suggests that when domestic constraints are strong (as during electoral periods), strategic thinking in triangular terms is neglected. Once the political leaders are relatively immune from domestic constraints (either popular or factional), they are free to think in triangular terms. In this way, domestic power maximizing and the strategic triangle take turns in determining the primary mode of thinking of the ruling elites in the three countries. As elections (or party congresses) approach, domestic constraints are strengthened and the country's security policy is comprehensible only through the prism of domestic political competition. When elections are over and the elites are less constrained in shaping foreign policy, either the ideological stance of the incumbents is stressed or strategic thinking along the triangular line is given primacy. Since elections and junctures of political competition in the three countries are not synchronized, however, it is always possible that when one player is deep in a domestic game, the others may be thinking in triangular terms. Although this brings further complexity to interactions among the three, complexity should not deter us from theorizing on cross-strait relations and the trilateral interactions among Washington, Taipei, and Beijing.

Now we can answer the question raised in the title of this chapter: "Does Chen's election make any difference?" If the major actors' behavior is constrained by domestic and international factors, it follows that a change of leadership alone would not bring about any change of the structure: The constraints remain in place; the actors behave in predictable ways. This is indeed what we saw in Chen's policies toward mainland China after his inauguration. A high degree of continuity is witnessed in Taiwan's mainland policy, Chen's pro-independence proclivity notwithstanding. In this way, the election of a DPP president does not lead Taiwan toward independence. It can even be argued that Chen's attitude toward Beijing is softer than that of his KMT predecessor, Lee Teng-hui. But if Chen has been tamed by domestic and international factors, a change in these factors would lead him toward a different route. If this happens, the structure is again at work, not Chen's personal ideological preferences. Chen's election really does not make a great difference. On the contrary, it shows the strength of the structure composed of domestic and international factors and their grip on realistic politicians.

Notes

1. See Lowell Dittmer, "The Strategic Triangle: A Critical Review," in *The Strategic Triangle: China, the United States, and the Soviet Union*, ed. Ilpyong J. Kim (New York: Paragon House, 1987).

2. Yu-Shan Wu, "Exploring Dual Triangles: The Development of Taipei–Washington–Beijing Relations," *Issues and Studies* 32(10) (October 1996):26–52.

3. Lowell Dittmer, "The Strategic Triangle: An Elementary Game—Theoretical Analysis," *World Politics* 33(4) (July 1981):485–516.

4. See Chi-cheng Lo, "Meiguo zai taihai liang'an hudong suo banyan de jiaose—jiegou pingheng zhe" [The role played by the United States in cross-strait relations: Structural balancer], *America Monthly* 1(10) (January 1995):39.

5. See Wu Yu-Shan, *Kangheng huo hucong: liang'an guanxi xinquan* [Balancing or bandwagoning: A new interpretation of the cross-strait relation] (Taipei: Chengchung, 1997), p. 183.

6. Bau Tzong-Ho, "Zhanlue sanjiao jiaose zhuanbian yu leixing bianhua fenxi—yi meiguo han taihai liang'an sanjiao hudong weili" [An analysis of role transition and type change in a strategic triangle: The case of triangular interaction between the U.S. and the two sides of the Taiwan Strait], in *Zhengbian zhong de liang'an guanxi lilun* [Contending theories in the study of cross-strait relations], ed. Bau Tzong-Ho and Wu Yu-Shan (Taipei: Wu-nan, 1999), p. 346.

7. Bau Tzong-Ho, "Zhanlue sanjiao jiaose zhuanbian yu leixing bianhua fenxi," pp. 347–356.

8. Yu-Shan Wu, "The Unintending Pivot: The U.S. in the Washington–Taipei–Beijing Triangle" (paper presented at the Twenty-eighth Sino-American Conference on Contemporary China, Duke University, 12–14 June 1999).

9. This is the true meaning of the "interim agreement" proposal.

10. Concerning the notion of a two-level game, see Peter Evans, Harold Jacobson, and Robert Putman, eds., *Double-Edged Diplomacy: International Bargaining and Domestic Politics* (Berkeley: University of California Press, 1993). The book tells how international bargaining that reflects domestic political agendas can be undone when it ignores the influence of domestic constituencies and explains how politics

between nations affects politics within nations and vice versa. See also Robert Keohane and Helen Milner, eds., *Internationalization and Domestic Politics* (Cambridge: Cambridge University Press, 1996), for empirical studies. For an application to the cross-strait relation, see Chia-lung Lin, "Lee Teng-hui and Cross-Strait Relations: A Two-Level Game Perspective" (paper delivered at the Twenty-ninth Sino-American Conference on Contemporary China, Taipei, 28–30 May 2000).

11. There are those who emphasize the compatibility of the two games or the instrumentality of one game for the other.

12. For a similar observation, see Li Yi, "Taiwan de liang'an zhengce 'sandang quyi'" [Taiwan's cross-strait policy: Three parties converging], *Jiushi Niandai* [The nineties] 339 (April 1998):35–36.

13. Besides the three main parties, the Taiwan Independence Party (TAIP) that was formed in October 1996 is still too small and wields too little influence to be counted as a significant political force. Among the big three, the NP split from the KMT in 1993 and has been competing with it for electoral support. The DPP is the other camp, subject to attrition by the TAIP, though not to the same degree that the NP encroaches on the KMT's electoral base.

14. See John Fuh-Sheng Hsieh, "Chiefs, Staffers, Indians, and Others: How Was Taiwan's Mainland Policy Made?" in *Inherited Rivalry: Conflict Across the Taiwan Straits*, ed. Tun-jen Chen, Chi Huang, and Samuel S.G. Wu (Boulder: Lynne Rienner, 1995).

15. To emphasize their pro-independence position, the DPP (as well as the TAIP) uses the term "China policy" rather than "mainland policy."

16. For a discussion on the momentum that drives the move to the middle point when there is standard distribution of preferences, see Anthony Downs, *An Economic Theory of Democracy* (New York: Harper & Row, 1957). For an application of Downs's theory to cross-strait relations, see Ming Chu-cheng, "Xiangxin jingzheng yu Zhonghuaminguo zhengdang zhengzhi zhi fazhan" [Centripetal competition and the development of party politics in the Republic of China], *Theory and Policy* 12(2) (May 1998):142–156. See also Kao Yung-kuang, "Zhengdang jingzheng yu zhengdang lianhe—yiti quxiang de fenxi" [Party competition and party alliance—Issue-oriented analysis], *Theory and Policy* 12(2) (May 1998):157–173.

17. To pacify non-mainstream opposition, Lee proposed appointing four vice-chairmen at the KMT's Fourteenth Party Congress in 1993. He nominated Li Yuan-zu, Hau Pei-tsun, Lin Yang-kang, and Lien Chan.

18. Lin Yang-kang, "A Bright Future for Cross-Strait Relations Is Not Far Away," *China Times*, 28 February 1998, p. 11.

19. See Yu-Shan Wu, "Taiwanese Elections and Cross-Strait Relations—Mainland Policy in Flux," *Asian Survey* 39(4) (July–August 1999):565–587.

20. For the content of the resolution, see www.dpp.org.tw/e/n-990508-2.htm.

21. In July 1999, Soong was interviewed by the *Washington Post* and expressed his support of the "three links" and political dialogue with mainland China. Soong also opposed Taiwan's "money diplomacy" and its bid for joining the United Nations. Furthermore, he questioned the necessity and desirability of deploying the theater missile defense (TMD). Soong's remarks soon became Lien and Chen's proofs that the former governor of Taiwan was betraying the interest of the Taiwan people. See *Washington Post*, 3 July 1999, p. A15.

22. The conditions are "peaceful solution of conflict" and "mutual respect in the international arena."

23. Chen Shui-bian loudly proclaimed that he was treading a "middle-of-the-road

line" when he visited Britain—obviously mimicking Tony Blair and Bill Clinton, the two international leaders who led their respective parties to power by toning down the leftist ideology and making the Labor Party and the Democratic Party acceptable to the majority of voters in the middle of the right-left ideological spectrum in Britain and the United States.

24. *United Daily*, 27 November 2000, p. 1.

25. On the dichotomy of idealism versus realism in the study of international relations, see E.H. Carr, *The Twenty Years' Crisis: 1919–1939* (New York: Harper & Row, 1946); for a recent debate on this issue, see David A. Baldwin, ed., *Neorealism and Neoliberalism* (New York: Columbia University Press, 1993).

26. Henry Kissinger, *Diplomacy* (New York: Simon & Schuster, 1994), chap. 1.

27. For the rise of China in the international arena, see Yan Xuetong et al., *Zhongguo jueqi: guoji huanjing pinggu* [The rise of China: An evaluation of the international environment] (Tianjin: Tianjin renminchubanshe, 1997).

28. On President Bush's China policy, see Strobe Talbott, "Post-Victory Blues," *Foreign Affairs* 71(1) (1991–1992):69.

29. See Alan Tonelson, "Prudence or Inertia? The Bush Administration's Foreign Policy," *Current History* 90(558) (1991):311–316.

30. For arguments favoring such a reorientation, see Ezra F. Vogel, ed., *Living with China* (New York: Norton, 1997).

31. For Beijing's perception of these developments, see Su Ge, "Shijimo guoji xingshi zhanwang: guoji geju yu meiguo guojia anquan zhanlue" [Prospects of the international situation toward the end of the century: International structure and national security strategy of the U.S.], *China Review* 14 (February 1999):8–10.

32. For the implications for Taiwan see Xiong Jie, "Ershiyi shiji zhongguo tongyi qianjing yuce" [Predictions on the prospects of Chinese unification in the twenty-first century], *China Review* 14 (February 1999):60–64.

33. Zhu knew he would meet with difficulties in his visit to the United States, that he would be an unwelcome visitor, but he still was willing to make the trip to enhance mutual understanding. See "An Interview with China's Zhu Rongji," *Wall Street Journal*, 6 April 1999, p. A23.

34. Condoleezza Rice once wrote that "American foreign policy in a Republican administration should refocus the United States on the national interest. . . . There is nothing wrong with doing something that benefits all humanity, but that is, in a sense, a second-order effect." See CNN Allpolitics, "Exceeding Expectations, Rice Returns to White House in Top Job," http://www.cnn.com/2000/ALLPOLITICS/stories/12/17/rice.profile.ap/index.html, accessed 31 December 2000. An expert on the Soviet Union, Rice was plucked from academia in 1989 by Brent Scowcroft to serve on the National Security Council of former President Bush, where she helped shape U.S. policy during the tumultuous time of the Soviet Union's collapse.

35. See Lowell Dittmer and Yu-Shan Wu, "The Modernization of Factionalism in Chinese Politics," *World Politics* 47(4) (July 1995):467–494.

36. Qi Mo, "Minzuzhuyi: Zhonggong de tidaixing yishixingtai" [Nationalism: The CCP's substituting ideology], in *Minzuzhuyi yu zhongguo qiantu* [Nationalism and the future of China], ed. Wang Pengling (Taipei: Shih-ying, 1996), p. 170.

37. Wu Hsin-hsing, "Cong Taiwan de guandian kan Zhongguo dalu de minzuzhuyi sichao" [The nationalist thinking in mainland China: A Taiwan perspective], in *Minzuzhuyi yu zhongguo qiantu* [Nationalism and the future of China], ed. Wang Pengling (Taipei: Shih-ying, 1996), p. 219.

38. Parris Chang, "Beijing's Policy Toward Taiwan: An Elite Conflict Model," in *Inherited Rivalry: Conflict Across the Taiwan Straits*, ed. Tun-jen Cheng, Chi Huang, and Samuel S.G. Wu (Boulder: Lynne Rienner, 1995).

39. On 30 January 1979, Deng Xiaoping said during his trip to the United States that the phrase "emancipation of Taiwan" should be dropped. On 11 January 1982, Deng first mentioned the "one country, two systems" formula as a solution of the Taiwan issue. See Pu Xingzu et al., *Zhonghua renmin gongheguo zhengzhi zhidu* [The political system of the People's Republic of China] (Hong Kong: Sanlian, 1995), p. 455; Li Jiaquan, *Yiguoliangzhi yu Taiwan qiantu* ["One country, two systems" and the future of Taiwan] (Beijing: Renminribao chubanshe, 1991), p. 3.

40. See Gao Xin, *Jiang Zemin de quanli zhi lu* [Jiang Zemin's road to power] (Hong Kong: Mingjing chubanshe, 1997), pp. 212–229.

41. In the Chinese New Year of 1995, Jiang announced his famous "eight points" offering negotiation with Taiwan on ending cross-strait hostility, stressing that "Chinese would not attack Chinese," extolling Chinese culture as a common heritage for both mainland China and Taiwan, respecting the Taiwanese way of life and their desire to control their own fate, and suggesting an exchange of visits by himself and Taiwan's leader. These are flexible measures embedded in Deng's "one country, two systems" formula. See Jiang Zemin, "Wei cujin tongyi dayie de wancheng er jixu fendou" [To continue striving for the enterprise of national unification], in *Jiang Zemin, Li Peng tan Taiwan wenti, 1990–1996* [Jiang Zemin and Li Peng discussing the Taiwan issue, 1990–1996], ed. Taiwan Affairs Office of the State Council (Beijing: Huayi chubanshe, 1997), pp. 1–7.

42. It was revealed in late July 2000, that Lee Teng-hui had sent his secret envoys Su Zhicheng and Zheng Shumin to meet with their mainland counterparts Wang Daohan, Jia Yibin, Yang Side, and others in Hong Kong through the mediation of Nan Huaijin, a Zen master and Confucian scholar, for at least nine times from 1988 to 1992. Su and Zheng went for further missions in the mainland thereafter. A secret hot line was opened between the envoys of the two sides until the secret channel was exposed by Taiwan's media. See *China Times*, 19 July 2000, p. 3; see also Wei Chengsi, "Lee Teng-hui shidai liang'an jiudu mitan shilu" [Documenting the nine secret meetings between the two sides of the strait during Lee Teng-hui's period], *Shangyie zhoukan* [Business weekly] 661 (24 July 2000):60–82.

43. The conservatives in the CCP, led by Li Peng, and the PLA generals led by Zhang Aiping reportedly made vigorous protests against Jiang's "soft line" toward Taiwan in the aftermath of Lee's visit. Under tremendous pressure, Jiang was forced to take strong measures. See Lin Gang, "Zhonggong neibu zhengjing qingshi yu duitai zhengce zhi guanxi" [The relation between the internal situation in the CCP and its Taiwan policy], in *Shuangying? Shuangshu?* [Win-win? Lose-lose?], ed. Ming Chucheng (Taipei: Chinese Association for Eurasian Studies, 1996), p. 79.

44. For an interpretation following this line, see Yun-han Chu, "Making Sense of Beijing's Policy Toward Taiwan: The Prospect of Cross-Strait Relations During the Jiang Zemin Era," in *China: Under Jiang Zemin*, ed. Hung-mao Tien and Yun-han Chu (Boulder: Lynne Rienner, 2000).

45. See Yu-Shan Wu, "Semi-Presidentialism Under Incongruence: Taiwan in Comparison" (paper presented at the Eighteenth World Congress of the International Political Science Association, Quebec, 1–5 August 2000).

6

Beijing and Taipei: Between a Rock and a Hard Place

Qingguo Jia

Shortly after the presidential election in Taiwan, Chen Shui-bian, the winner, claimed that under his leadership relations between Taiwan and the Chinese mainland may experience *"liu'an huaming you yicun"*—that is, a dramatic turn for the better. More than a year has passed, however, and the miracle has not happened.

Contrary to Chen's claims, the relationship across the Taiwan Strait has been stuck between a rock and a hard place. Adopting a carrot-and-stick approach, Beijing has been urging Chen to embrace the "one China" principle as the basis for resuming cross-strait dialogue. In fact, it has offered to negotiate unification with Taipei on an equal footing should the latter accept the "one China" principle. Simultaneously the People's Republic of China (PRC) has sought to isolate Chen and actively prepare for a military showdown should Taipei drag its feet indefinitely or make significant further moves toward independence. Taipei has stubbornly refused Beijing's demand. While trying to avoid making fresh provocations on the question of independence, it has left Taiwan's status open for future determination. As the two sides adhere to their respective stance, cross-strait relations have remained tense. In the short to medium term, as we shall see, the chance for reconciliation between the two sides appears remote.

What are the implications of Chen Shui-bian's election for Taiwan's mainland policy? How has it contributed to the development of Beijing's Taiwan policy? In what ways has it affected the political and security relations across the Taiwan Strait? Are the two sides heading for a military confrontation? Or will they find a solution to manage the ongoing crisis in the strait? This chapter addresses these questions. After analyzing the election result, especially as viewed in Beijing, we will look at the ways the election is likely to affect Taipei's mainland policy and Beijing's Taiwan policy. Finally, we will examine the implications of the election on cross-strait relations and explore the prospect of the relationship's development in the months and years to come.

Analyzing the Election's Outcome

The 2000 presidential election in Taiwan is undoubtedly an important historical event. For the first time since Chiang Kai-shek fled to Taiwan in 1949, the people in Taiwan elected an opposition party leader to be their president. For the first time in Chinese history, political power was peacefully transferred from the ruling party to the opposition. Taiwan's democratization process has now entered a new stage in which democratic institutions are strong enough to give the people—rather than powerful figures in the ruling party— the final say about who should lead them in their search for a better life.

Despite its historical significance, however, the election's outcome was by and large an accident. Under normal circumstances, Chen Shui-bian would not really have had a chance to get elected. By the time of the election, political democratization had given the Taiwanese people sufficient power to decide who should serve as their leader. Increasing economic and culture contacts across the Taiwan Strait had increased their stake in a stable relationship with the Chinese mainland. And Beijing's increasing military power and its refusal to abandon the right to use force against Taiwan separatism had made Taiwan's independence a highly risky and irrational policy option. Under these circumstances, then, most people in Taiwan regarded an active pro-independence candidate a serious political liability. Accordingly, whoever wanted to get elected had to forget about advocating independence—and whoever wanted to advocate Taiwan's independence had to forget about getting elected.[1] It was against this background, years before the election, that some in Chen Shui-bian's party, the Democratic Progressive Party (DPP), recognized the political dilemma and tried to change their party's constitution to delete Taiwan's independence as a goal of the party.[2] In light of all this, Chen's chances of being elected were indeed very small.

In the end, neither the DPP nor Chen had openly abandoned the cause of independence. Yet Chen did get elected. How can we explain this? Careful analysis of the situation reveals that this unexpected turn of events is the result of a series of unusual developments in Taiwan. To begin with, during his twelve-year chairmanship of the Kuomintang (KMT), one after another, Lee Teng-hui drove the best and brightest people out of the KMT or from key positions within the party, leaving behind mundane and less charismatic figures like Lien Chan and Hsiao Wan-chang in top leadership positions. Among the people he managed to push aside were Jaw Shao-kong, Wang

Chien-hsuan, Ma Ying-jeou, Wu Po-hsiong, and James Soong. Since Lien Chan, Lee's chosen candidate for the election, had little popular appeal, he lagged far behind other candidates from the very beginning of the presidential campaign. Despite the immense political and financial resources the KMT could mobilize and despite the strenuous efforts he had made during the campaign, Lien's chances were much less significant than many believed at the time.

Moreover, in his pursuit of Taiwan's independence, Lee Teng-hui had successively created two major splits within the KMT and crippled the party in the election. After he consolidated power in the early 1990s, Lee Teng-hui began to push for a pro-Taiwan independence line within the KMT. Lee's efforts frustrated and angered quite a few party members who believed in ultimate reunification with the mainland. In protest, people like Jaw Shao-kong and Wang Chien-hsuan decided to withdraw from the KMT and set up their own political party: the New Party.

Perhaps out of jealousy of James Soong's popularity or fear of it (or both), Lee Teng-hui then made concerted efforts to wrest power from Soong. Among other things, he collaborated with the DPP in an attempt to abolish Taiwan's provincial government of which Soong was the popularly elected governor. Although Lee did not quite succeed in getting rid of the provincial government, he did manage to freeze it—leaving Soong with little real power, a most embarrassing position. Next, although Soong was the most popular political leader in the KMT, Lee blocked his nomination as the party's presidential candidate. Consequently, Soong found himself with no alternative but to run independently and later set up his own party, the People First Party. The two political splits of the KMT that Lee Teng-hui engineered not only weakened the party, but seriously diluted its votes presenting Chen Shui-bian with a golden opportunity. If Lee had not blocked James Soong's candidacy in the KMT, Chen would have had little chance to win the election.

Further, unlike most leaders of political parties, Lee Teng-hui showed little interest in helping his own party's candidate, Lien Chan, to succeed. In retrospect it appears that he selected Lien in part because he wanted to block James Soong from running for president and in part because he did not want the KMT to win the election. During the election, he spoke little in favor of Lien Chan in public—indeed he openly praised Chen Shui-bian, the DPP candidate—and refrained from campaigning for Lien until the very last moment. Lee's abnormal political behavior amounted to nothing less than political betrayal of his own party, the KMT, and its candidate. Certainly it reduced Lien's chance to get elected. Ultimately, it was also to cost Lee his chairmanship of the KMT. In the wake of the election, angry KMT members forced Lee to step down as chairman of the party.

Finally, in his attempt to win office Chen Shui-bian issued a seven-point statement announcing that, if he got elected, he would not declare independence, nor initiate a plebiscite on Taiwan's future, nor revise the Taiwan constitution to incorporate Lee Teng-hui's special "state-to-state" doctrine. Instead, he would seek reconciliation and accommodation with the Chinese mainland.[3] Although Chen had not quite accepted the "one China" principle, his statement helped alleviate fears of the potential risk of his election and indeed might have won him the critical votes he so desperately needed.

Chen Shui-bian's election was not only a historical accident. It also gave him a very limited mandate. Despite the unusual and enormous help he got from Lee Teng-hui before and during the election campaign and despite his own vigorous campaign efforts, Chen was voted into office by an extremely narrow margin. He only managed to get 39.3 percent of the votes—far below the 50 percent mark. Some 61 percent of the people, in other words, did not vote for him. In some countries, he would have had to go through a second round of election in order to claim the office. His competitor, James Soong, got 36.84 percent of the votes, only two and a half percentage points less than Chen.[4] Moreover, the KMT still constitutes the majority in the Legislative Yuan. With a limited mandate and the DPP as the minority party in parliament, Chen has to be very cautious in pushing for major policy changes in order to avoid a political backlash.

Furthermore, the election was by no means a referendum on Taiwan's independence. It is true that both Chen Shui-bian and his own party, the DPP, did not abandon independence as their objective during the election. But it is also true that Chen tried very hard to downplay independence as an issue during the election. In his final and desperate drive to get votes, Chen made great efforts to assure voters he would not do anything to provoke the mainland on the question of independence and promised he would promote dialogue across the Taiwan Strait. Clearly he recognized that if he continued to push for independence he would have lost the election.

Moreover, international reaction to the election has been a mixture of strong support and grave concern. On the one hand, countries (especially in the West) were glad to see the election in Taiwan go so smoothly. They regard this as another major breakthrough in their efforts to spread democracy worldwide. They particularly feel relieved that the power transition took place without much problem even though Chen barely won. Prior to the election, some people worried that the losing candidates would not accept the result of the election if it turned out to be a close call. On the other hand, many in the international community are concerned about the implications of the election on relations across the Taiwan Strait. They worry that Chen Shui-bian might provoke the Chinese mainland on the question of independence and cause a military crisis that would damage regional peace and stability in East Asia. Accordingly, they have tried to influence Chen to take a rational course. Although Chen's moderate and seemingly conciliatory inaugural speech calmed their fear somewhat, continuing tension in the Taiwan Strait has left them concerned. Accordingly, they have been trying to exercise pressure on both Taipei and Beijing to be cautious in dealing with one another.[5]

Finally, not only did the election catch many observers by surprise, but it even caught Chen Shui-bian unprepared. Given that the KMT had so many resources, James Soong was so popular, and the DPP still held onto Taiwan's independence as its ultimate objective, Chen's chances of being elected were not at all obvious until the very last moment. Only after the election did Chen begin to think seriously about forming a government. To make up for his limited mandate, Chen tried to draw people from both the DPP and other political parties in setting up his government. For instance, he invited Tang Fei, a senior general affiliated with the KMT, to serve as his premier. Tang Fei's subsequent resignation and the political problems Chen is facing today can be regarded as a logical consequence of his lack of preparation and inexperience in government.

In sum, then, while the election is of historical significance, it is also a historical accident. Despite his electoral victory, Chen's popular mandate is very limited. And he has neither internal nor international support for pushing for independence.

Implications for Taiwan's Mainland Policy

On the surface, Taiwan's presidential election was likely to bring about a dramatic shift in Taipei's mainland policy. To begin with, it put an end to the KMT's long-term rule over Taiwan following its flight there in 1949. For the first forty years, the KMT actively pursued a "one China" policy under Chiang Kai-shek and his son Chiang Ching-kuo. After Lee Teng-hui came to office in 1988, he gradually undermined this policy through subtle and repeated redefinition. By the time of the election, however, Lee still had not had sufficient time to change the KMT's "one China" policy altogether. As a political party, the KMT was still formally committed to China's reunification. Given the political atmosphere in Taiwan, the departure of the KMT meant at least uncertainty for the fate of the "one China" principle.

Moreover, the election made the DPP, a pro-independence party, the ruling party. Although in its efforts to seek power the DPP has moderated its tone on the question of independence over the years, it is still by and large a party of independence. Its party constitution still makes Taiwan's independence one of its main objectives, and many of its leaders still openly advocate such a policy. When in opposition, the DPP repeatedly condemned the KMT for adhering to the "one China" policy against the alleged interests of the Taiwanese people. Now, as the ruling party, it finally has an opportunity to realize its ambitions.

The newly elected leaders of Taiwan have a pro-independence track record. Chen Shui-bian had been an outspoken advocate of Taiwan's independence until quite recently. Only on the eve of the election did he soften his tone on the question of independence, and even then he still claimed that Taiwan was already an independent sovereign state. Thus, one has good reason to suspect that his moderation on the question of independence was no more than a tactic rather than a shift of policy. Certainly his running mate, Annette Lu, is a reckless champion of Taiwan's independence who is willing to fight a war with the mainland over independence. And Tsai Ying-wen, the newly appointed chair of the Mainland Affairs Council, is believed to be one of the people responsible for drafting the policy proposal on the basis of which Lee Teng-hui made his highly controversial remark to the effect that the cross-strait relationship is one between states.

A closer look, however, does not warrant such a conclusion. To begin with, Beijing has become deeply frustrated with Taipei's mainland policy and it is highly dangerous for Chen Shui-bian to take further steps to push for Taiwan's independence. After twelve years of deft political manipulation by Lee Teng-hui—especially after his depiction of the cross-strait relationship as one of "state to state" in July 1999—Taipei's mainland policy has already moved to a position between de facto and de jure independence. Confronted with this situation, Beijing has repeatedly warned Taiwan not to make further moves toward independence. On 21 February 2000, Beijing published a white paper on its Taiwan policy. This document states that while Beijing still adheres to the policy of peaceful reunification, it would rather fight a war than tolerate Taiwan's independence.[6] In his talk at the conference of the directors of the Office of Taiwan Affairs in March 2000, Qian Qichen, China's vice-premier in charge of Beijing's Taiwan policy, declared that the Chinese government would never compromise on the "one China" principle.[7] In the wake of Chen Shui-bian's inaugural speech, the mainland's Office of Taiwan Affairs issued a statement to the effect that the Chinese government would not tolerate Taiwan independence activities.[8] In the meantime, Beijing actively made military preparations for a possible showdown in the Taiwan Strait.[9] Hence, there is little room for Chen Shui-bian to maneuver on the question of independence without provoking military confrontation across the strait.

In the second place, balancing the pros and cons of Taiwan's independence, the international community has opted to oppose it. Most countries in the world including the United States have publicly endorsed the "one China" principle. Only a handful of states, for economic reasons, still maintain diplomatic relations with Taipei. As Taiwan's only international supporter able and willing to fight a war with the Chinese mainland in defense of Taiwan, the United States does not think it is in its national interest to let the Taiwan independence activists drag the United States into a war with China. For if war breaks out in the Taiwan Strait, the United States would be confronted with two equally unpalatable choices. One alternative is to intervene and risk a war with China, a state with strategic nuclear weapons. Because of the unacceptable consequences of nuclear war, no two states with nuclear weapons have ever fought one another. Even if a Sino-American military confrontation did not lead to nuclear war, it would destroy the regional arrangements the United States has painstakingly built since World War II. As the United States is the biggest beneficiary of such arrangements, it has no interest in seeing them unravel. The other alternative is not to intervene. In this case the U.S. government would suffer a loss of credibility in the region and moral and political consequences at home. For obvious reasons, Washington finds neither scenario acceptable. Accordingly the United States must do all it can to prevent Taiwan's independence. Therefore, while Washington has made it clear that it is opposed to Beijing using force to achieve reunification, it has also repeatedly stated that it will adhere to the "one China" principle—and will not support Taiwan's independence, will not support the practice of "two Chinas" or "one China, one Taiwan," and will not support Taiwan's admission to any international organization that is based on statehood.[10] Without U.S. support, pushing Taiwan's independence is equivalent to committing suicide for Taipei.

In the third place, given that Chen has only a limited mandate to rule, he must be extremely cautious in pushing independence. Some people did not vote for him because they were concerned that his pro-independence stance might provoke a war with the mainland and jeopardize their lives and welfare. Consequently, if he does push for independence he runs the risk that these people may oppose him. And since the DPP is a minority party in the Legislative Yuan, it is doubtful that Chen Shui-bian could get his way there even if he presses for independence. If he pushes for independence and political opposition rises against him, he could find himself in deep trouble. The island might well descend into political discord and conflict.

In the fourth place, it is not in Chen Shui-bian's best interest to push for independence. After all, independence is likely to bring about war across the Taiwan Strait. No rational political leader in Taiwan would want that to happen. Even if war does not occur, prolonged tension across the strait would hamper Taiwan's economic development. Certainly Taiwan has benefited from its economic relations with the PRC in terms of trade and investment in the mainland.[11] Persistent tension in the Taiwan Strait may well lead to denial of trade and investment opportunities for Taiwan. Moreover, independence is not the only political objective of Chen Shui-bian. He also wants to reform Taiwan's money politics, promote economic development, improve human rights, and clean up the environment. Just as important, he wants to get reelected in four years' time. If tension persists in the Taiwan Strait, Chen Shui-bian would have to devote much of his attention and Taiwan's valuable assets to deal with it. Consequently, he would find little time and resources to realize his other objectives—and this may jeopardize his chance for reelection. Seeking independence would therefore mean allocating all his time and resources on a hopeless and most probably disastrous enterprise. Given that most people in Taiwan do not believe it is in their interests to fight a war over independence, if Chen wants to get reelected in four years' time he will have to give up pushing independence at least for the time being.

Finally, Chen Shui-bian's own party, the DPP, is divided on the question of independence. Pressures for abandoning independence within the party have always been there. In fact, right after Chen's election some DPP members again raised the issue of removing the independence clause from the party's constitution. Although the issue was eventually dropped at the party's ninth congress for various reasons, division remained within the party as to the feasibility of a push for independence.[12] Should Chen press for independence, therefore, he may even face serious challenges from his own party.

In light of these factors, it is not surprising to find Chen Shui-bian extremely cautious on the question of independence. Since his election, while refusing to endorse the "one China" principle, he has also refrained from explicitly urging Taiwan's independence in his public addresses. Indeed, he has tried to appear flexible and pragmatic on the independence issue; and he has made it clear that he will not give the mainland any excuse to use force against Taiwan.

Caution on the question of independence, however, does not mean that Chen Shui-bian is preparing to embrace the "one China" principle. He has several other considerations weighing against it. As a person devoted to the cause of independence for a long time, he does not identify himself with China emotionally. While he does not wish to jeopardize his ambition to promote the welfare of the Taiwanese people as well as his own political career by provoking a war with the mainland, he is by no means in a mood to accept the "one China" principle either. Long before the election, he had been a vocal advocate of Taiwan's independence. Before the election he repeatedly claimed in public that Taiwan is an independent and sovereign state. If he were to accept the "one China" principle now, he would contradict himself—which would undermine his political credibility in the eyes of the public and damage his image. His political opponents would condemn him as unprincipled and unreliable. They might call him a coward, as well, for caving in to mainland pressures and threats.

Moreover, short-term political calculations counsel against accepting the "one China" principle. Among those who voted Chen into office, about 15 percent support Taiwan's independence. If Chen accepts the "one China" principle, he risks alienating these people and losing their support. In the meantime, he has no assurance that his acceptance of the "one China" principle would gain him as much support from supporters of James Soong or Lien Chan. Hence, he is likely to end up with a net loss in popular support. Given that he was elected into office by only 39 percent of the vote, he might well consider this option too risky.[13]

Finally, if Chen opts for the "one China" principle before the DPP deletes the Taiwan independence provision from the party's constitution, he will be violating his own party's constitution and may lose the support of the party or at least cause a split in its support for him. Certainly people like Annette Lu, the vice-president, as well as some DPP legislators who have been very aggressive in pushing for independence, are going to condemn him for this perceived act of betrayal to the party.[14]

Against this background, Chen does not appear to have many policy options. The best he can do is to steer a course ambiguous enough to avoid military confrontation with the mainland and at the same time not abandon Taiwan's independence as an option. To reduce the risk of military confrontation, he has tried to appear moderate and conciliatory. Immediately following his election, he assured people that he would not push for independence. He also made it known that he favors the three direct links across the Taiwan Strait: post, travel, and trade. In his inaugural speech on 20 May, he acknowledged the mainland's economic miracle over the past twenty years and announced that he would not press for Taiwan's independence during his presidency. He acknowledged, too, that people on both sides of the strait share the same blood, culture, and historical origins. He urged mainland leaders to work with him to develop cooperation on the basis of equality and deal with the question of "a future China."[15]

In an attempt to please his pro-independence supporters, Chen repeatedly used the word "Taiwan" in place of the Republic of China (ROC). The choice of words is important because the ROC stands for all China, not just Taiwan. He also made his inaugural speech sound like a declaration of independence by repeatedly talking about Taiwanese "standing up." He deliberately avoided the question of "one China," even a historical "one China." As well, he made a special effort to suggest that Taiwan is at the moment an independent sovereign state when he announced his intention to deal with the mainland government on the question of "a future China."[16]

In a word, contrary to popular expectations, the election of Chen Shui-bian is unlikely to bring about fresh attempts by Taipei to push for Taiwan's independence. At the same time, Chen is unlikely to accept the "one China" principle in the short run. Most probably, he will avoid the question of either reunification or independence for the time being and make a decision later when opportunities open up.

Implications for Beijing's Taiwan Policy

Chen Shui-bian's election took many in Beijing by surprise. Until the very last moment most people shared the belief, perhaps wishfully, that Chen could not win. Because the KMT enjoyed such unparalleled election resources, many thought Lien Chan had a better chance. When news of Chen's election broke out, therefore, many felt dismayed and frustrated.

Almost everyone in Beijing agrees that if Taiwan declares independence, the Chinese government will have no alternative but to resort to force to defend China's territorial integrity and national sovereignty. After all, the Taiwan issue is a matter not only of national dignity but also of national survival. First, it is a question of the regime's legitimacy. Half a century ago, the PRC was founded on a promise that the new government would not lose additional Chinese territory as previous governments had done throughout China's modern history. Hence, it cannot lose Taiwan without jeopardizing its legitimacy. Second, it is a question of political legitimacy. Given overwhelming popular support for national reunification, no Chinese political leader can afford to remain inactive if Taiwan declares independence. Third, it is a question of national unity. China is a country with many minority nationalities and its development is still quite uneven in regional terms. If the central government tolerates Taiwan's independence, it would be difficult to keep the country together. On top of all this, it is a question of China's modernization. Modernization has been a dream for generations of Chinese; and a crucial aspect of modernization is national confidence. If China cannot even keep its territories together, how can the Chinese hope to catch up with more developed countries?

This does not mean that Beijing prefers using force in settling the Taiwan problem. On the contrary, it regards force as the very last alternative. It fully appreciates the terrible consequence of a military showdown in the Taiwan Strait. It understands that if war breaks out in the strait, it is by no means certain that the People's Liberation Army (PLA) would be able to take over Taiwan or compel Taipei to surrender quickly and at a reasonable cost; and if it cannot, it is likely to face a protracted and highly destructive war. Nor is Beijing certain that the United States would not intervene militarily. If the United States does intervene, the war could be even more costly and destructive. Even if the PLA could take over Taiwan or compel Taipei to surrender without the United States intervening militarily, China's foreign relations would be in disarray. As China has already become highly integrated with the world economy, a drastic deterioration of Beijing's foreign relations could bring unacceptable damage to its economy and political stability, indefinitely postponing its modernization program. That is to say, a military showdown in the Taiwan Strait threatens to destroy China's only realistic chance for modernization since the Opium War.

Caught between two equally unpleasant alternatives, Beijing's best hope is to avoid them; but Lee Teng-hui's provocations and Chen Shui-bian's election have forced the issue to the front. Confronted with this new development, policy analysts in Beijing have been divided. Some are beginning to question the effectiveness of Beijing's policy of peaceful reunification. They argue that Beijing's conciliation and patience over the past twenty years have not brought Taiwan anywhere closer to reunification with the mainland. On the contrary, Taipei has been moving further and further away from the "one China" principle and peaceful reunification is becoming increasingly untenable. In their eyes, the election of Chen Shui-bian as president might be the beginning of Taipei's final push for independence. Some even believe that war across the strait is unavoidable. Although they agree that Beijing should continue to seek peaceful reunification with Taiwan, they also argue that Beijing should take a tougher position on the independence issue and prepare for a military showdown if Taipei continues to drag its feet on the question of reunification.[17]

While sharing the view that Taiwan's independence would indeed constitute war, others in Beijing deny that Chen's election will lead to Taiwan's independence. Nor do they believe that a military showdown across the Taiwan Strait is inevitable. They argue that Chen fully understands that Taiwan's independence means war. Despite his pro-independence inclination—unlike Lee Teng-hui, an aging pro-independence fundamentalist who has nothing to lose except his remaining years of lonely retirement—Chen is a young and pragmatic politician with a long career ahead of him. Most people in Taiwan are opposed to independence, although they are not interested in immediate reunification with the mainland. The international community, including the United States, does not support Taiwan's independence. Thus, Chen is unlikely to let the independence issue jeopardize his political career as well as the welfare of the Taiwanese people. In light of his own interests as well as the interests of all Taiwanese, he is likely to remain cautious on the independence issue. On the question of peaceful reunification, these analysts believe that the policy has been successful in general. It has won twenty years of peace for the mainland to engage in economic development and reforms. And it has enabled the mainland to enhance its capacity to prevent Taiwan's independence over the years. Accordingly, they argue that China should continue to adhere to the policy of peaceful reunification unless Taiwan takes major steps toward independence.

Although the two groups differ regarding the significance of Chen Shuibian's election for the question of independence, both sides agree that Taipei has already abandoned the "one China" principle in substance if not in form, that China cannot afford to let this development continue, and that consequently Beijing must take active measures to block further steps toward independence on the part of Taipei. Both sides share the view that Beijing should take a tougher stance on the "one China" principle. Both concur that China should devote more resources to its military capacity to deter Taiwan separatism and be ready for a military showdown should Taipei dare to move any closer toward independence.

Beijing's behavior on the Taiwan question since Chen Shui-bian's election is a reflection of the interaction between these two approaches. On the one hand, Beijing has stated that it will continue to adhere to the policy of peaceful reunification. It is willing to hold negotiations with Taipei on any issue including exchange of visits by top leaders of the two sides provided Taiwan accepts the "one China" principle. As the first step, the two sides can negotiate on the question of ceasing hostilities in the Taiwan Strait under the "one China" principle.[18] In response to Taipei's concern that the Taiwan side may not enjoy equal status in the proposed talks, Tang Jiaxuan, China's minister of foreign affairs, stated that Beijing is willing to hold talks on an equal basis. It is also willing to allow some ambiguity as to the question of whether "one China" means the PRC or ROC, as long as both sides recognize that there is only one China and both sides of the Taiwan Strait belong to China.[19]

On the other hand, Beijing has stepped up pressures on Taipei to return to the "one China" principle. On several occasions, it has issued stern warnings against further moves on the part of Taipei toward independence. It has also announced that it will not tolerate Taipei's indefinite foot-dragging on the question of reunification.[20] An article in *Renmin Ribao*, the CCP's official news organ, even insisted that Beijing must set a timetable for resolution of the Taiwan problem.[21] In its official response to Chen Shui-bian's inaugural speech, Beijing's Taiwan Affairs Office dismissed Chen's call for dialogue and negotiation as gestures without substance. It demanded that Chen return to the "one China" principle or face the dire consequences. Beijing could wait and see what Chen was up to, it stated; but it could not wait forever.

Meanwhile, Beijing has adopted a series of measures to pressure Chen to accept the "one China" principle. Politically it has refused to engage in talks with Taipei before Taiwan accepts the "one China" principle. Chinese Premier Zhu Rongji said that Taiwan's new leaders do not accept the "one China" principle and indeed do not even regard themselves as Chinese. Thus, there really is nothing the two sides can talk about.[22] In the meantime, Beijing has reached out to other political parties and figures from Taiwan who have openly accepted the "one China" principle—including those from the People First Party headed by James Soong, the New Party led by Feng Hu-hsiang, and even Hsieh Chang-ting, the mayor of Kaohsiung and the person to assume the chair of the DPP, because he appeared to be flexible on the "one China" principle.[23] Beijing has publicly stated that it invites any individual or political party to visit the mainland and hold talks on the Taiwan question as long as he/she/it accepts the "one China" principle.[24] Recently, Qian Qichen indicated that Beijing is willing to see civilian contacts to promote the three links—travel, trade, and communication—across the Taiwan Strait on the basis of the principle of "one China."[25]

While applying political pressures on the Taiwan authorities, Beijing has redoubled its military preparations for a possible showdown in the Taiwan Strait. It has reviewed military plans for various contingencies. It has redeployed missiles to Fujian province across the strait; and it has conducted various military maneuvers, including amphibious landing exercises along the coast. Moreover, Beijing has voiced its intention to restrict the economic activities of Taiwanese enterprises whose owners support Taiwan independence activities. China has made it clear that it will no longer put up with businessmen who want to make money on the mainland while promoting Taiwan's independence at home. If they want to make money in China, Beijing warned, they should abandon their support for Taiwan's independence. Otherwise, they should pack up and leave the mainland.[26]

In sum, then, Beijing hopes it can bring Taipei back to the "one China" principle through selective use of carrots and sticks. It has no interest in a war in the Taiwan Strait. In fact, it considers war as the last resort in resolving the Taiwan problem. All it has done is to prevent such a development from happening. This is why China still adheres to the policy of peaceful reunification. But if Taipei continues to push for Taiwan's independence, Beijing wants to be ready for it. Given the high stakes involved in the event of independence, China would rather fight a war to defend its territorial and national sovereignty than allow Taiwan to become independent.

In the short run, Beijing is simply waiting for Chen Shui-bian to come back to the "one China" principle and hoping for the best. As time passes, however, its patience is likely to wear thin. Meanwhile, political pressure on the mainland for tougher action is likely to mount. Unlike the Lee Teng-hui era, Beijing is not going to wait another ten years. Some in Beijing have already warned that China should not let itself be tricked by the Taiwan authorities twice.[27] Increasing numbers of people on the mainland have lost faith in the effectiveness of peaceful overtures for reunification and public warnings against Taiwan separatism. Should the Taipei leadership choose to push for independence in the days to come, one is more likely to hear the sounds of war than the music of peace in the Taiwan Strait.

Implications for Cross-Strait Relations

With Chen Shui-bian sticking to a policy of ambiguity on the "one China" principle and Beijing insisting that Chen must accept the "one China" principle in the near future, relations across the Taiwan Strait are at an impasse. Although Chen may appear flexible and conciliatory in rhetoric and posture, Beijing is unlikely to reciprocate so long as Chen refuses to accept the "one China" principle.

The impasse in cross-strait relations, it should be pointed out, is different from the stalemate during the better part of the Lee Teng-hui period in that it is highly unstable. Before Lee Teng-hui came up with the controversial concept of a "special state-to-state relationship," both sides managed to maintain the "one China" principle at least in formal terms even though Lee and his supporters had been chipping away at that concept. At the time, Beijing could still try to manage cross-strait relations largely through peaceful means with a hope that it would not have to face the question of Taiwan's independence. Ever since Lee raised the issue of "a special state-to-state relationship," however, Taipei has departed from the "one China" principle both in substance and in name although it has not quite announced Taiwan's independence. At this point, Beijing can no longer avoid confronting the question of Taiwan's independence and thinks it must do something to reverse the trend of development. Accordingly it has issued repeated warnings to Taipei and made active preparations for a military showdown in the event of Taiwan's independence.

Beijing's warnings and military preparations alarmed both Washington and Taipei. Washington was clearly annoyed by Lee's fresh provocations to Beijing, particularly when it was not advised ahead of time. It was concerned that Lee's new maneuver might give Beijing a good reason to take military action against Taiwan and jeopardize U.S. national interests. To manage the escalating crisis, Washington immediately issued statements to the effect that it would still uphold the "one China" principle. At the same time, it expressed hope that Beijing would exercise restraint in the face of Lee's provocations.[28]

While Lee Teng-hui might have wished to set the tone for his successor's mainland policy, he was not ready for war, especially one without U.S. backing. Consequently, his aides began to explain the concept of "special state-to-state relations" in more innocuous terms. Meanwhile, Lee and his people decided not to stress the concept in subsequent talks.

Although Beijing did not resort to force to compel Lee Teng-hui to abandon his concept of "special state-to-state relations," it began to attach greater importance to a military solution in case Taipei declared independence. As we have seen, reunification through peaceful means remained Beijing's objective, although military readiness gained weight as a necessary means to deter and in the case of independence fight against Taiwan separatism. Against this backdrop, Chen Shui-bian's election only aggravated Beijing's concern. Given Chen's pro-independence track record, Beijing had good reason to believe that the chances for Taiwan's independence—and war—had increased. Accordingly it stepped up preparations for a military showdown in the Taiwan Strait.

Chen Shui-bian's policy of ambiguity or flexibility on the "one China" principle, demonstrated in his inaugural speech, may have arrested the trend of escalating tension across the Taiwan Strait. It has not solved the problem, however, and at best has only postponed it. So long as Chen refuses to accept the "one China" principle, Beijing is likely to find it impossible to deal with him. For the moment, Beijing has adopted a wait-and-see approach in the hope that its pressures on Chen will eventually make him see the light and accept the "one China" concept. But given that Chen has already abandoned the "one China" principle, Beijing cannot afford to wait too long. Domestic political pressures for action have been increasing. Many in Beijing insist that prolonged waiting will only solidify the situation created by Lee Teng-hui and continued by Chen Shui-bian. If Chen Shui-bian drags his feet, Beijing is likely to step up pressures to compel him to accept the "one China" principle.

Despite Beijing's pressures, Chen Shui-bian appears to be in no hurry to give in to Beijing's wishes. While maintaining an apparent conciliatory posture, he has stubbornly refused to accept the "one China" principle. In the meantime, he has tried to limit unofficial interactions across the strait. He refused, for example, to allow Taiwan groups to travel by ship to the mainland directly from Jinmen, an offshore island under the control of the Taiwan authorities.[29] He obstructed the planned visit to Xiamen by Hsieh Chang-ting, the mayor of Kaohsiung and aspiring chairman of the DPP.[30] He also made it impossible for the mayor of Xiamen to visit Kaohsiung when Hsieh's visit to Xiamen failed to get approval from the Taiwan authorities.[31] At the same time, he went ahead with the lobbying efforts at the United Nations to seek Taiwan's membership. He also visited Latin America to pursue Lee Teng-hui's so-called pragmatic diplomacy. In response to Beijing's criticisms of him, Chen retorts that the two sides should not play the rhetoric game.[32] He has already made all the concessions he can make, he says, and the ball is on the mainland's court.[33]

Confronted with Chen Shui-bian's maneuvers, Beijing has become increasingly frustrated—as shown by its increasingly critical comments on Chen and his government. On 26 July, Xinhua News Agency published an article condemning Tsai Ying-wen, chair of Taiwan's Mainland Affairs Council, charging that Tsai did not consider herself to be Chinese; that she claimed that even though Lee Teng-hui's "special state-to-state relations" concept is no longer discussed it is still an appropriate description of reality; that she denied the two sides had reached consensus on the "one China" principle in 1992; and that she had exerted herself in obstructing the three direct links (postal communication, trade, and travel). The article charged further that Tsai Ying-wen used to work for Lee Teng-hui and had been pursuing Lee's policy ever since she was appointed to her current position.[34]

Another article published in a military newspaper aimed criticism directly at Chen Shui-bian himself. Despite his seemingly friendly rhetoric, the article alleges, Taiwan's new leader has been deliberately evasive on the "one China" principle. His words and deeds during his two months in office demonstrate that he is still pursuing Taiwan's independence. He is playing a dangerous game: He can deceive some of the people some of the time, but not all of the people all of the time. And he will pay for what he has been doing.[35]

Looking to the future, one can foresee three possible scenarios. In the first scenario, Chen Shui-bian caves in under Beijing's pressures and eventually accepts the "one China" principle. Although he may appear a coward in the eyes of many in Taiwan, he can explain his decision on the ground that the alternative is war and he has to protect what the Taiwanese people have achieved over the years. By doing so, he is likely to resume cross-strait talks and may even realize exchanges of visits by leaders of both sides. Eventually this policy may lead to some kind of peaceful settlement of the Taiwan problem in the spirit of the "one China" principle.

In the second scenario, Chen Shui-bian opts for Taiwan's independence. His policy of ambiguity and conciliation may have been simply for tactical purposes. He needed time to consolidate his power because he was elected by only a minority and lacked experience to govern and simply could not afford to take on another Taiwan Strait crisis for the time being. Once he consolidates his position in Taiwan, however, he will push for independence again. After all, this is one of his long-held political ambitions. In doing so, he understands the risk of provoking Beijing. But with the United States behind him, he may think that Beijing would not dare risk a war with the United States. If this is the case, a war in the Taiwan Strait is likely to follow since Beijing, for the reasons cited earlier, would have to fight whether the United States intervenes or not.

In the third scenario, Chen opts for a policy of ambiguity and evasiveness just as he has done since his election. Certainly the United States has no problem with the policy and Beijing, despite its distaste, has been putting up with it. In doing so Chen can avoid alienating his political support from the pro-independence people and at the same time give Beijing no additional reason to use force. As time passes, his current stance between de facto and de jure independence of Taiwan will solidify as people get used to the idea that Taipei has abandoned the "one China" principle. Where this policy will lead in the future is not certain. For the time being, however, it will help Chen to avoid facing a tough political dilemma: accepting the "one China" principle or fighting a war with the mainland.

Among the three scenarios, it appears that the third is most likely to occur. In the first scenario, Chen Shui-bian may regard acceptance of the "one China" principle as too costly in political terms. After years of political maneuvering, Lee Teng-hui has created an atmosphere in which the average politician in Taiwan dares not admit he or she is a Chinese. Acceptance of the "one China" principle would not only make Chen, a long-term advocate of Taiwan's independence, appear to be buckling under mainland pressure but also give others the impression that he is unprincipled. Under the circumstances, Chen would have to have great political courage and the foresight to accept the "one China" principle for the long-term good of Taiwan. His past track record and current behavior, however, do not suggest he has either the courage or the foresight to do so. He is merely a politician, not a statesman.

In the second scenario, Chen may find the risk of pushing for Taiwan's independence unacceptable. Beijing has made it clear that independence is equivalent to war. Any realistic analysis of the political atmosphere on the mainland regarding the Taiwan question will show that Beijing is not bluffing. Appreciating this reality, Washington has clearly stated that it will not support Taiwan's independence—implying that Taipei would be on its own should it push for independence. Moreover, most people on Taiwan are opposed to independence at the expense of their interests and personal welfare. Thus, pushing for Taiwan's independence is a hopeless and highly risky project. Unless Chen behaves irrationally, he is not likely to take this on.

In the third scenario, Chen does not have to worry about the problems of either scenario discussed previously—that is, not to appear spineless under Beijing's pressure, alienating his pro-independence supporters, and at the same time not to be unnecessarily provocative to Beijing, bringing dire consequences for Taiwan. Hence, he is likely to get American support, avoid a political split within Taiwan, and give Beijing no good reason to use force. And as time passes, he may even solidify the situation into a new status quo, which opens the possibility of seeking independence in the long run.

If the third scenario is the most likely, we may expect one of two possible avenues of development. Consider the first avenue. As domestic political pressures for action begin to mount, Beijing is likely to decide that it cannot wait and let Chen Shui-bian determine the course of events. Since it has no good reason to trust Chen, it would interpret his rhetoric and behavior from the worst possible angle. Chen, however, is likely to find it necessary to respond to Beijing's criticisms in a less conciliatory manner. Confronted with this situation, more likely than not, sooner or later Beijing would conclude that Chen is pushing for Taiwan's independence and give up on him altogether unless Chen does something significant to impress them otherwise. Under the circumstances, Beijing may launch a public campaign to discredit Chen's policy and eventually Chen himself for promoting Taiwan's independence. This, as we have seen, is precisely what is happening.

Confronted with a rhetorical assault from Beijing, Chen would probably find it more difficult to make concessions. As a person, he may not be able to swallow the harsh attacks. As a politician, he may not want to look like a coward buckling under Beijing's pressure. Thus, he may respond with equally harsh rhetoric or even efforts to push for independence. Beijing in turn would take this as evidence that Chen is pushing for independence and follow it up with even more strenuous military preparations.

As Beijing steps up its military preparations for such an eventuality, Taipei is going to feel increasingly insecure. Taiwan is likely to appeal to the United States or other Western countries for permission to buy more advanced and sophisticated weapons. It will also try harder to seek U.S. military protection, including joining the U.S. theater missile defense (TMD) system. Confronted with this situation, Beijing may have no alternative but to develop countermeasures against the TMD system by developing new weapon systems or purchasing advanced systems from Russia. In doing so, Beijing is also likely to work more closely with Russia militarily in its efforts to develop countermeasures. The arms race across the strait is likely to intensify.

If the arms race accelerates, a war across the Taiwan Strait becomes more likely. Conceivably it is likely to happen under two circumstances. First, if Beijing perceives that the military balance is turning against it, it may consider launching a preemptive strike. Second, if Beijing believes that Taipei refuses to accept the "one China" principle, it may try to overwhelm Taiwan within a short period of time at a reasonable cost. If war erupts, Taiwan would become a battlefield. The worst thing to happen would be U.S. military intervention. In this case, China and the United States may find themselves for the first time in history fighting an all-out war with a possibility of escalation into nuclear war. Then China and the United States would be reduced to battlegrounds. This process, of course, is the worst-case scenario.

But escalation might not go right through to its logical end—that is, war in the Taiwan Strait. This possibility leads us to the second avenue of development. As the chance of war increases, Chen Shui-bian may find acceptance of the "one China" principle increasingly preferable to war with the mainland. After all, in the event of a military showdown, it does not really matter whether Taiwan could hold out against the mainland and whether the United States would intervene on Taiwan's side or not. In either case, Taiwan would be reduced to rubble.

Even if a war is not going to be fought over Chen's refusal to return to the "one China" principle, relations across the Taiwan Strait will remain tense and volatile. The mainland is likely to apply economic pressure on Taiwan. This would affect investors' confidence in Taiwan and hurt the economy— just the situation Taiwan has been experiencing in recent months. Moreover, Chen Shui-bian would have to devote most of his attention to the mainland. With investors' confidence low and Chen spending most of his time and resources on coping with cross-strait tension, Chen would have little left for delivering his campaign promises: cleaning up Taiwanese politics, promoting social welfare, improving human rights, protecting the environment. Under the circumstances, he might find it difficult to retain power in the next election in four years time.

In view of all this, Chen is likely to see great incentives to return to the "one China" principle. In the short run, such a move might reduce tension and restore some level of good faith across the Taiwan Strait. This in turn would improve Taiwan's security and restore investors' confidence. Moreover, it would help make him a responsible leader who is not going to let his personal preference for independence jeopardize the security of the Taiwanese people. In the long run, such a move would lead to mutually beneficial relations across the Taiwan Strait and contribute to long-term peace, prosperity, and progress throughout China.

Recent developments suggest that Chen and certain DPP heavyweights have begun to appreciate the benefits of reaching a compromise across the Taiwan Strait on the basis of the "one China" principle. In his meeting with an Asia Foundation delegation on 27 June 2000, Chen said he was willing to accept a "one China, different interpretations" formula as the basis for handling cross-strait relations.[36] Although he and his aides later explained that this did not represent a major change in Chen's mainland policy, the event can be interpreted as a trial balloon to sound the reactions should he accept the "one China" principle. In a way, the recent remark by Hsieh Chang-ting, the DPP's newly elected chairman—that both Kaohsiung and Xiamen are cities of the same country—suggests the inclinations of pragmatic politicians within the DPP on the question of "one China."[37] Recently, the Taiwan authorities finally approved opening up direct travel between Kinmen/Matsu islands and certain mainland coastal areas—although it still limits travel by people from the mainland to Kinmen and Matsu, two groups of offshore islands under Taiwan's control.[38] In his New Year's address, Chen Shui-bian said that according to the constitution of the ROC, "one China" was not a problem and he would be willing to discuss it with the mainland leaders on the basis of equality and goodwill.[39]

It is still too early to predict which avenue of development the cross-strait relationship will follow. In the short run, Chen Shui-bian is still likely to pursue the policy of ambiguity and evasion. And Beijing is still likely to apply various pressures, including speeding up military preparations, both to prevent Taiwan's independence and to deter U.S. military intervention in the event of war in the Taiwan Strait. In the long run, the chances that Chen will accept the "one China" principle are likely to improve and from this acceptance some kind of peaceful arrangement is likely to emerge.

Chen: Statesman or Politician?

Chen Shui-bian's election turned a new page both in Chinese politics and in cross-strait relations. The situation across the Taiwan Strait, however, has not turned for the better since his election. As we have seen, in the short run the situation is likely to remain uncertain before it takes a turn for the better. For that to happen, Chen must accept the "one China" principle. If he fails to do so, the cross-strait relationship might well end like a typical Greek tragedy in which the protagonists march helplessly to the tragic end despite their desperate efforts to avoid it.

At the moment, Chen is still refusing to accept the "one China" principle and the cross-strait relationship is still tense. Yet history is full of possibilities. In the end, one may still be able to find a satisfactory conclusion to this historical drama. In this process, Chen Shui-bian plays a crucial role. As Chinese often say: *"Tui yibu hai kuo tian kong"* (take a step back and you will find endless possibilities). Chinese on both sides of the Taiwan Strait hope that Chen turns out to be a statesman who has the courage to take up the challenge of leadership instead of a mere politician who follows short-term political interests. The former requires acceptance of the "one China" principle now; the latter means continuation of a policy of evasion and ambiguity.

Notes

1. Jia Qingguo, "Toward the Center: Implications of Integration and Democratisation for Taiwan's Mainland Policy," *Journal of Northeast Asian Studies* 13(1) (Spring 1994):49–63.

2. Fan Liqing, *Taiwan bianju: Minjindang yu guomindang de zhengquan zhengzhan* [Political change in Taiwan: The power struggle between the DPP and the KMT] (Beijing: Xinhua, 1998), p. 32.

3. Wu Liying, "Chen Shuibian zaici tiaozheng dalu zhengce" [Chen Shui-bian adjusted his mainland policy again], *Lianhe Zaobao*, 31 January 2000, reproduced at http://www.zaobao.com.sg.

4. Wu Liying, "Chen Shuibian dangxuan Taiwan biantian" [Chen Shuibian is elected and Taiwan's power changes hands], *Lianhe Zaobao*, 19 March 2000.

5. The Asia Foundation, the New York Council for Foreign Relations, the National Committee on American Foreign Policy, and others had been trying to engage Taiwan and the Chinese mainland to talk to each other even before Chen Shui-bian's election.

6. Office of Taiwan Affairs and Information Office of the State Council of the People's Republic of China, "The One-China Principle and the Taiwan Question," *Renmin Ribao* [People's daily], 21 February 2000, p. 1.

7. *Renmin Ribao*, 25 March 2000, p. 2.

8. *Renmin Ribao*, 21 May 2000, p. 1.

9. *Lianhe Zaobao* (Singapore), 5 and 23 June and 23, 26, 27 July 2000.

10. *Renmin Ribao*, 6 February 2000, p. 1; *Lianhe Zaobao*, 23 June 2000.

11. Taiwan's balance of trade would have been in the red had it not enjoyed an enormous trade surplus with the mainland. See *Liangan Jingmao* [Straits business monthly] 6 (2000):48–49.

12. "Minjindang jiuci quandaihui pingshu" [Analysis of ninth party congress of the DPP], *Taiwan Zhoukan* [Taiwan weekly] 39 (2000):1–3.

13. My conversation with two DPP cadres.

14. In fact, soon after Chen said on 27 June 2000 that he was willing to accept the consensus on the "one China" principle reached by Taiwan and the mainland in 1992, some DPP legislators openly voiced criticisms of Chen even though he had carefully avoided defining what he understood as the 1992 consensus. See "Chen Shuibian '6.27 jianghua' jiqi fanying" [The 27 June talk by Chen Shui-bian and reactions], *Taiwan Zhoukan* [Taiwan weekly], 5 July 2000, p. 2.

15. *Taiwan Zhoukan*, 31 May 2000, p. 8.

16. Ibid., pp. 3–9.

17. This view is partly reflected in Beijing's white paper on Taiwan published on 21 February 2000, which states that it will not tolerate Taiwan's indefinite procrastination on the question of reunification. See Office of Taiwan Affairs and Information Office of the State Council of the People's Republic of China, "The One-China Principle."

18. Ibid., p. 1.

19. "Tang Shubei zai liangan guanxi yantao hui shang zhichu liangan guanxi fazhan dengfou zhengqu heping wending qianjing qujueyu taiwan dangju shifou chengren yige zhongguo yuanze" [Tang Shubei pointed out that the key to peace and stability in cross-strait relations lies in whether Taiwan authorities will accept "one China" principle at forum on cross-strait relations], *Renmin Ribao*, 10 May 2000, p. 4.

20. Office of Taiwan Affairs and Information Office of the State Council of the People's Republic of China, "The One-China Principle," p. 1.

21. "Zhuajin zaori jiejue Taiwan wenti de gongzuo" [Step up efforts to prepare to solve Taiwan problem at earliest possible time], *Renmin Ribao*, 3 March 2000, p. 3.

22. *Huanshengbao* [Huansheng daily], 7 July 2000.

23. "Haixiehui yu xindang dui yige zhongguo yuanze dacheng gongshi" [ARATS and New Party reached consensus on "one China" principle], *Wenhuibao* [Wenhui daily (Hong Kong)], 11 July 2000.

24. "Beijing Welcomes Taiwan People to Visit the Mainland," http://www.chinadaily.com.cn/highlights/taiwan/y718welcome.html.

25. *Lianhe Zaobao*, 6 January 2001.

26. "Guanyu dangqian liangan jingji guanxi fazhan de ruogan wenti zhonggong zhongyang taiban guowuyuan taiban fuzeren da jizhe wen" [Answers to press by the official in charge of Office of Taiwan Affairs of CCP Central Committee and Office of Taiwan Affairs of State Council], *Renmin Ribao*, 9 April 2000, p. 1.

27. Li Jiaquan, "Shixi chenshuibian dangzheng hou de liangan guanxi" [Analyzing cross-strait relations following Chen Shui-bian's rise to power], *Tianjing Taiwan Yanjiu Tongxun* [Newsletter on Taiwan studies in Tianjing] (2000:4), p. 4.

28. "Geguo fenfen chongshen yige zhongguo de lichang" [Countries repeat "one China" principle], *Renmin Ribao*, 23 July 1999, p. 6.

29. "Taibei quxiao beigang mazu xing" [Taipei canceled trip to worship Mazu from north port], *Lianhe Zaobao*, 22 June 2000.

30. Li Qihong, "Xiechangting qu bu liao xiamen" [Hsieh Chang-ting cannot go to Xiamen], *Lianhe Zaobao*, 8 July 2000.

31. "Xiamen shizhang quxiao fang gaoxiong" [Mayor of Xiamen canceled visit to Kaohsiung], *Lianhe Zaobao*, 21 July 2000.

32. Li Qihong, "Chen Shuibian: Liangan buying zai hua shijian gao wenzi youxi" [Chen Shui-bian: Two sides across strait should not waste time playing word games], *Lianhe Zaobao*, 1 August 2000.

33. "Chen Shuibian: Yizhong yi shuodao dixian" [Chen Shui-bian: He has already said all he can on one China principle], *Lianhe Zaobao*, 20 July 2000.

34. Tai Hai, "Gao fenlie zhe zhongjiang pengbi—ping caiyingwen jinlai yanxing" [Those who engage in separatism are doomed to fail: On Tsai Ying-wen's recent words and deeds], http://www.xinhua.net, 26 July 2000.

35. Hong Bing, "Shi shanyi haishi weizhuang? Ping Taiwan dangju xin lingdaoren jinlai de yanxing" [Goodwill or pretence? On recent behavior of Taiwan's new leader], *Zhongguo Guofang Bao* [Chinese national defense daily], 21 July 2000.

36. "Chen Shuibian yuan jieshou 'yi zhong gezi biaoshu'" [Chen Shui-bian said he would accept "one China and different interpretations"], *Lianhe Zaobao*, 28 June 2000.

37. "Xie Changting: Xiamen yu gaoxiong ying tong shu yige guojia guanxi" [Hsieh Chang-ting: Xiamen and Kaohsiung should belong to same country], *Lianhe Zaobao*, 2 July 2000.

38. *Lianhe Zaobao*, 3 January 2001.

39. *Lianhe Zaobao*, 31 December 2000.

7

Cross-Strait Economic Relations: Can They Ameliorate the Political Problem?

Tain-Jy Chen and C.Y. Cyrus Chu

Shortly after Chen Shui-bian's historic election as president of Taiwan on 18 March 2000, several Taiwanese business leaders stationed in various cities in mainland China were interviewed by reporters from the *Commercial Times*, a Taiwan newspaper, for their immediate feelings about the election's outcome. Unanimously the businessmen expressed worries about the future relationship between the two sides of the Taiwan Strait. And since all future economic interactions hinge on the stability of the overall environment, their worries are neither irrational nor impractical.

The Taiwanese businessmen feel anxious, not because of their personal opposition to the Chen ideology, but because such opposition is currently the mood in mainland China. Indeed, due to President Chen's stereotyped anti-China image, along with his prior endorsement of independence for Taiwan, the mainland Chinese authorities tend to regard Chen's victory as a signal of the soaring spirits of the pro-independence movement. Authorities in mainland China have also blamed a number of influential businessmen in Taiwan for their support of Chen during the presidential campaign. According to the *Commercial Times*,[1] there were several cases of unscheduled tax audits, invalidation of prior investment approvals, and postponement of scheduled reviews of investment projects all targeted at business branches in China

The authors would like to thank Marcus Noland, Tianshu Chu, and participants at the East-West Center conference on "Taiwan Presidential Elections: Outcome and Implications" for useful comments.

owned by businessmen suspected of having supported Chen. In newspaper interviews, these businessmen have denied their roles in the campaign; without exception they all insist that they are neither supporters nor proponents of Taiwanese independence. Later, the Chinese authorities announced they had been fair and evenhanded to all businesses in China and did not practice discrimination against any particular business groups.

These anecdotal incidents of business interference reveal several economic realities worthy of attention. First of all, Taiwanese businesses have invested a significant amount of capital in mainland China. Since much of this is in the form of direct investment, rather than portfolio investment, the end result is an increase in the mutual dependence of the two economic communities across the Taiwan Strait and, at the same time, an increase in the vulnerability of the Taiwanese economy to Chinese government interference. Second, one reason for the injection of significant amounts of foreign direct investment (FDI) into mainland China by these Taiwanese businesses is the trade restrictions imposed by the Chinese authorities over the past few years. Third, from a strategic point of view this mutual dependence is in fact tilted against Taiwan. The major source of FDI flows from Taiwan to China, and China has a much larger capacity for absorbing economic shocks than Taiwan. Thus, if China imposes economic sanctions against Taiwan, the island will be particularly vulnerable.

But as both Taiwan and China are expected to gain entry into the World Trade Organization (WTO) soon, trade barriers between the two sides will have to be removed. The government in Taiwan currently regulates all FDI going to mainland China with its "go slow, be patient" policy: Taiwanese businessmen intending to invest in mainland China are urged to "slow down, don't move too fast." This was a policy conceived and implemented by Lee Teng-hui, the former president of Taiwan. Since Lee was viewed by mainland China as a major obstacle to the development of cross-strait relations, if President Chen intends to appease China he will have to relax or remove the regulatory controls imposed by Lee.

Our purpose here is to analyze current and future economic relations between China and Taiwan. Today the trade environment in Taiwan is generally open, but the Taiwan government has adopted certain discriminatory policies toward trade with China; meanwhile, the trade environment in China is generally closed, but the Chinese government does not discriminate against trade with Taiwan. Our focus, therefore, is on the deregulation of Taiwan's investment and trade regimes specific to China and on China's general trade liberalizations.

China's Economic Development and Cross-Strait Relations

Before 1979, China was isolated from the rest of the world and there was no economic interaction across the Taiwan Strait. Since 1979, China has adopted an open-door policy that completely reshaped the landscape in which Taiwan's businesses played an important role, particularly in the area of foreign investment.

Background

In 1979, China announced its policy of "reform on the inside, open to the outside," which set out the stages of its economic reforms. Since then China's economy has experienced an astonishing lift: from a poor, largely state-controlled, stagnant, and closed economy to one that has embraced a whole new outlook. Although income levels do not yet approach those of the developed countries, the income growth rate over the past twenty years has been roughly 9 percent a year and per capita income is growing over 7 percent a year— rates of growth higher than almost any other country in the world over the same period. In 1979, the total value of trade accounted for less than 10 percent of China's gross national product, but this ratio quickly rose to its recent high of more than 40 percent. In terms of the government's role in the economy, the ratio of the value of goods and services produced by state-owned enterprises has fallen from 85 percent in 1979 to less than 75 percent in 1998.[2] More important, the direction of resource allocation has shifted from the hard command of the government to the soft attraction of the market. Compared with the cases of Russia and former Eastern Bloc countries, economic reforms in mainland China have undoubtedly been much more effective.

After forty years of being closed to the outside world and thus lacking physical capital, mainland China's economic reform strategy was to adopt policies that would attract foreign capital. Such policies included tax deductions or exemptions for foreign firms, creation of special economic zones in which administrative bureaucracy was minimized, and "special privileges" permitting foreign firms to hold and trade foreign exchanges. Leaving aside the slow capital inflow immediately after 1979—most businessmen were still watching and waiting—China's overall policy of attracting capital inflow has been quite successful over the past twenty years. According to the UNCTAD *World Investment Report*, since 1993 China has consistently attracted in excess of 11 percent of the world's total flow of FDI. From China's perspective, more than 10 percent of its annual fixed capital formation has come from investment by foreign nationals. Thus, China may well stand as a model country in the history of economic development—a testament to the theory of Ragnar Nurkse, who argued that countries could escape the vicious circle of poverty by attracting foreign capital.[3]

In the process of China's economic development over the past twenty years, the role of Taiwan has been both important and intriguing. Apart from the regular rules encouraging capital inflow from foreign countries, the Chinese authorities have, since 1983, announced special incentives applicable to direct investment from Taiwan: tax deductions (in 1983), enlarging the scope of industries allowed for direct investment (in 1988), opening special industrial parks (in 1989), and expediting the settlement of legal disputes (in 1994) for Taiwanese investors. Other than these incentives, the familiar language and cultural affinity appeal to Taiwanese businesses. As a result, by the end of 1999 the accumulated direct investment from Taiwan accounted for 7.1 percent of China's total FDI making Taiwan the fourth-largest investing country in China. And if we take approved investment, as opposed to actual investment, as the basis of comparison, then Taiwan ranks third. These rankings are particularly high when we consider that Taiwan's economic capacity is in fact relatively small.[4]

Table 7.1 shows the statistics of Taiwan's direct investment in China. There is a large discrepancy between the statistics collected by Taipei and those gathered by Beijing, although both are based on approvals. According to the Taiwan statistics, by June 2000 a total of 22,475 projects had been approved to invest in China with a total investment reaching US$15,598 million. The Chinese recorded 44,915 investment projects during the same period, with a total amount of investment reaching US$45,758 million. This suggests that about half of Taiwan's investment projects in China have circumvented the Republic of China's (ROC) capital control regulations. There is also a tendency for Taiwanese investors who did register with the Taiwan government to underreport their investment amounts.

Transport, Trade, and FDI Barriers

Several aspects of the economic relationship between China and Taiwan are worthy of further investigation. First of all, since 1978 when China started its economic reforms, no direct trade between China and Taiwan has been allowed. As a result of the overwhelming amount of illicit trade going on across the strait, however, Taiwan eventually allowed certain elements of official trade with China in 1987. But all trade was to be carried out "indirectly"—that is, the shipment of goods between Taiwan and mainland China had to go via a third port, usually Hong Kong, Ishigaki (Japan), Pusan (South

Table 7.1

Taiwan's Direct Investment in China

Year	Taiwan's statistics		China's statistics	
	Cases	Amount (US$ million)	Cases	Amount (US$ million)
1991[a]	237	174	3,446	2,783
1992	264	247	6,430	5,543
1993	1,262 (8,067)	1,140 (2,028)	10,948	9,965
1994	934	962	6,247	5,395
1995	490	1,093	4,778	5,777
1996	383	1,229	3,184	5,141
1997	728 (7,997)	1,615 (2,720)	3,014	2,814
1998	641 (643)	1,519 (515)	2,970	2,982
1999	488	1,253	2,499	3,374
2000[b]	341	1,102	1,399	1,984
Total	22,475	15,598	44,915	45,758

Sources: Taiwan's statistics are from *Statistics on Overseas Chinese and Foreign Investment, Outward Investment, Outward Technical Cooperation, Indirect Mainland Investment, Guide of Mainland Industry Technology*, Ministry of Economic Affairs (Taiwan); China's statistics are from *Almanac of China's Foreign Economic Relations and Trade*.
Note: Numbers in parentheses are investment projects recorded through makeup registration rather than prior approval.
[a]Includes cases prior to 1991.
[b]Statistics are up to June only.

Korea), or Singapore. This rule is a symptom of the Trojan Horse syndrome, whereby the Taiwan government fears an armed invasion of Chinese troops aboard ships or airplanes directly approaching Taiwanese ports. Although this rule can be enforced when the transaction amount is significant, small-scale trading can easily circumvent the regulations.

Second, although direct investment in China has been allowed by the Taiwan government since 1991, all investment projects have to obtain prior approval from Taipei, which restricts the amount of investment and the target industry. In 1995, Taiwan's FDI in China accounted for almost 50 percent of its total capital outflow. Taipei's reaction was to impose tougher regulations. According to the regulations imposed in 1996, other than a few sectors in which FDI is totally prohibited, regular investments are more likely to be approved if they are low-tech and not capital-intensive. This FDI restriction was dubbed the GSBP policy ("go slow, be patient").

Although it is difficult to assess the impact of these regulations on ordinary economic activities, trade restrictions seem to have been more effective than investment restrictions. Since commodity transactions are highly visible, subject to customs inspection, and liable to criminal charges, few businessmen would take such a high risk in an effort to bypass the trade regulations. And although "direct" trade (commodities shipped directly between Taiwan and China without entering a third-country port to comply with the regulation) is perhaps substantial, it is unlikely that firms engaged in large-scale trade will violate the regulation. But FDI is different. Since capital funds can easily be rerouted, the GSBP policy cannot hope to block the capital outflow from Taiwan. This explains why direct export from Taiwan to mainland China (and direct import from China to Taiwan), as estimated by Kao,[5] has only risen to 6.72 percent (1.47 percent) of Taiwan's overall exports (imports), whereas the FDI from Taiwan to China accounts for almost 50 percent of Taiwan's outward investment.

For most Taiwanese investors, it is only rational to invest in areas with lower production costs and China is most satisfactory in this respect. Indeed, China's abundant cheap labor, inexpensive materials, tax incentives, vast domestic market, and lax environmental regulations are all much more attractive than in most other countries. Moreover, as noted earlier, the familiar language and cultural affinity represent a further pulling force for Taiwanese firms. Faced with increasing labor costs at home and ever increasing competition from low-wage countries, they find it natural to move their sunset industries to mainland China where they can rejuvenate their declining competitiveness. But the Taiwanese government's idea is somewhat different. The GSBP policy has been driven by two main ideas: Rapid outflow of FDI from Taiwan to mainland China might "hollow out" Taiwan's industries; and businessmen putting too many eggs in one basket in mainland China might render Taiwan vulnerable to future antagonistic moves by China. The scenario of mainland China "forcing policies by economic interests, influencing politicians by pro-China businessmen" is in fact what Taipei has been trying to avoid. The most undesirable scenario, however, is exactly what happened after the presidential election in March 2000, when the pro-Chen businessmen were coerced to make statements that Taiwanese politicians did not want to hear. In the next section, we analyze the economic impact of FDI and examine the political factors that led to Taipei's imposition of regulations.

The Political Economy of FDI

As we have seen, the fundamental rationale behind Taiwan's GSBP policy was the fear that local industries could be hollowed out by the capital outflow to China. But if we look at the experiences of developed countries, Taiwan is not the only place where businesses face the option of moving their capital abroad. Even though mainland China is a nearby place with a familiar language and culture, similar situations arise in Europe. Yet no European country has imposed FDI restrictions as severe as Taiwan's GSBP policy. In fact, the main reasons behind Taiwan's tough economic regulations are concerns over national security—that is, worries that China could use its economic power to make Taiwanese businessmen in China further the People's Republic of China's (PRC) policy aims. Although such worries are somewhat understandable, we should distinguish the economic factors from the political factors in FDI.

Theoretical Reasons for FDI

The literature offers several reasons why firms invest directly in a foreign country. The first motive is to shift capital to places with a higher rate of return.[6] When two countries have no significant differences in technology—probably the case for traditional industries with low technology content—it is natural for the capital to flow to areas with higher rates of return. Typical examples in Taiwan include the textile, clothing, wooden furniture, plastics, and leather product industries, all of which have returned a very low rate of capital accumulation in recent years. These industries, according to Kao,[7] have indeed contributed a significant proportion of capital outflow to mainland China. Firms in industries with a high technology content, or those needing sophisticated managerial support, would have no reason to move to mainland China in its current stage of development.

The second reason why firms set up plants abroad is to save on transport costs.[8] Since the market for everyday commodities in China is huge, it is rational for firms to consider producing these commodities close to the markets. But if the production of a commodity needs certain critical inputs that are not available in China and would entail high transport costs, these producers are unlikely to shift their production to mainland China. Of course firms may differentiate their production of the same goods, with different grades of quality, and locate them in different places, so that consumers with different tastes can all be satisfied. In a sense, this kind of intra-industry separation of production across countries is a variant form of saving transport costs.

The third cause of FDI, as pointed out by Barrell and Pain,[9] is that FDI is an effective means of bypassing trade barriers. This also explains why most FDI occurs in the manufacturing industries; for service industries, barriers to trade do not constitute an inducement for FDI.[10] Beijing, for example, imposes licensing and foreign exchange controls on the importation of goods such as plastic and textile materials—controls that constitute major trade barriers. In response, many investment projects from Taiwan, as well as other countries, have targeted local production of such materials as a way to jump the trade barriers. Investments induced by trade barriers can also be observed in the case of consumer electronics and telecommunication equipment.

The fourth reason for FDI is particularly relevant to markets character-ized by imperfect competition. Firms may want to invest abroad in order to grow abroad. If the market in question is not competitive, then it is certainly important to increase the market size and secure monopoly power.[11] In this case, FDI and exports are not substitutes.[12] Firms in imperfect markets seek first-mover advantage on new frontiers, which in turn will attract follow-up investments.

Matching Theory with Practice

Now that we know why Taiwanese businesses move to China, we are ready to investigate how governments should react to FDI. From the viewpoint of a host country, inward investment was once feared as a possible source of foreign influence, competition, and control. Such fears have diminished in recent years; indeed this is why, in 1979, China announced its policy of welcoming foreign capital. After twenty-two years of development leading to a fourfold increase in China's per capita income, the tide can no longer be turned back. Moreover, Barrell and Pain have shown that FDI has a positive influence on domestic technological progress and hence can assist in China's industrial upgrading.[13] As there is no reason for mainland China to oppose FDI from Taiwan, our attention focuses mainly on the policies of Taipei.

As Blomstrom et al. point out,[14] outward investment has been opposed by many home countries because it may substitute for exports and domestic employment and reduce domestic capital formation. As for the argument that FDI reduces exports and employment, we cannot find any solid support for this statement. Indeed, Lipsey and Weiss conclude there is "no evidence that on net balance a country's production in overseas markets substitutes for its own domestic production and employment."[15] The reason for such a conclusion is clear once we know more about the context of the economy. As we have seen, a Taiwanese firm moving its capital to China has probably lost its competitiveness in Taiwan and is forced to move to a place with lower labor and material costs in order to survive. Chen and Ku have shown that FDI reduces the risk of business failure in the home country.[16] Without such an opportunity for capital outflow, therefore, the firm's production or-ders and jobs may well disappear anyway; and even if the firm moves to

China, its intermediate inputs, particularly those with high technological content, may well be produced in Taiwan and exported to China in support of its operations there. According to a government survey, Taiwanese firms in China import 47.5 percent of their parts and semifinished products from Taiwan.[17] If the final demand in China is large, the derived demand for such intermediate inputs would be even larger than the original amount—which would benefit rather than hurt Taiwan's production and job opportunities. Finally, when Taiwanese firms move to China the middle- and high-level managerial staff positions are often filled by expatriates from Taiwan. Thus, even though the local job opportunity for blue-collar workers may indeed be reduced by FDI, the need for white-collar workers increases.[18] To say the least, then, the net effect of Taiwan's FDI outflow to China is uncertain.

Now we turn to the contention that FDI may reduce the home country's domestic investment. The basis for such an argument is the financial constraints that a firm faces. When a firm invests abroad, where the return is higher, credit constraints sometimes crowd out its domestic investment. Stevens and Lipsey have shown a correlation between domestic and foreign investments: When the parent firm faces an exogenous shock, the better opportunity abroad usually induces the firm to reduce its domestic investment.[19] But what holds at the micro-level may not hold at the macro-level. When it is argued that there is a substitution relationship between domestic and foreign capital accumulation, this refers to the phenomenon at the macro-level. This worry, though legitimate, must be evaluated not from the perspective of individuals but from that of the country as a whole. According to the Council for Economic Planning and Development (CEPD),[20] Taiwan's direct investment in China between 1992 and 1999 accounted for an average of 2 percent of Taiwan's GDP. Given that Taiwan's excess savings ratio during the same period averaged 3 percent, the investment in China can hardly be blamed for crowding out domestic investment. The Taiwan authorities, however, worry that if a lot of businessmen invest in China instead of Taiwan, the Taiwan economy will be under-invested and labor productivity will subsequently decline.

Although we cannot say this reasoning is wrong, it is incomplete. Resource allocation in a free economy is dictated by the market. Without referring to market competition, it is paradoxical to base the GSBP policy on the government's assessment that FDI to China is harmful to Taiwan and needs to be curbed. When capital in one industry moves out, there are always other industries to fill the vacuum. In particular, the product life cycle theory says that the world's comparative advantages change over time.[21] The fact that most investments in China are targeted at low-technology industries—and that the degree of capital intensity of direct investment in China is increasing with the pace of China's economic development—indicates changing comparative advantages across the Taiwan Strait. If there is anything to be worried about, it should be the domestic economic environment that is needed to nurture Taiwan's new comparative advantages. This environment includes the adequacy of public infrastructure, the efficiency of the government, and the quality of the labor force. The search for new comparative advantages, however, does not have much connection with the FDI practices.

Finally, a noneconomic reason for implementing the GSBP policy is often cited: national security. When Taiwanese businessmen invest most of their resources in China—even though these investments are profit-oriented and match the international tide of product life cycle—Taiwan's economy becomes highly vulnerable to antagonistic moves by China. With respect to such an argument, we have two comments. The first concerns the problem of protecting national interests against a move by China forcing Taiwanese businessmen to do something harmful to the political balance across the strait. The second concerns the problem of mitigating the mutual antagonism between the two sides of the strait. We discuss the first point now and leave the second to later.

If Taiwan's focus is on protecting itself from China's harassment—auditing the tax returns of Taiwanese firms in China, canceling approval of various applications already granted these firms—there are better ways to achieve such a goal. Since harassment is not something Taiwanese firms can predict or avoid, the best way to deal with the problem is to ensure against these events rather than abandon the investment projects altogether. One way to ensure against such harassment is to encourage Taiwanese firms to invite foreign companies, particularly from the United States and Europe, to undertake joint investment in China. Because such a scheme provides a mechanism for businessmen to share risks, it should be eminently acceptable to them. The government could encourage such joint ventures with tax incentives or administrative dispatch in approving the projects. Once the joint venture between a Taiwanese and a foreign firm is formed, the entity that invests in China is no longer a "Taiwanese" firm. Such joint ventures should be welcomed by the Chinese government since they do not deter the inflow of FDI. And because hybrid ownership of the joint venture would make the Chinese authorities reluctant to pursue harassment, the interests of Taiwan's investors would be protected.

The Impact of China's Entry into the WTO

China applied in 1986 to join the General Agreement on Tariffs and Trade (GATT), the predecessor to the WTO, and lengthy negotiations had been going on for some thirteen years when finally, in November 1999, China struck a major deal with the United States regarding a package of concessions it was willing to make upon its accession into the WTO. According to the U.S. trade representatives' news release (2 February 2000), China is committed to cutting tariffs on industrial goods (from an average of 24.6 percent to 9.4 percent), expanding market access opportunities for foreign agricultural products, eliminating discriminatory taxes and regulations, abolishing trade-distorting export subsidies, and phasing out import quotas. Moreover, China will grant foreign nationals trading and distribution rights that had been reserved for Chinese enterprises.

To calm American fears over surging imports from China after its accession, China has even agreed to allow the U.S. authorities to treat China as a nonmarket economy in its antidumping litigation for a further fifteen years and to apply textile safeguards until 2008, even though the relevant WTO provisions for such measures are due to expire at the end of 2005. In return, the United States has granted China normal trading relations (NTR), whereby China will be granted permanent most-favored-nation (MFN) status upon entry to the WTO and become eligible for all U.S. concessions committed under the purview of the WTO.

Relaxing Restrictions on Chinese Imports

Taiwan's and China's accession into the WTO has important implications for cross-strait relations in the future. Above all, Taiwan's current restrictions on cross-strait trade will violate the WTO's nondiscriminatory principle unless Taiwan invokes the WTO's Article 13 (the nonapplication clause) to exclude China from the beneficiary list. Assuming Taiwan does not do so, Taipei's indirect shipping requirement and its prohibition of sensitive imports from China will have to be abolished. Taipei's unilateral removal of the indirect shipping requirement may not automatically translate into direct shipping practices, however, because direct shipping across the Taiwan Strait is a complex political issue. Only political dialogue can resolve such issues as flagging, documentation, legal jurisdiction, and customs procedures, and the WTO can hardly be expected to precipitate a political dialogue between Taiwan and China. Beijing maintains that cross-strait shipping is a domestic matter, but Taipei has consistently rejected this idea. Since 1997 Taiwan has allowed Chinese and multinational ship lines to navigate between Taiwanese and Chinese ports, but the commodities they carry are not allowed to enter Taiwan's customs territory. Thus, the removal of Taiwan's shipping restrictions will only benefit multinational ship lines that have been allowed to travel between Taiwanese and Chinese ports, and concern for domestic lines is likely to foster protectionist measures to prevent foreign lines from

Table 7.2

Taiwan's Trade with China

	Taiwan's exports to China		Taiwan's imports from China	
Year	Volume (US$ million)	Share (%)	Volume (US$ million)	Share (%)
1991	6,928	9.1	1,126	1.8
1992	9,697	11.9	1,119	1.6
1993	12,728	14.9	1,016	1.3
1994	14,653	15.7	1,859	2.2
1995	17,898	16.0	3,091	3.0
1996	19,148	16.5	3,060	3.0
1997	20,518	16.8	3,915	3.4
1998	18,380	16.6	4,111	3.9
1999	21,221	17.5	4,526	4.1
2000	26,162	17.6	6,223	4.4

Source: Data are from *Liang-An Mao-I Ching-Shih Fen-Hsi* [Trends in Taiwan-China trade], various issues, Board of Foreign Trade, Taiwan.

Note: "Share" refers to shares in Taiwan's total exports and imports respectively.

taking a free ride. This means that little progress can be expected unless there is a breakthrough in the political arena.

Now we come to the prohibition of Chinese imports. Taiwan currently applies separate regulations on imports from China. At present, about 56 percent of tariff lines are allowed to be imported from China. The rest are prohibited, including most agricultural products and certain industrial goods such as textiles and clothing, footwear, and electronic goods. In general, goods geared toward final consumption are prohibited from importation; only semifinished products and intermediate goods that do not present a threat to the domestic industry are permissible. Therefore, semifinished electronic and metal products, machine parts, and minerals form the mainstay of Chinese imports. Moreover, some imports from China need to be licensed even though the same items can be freely imported from the rest of the world.

Unlike the stringent regulations on Chinese imports, Taipei imposes no particular restrictions on Taiwanese exports to China. As a result, cross-strait trade has been unevenly in Taiwan's favor. In 2000, for example, Taiwan exported US$26,162 million worth of goods to China while importing just US$6,223 million in return. Exports to China accounted for 17.6 percent of Taiwan's total exports, while imports from China accounted for only 4.4 percent of Taiwan's total imports (Table 7.2). Industrial goods such as textile materials, machinery, electronic components, and metal parts supporting Taiwanese firms' Chinese operations constituted the mainstay of Taiwan's exports.

If Taiwan were to abolish the discriminatory import control regime that currently applies to China and began to treat China as an MFN trading partner, cross-strait trade figures would be drastically redrawn. No doubt imports from China would surge by several times. Indeed Hui-tzu Shih estimates that imports from China would surpass Taiwan's exports to China, turning Taiwan's current cross-strait trade surplus into a trade deficit.[22] Shih, however, also predicts that the overall trade balance for Taiwan would remain in the black since increased Chinese imports would mainly replace imports from Southeast Asian nations and other developing countries. Nonetheless, there would be structural changes in the composition of imports (notably an increase in textiles and agricultural imports) to the extent that they would seriously threaten the domestic industry. Consequently, there will be immense adjustment costs for Taiwanese society to bear.

Liberalization of China's Markets

Upon joining the WTO, China will lower its tariff barriers, provide market access, and remove domestic taxes and regulations that discriminate against imported goods to conform with the principle of national treatment. This, of course, creates new market opportunities for Taiwan. But how much benefit can Taiwanese enterprises garner from this unprecedented market opening?

At present, Taiwan's exports to China comprise mainly industrial materials that support Chinese export industries, including those operated by Taiwanese enterprises. In 1999, for example, machinery and electronic components accounted for 38 percent of total exports, textiles for 16 percent, and plastic and rubber products for 16 percent.[23] Electronics, textiles, and plastic and rubber products, are incidentally, also the three major sectors in which Taiwanese FDI is concentrated. Typical Chinese import tariffs on these items exceed 20 percent. Moreover, a 17 percent value-added tax is levied on the tariff-cum-value of imports, making the imports prohibitively expensive. Taiwan was able to export these materials to China because customs duties and value-added tax are exempted if the imported materials are processed for export. Therefore, it is understandable that most Taiwanese exports to China are eventually exported to the rest of the world after some processing in China. Exports of this nature will not be affected by China's tariff concessions when it enters the WTO.

Trade will be created, however, when China removes nontariff measures (NTMs) on selected imports. China currently imposes quotas and licensing controls on a wide range of sensitive imports, notably those designated as import-substitution industries. China is committed to phasing out most import quotas by 2002 and all quotas by 2005. According to a study by Taiwan's

Board of Foreign Trade (BOFT),[24] Taiwan stands to gain a great deal from China's elimination of NTMs. The BOFT points out that Taiwan was among the top suppliers of NTM-restricted items such as cathode-ray tubes (used in TV receivers and computers), plastic molding, metal molding, polyester filament, and metalworking machine tools. These items are relatively capital intensive in production and, therefore, are not yet ripe for relocation to China. Quota and licensing controls have forced some Taiwanese firms to invest in China prematurely. When these measures are eliminated, normal trade can be carried out and the volume of export is expected to increase.

More trade will be created in sectors where imports are destined for the domestic market. At present, the Chinese government denies foreign nationals the right to import and distribute products in the Chinese market. Foreign-owned enterprises may distribute only the goods they produce in China. Even if they do so, goods purchased from them cannot be deducted from the value of sales in calculating the tax base on which the value-added tax is to be assessed. These practices are important measures for the protection of Chinese state-owned enterprises and constitute insurmountable hurdles for foreign enterprises interested in penetrating the Chinese market.

Upon entering the WTO, China is committed to offering trading and distribution rights to foreign nationals and rendering national treatment to foreign-produced goods. If faithfully implemented, this measure will have far-reaching impacts on competition in the Chinese market. With respect to consumer durables, for example, the monopoly power of state-owned enterprises is likely to be challenged by brand-name multinationals that invest and market in China. Under the competitive pressure, state-owned enterprises that dominate the market at present will have to restructure themselves, ally with multinationals, or face elimination. Although China has not agreed to sign the WTO Government Procurement Agreement, it has promised not to intervene in the commercial transactions of state-owned enterprises. This implies that the markets for durables such as consumer electronics and automobiles will enter a new era of competition and industrial shakeout. Taiwanese firms are relatively weak in these sectors; the major benefits they may expect are probably in the areas of components and parts, which can be exported from Taiwan or produced inside China. The tariffs on auto parts, for instance, will be dropped to an average of 10 percent by mid-2006 according to the China-U.S. bilateral agreement signed in November 1999.

Taiwanese firms, however, will benefit enormously from China's participation in the Information Technology Agreement (ITA), although the exact date of its participation has not yet been spelled out. The ITA binds the signatory nations to applying zero tariffs on products such as computers, telecommunication equipment, semiconductors, and Internet applications. In recent years, Taiwanese computer-related firms have generated a new wave of FDI in China, aiming at the local market, and the products manufactured in China include computers, computer peripherals, multimedia equipment, cellular phone handsets, and all sorts of components. Due to the administrative barriers and market segmentation, domestic sales of information products have not lived up to expectations. But China's entry into the WTO, and particularly its participation in the ITA, will blow the entire market open to Taiwanese firms that have established a foothold there. Even multinational firms such as Compaq and Dell, which already manufacture in China, will have difficulty competing because of the Taiwanese firms' advantage in language and cultural affinity. This advantage will give Taiwan's computer industry a further lift and secure its position on the world map. The Chinese market will prompt Taiwanese firms to integrate backward and forward along the value chain, as well, enticing them to devote more resources to R&D and marketing.

Trade and Investment Nexus

Robert Mundell has argued that trade and direct investment are perfect substitutes, so that prohibition of trade can induce capital flow, which produces exactly the same result as trade.[25] The real world, of course, falls short of the perfect settings in the theoretical model that underpin the equivalence. For one thing, direct investment entails more risks than trade. It also provides proximity to the market that enables investors to beat out the exporters in serving consumers. Most Taiwanese investments in China are export-oriented and aimed at utilizing China's cheap labor. Since the mid-1990s there have been increasing cases of investment aimed at producing intermediate materials and components to be incorporated into Chinese exports. Some of these investment projects are indeed induced by trade barriers, particularly nontariff measures, but they constitute only a fraction of the total Taiwanese FDI. Most investment projects are still aimed at exploiting China's immense labor pool, including skilled workers.

Although there has been much talk about the potential of the Chinese market, which is now the world's sixth-largest economy in terms of GNP, few genuinely local-market-oriented investment projects have been implemented. Notable exceptions appear in food processing, motorcycles, and home appliances, where import controls have effectively locked out foreign competition. Therefore, as Mundell's model would predict, if China's entry in the WTO does result in a lowering of trade barriers, it will only facilitate trade to substitute for a small proportion of Taiwanese FDI. On the contrary, China's market opening is likely to induce a substantial amount of new investment into that country.

Local presence is essential for a Taiwanese firm interested in penetrating the Chinese markets, particularly for durable goods and expensive items. Lacking a brand-name image, Taiwanese firms have to rely on local presence to win over local consumers. As an unexploited market dominated by state-owned enterprises, China is also a perfect launching ground for new brands, and a few Taiwanese firms in the apparel and home appliance industries have succeeded in such initiatives. Many computer-related firms are prepared to embark on the same endeavor. The tariffs currently levied by China on durable goods are high enough to create an advantage for local manufacturers in spite of the future concessions. Therefore, FDI in this sector will increase rather than decrease after China's accession to the WTO.

Moreover, when China conforms to the WTO rules on trade-related investment measures (TRIMs), FDI in China becomes even more attractive in the manufacture and sale of durable goods, since conforming to TRIMs means that China must remove trade-distorting regulations such as local content ratio and the requirement that foreign exchange payments must balance earnings. The latter requirement forces foreign-owned firms to export some products to support their need to import raw materials even if their operations are completely oriented toward the local market. Removing this requirement will reduce the costs of genuinely local operations.

Intermediate goods used in downstream processing for the Chinese export industries, such as textiles and petrochemical materials, can be exported to China with fewer restrictions after China enters the WTO. Production of these goods, which is capital-intensive, can remain in Taiwan without losing market opportunities. Trade, therefore, will substitute for direct investment in this case. The pressure on Taipei to relax the GSBP policy in these areas will be vented when China is admitted to the WTO.

Two Constructive Views of the Cross-Strait Relations

As GSBP policy has failed to curtail Taiwan's direct investment into China and the WTO presents an opportunity for redrawing the policy, we will present two constructive views of the cross-strait relations in this section.

Self-fulfilling Expectation and Its Policy Implications

A self-fulfilling expectation is a common expectation of economic agents that changes their behavior, which in turn leads to the realization of their original expectation. If all agents expect a stock's price to rise, for instance, they will rush to buy the stock causing an excess demand for the stock and, hence, a price increase just as they had expected. If all agents expect British sterling to depreciate, then all agents will sell sterling causing an excess supply of sterling and eventually its depreciation. A brief analysis of self-fulfilling equilibria can be found in C.Y. Cyrus Chu.[26] We believe that the same logic applies to the development of cross-strait affairs.

Consider the proposal put forth by S.M. Chen, deputy governor of the Central Bank of Taiwan, to levy a "national security tax" on investment in China by Taiwanese firms. The idea was roughly as follows: Since investment in China by Taiwanese firms gives the Chinese government a "hostage" it can use to blackmail the government of Taiwan, the parent firms are in fact exercising an activity with negative externalities. Thus, GSBP is not enough; firms undertaking these investments should be subject to a corrective Pigouvian tax. We see this as a naive way of dealing with cross-strait economic problems.

Under the current GSBP policy, many firms already bypass the review procedure when investing in China just to avoid the tedious bureaucratic details. How many businessmen would be foolish enough to come to the government desk and register for a national security tax—given that there are ways of circumvention? Even if we leave aside the technical difficulty of collecting this tax, the idea itself is problematic. Levying a national security tax sends the message that investing in China is a bad thing. In view of this unfriendly policy, Beijing would certainly respond in an equally unfriendly way against Taiwan—which in turn would demonstrate that China is indeed antagonistic. This is a kind of self-fulfilling expectation.

China's missile tests in 1995 provide clear evidence of its aggressive attitude, and we do not seek to justify or defend its position. Our suggestion is, not to look backward and ascertain which side initiated the vicious circle, but to look forward and see how the vicious circle and the current mistrust in cross-strait affairs can be finally put to rest. The political entanglement across the strait can be dissolved only by ever increasing, mutually beneficial, economic transactions. Thus, the current economic interests should be allowed to further the future development of friendship; the current lack of friendship should not be allowed to void both countries' mutual economic interests. If both sides insist that economic interests must be subordinated to political purposes, there will be no development of economic activities. But if both sides look at the problem differently and hold out different expectations, the results are likely to be different.

Distinguishing Between Processes and Outcomes

In economics there are two distinct ways of policy analysis: One is to calculate the possible outcomes and then determine how a desirable outcome can be achieved by the correct choice of policy; the other is to study the dynamics of the process and see how different policies may change them. When the environment is simple and exogenous factors are few, the former approach is possible. In a sophisticated environment, however, the former approach is almost impossible. All we can do is choose a controllable process and let time decide the outcome.

A common doctrine of liberalism everywhere is citizen sovereignty. From this we derive two beliefs: First, a government should not impose any prespecified outcome on its citizens and use it to constrain their right of dynamic development; second, the purpose of all government policies should be the improvement of citizens' welfare, and there should be no objectives above and beyond such a concern. Consider the formation of the European Union. It has indeed gone through the stages of customs union, common market, and monetary and political unions. The move from one stage to the next certainly implies the approval of all governments involved. More important, the process should be viewed as economic rather than political, for it is economic welfare, not political ideology, that drives the evolution of the various stages. Liberalist philosophy may fail to persuade the leaders of either side of the Taiwan Strait. But we think it is unreasonable and even harmful for either side to withhold economic exchanges simply because the political outcomes are still being debated.

Chen Shui-bian's new administration has not done a good job of sustaining Taiwan's economic prosperity. Halting and resumption of the construction of the fourth nuclear power plant has given an impression of policy inconsistency. The "nonperforming loan" ratio of many financial institutions has exceeded the level of financial prudence. In November and December 2000, foreign publications such as the *Economist*, *Business Week*, and the *New York Times* independently raised their concerns about a possible financial crisis in Taiwan. The third-quarter unemployment rate in 2000 reached a historic high of 3.19 percent. Threats of an imminent economic recession have put pressure on the Chen administration to open up economic exchanges with China as a stimulus to Taiwan's sliding economy, such as lifting the ban on Chinese tourists to Taiwan. Given such pressure, Taipei's GSBP policy and trade regulations may be relaxed in the near future, even before both sides enter the WTO.

Reasons for Optimism

In recent years we have witnessed the increasing integration of the whole world, and we note it is economic interests that tend to drive this integration. Economic interests, while providing a common ground for countries to share, also allow for the peaceful coexistence of countries of a wide diversity. Diversity of race, culture, language, and even political ideology is possible under the umbrella of economic prosperity. Indeed, the European Union is a classic case of an integrated economy encompassing political diversity.

The adversarial relationship between Taiwan and China will undoubtedly be softened by the sharing of irresistible economic interests. Despite Taiwan's stringent restrictions, trade and investment between the two sides have created enormous benefits for both. Taiwan's regulations on trade and investment were underpinned by a sense of insecurity arising from its asymmetry with mainland China. This sense of insecurity can only be dispelled if China denounces the use of force against Taiwan. Otherwise, Taiwan's policy toward China is likely to be dominated by concerns for its own security.

We, however, find that the sharing of economic interests generally contributes to national security. Certainly there is no hard evidence that foreign direct investment in China has hollowed out Taiwan's domestic industry. Overdependence on the Chinese market can be avoided if Taiwanese firms invest in China as part of a globalization process rather than a simple relocation of production facilities to a labor haven.

Given that China is a large and growing member of the world economy, increasing dependence on the Chinese market seems inevitable. One way for Taiwan to prevent one-sided dependence on China is to build up technological capabilities that can serve the Chinese market but can also be switched to alternative ends at low cost. The other solution for Taiwan is to integrate regional economies, such as those in the Asia Pacific Economic Cooperation (APEC), into one common market so that bilateral relations with China are subsumed in a regional framework.

To this end, Taiwan's and China's expected accession into the WTO serves a useful purpose. Upon accession both sides will relax trade restrictions to promote exchange of goods and services. Moreover, trade disputes can be resolved within the purview of the WTO to avoid the sensitive issue of sovereignty. We expect bilateral trade to increase after the WTO accession. Compared to the current lopsided situation, trade will become more balanced and China may even end up on the surplus side. Without increasing the stringency of investment regulations, Taiwan's FDI in China can also be expected to increase, particularly with respect to durable goods.

We therefore propose a positive view of the cross-strait relationship and offer two suggestions. First, bilateral relations may be a self-fulfilling process in which good intentions drive a virtuous cycle and evil intentions drive a vicious cycle. At this difficult time, it is important to embark upon a course of confidence building on the basis of common economic interests. Second, neither government should impose a political outcome on its citizens and force a choice of economic course that leads to that outcome. Instead, both governments should choose economic courses that are controllable, with calculated risks, but that may lead to outcomes determined by their citizens.

Notes

1. See *Commercial Times*, various days in mid-April 2000.
2. For various statistics and references, see C. Kao, "A Study of the Impact of Changing Economic Environment in Mainland China on Taiwanese Investment" (research report prepared for Ministry of Economic Affairs, Legislative Yuan, 1999).
3. R. Nurkse, *Problems of Capital Formation in Underdeveloped Countries* (Oxford: Blackwell, 1953).
4. For a further discussion, see C. Kao, "An Investigation of the Economic and Trade Interactions Between Taiwan and China" (in Chinese) (paper presented at the Fifth Conference of Cross-Strait Academics held at Da Yeh Technical College, 2000).
5. Ibid.
6. R. Barrell and N. Pain, "Foreign Direct Investment, Technological Change, and Economic Growth Within Europe," *Economic Journal* 107 (1997):1770–1786.
7. See Kao, "Impact of Changing Economic Environment."
8. S.L. Brainard, "A Simple Theory of Multinational Corporations and Trade with a Trade-off Between Proximity and Concentration," National Bureau of Economic Research Working Paper 4269 (Cambridge: National Bureau of Economic Research, 1993).
9. Barrell and Pain, "Foreign Direct Investment."
10. I.B. Kravis and R.E. Lipsey, "The Effect of Multinational Firms' Foreign Operations on Their Domestic Employment," NBER Working Paper 2760 (Cambridge: NBER, 1988).
11. J.A. Cantwell, "A Survey of Theories of International Production," in *The Nature of the Transnational Firm*, ed. C. Pitelis and R. Sugden (London and New York: Routledge, 1991).
12. R.E. Lipsey and M.Y. Weiss, "Foreign Production and Exports in Manufacturing Industries," *Review of Economics and Statistics* 63 (1981):488–494.
13. See Barrell and Pain, "Foreign Direct Investment."
14. M. Blomstrom, G. Fors, and R.E. Lipsey, "Foreign Direct Investment and Employment: Home Country Experience in the United States and Sweden," *Economic Journal* 107 (1997):1787–1797.
15. Lipsey and Weiss, "Foreign Production and Exports," p. 494.
16. Tain-Jy Chen and Ying-Hua Ku, "The Effect of Foreign Direct Investment on Firm Growth: The Case of Taiwan's Manufacturers," *Japan and the World Economy* 12 (2000):153–172.
17. Ministry of Economic Affairs, "Chih tsao yeh tui wai tou tzu tiao cha pao kao" [Survey of foreign direct investment by manufacturing firms] (Taipei: Ministry of Economic Affairs, 1998).
18. Blomstrom et al., "Foreign Direct Investment and Employment."
19. G.V.G. Stevens and R.E. Lipsey, "Interactions Between Domestic and Foreign Investments," *Journal of International Money and Finance* 11 (1992):40–62.

20. Council for Economic Planning and Development, "The Effect of Foreign Direct Investment on Domestic Economy" (unpublished report, 2000).

21. R. Vernon, "International Investment and International Trade in the Product Cycle," *Quarterly Journal of Economics* 83 (1966):190–207.

22. H.T. Shih, *The Impact of Trade Deregulation Across the Taiwan Strait* (in Chinese), Economic Monograph 193 (Taipei: Chung-Hua Institution for Economic Research, 1999).

23. Chung-Hua Institution for Economic Research, *Quarterly Report on Industrial Development in China*, no. 20 (Taipei: Chung-Hua Institution for Economic Research, 2000).

24. Board of Foreign Trade, "The Impact on Taiwanese Firms of Chinese Economic Reforms upon Accession to WTO," as posted on the BOFT website, moeaboft.gov.tw, dated 24 April 2000.

25. R. Mundell, "International Trade and Factor Mobility," *American Economic Review* 67 (1957):321–335.

26. C.Y.C. Chu, "Introducing the Soros Bond: Insuring Against Self-Fulfilling Financial Crises" (working paper, Institute of Economics, Academia Sinica, 2000).

8

America's Taiwan Quandary: How Much Does Chen's Election Matter?

Alan M. Wachman

For the United States, the election of Chen Shui-bian exacerbated a long-standing quandary that reflects competing political impulses. Americans are certainly wont to oppose governments that restrict the right of citizens to express their political will or impose on them a sanctioned dogma to which they must adhere. Thus, the United States has welcomed the emergence of pluralism and democracy on Taiwan. Nevertheless, the United States has also discouraged Taiwan from invoking the principle of self-determination and declaring independence—even if the ambition to preserve an independent state accords with the will of the majority on Taiwan expressed through the same democratic processes the United States has otherwise acclaimed. For the United States to do otherwise would risk confrontation with the People's Republic of China (PRC), which maintains that Taiwan is part of China and warns that a declaration of independence by Taiwan is a casus belli. For reasons of history and concern for U.S. credibility, among other explanations, the United States would likely feel compelled to respond to an attack by the PRC on Taiwan, perhaps leading to direct military conflict between Washington and Beijing. To avoid this outcome, the United States has adopted an ambiguous policy about the status of Taiwan and U.S. intentions. By remaining ambiguous, the United States aims to deter Taiwan—its government and population—from declaring independence, on the one hand,

I am indebted to Muthiah Alagappa, Chu Yun-han, Larry Diamond, Harry Harding, Jia Qingguo, Denny Roy, and Wu Yu-Shan, all of whom responded with insight and suggestions to an initial draft of this chapter presented at "Taiwan Presidential Elections: Outcome and Implications," a conference sponsored by the East-West Center, Honolulu, Hawaii, 20–22 August 2000.

while deterring the PRC, on the other, from using force to settle the unresolved controversy about sovereignty over Taiwan.

This ambiguous policy seemed easier to sustain before the election of Chen Shui-bian. While the Kuomintang (KMT) was in power, the government of the Republic of China (ROC) was explicitly committed to the unification of Taiwan and the mainland—even though Lee Teng-hui strained credibility at times by appearing determined to preserve Taiwan's autonomy. The official stance of the ROC government made it possible for the United States to maintain its own version of a "one China" policy and thereby minimize friction with the PRC over the Taiwan issue. But Chen's election prompted worries that he might act in accordance with the posture of the Democratic Progressive Party (DPP) from which he arose. Even though Chen was not elected with a mandate to pursue independence, his history as an independence activist was deeply troubling, as was the DPP's long-standing determination to promote independence for Taiwan.

The United States has carefully calibrated its actions and statements to avoid provoking the PRC—as support for independence undoubtedly would.[1] With the victory of Chen Shui-bian, however, the United States was confronted by a perplexing contest between its reflexive identification with democracy and its recognition that its other national interests are not served by military confrontation with the PRC. For this reason, the election of Chen Shui-bian has serious implications for the U.S. policy. The question addressed in this chapter, then, is not whether Chen's election matters to the United States, but *how much* it matters compared with other factors that affect the U.S. role in the cross-strait controversy.

Since 1972, the policy of the United States toward China and Taiwan has been relatively stable, though not absolutely so. Incremental adjustments of tone or emphasis contribute to a sense that the U.S. role has evolved. Such changes, however, have generally reinforced the fundamental architecture of the relationship between Washington, Beijing, and Taipei. Indeed, the parameters of the triadic relations among the three states have not changed much in this period. Certain enduring features of the relationship contribute to stability:

- The triadic dynamics of interaction
- The primacy of security as a motivating factor for each state
- The dominance of the Sino-U.S. relationship

Incremental changes have also affected the enduring features of the triadic relationship—changes brought about by evolving forces in politics, economics, and the realm of ideas. These, in turn, help to determine the way in which each state perceives the others. Among the evolving forces that affected relations between the United States and the PRC and Taiwan in the 1980s and 1990s are

- The democratization of Taiwan
- The economic liberalization of the PRC
- The emergence of a new international order after the demise of bipolarity

Such factors affect policy in a gradual manner, but not so slowly as to be imperceptible. Democratization in Taiwan has, among other things, increased the number of voices that participate in determining Taiwan's posture toward the PRC. Economic liberalization in China has enhanced the PRC's integration into a broad community of states with comparable objectives for development and enrichment, and has shifted the values that motivate leaders in Beijing. Finally, the demise of bipolarity has prompted a sense that the international order is undergoing a rapid transformation that affects the status of the United States and its relationship to other states and institutions. This transformation has generated debate within the United States about its role abroad and has changed the way that the United States and the PRC view each other.

Evolving influences such as these may also engender more ephemeral effects, some of which are utterly transitory, others of which may reinforce the gradual changes already under way. Perhaps a catastrophic event, such as the PRC's suppression of demonstrations in 1989 or the missile "crisis" of 1996 have the potential of abruptly reorienting the relationship among the states as well.[2] The election of Chen Shui-bian, however, is not such a political shock, even though, in principle, a change of government might bring on such a cataclysmic reorientation of policy. Thus, the implications of Chen's election for the United States can be elucidated by considering it in the context of the triadic relationship and other factors that may affect the U.S. role.

Enduring Constraints

In chapter 5, Yu-Shan Wu describes the dynamics of interactivity in the Washington–Beijing–Taipei triad by reference to the "strategic triangle" model proposed by Lowell Dittmer.[3] One may quibble about whether Dittmer's concept corresponds fully to this triad, but it does identify characteristics of the U.S. relationship with the PRC and the Soviet Union during the Cold War that offer a useful way of thinking about the dynamics of the U.S. relationship with the PRC and Taiwan. In the Washington–Beijing–Taipei triad, for instance, it does appear that each of the three states perceives the "strategic salience" of the other two and in its relations with them is primarily motivated by a concern for security. Moreover, all three states appear to be looking over their shoulder, at the second state when dealing with the third. For this reason, actions taken unilaterally by any one of the three states in pursuit of security tend to have an effect on relations among all three.[4]

Perhaps, in the context of Washington's relations with Beijing and Taipei, security should be broadly defined to extend beyond territorial security to include such matters as economic viability and national prestige. Even so, the rhetoric of ideology or the claims of nationalism should not prevent us from recognizing that Washington, Beijing, and Taipei act primarily, even if not solely, to enhance a sense of security. Expressions of determination to advance high ideals (unification, independence, peaceful resolution of the cross-strait controversy, stability in the Western Pacific) and stirring principles (no interference in internal affairs, more international space, democracy) may mask a deeper purpose: to make the state feel more secure.[5]

Security from Washington's Vantage

For the United States, the anxiety about security is a reaction to the PRC, not a concern about Taiwan. Despite solemn and self-righteous nods in Washington to the idea that the United States cannot play the role of global policeman by stopping every bad guy and serving as a referee in every conflict, the United States has already invested a good deal of political capital and risked other interests to deter the PRC from imposing its will on Taiwan by force. During the second half of the 1990s and into the new century, inflamed rhetoric on Capitol Hill, outraged editorials in the nation's journals, and a flood of policy prescriptions from think tanks and pundits might lead one to conclude that the PRC was swiftly becoming a menace to U.S. national security. Not all analysts share this view of the PRC, to be sure, but the undercurrent of wariness has had the effect of bolstering a sense among some of Beijing's detractors in Washington that the United States must stand up to the PRC. This, in turn, has resulted in efforts to provide Taiwan with more effective ways of defending itself.

Even for analysts and policymakers who do not view the PRC as an immediate threat to the United States, one suspects that the rationale for assisting Taiwan has something to do with Beijing's propensity to use force and its effort to intimidate Taiwan by references to the potential of a forceful settlement of cross-strait differences. Beijing's refusal to renounce the use of force, its missile exercises in 1995 and 1996, the "third if" in the white paper of February 2000 (which appeared to add a new condition that would prompt the use of force),[6] Zhu Rongji's chilling warning to Taiwan prior to the 2000 elections,[7] and the buildup of missile forces on China's southeast coast have left many American analysts with a concern that if it is not managed well, the cross-strait dispute could spark a military conflagration. This the United States positively hopes to deter. For this reason and others, it positions itself as a not-quite-disinterested balancer. While the PRC may attribute other, insidious motives to U.S. involvement, since the end of the Cold War the United States has remained a feature of this controversy largely, though not entirely, because of the PRC's threats to use force.

In reality, it has been decades since the PRC has employed force to harm the interests of Taiwan or destroy targets of value to Taiwan. The perception of observers in Washington and Taipei, though, is of a PRC that has, perhaps unwittingly, come to rely on belligerence more than blandishments to assert its determination to unify China. One strongly suspects that U.S. policy toward Taiwan is motivated less by a genuine concern for the autonomy of Taiwan's citizenry and more by a sense that Beijing should not be permitted to "get away with" a forceful absorption of a democratic state. Such a takeover would be devastating for U.S. credibility and undermine American alliances elsewhere in the Pacific. It would also disrupt the stability of the Western Pacific from which the United States, and its allies, derive much that they wish to preserve. It is hard to escape the conclusion that for American policymakers, the Taiwan issue is not so much about Taiwan as it is about constraining the choices made by the PRC.

In the abstract, it makes little difference to the United States whether Taiwan remains autonomous or is unified with other parts of China—as long as the resolution of the dispute is achieved by mutual consent and without the use or threat of force. According to the chairman and managing director of the American Institute in Taiwan, Richard Bush:

> The government of the United States takes no view on the substance of the ultimate outcome of the Taiwan Strait issue. What the United States cares about—its true interest—is process and context. . . . What is important is how decisions are made, not what those decisions are.[8]

By emphasizing process and "a willingness to support any outcome voluntarily agreed to by both sides of the Taiwan Strait,"[9] the United States emphasizes "peace and stability." This is a euphemism indicating Washington's hope that it can avoid being placed in a situation where it is compelled to choose between Beijing and Taipei. Even more than that, the United States wants to avoid getting sucked into a conflict between the two adversaries. Hostilities across the strait have, in the past, drawn the United States in. To preserve its credibility, the United States would likely feel compelled to restrain the PRC again if it assaulted Taiwan in a way that Washington judged to be unprovoked. Certainly the Taiwan Relations Act (TRA) that Congress made law in 1979 anticipates that the president and Congress would be motivated to respond. Moreover, by the end of the 1990s and early in the twenty-first century, there was a rising sense in Washington that the United States should do more to protect Taiwan from the PRC—hence, the efforts to enhance the TRA with the Taiwan Security Enhancement Act (TSEA) and the discussion concerning Taiwan's role in a theater missile defense (TMD) system.

Security from Beijing's Vantage

Beijing too is motivated principally by concerns about national security. That the unification of the state should be considered the path to security when the attainment of that goal puts Beijing's security at risk may seem counterintuitive. Yet the leadership of the PRC has come to see its legitimacy tied to the unification of the state. Whether popular nationalism in support of unification emerged spontaneously—or is itself a product of Beijing's effort to arouse domestic support—is difficult to gauge in a state where popular opinion cannot be reliably measured. What is clear, though, is that Beijing regards the Taiwan issue as one on which there is consensus among the Chinese people. The implication, of course, is that the government is compelled to adopt the posture it does to satisfy popular demands for unification. The leadership has staked an enormous share of credibility on its determination to resist prolonged division of the Chinese state and to override efforts to enable Taiwan to remain independent.

If it could, Beijing would surely rein Taiwan in. That it cannot do so reveals Beijing's impotence in the face of American interference. This is a painful reminder of the PRC's comparative weakness and vulnerability as well as China's experience at the hands of foreign predators prior to the establishment of the PRC. At stake for Beijing, therefore, is more than extending effective control over territory per se. Beijing hopes to erode Washington's support for Taiwan because that support is a symbol of China's victimization. In other words: How can the PRC regard itself as having cast off the yoke of imperialism as long as the United States shelters Taiwan and impedes Beijing from governing territory it claims as its own?

The PRC's stance is not motivated by a sense that the state itself is under threat. Rather, the division of China and the interference of the United States constitute an affront to the credibility and legitimacy of the Chinese Communist Party (CCP). Although PRC leaders express interest in unification, it appears from their behavior that a unified Chinese state is not as desirable as a unified state under the control of the CCP. Taiwan's autonomy is not a threat to the physical security of China, but to the security of the regime that rules it. The leadership of the PRC is not motivated simply by a wish to unify China, but by the desire to sustain itself in power.

Judging from the public utterances of PRC leaders, one senses in Beijing that there is a hierarchy to which the PRC expects Taiwan to conform. In this framework, Beijing is the superior and Taiwan the inferior. From the moment Chen Shui-bian was elected, Beijing arrogated to itself the privilege of asserting a precondition for negotiation: Chen must accept the "one China" principle before discussions can proceed about the nature of unification. Moreover, Chen must state his commitment in a manner that Beijing sees as sincere.

Even though Beijing ultimately found Lee Teng-hui untrustworthy and provocative, he at least acknowledged that there is "one China." From 1992 until 1999, Lee accepted the agreement about "one China" that was reached by negotiators from both sides. Then, on 9 July 1999, Lee's publicized comments about a "special state-to-state relationship" struck Beijing as violating the 1992 consensus. The PRC has been waiting ever since for Taipei to reaffirm the critical "one China" mantra.[10] That China is unified is not as important to Beijing as its determination that the PRC remain orderly and under the firm hand of the current regime. Taiwan's acquiescence to Beijing's legitimacy contributes to this end; Taiwan's autonomy or defiance detracts from it.

The PRC has articulated a formula for unification that it calls "one country, two systems." Under this formula Taiwan would be permitted a wide array of liberties—including the right to maintain its own government and even its own military—as long as it acknowledges there is "one China." This concept suggests a minimal degree of effective control by Beijing over the island itself. According to Andrew Nathan, the PRC does not need to control Taiwan internally "but it needs enough influence to guarantee Taiwan's deference to mainland security needs."[11] This means severing the ties between the United States and Taiwan that enable Taipei to use Washington against Beijing and to prevent Taiwan from serving U.S. security objectives in East Asia directly. That is, among other aims, Beijing wants to ensure that the island that lies ninety miles off its southeastern flank is not home to U.S. troops or a port for U.S. ships or a "stationary aircraft carrier" for U.S. planes.

American "hegemony," especially as it appears to restrain the PRC's hand in its own backyard, is intensely threatening. The PRC is also quite wary of the U.S.-Japan alliance, especially in the wake of the Revised Defense Guidelines and the ongoing discussion about the possibility of a Japanese role in

TMD. The PRC has sought to counterbalance this perceived threat with overtures to Russia and Europe as a means of creating a multipolar world, rather than allowing the United States to dominate in a unipolar world.[12] It is from this vantage that the PRC views its relations with the United States.

Security from Taipei's Vantage

Nowhere is the search for security more obvious than in Taiwan. Taipei wants to maintain and enhance its autonomy because it does not wish to give up a way of life it now enjoys. This is not about the security of the regime; it is about survival as a political entity. The desire for autonomy is not accompanied by an interest in threatening the security of the PRC. The rivalry over Taiwan's status does not imply an inherent hostility in Taiwan toward the PRC's existence. During the heyday of the KMT, such hostility did exist. However, since President Lee Teng-hui terminated the "Temporary Provisions Effective During the Period of Communist Rebellion" in 1991, not even the Nationalist Party of China has been prepared to contest Beijing's legitimacy to rule the territory it now governs.

At present Taiwan has only one adversary. It is a poignant paradox that its sole adversary, the PRC, claims a sacred historical mission to absorb Taiwan into a greater Chinese state because of common cultural and historical ties linking Chinese people on both sides of the Taiwan Strait, regardless of how the people on Taiwan feel about being absorbed. To safeguard itself from absorption and deflect military assaults or other pressure from Beijing, the ROC vigorously nurtures its relationship with Washington to remain in the protective embrace of the United States.

For Taiwan, the commitment to preserve a distinct political entity grows from a widespread sense that Taiwanese are distinct from the Chinese who reside on the mainland.[13] This distinction is not one of ethnicity, though extremists on Taiwan have made exaggerated claims of a distinct cultural division. It is a question of national identity. Many people on Taiwan wish to govern themselves because the history of Taiwan is a history of political authority imposed on the population by rulers coming from afar. This is not to suggest that all residents of Taiwan oppose unification. Under certain conditions, certain segments of the population might welcome union. Few of them, though, are prepared to consider such a thing on Beijing's terms or while the PRC is still ruled by an authoritarian government.

Most people on Taiwan still prefer to live apart from China and govern themselves while fostering less combative relations with their cousins across the strait. To some degree, this attitude reflects the emergence over decades of a distinct Taiwanese identity. The KMT's rigid cultural policies that superimposed a national Chinese culture on the local culture of Taiwan—coupled with the KMT's stifling authoritarian suppression of political dissent—had the unintended consequence of encouraging the majority of the island's population to see itself as distinct from the Chinese civilization represented by the KMT rulers, who arrived on the island only after the Japanese surrender in 1945.

The PRC leaders do not seem to appreciate the origins or intensity of the national identity of Taiwanese. Beijing dismisses those who cling to a separate identity on Taiwan with the disparaging label "separatist" or "splittist"—as if the Taiwanese are to be blamed for the civil war that erupted between the KMT and the CCP and divided the Chinese state. The leadership of the PRC seems unconcerned that the sense of separateness many Taiwanese feel is an outgrowth of hostility directed at them by the KMT and other elites who came from the mainland in the 1940s.

The tragic element in this cross-strait conflict is that the PRC leadership knows that what it does and says has consequences for policies and behavior on Taiwan. Beijing is exquisitely skilled in the art of diplomatic signaling. Yet leaders in Beijing seem not to see—or choose not to acknowledge—that by seeking to impose their political will on Taiwan they encourage the separate identity that Taiwanese already feel and reinforce the division between Taiwan and the mainland. The inclination to impose is itself a reflection of the highly emotional quality of Chinese nationalism in the PRC and the fervent belief, expressed by officials and other elites, that the government will do what it must to ensure that China does not remain divided. Of course, one senses that the trigger of these nationalist sentiments is not just Taiwan's defiance of Beijing's demands, but the involvement of the United States as an impediment to Beijing's objectives.

The Shrill Tenor of Sino-U.S. Relations

Perhaps it is axiomatic to observe that when the tenor of relations between Beijing and Washington is good, relations between Beijing and Taipei are less hostile than when Sino-U.S. relations deteriorate.[14] The "Taiwan problem" is only partly about Beijing's ambition to reassert control—however tenuous—over territory. It is also about Beijing's appetite for unimpaired sovereignty broadly envisaged and national dignity measured by international prestige. The appetite for these intangible attainments cannot be fully satisfied so long as the PRC leadership believes that the United States seeks to undermine these ambitions.

Before the election of Chen Shui-bian, relations between Washington and Beijing had grown decidedly shrill. The Cox Committee Report, the Wen-ho Lee affair, and the struggle over WTO negotiations in 1999 gave way in 2000 to the struggle over permanent normal trading relations (PNTR) and a

raft of accusations that Beijing has engaged in arms sales to America's adversaries, especially Iran and Pakistan.[15] In this period, relations were strained
to an extreme by the U.S. bombing of the PRC embassy in Belgrade. While
Americans may have responded with chagrin to news of the intelligence
failure that resulted in the bombing, they were not prepared for the explosion
of hostility directed at the United States and its facilities in the PRC by crowds
of protesters, apparently with the encouragement of the Chinese authorities.
To those Americans who failed to heed earlier signals of Chinese frustration
over the Sino-U.S. relationship, the anti-Americanism seemed to erupt out
of nowhere, revealing a nasty, nationalist sentiment that many, perhaps un-
justifiably, attributed solely to official machinations. It seemed difficult for
some in the United States to consider that such fury could be the unpremedi-
tated popular response to what was, in American eyes, simply a colossal
manifestation of bureaucratic ineptitude. A palpable, though more muted,
anti-American response affected the PRC's reaction to the April 2001 colli-
sion of a Chinese F-8 and a U.S. Navy surveillance plane.

From Beijing's point of view, the bombing of the embassy and the "spy
plane" incident confirmed a creeping view that the United States has become an unrestrained hegemonic force to which the PRC must not bend.
Chinese are eager to have amicable relations with the United States. Generally they are determined to avoid conflict. They do not understand why the
United States involves itself in what China sees as its internal affairs (human
rights, Tibet, Taiwan), and hence they fasten on conspiratorial explanations
having the common theme that the United States hopes to preserve its international influence by keeping China, a potential competitor, weak and divided. Such thinking gives rise to a Chinese stridency that many in the United
States do not understand. Paul Heer warns: "Washington should recognize
that Beijing's diplomatic behavior is, to some extent, a function of
Washington's own, and it should examine more closely the basis for China's
suspicions that the United States wants to contain and subvert it."[16]

Among the many irritants in Sino-U.S. relations that cause the PRC to be
suspicious, the Taiwan issue is the one that Chinese and Americans see as
most volatile. The United States cannot avoid the dilemma posed by the
conflicting objectives of forging amicable relations with the PRC while ensuring that the cross-strait controversy is resolved without force. However,
to maximize its political maneuverability, the United States has labored to
remain noncommittal about the unification of the PRC and Taiwan. The three
joint communiqués that the United States and the PRC signed in 1972, 1979,
and 1982, and the Taiwan Relations Act, seem to reflect competing objectives of the United States. There is no question that the United States still
hopes to have cooperative and profitable relations with the PRC. Yet it is
equally evident that many Americans of influence are not prepared to sacri-

fice Taiwan's interest as the price for healthy Sino-U.S. relations.

The United States has maintained what it calls a "one China" policy, but by this it means something rather different than Beijing does. Beijing's view of "one China" is normative and declarative: There is only one China in the world and Taiwan is an inalienable part of it.[17] The United States has adopted a procedural approach to "one China" by recognizing the government of the PRC as the sole legal government of China, acknowledging the Chinese view that there is only one China of which Taiwan is a part, and establishing that the United States has a strong interest in ensuring that the process by which the Taiwan problem is resolved is peaceful. The United States remains noncommittal about whether Taiwan is now or should become subject to the jurisdiction of the PRC.

Despite its public enunciation of a "one China" policy, U.S. support for Taiwan did not diminish appreciably during Clinton's presidency. It was on Clinton's watch that Lee Teng-hui was granted permission to visit the United States in 1995. Then, in 1996, when the PRC employed missile diplomacy to intimidate Taiwan's voters prior to that year's presidential elections, a powerful American naval armada was positioned near the Taiwan Strait to convey the message that Washington is prepared to act if Beijing engages in hostilities aimed at Taiwan. Moreover, the United States has continued to sell armaments to Taiwan and effectively blocked Israel's sale of a sophisticated airborne radar system to the PRC that could have significantly augmented Beijing's strategic advantage vis-à-vis Taiwan. President George W. Bush approved the sale of a considerable package of arms to Taiwan in April 2001 and his administration has taken further steps to enhance Taiwan's security.[18] In operational terms, therefore, the United States continues to support Taiwan in accordance with the TRA.

Taiwan's champions—and the PRC's detractors—have reacted with vigilance to any hint that the United States may be softening its resolve to defend Taiwan from absorption by China. Members of Congress, for instance, have spoken forcefully in support of Taiwan, they have introduced nonbinding resolutions sympathetic to Taiwan, and Congress has considered potentially significant changes in the U.S. posture toward Taiwan, most notably the TSEA. Finally, just before Taiwan's presidential election of March 2000, President Clinton made clear in a speech on 8 March that the cross-strait controversy must be resolved "peacefully and with the assent of the people of Taiwan."[19] He reiterated this point several days after Chen Shui-bian was elected. This was a significant new twist in U.S. policy that underscored the importance of considering the popular will in Taiwan. It corrected a misimpression created by earlier U.S. assertions of the "one China" policy that the United States would concur with a coercive—even if peaceful—imposition of terms on Taiwan by Beijing.

While the United States has enjoyed productive relations with both Beijing and Taipei on the basis of this precarious tangle of commitments, the effort to preserve a flexible posture has become increasingly difficult to sustain. During the 1990s, a number of incremental changes in China, Taiwan, and the international arena exposed and exacerbated the underlying tensions in Washington's relations with Beijing and Taipei. American flexibility was further constrained by domestic public opinion—which is generally sympathetic toward democratic Taiwan—and concern about the potential of the PRC to become a competitor or even an adversary.

With this potential and other threats in mind, the United States has gone out of its way to demonstrate its resolve to live up to both explicit and implicit security and economic guarantees in East Asia—a posture that has contributed to three decades of peace and rapid economic growth in the region. One keystone of the region's stability is a U.S. commitment to deter military hostilities in the Western Pacific generally and in the Taiwan Strait especially. A war in the Taiwan Strait would likely affect the continued growth and prosperity from which so many states—the United States, PRC, and Taiwan included—have benefited. It would threaten American commercial and other interests in Taiwan, on the Chinese mainland, and in Hong Kong and Japan, to say nothing of the interests of U.S. allies in the region. If hostilities broke out between Beijing and Taipei and the United States failed to intervene with military force, the security guarantees on which Washington has premised its forward presence in the region might well be undermined.

Despite various American concerns about the PRC, on the whole the U.S.-PRC relationship is hardy. It continues to grow in a wide array of official and unofficial interactions that make it a far more complex and reciprocal relationship than it was when diplomatic relations were established in 1979. Despite persistent friction over the issue of Taiwan's sovereignty, commercial, social, cultural, scholarly, and other links have proliferated and entail significant commitments by American institutions to engage in continued interaction with the PRC. As the PRC pursues economic and social reform, it too has become involved in a host of international and nongovernmental arenas in which it and the United States have common objectives. Washington and Beijing, though often at odds, have found ways to cooperate in the handling of such sensitive matters as North Korea, terrorism, international crime prevention, environmental preservation, and drug trafficking, to name just a few issues.

It is the Taiwan problem, however, that most often threatens to push the U.S.-PRC relationship to the brink of open conflict. To avoid armed confrontation with the PRC or between the PRC and Taiwan, some analysts argue that the United States should recalibrate its policies to add definition both to the ends and the means. Some argue that the election of Chen Shui-bian and the defeat of the KMT mean that the ambiguous, noncommittal posture of the United States is now anachronistic.

These developments have, naturally, complicated American policy toward Beijing and Taipei. In response to changes in Taiwan, the PRC has intensified pressure on the United States to toe the "one China" line. Increasingly, the United States has found itself torn between a principled defense of Taiwan's democratic expression of self-determination and Beijing's ever more insistent demands that the United States honor the agreements it signed with the PRC to maintain no more than an unofficial relationship with Taiwan and to end arms sales. Having encouraged democratization on Taiwan, it is difficult for the United States to ignore pleas for autonomy or resistance to unification when they amount to expressions of popular will. It is equally difficult for the United States to ignore Beijing's sensitivities about Taiwan and Washington's extensive, though unofficial, relations with Taipei.

Incremental Changes, Transitory Effects

The enduring features of the triadic relationship between Washington, Beijing, and Taipei have certainly been affected by incremental changes—changes resulting from the opening and liberalization of the PRC's economy, the end of the Cold War, and the dissolution of the bipolar system of international relations.[20] While these factors have certainly exerted considerable influence on the three states and have created new pressures on all three, the salutary effects of these trends may balance or even outweigh the tensions they have generated.

As for the democratization of Taiwan, while the populace has liberated itself to govern as it chooses and has demanded the expansion of the realm of liberties it enjoys, one would have to conclude that democratization has also eroded the stability of the triadic relationship. Democracy has many merits, but it does complicate relations with other states. It enables domestic interest groups with conflicting objectives to compete for prominence in the policy arena. It obliges policymakers to consider how their policies will be perceived not only abroad but also at home among voters whose support is vital. It encourages the press and other such communities to examine the government policy and expose hypocrisy, contradictions, and venal self-interest. None of this is helpful when a state must also navigate cautiously through the shoals of controversy with a potentially violent adversary and a potentially fickle advocate. Yet, this is indeed the condition in which Taiwan finds itself.

In the days that followed the election of Chen Shui-bian, analysts began to interpret the election as having a destabilizing effect on the triad.[21] Other observers have noted the possibility that Chen, like Richard Nixon, might override his political past and manifest a statesmanlike demeanor—enabling him to choreograph a grand gesture of reconciliation, prompting a break-through in the stalemate across the Taiwan Strait, and becoming a catalyst for positive change in the tense standoff.

Pessimists read the PRC's white paper on Taiwan, heard Premier Zhu Rongji's jingoistic warning of March 2000, and concluded that Beijing's perspective was: "If Chen, then war."[22] Optimists, by contrast, bank on the insuperable practicality of PRC leaders and trust that Beijing barked loudly before the election so that it would not have to bite afterward. They note that the PRC's overwhelming concerns about economic development will mili-tate against bellicose adventurism and, in any event, Beijing knows it cannot yet prevail in a head-to-head conflict with Taiwan as long as Taiwan has the United States behind it. In Washington, Chen's election prompted such con-cern about whether Beijing would be aroused to respond with force that President Clinton immediately dispatched emissaries to Beijing and Taipei to counsel moderation.[23] The United States extended itself to both Beijing and Taipei in order to urge cautious relaxation of tensions and assure both sides that U.S. policy had not changed.

The first year of Chen Shui-bian's tenure was not a period of substantial change in the triadic relationship or in the underlying predicament. The sta-bility may have resulted, in part, from the tumult that Chen and his new administration faced at home. The sense of disarray and rudderless policy toward the PRC was magnified by the simultaneous and unexpected adjust-ments that both the DPP and the KMT had to make after the election. Just as the DPP had had no experience governing Taiwan or managing its foreign and cross-strait policies, the KMT had had no experience serving in opposi-tion or internalizing the wisdom embodied in the notion that "politics stops at the water's edge." Chen's slim electoral victory, the economic downturn, and political crises at home all undermined his effectiveness. Worse, promi-nent figures in rival political parties traveled to Beijing to consult the PRC leadership about matters of cross-strait relations, enabling Beijing to revive United Front tactics while undercutting Chen's position on cross-strait rela-tions. These partisan activities—quite likely an effort to pander to Taiwan's voters—are among the inefficiencies that must be tolerated in a democracy.

Certainly the PRC was delighted to exploit the dynamics of partisan com-petition in Taiwan. Indeed, that Taiwan's major opposition parties accept the "one China" principle serves Beijing's cause well by pressuring Chen Shui-bian to follow suit and acknowledge Beijing's demand or else become irrel-evant. Despite the PRC's shrewd handling of visitors from Taipei, however, Beijing has not fully accommodated to a democratic Taiwan. While there are many well-informed and sensible analysts in the PRC who understand some-thing of the dynamics of a democratic system, the centrally regulated system by which the PRC operates is so starkly different from that of Taiwan that one senses few decision makers or their advisers have a visceral feel for how government operates in Taiwan. Notwithstanding Beijing's efforts to pressure Chen Shui-bian to accept the "one China" principle by courting partisans from other camps, Beijing does not seem to understand how to exert leverage effectively over its counterparts in Taipei. It certainly does not seem adept at influencing popular opinion in Taiwan in ways that lead constructively toward unification. By "mirror imaging," Beijing may underestimate the need for compromise between the president and other interest groups and overestimate the degree to which the president in Taiwan is at liberty to establish policy as he likes.

One senses in Beijing, for instance, a skepticism about statements made or actions taken in Taipei that appear instrumental, not a reflection of Chen Shui-bian's genuine intent. Apparently the depth of popular sentiment in Taiwan about issues of identity and resistance to unification is not well understood in the PRC. This is problematic because it leads to Beijing's misreading of intentions, signals, and trends in Taiwan. This, in turn, causes Beijing to act on its misperceptions in ways that may exacerbate the underlying tensions in the cross-strait relationship.

For the United States, too, the democratization of Taiwan has complicated the management of policy toward the triadic relationship. From 1972 until the early 1990s, it was possible for the United States to hide, disingenuously, behind the shield provided by the ROC government. With a straight face the United States could state, as it did in the Shanghai communiqué of 1972, that "Chinese on either side of the Taiwan Strait maintain there is but one China and that Taiwan is part of China." With the democratization of Taiwan that shield has been withdrawn—highlighting the contradictions in U.S. policy and prompting debate in the United States about what Washington should do.

Those who value the projection of a muscular American demeanor in international relations, those who cherish clear and principled solutions to problems, and those who advocate the application of these standards to Sino-U.S. relations urge that Washington dispense with its coy and ambiguous policy toward Taiwan. The democratization of Taiwan has revived interest in stating unambiguously that the United States will defend Taiwan from the PRC's use of military pressure or coercive diplomacy as a way of pressing Taiwan to comply with Beijing's wishes. On the other hand, Americans who see a range of options between black and white extremes, those who see merit in encouraging cooperative relations with the PRC, those who are not sanguine about igniting a conflict with Beijing, and those who are prepared to maximize benefits arising from conflicting interests even if this means failing to attain any single objective are, therefore, prepared to compromise their ideals. For them the ambiguity of U.S. policy is worth preserving because it provides flexibility. When, in an interview with ABC News on April 25, 2001, President Bush expressed his view of the U.S. commitment to Taiwan, he was unambiguous. Replying to "Good Morning America" host, Charlie Gibson, President Bush said that if the PRC attacks Taiwan the United States does have an obligation to defend the people of Taiwan. He said that the United States would do "Whatever it took to help Taiwan defend herself."[24]

Immediately afterward, administration officials dispelled the impression that the president had abandoned the ambiguous U.S. stance. Later that day, in an interview with CNN, President Bush reformulated his view of U.S. commitments in a way that conformed with the ambiguous posture that the U.S. has adopted.[25]

In sum, then, the democratization of Taiwan has had a corrosive effect on the stability of the triadic relationship. It has complicated the message that emerges from Taiwan and given voice to advocates of independence or indefinite division who would have been silenced in the days before political reform. It has confounded the PRC—which had in the authoritarian KMT an adversary that, fundamentally, shared Beijing's view of China as indivisible. It has also made it more difficult for the United States to abandon Taiwan at a time when it is also more dangerous for the United States to assert that it will not abandon Taiwan.

The effects of democratization on the triadic relationship have been gradual. For instance, the transformation of the KMT—from a party dominated by Chinese concerned about unification to a party dominated by Taiwanese hoping to forestall it—came about by degrees. The transformation of Lee Teng-hui—from a president who walked the fine line of representing the sentiments of Taiwan's majority while advocating unification to the man who taunted the PRC with his campaign for pragmatic diplomacy, widening the international space in which Taiwan operated—also occurred gradually. Finally, the victory of Chen Shui-bian and the emergence of the DPP from a campaign dominated by the fractured KMT was a development brought about by the incremental forces of democracy and succession politics.

The accidental presidency of Chen Shui-bian is the outgrowth of democracy and probably not as significant an influence on the triadic relationship as is the democratization of Taiwan itself. While Chen's presidency may herald a dramatic reorientation of the dynamics that govern relations between Washington, Beijing, and Taipei, it is equally plausible that his tenure will have no greater effect on the underlying dynamics than did that of his predecessor. After all, Lee Teng-hui did provoke outrage and belligerence from Beijing that was met with Washington's firmness and efforts to conciliate. However, Lee did not fundamentally alter the triadic relationship or change the dynamics of interaction or the interests of any of the three states. His influence was transitory, not transformative. Despite the high state of anxiety in Washington, Beijing, and even Taipei that attended the election of Chen Shui-bian, there is no reason to assume that Chen's presidency will be transformative either.

Another way of thinking about the implications of Chen Shui-bian's election is to ask how a Soong or a Lien victory would have altered cross-strait relations.[26] Perhaps Soong or Lien might have embraced the "one China" principle in a manner that soothed Beijing's anxieties, but the fundamental problem in cross-strait relations would have remained. Taiwan is not prepared to unify with the PRC under present circumstances. While the tension and distrust surrounding the relationship between Beijing and Taipei since Chen's inauguration might have been avoided, there is no reason to imagine that the whole problem would have been resolved or even fundamentally altered.

By targeting Chen Shui-bian's candidacy so vigorously before the election, Beijing appears to have missed the point: On cross-strait relations, the three principal candidates held substantially comparable views, even if they emerged from parties that did not.[27] Each laid claim to the middle ground of Taiwan's political spectrum. Thus, even if Beijing is slow to recognize it, the underlying cause of the PRC's frustration with Taiwan should not be tied to the person who serves as president, but to the democratic system that enables the populace to make its own choice about how cozy it wishes to be with the PRC. Regardless who was elected president in 2000, relations with the PRC would probably have been contentious and unification a remote possibility.

Moreover, it is difficult to imagine that the PRC would have pursued a policy regarding unification substantially different from the one the PRC is currently pursuing. Regardless who had won the presidential election, the PRC would very likely have advocated that the new president publicly acknowledge the "one China" policy, that the new president renounce the "state-to-state formula" that Lee Teng-hui articulated, and that the new administration engage in negotiations with the PRC under the "one China" principle and on the basis of the "one country, two systems" model for unification.

Beijing made an abrupt about-face when it realized that the candidate it had worked hardest to undermine had been elected. It then adopted a temperate approach to Chen Shui-bian, which the PRC calls "listening to his words while observing his actions." What Beijing has been waiting for is Chen's unambiguous declaration that he endorses the "one China" principle. Beijing was disappointed not to find the magic words in Chen's carefully crafted inaugural address and in his even more craftily worded New Year's speech of 2001. Yet observers in Beijing proudly point out that the PRC government resisted criticizing Chen by name. Indeed, this restraint was so evident that the first time Chen was repudiated in the PRC press by name the occasion was seen to warrant a report in the press.[28]

Perhaps the atmospherics of cross-strait relations would have differed had Lien or Soong won. Still, there is no assurance that a Lien presidency (with Lee Teng-hui hovering in the KMT wings) would have pleased Beijing any more than Chen's presidency does. At least with Chen Shui-bian, his vulnerability as the DPP candidate led him to take the independence issue off the table at the outset, pledging in his inaugural address that unless the PRC had the intention of using force, he would not declare independence.[29]

Thus, even though the election of Chen Shui-bian may prove to have only transitory influence on the underlying contest between Beijing and Taipei and on the triadic relationship with the United States, the PRC has acted as if Chen is the issue. This behavior reflects the propensity of the PRC's analysts and decision makers to overemphasize the influence of personality on policy—yet another case of "mirror imaging." Observers in the PRC find it hard to dislodge memories of Chen Shui-bian as an advocate of independence. In Beijing there is a strong sense that one can gauge a person's character from his past behavior and anticipate his future actions from his present behavior. In the case of Chen Shui-bian, there is a sense that he manifests a lawyerly way with words, that he is slippery and insincere, and that his public statements about "one China" have vacillated without expressing his genuine intent.

While analysts and observers in Beijing consider Chen to be untrustworthy, it is hard for them to see why people in Taiwan might draw the same conclusion about Beijing's policies toward unification and "one China." Evidently there is a sense in Beijing that the PRC has been reasonable, patient, even generous, in its overtures and responses to Taiwan since Chen Shui-bian was elected. Beijing does not perceive itself as contributing to the stalemate in cross-strait relations.

Indeed, a significant signal was sent in early January 2001. Not quite a year after the saber rattling of February and March 2000, Qian Qichen, a Politburo member whose views on foreign affairs are regarded as authoritative, assumed a much more conciliatory mien in an interview with the *Washington Post*. Qian allowed that the standing formulation of the "one China" principle caused doubt in Taiwan about Beijing's intentions. His ostensible clarification provided a new formulation that was, one assumed, intended to be much more palatable in Taipei and less threatening in Washington, coming as it did on the eve of George W. Bush's inauguration. Qian stated:

> In order to ease their doubts . . . we said "one China" not only includes the mainland, but also Taiwan. We think of this China as an integral whole

254 ALAN M. WACHMAN

which can't be separated in sovereignty or territory. This is the true meaning of "one China." . . . And they had another doubt. . . . They think that
Taiwan being part of Chinese territory means Taiwan and China are not
equal. . . . To ease this doubt, we said the mainland and Taiwan belong to
the same one China. At least, it shows some kind of equality. I think it can
help ease their doubt.[30]

In the same interview, another official observed, anonymously, that in the past
the PRC had said "we would liberate Taiwan, then we said Taiwan was just a
province of China, now we are saying Taiwan can be our equal. . . . For the
mainland to make these kinds of adjustments in policy is not an easy thing."[31]

Indeed, it is unlikely that Qian's reformulation of the long-standing "one
China" principle was made casually. The PRC's foreign policy system is so
centralized that there is little doubt the statement reflects a well-considered
effort to adjust Beijing's stance and indicate the direction in which the central leadership expects to guide its policy. It is plausible that Beijing also had
in mind the benefit of making a favorable overture to the incoming Bush
administration, which was confronted from the start with a need to consider
Taiwan's request to purchase *Aegis*-class destroyers and other weapons opposed by Beijing.

Finally, regarding the proposition that Chen's election has had only transitory implications for the triadic relationship, consider how the United States
would have reacted if Lien or Soong had been elected. It is difficult to imagine that the U.S. posture toward either Beijing or Taiwan would have differed. After all, the United States has been in the business of urging the value
of restraint and dialogue by both sides. This position underscores the view
one hears in Beijing: As far as the stability of the cross-strait relationship is
concerned, whether Taiwan seeks independence or resists unification is less
important than whether the United States will support Taiwan's bid for independence or resistance to unification. While we cannot know what might
have happened under other circumstances, it seems unlikely that Washington would have been shaken from its long-standing posture had Lien or Soong
prevailed.

Implications for the United States

Chen Shui-bian's victory was a symptom of political trends that have been
evolving on Taiwan for decades. His election reflects not only the consolidation and maturation of democracy on Taiwan, but the empowerment of the
Taiwanese people and the drive for self-governance that prompted opposition
to the KMT. That the KMT collapsed in 2000 into self-destructive rivalry is

itself a sign that the political life of Taiwan has been transformed. Whether the KMT rises again or not, it is the democratization of Taiwan, not Chen's election, that has the most significant implications for the United States.

As for the dynamics of the triadic relationship, the fundamental issue is the nature of Sino-U.S. relations. Thus, the election of George W. Bush in the United States and the return to power of the Republican Party is simply another transitory influence on stability. Whichever party is in office and whoever is president of the United States, in the long run it seems that an initial period of muscle flexing gives way to a U.S. policy that generally seeks to preserve the status quo. One is reminded of Ronald Reagan's pledge during the 1980 campaign that, if elected, he would essentially reestablish diplomatic relations with the ROC. Ultimately, he made his peace with the PRC and did not change the status of relations with Taiwan. One recalls, also, the sharp campaign rhetoric of candidate Bill Clinton who chastised George Bush for his handling of China. Clinton declared that he would not "coddle dictators from Beijing to Baghdad." When he took office, though, Clinton tried in vain to link the granting of most-favored-nation status for Beijing with the need to demonstrate that the PRC's protection of human rights was improving. In the end, Clinton too recognized that his stridency was infeasible and destabilizing and, in 1994, he backed down.[32]

The point is that temperamental and philosophical differences about how the United States should deal with the PRC and Taiwan have, in the end, given way to a generally consistent, even if contradictory, pattern of behavior. The United States asserts its support for the notion of "one China" and conducts relations with Taiwan on an unofficial, rather than official, basis to appease Beijing. At the same time, it sells arms to Taiwan in accordance with a strong popular inclination to protect the viability of a democracy threatened by a strong authoritarian adversary—a sentiment manifested in the Taiwan Relations Act—and does so despite Beijing's severe disapproval. This has been the middle ground of U.S. policy since 1979. Advocates of closer ties to the PRC suggest that the United States do less for Taiwan; proponents of a strong hand in foreign policy advise that the United States do more. In the end, though, the default position is to balance these competing inclinations and do what is possible to preserve the stability of relations across the Taiwan Strait at as low a cost to the United States as possible.

This is not to suggest that the United States has an interest in keeping Taiwan and the PRC from accommodation. It is difficult to imagine a settlement across the Taiwan Strait that would not accord with U.S. interests, as long as the settlement was reached by mutual agreement between Beijing and Taipei and without the threat of force. It does mean that the United States has acted against precipitous or unilateral efforts by either side to fundamentally alter the cross-strait relationship. Thus, the United States can be seen to prefer the status quo—even though none of the parties is completely content —to a violent or imposed resolution of the conflict that will satisfy only the victor. Put bluntly: A win/win situation for Beijing and Taipei is likely to be a situation in which the United States also wins. A win/lose situation for Beijing and Taipei is likely to be one in which the United States will also lose. The status quo is a "no win/no lose" situation for all three states.

As the Bush administration considers how to satisfy itself that the United States is doing enough to defend Taiwan's autonomy, it will have to address the following questions:

- Is cross-strait stability fostered or hindered by a U.S. policy that is ambiguous?
- Does the supply of sophisticated U.S. arms to Taiwan embolden advocates of independence as Beijing fears? Or does it make Taiwan feel secure enough to negotiate with the PRC?

As for the matter of ambiguity, if the interests of the United States lie in preserving the status quo until both Beijing and Taipei are ripe to make serious compromises and hammer out a win/win settlement, any change of Washington's posture, no matter how well intended, may be destabilizing. Even though the U.S. policy is contradictory and unsatisfactory, it may have the merit of helping to preserve stability.

With respect to the sale of sophisticated arms to Taiwan, the United States finds itself in the awkward position of knowing that these arms are unlikely to enable Taiwan to defend itself. As Taiwan cannot prevail in a prolonged arms race with the PRC, the arms it receives from the United States may do more to enhance morale on Taiwan than anything else. If the principal value of these arms sales is to offer Taiwan a *sense* of security, rather than a means of self-defense, the United States must weigh carefully how much is enough. Those who advocate that the United States should do even more to help Taiwan defend itself may unwittingly undercut Taipei's security by triggering the security dilemma and Beijing's determination to overcome Taiwan's marginal defensive advantage. Indeed, there is something to the argument advanced in Beijing that the more sophisticated Taiwan's weapons become, the more incentive Beijing has to eliminate them in a preemptive strike that will neutralize Taiwan's advantage.

How these questions are resolved in Washington depends, in part, on the quality of collaboration or the intensity of competition between the executive and legislative branches and between the two major parties. Just as precipitous or unilateral actions by either Beijing or Taipei are likely to disrupt a fragile stability in triadic relations, so too must the United States avoid tipping the balance by well-meant but ill-considered efforts to make things better. Tolerable changes in the dynamics of the triadic relationship have emerged slowly from the incremental forces of economic liberalization, political transformation, and social integration. In many respects, tensions in cross-strait relations have subsided in the past decade as the two sides have become intertwined in a web of cooperative interchange.[33]

The potentially destabilizing moments in the past decade have arisen from the unilateral actions of one state that sought suddenly to enhance its advantage or reinforce its position. In each case, during the 1990s, the balance was restored. However, the return to balance after a destabilizing act is by no means assured. Passions run deep in Washington, Beijing, and Taipei. The potential for devastating conflict is still present.

Chen Shui-bian's election certainly aroused concerns about the erosion of stability and the likelihood of conflict. It was so unexpected that many feared it would cause a cataclysmic change. Among the factors that prevented it from having more than a transitory influence was the measured response of the United States, which quelled Beijing's anxieties that Washington would suddenly support Chen's desire for independence. Perhaps the best contributions the United States can make to the preservation of stability are these: wisdom about the costs and benefits of change; skill in managing the fears and anxieties of both Beijing and Taipei; leadership at home to encourage ardent advocates that their aims are best served by moderation; and calm and consistent diplomacy designed to reinforce the gains that have been made in Sino-U.S. relations. In the end, Washington's capacity to overcome the insidious distrust that has characterized Sino-U.S. relations is a key to stability.

Notes

1. Alan M. Wachman, *Challenges and Opportunities in the Taiwan Strait: Defining America's Role*, Conference Report: China Policy Series 17 (New York: National Committee on United States–China Relations, 2001), pp. 1–15.

2. Gary Goertz and Paul F. Diehl, "The Initiation and Termination of Enduring Rivalries: The Impact of Political Shocks," *American Journal of Political Science* 39(1) (1995):31.

3. Lowell Dittmer, "The Strategic Triangle: An Elementary Game—Theoretical Analysis," *World Politics* (July 1981):485–516, and *Sino-Soviet Normalization and Its International Implications* (Seattle: Washington University Press, 1992).

4. Alan Collins, *The Security Dilemma and the End of the Cold War* (New York: St. Martin's Press, 1997); Alan M. Wachman, "Taiwan: Trapped in a Tempestuous Triad," in *Small States in a Shrinking World: Explaining Foreign Policy*, ed. Jeanne A. Hey (Boulder: Lynne Rienner, forthcoming).

5. Andrew J. Nathan, "Taiwan's New Political Order: Implications for Cross-Strait Relations" (paper delivered at the seminar "Taiwan's New Political Order: Short-

Term Prospects and Implications for China and the United States," National Intelligence Council and Federal Research Division of the Library of Congress, 9 June 2000), p. 2.

6. The white paper stated three conditions under which the PRC would consider using force against Taiwan. The third of these struck many readers as a new condition, although Chinese commentators have identified it as a revival of something Deng Xiaoping said in 1984. The portion of the white paper that drew attention reads: "If the Taiwan authorities refuse, sine die, the peaceful settlement of cross-strait unification through negotiations, then the Chinese government will only be forced to adopt all drastic measures possible, including the use of force, to safeguard China's sovereignty and territorial integrity and fulfill the great cause of reunification." (The Latin term "sine die" means indefinitely.) See Taiwan Affairs Office and Information Office of the State Council, "White Paper—The One China Principle and the Taiwan Issue" (21 February 2000), as reproduced at http://www.fmprc.gov.cn/english.

7. On 15 March, PRC Premier Zhu Rongji stated: "Some people are calculating how many aircraft, missiles, and warships China possesses, and have concluded that China dare not and will not use force. . . . People making such calculations don't know Chinese history. The Chinese people are ready to shed blood and sacrifice their lives to defend the unity of their motherland and the dignity of the Chinese nation." See "Chinese Premier Warns Against 'Taiwan Independence'" (15 March 2000), as reproduced at http://www.china-embassy.org/taiwan/zhu001.htm.

8. Richard C. Bush, "United States Policy Toward Taiwan," *American Foreign Policy Interests* 22(3) (2000):3.

9. Ibid., p. 2.

10. Alan M. Wachman, "The 'State-to-State' Flap: Tentative Conclusions About Risk and Restraint in Diplomacy Across the Taiwan Straits," *Harvard Asia Quarterly* 4(1) (2000): 37–40.

11. Nathan, "Taiwan's New Political Order," p. 2.

12. Ralph A. Cossa, "Long-Term Visions of Regional Security: A U.S.-China Strategic Dialogue," *PacNet* 21 (Honolulu: Pacific Forum Center for Strategic International Studies), p. 1.

13. Alan M. Wachman, *Taiwan: National Identity and Democratization* (Armonk, NY: M.E. Sharpe, 1994), pp. 56–127.

14. This section draws on material I published previously as *Challenges and Opportunities in the Taiwan Strait: Defining America's Role*. I am grateful to the National Committee on United States–China Relations, those who reviewed and edited the document, and especially to John Holden, president of the National Committee, for his many suggested refinements and permission to republish portions of the report.

15. Susan V. Lawrence, "Non-Proliferation: China's Perspective," *Far Eastern Economic Review* (20 July 2000):18.

16. Paul Heer, "A House United: Beijing's View of Washington," *Foreign Affairs* 79(4) (2000):23.

17. Taiwan Affairs Office and Information Office of the State Council, "White Paper."

18. Steven Mufson and Dana Milbank, "Taiwan to Get Variety of Arms but U.S. Withholds Aegis Radar that China Strongly Opposed," *Washington Post* (24 April 2001), as reproduced at http://Taiwan security.org/wp/2001/wp-042401.htm.

19. William Clinton, "Remarks by the President on China" (8 March 2000), as

reproduced at http://www.chinapntr.gov/messages/pressspeech0308.htm.

20. This section is informed by a sequence of interviews conducted in Beijing during January 2001 with leading figures in the PRC's foreign affairs community including civilian and military officials, academics, and think tank analysts.

21. James Kynge and Mure Dickie, "Defying the Dragon," *Financial Times* (19 March 2000), as reproduced at http://taiwansecurity.org/News/FT-031900.htm; "Political Earthquake in Taiwan," editorial, *New York Times* (20 March 2000) as reproduced at http://taiwansecurity.org/NYT/NYT-032000.htm; "Taiwan Steps Forward," editorial, *Washington Post* (19 March 2000), as reproduced at http://taiwansecurity.org/WP/WP-031900.htm.

22. "Chinese Premier Warns Against 'Taiwan Independence'" (15 March 2000), as reproduced at Embassy of the People's Republic of China in the United States at http://www.china-embassy.org/taiwan/zhu001.htm; "Premier Zhu Don Corleone," editorial, *Washington Post* (16 March 2000), as reproduced at http://taiwansecurity.org/WP/WP-031600–Zhu.htm.

23. John Pomfret, "Taiwan Makes Goodwill Bows Toward China: Links Opened Between Islands, Beijing; Party May Strike Independence Plank from Platform," *Washington Post* (22 March 2000), as reproduced at http://taiwansecurity.org/WP/WP-032200.htm.

24. "President Milestone: U.S. Must Defend Taiwan, Bush Says," ABCNews.com as reproduced at http://ABCNews.go.com/sections/GMA/GoodMorningAmerica/GMA010425 Bush_100days.html.

25. "Relaxed Bush Cites Progress on Tax, Education Plans," April 25, 2001 as reproduced at http://cnn.com/2001/ALLPOLITICS/04/25/bushinterview.02/index.html.

26. Studying history, one is often tempted to ask "what if" while knowing that such questions cannot be answered satisfactorily. Looking back in time to ask what might have happened if only one factor had been different—if Soong or Lien had been elected, for instance—presupposes that all other facts about the past would have remained the same. For Soong or Lien to have been elected, of course, other factors would *not* have been the same. Since one cannot know what the differences would have been or what consequences might have ensued, the enterprise of asking oneself "what if" can lead only to empty speculation.

27. "Three Leading Candidates Stress Sovereignty of the Island," *Taiwan News* (25 February 2000), as reproduced at http://taiwansecurity.org/News/TN-022500–Sovereignty.htm.

28. "China Criticizes New Taiwan Leader," Associated Press (19 July 2000), as reproduced at http://taiwansecurity.org/AP/AP-071900.htm.

29. Chen Shui-bian, "Taiwan Stands Up: Advancing to an Uplifting Era," *Exchange* 51 (June 2000):18–21.

30. John Pomfret, "Beijing Signals New Flexibility on Taiwan," *Washington Post* (5 January 2001), as reproduced at http://taiwansecurity.org/WP/2001/WP-010501.htm.

31. Ibid.

32. James Mann, *About Face: A History of America's Curious Relationship with China, from Nixon to Clinton* (New York: Knopf, 1999), pp. 116, 262, 292–315.

33. Ralph Clough, *Cooperation or Conflict in the Taiwan Strait?* (Lanham, MD: Rowman & Littlefield, 1999).

9

Japan's Taiwan Policy: Beyond the 1972 System?

Yoshihisa Amae

1. In today's "presidential" election held in Taiwan, Mr. Chen Shui-bian was elected as the new leader.

2. Japan expects that under such new circumstances the issue relating to Taiwan will be settled peacefully through direct dialogue between the parties on both sides of the Taiwan Strait and that this dialogue will be promptly resumed.

3. Japan, based on the joint communiqué of the government of Japan and the government of the People's Republic of China (PRC) of 1972, will maintain its exchanges of a private and regional nature with Taiwan as nongovernmental working relations while furthering stable and cooperative relations with China.

Kono Yohei,
Japan's Foreign Minister[1]

Taiwan's presidential election of March 2000 symbolized the maturation of Taiwanese democracy. For the first time in the history of Taiwan—including the Republic of China (ROC)—an opposition party came into power through democratic procedures. This democratic achievement was not fully acknowledged by the Japanese government, however. In the statement cited above, which was announced soon after the election, the Japanese foreign minister not only failed to congratulate Chen Shui-bian on his victory, but also be-

I am indebted to Muthiah Alagappa, Sheila Smith, Yoshihide Soeya, Benjamin Self, and Fumiko Halloran for their insights and suggestions on the initial draft of this chapter. I also thank Yasuhiro Matsuda for kindly arranging the interviews for me in Japan.

littled its significance by parenthesizing the term "presidential." This reaction stands in sharp contrast to American President Bill Clinton's statement congratulating Chen Shui-bian's victory in an election that "clearly demonstrates the strength and vitality of Taiwan's democracy."[2]

The Japanese official statement also underlined that the election's outcome will not affect its policy toward Taiwan. When Japan normalized diplomatic ties with the People's Republic of China (PRC) in 1972, its relationship with Taiwan was downgraded to "nongovernmental working relations." At the same time, no legal adjustment was made to replace the treaty that had provided the legal basis of diplomatic relations since 1952. To this date, therefore, Japan's relationship with Taiwan has been constrained by the joint communiqué of 1972 that states that Japan recognizes the PRC as "the sole legal government of China," that it "fully understands and respects" Beijing's position, and that Taiwan is "an inalienable part" of the PRC.[3] As a result, Japan has maintained strictly nongovernmental economic and cultural relations with Taiwan since 1972. To date the Japanese government has never allowed its ministers to officially visit Taiwan, and it has retained rigid control over Taiwanese officials' visits to Japan. The United States, by contrast, has allowed President Lee Teng-hui to visit Cornell University—although at a "private" level—in 1995, and sent its Trade Representative Carla Hills to Taiwan in 1992. Other countries such as France, Canada, Italy, and the Philippines sent cabinet members to Taiwan in the early 1990s.

Yet Japan's relationship with Taiwan extends beyond the legal constraints of the 1972 joint communiqué. It has a political dimension as well. Acknowledging Beijing's claim that Taiwan is an internal affair of China, Japan has therefore abstained from actions that Beijing opposes, even though they may not violate the communiqué. This explains why Tokyo did not allow former Taiwanese President Lee Teng-hui to visit Japan in October 2000 even though Lee no longer holds any position in the government. Since Lee's retirement, Beijing has been pressuring Tokyo not to permit his entry under any circumstances, insisting that Lee Teng-hui is not "an ordinary individual." The Japanese foreign minister concurs: "A person with great political influence cannot necessarily be considered a private citizen."[4] The Japanese government remains prudent, if not negative, on the question of Lee's visit to Japan due to the damage it might inflict on Japan's relationship with the PRC.[5]

Under the 1972 system it has been Japan's consistent policy to develop a friendship with the PRC while maintaining economic and cultural relations with Taiwan. Heretofore, Japan's interest in Taiwan has been basically economic. When Japan and Taiwan severed formal diplomatic ties in 1972, the total trade between the two countries was US$1.4 billion. By 1986, however, it had surpassed US$10 billion and then reached US$20 billion in the next two years, amounting to US$41.6 billion in 1999. The total trade between Japan and Taiwan has increased by almost thirtyfold in nearly three decades. More important, Japan has benefited significantly from its trade with Taiwan. In 1999, Japan's exports to Taiwan amounted to US$28.8 billion while its imports were US$12.8 billion, less than half of what it exported. In fact, over the two decades since 1972 Japan's cumulative surplus was US$67.5 billion and the figure has continued to grow.[6] Thus, Japan has a strong incentive indeed to maintain economic ties with Taiwan. At the same time, however, Japan wants to distance itself from the dispute between Taiwan and the PRC over Taiwan's status. Getting involved in a military conflict in the Taiwan Strait is Tokyo's nightmare. Therefore, Japan has isolated itself from the "Taiwan issue"—that is, Taiwan's international status—on the basis of Beijing's claim that Taiwan is an internal affair of China.

As we shall see, Taiwan's democratization and the ensuing increase in tension across the Taiwan Strait have made it difficult for Japan to confine its relationship with Taiwan to the realm of "low politics"—nongovernmental, economic, and cultural affairs—under the 1972 system. The prominence of Lee Teng-hui in Taiwan's politics has contributed to changing Japan's negative image of Taiwan. Moreover, the growing tension between Taipei and Beijing, especially the 1996 Taiwan Strait crisis, has made Tokyo recognize the serious implications that Taiwan represents for Japan's security. Taiwan is no longer just an economic matter for Japan.

Certainly the election of Chen Shui-bian and the Democratic Progressive Party (DPP), which I view as the culmination of Taiwan's transformation, further challenges the 1972 system. It has important implications for Japan in two dimensions: Japan's Taiwan policy and its relationship with Taiwan. First, Japan is likely to pursue a more autonomous policy toward Taiwan since Chen's victory is challenging Japan's perception of the Taiwan issue. Since 1972 the Japanese government has acknowledged Beijing's claim that Taiwan is a Chinese internal affair because its origin goes back to the Chinese civil war between the Kuomintang (KMT) and the Chinese Communist Party (CCP) (1946–1950). With the ascension of a non-KMT leader, however, one can now say that Taiwan is no longer a "Chinese" internal affair. Moreover, a soft landing of the Taiwan issue has become more difficult because the CCP and the DPP have no consensus on "one China." Instability and the possibility of a military conflict in the Taiwan Strait are of great concern to Japan, which deems cross-strait peace and stability vital to its national interest. Second, the relationship between Japan and Taiwan is likely to strengthen as the KMT's defeat and the retirement of Lee Teng-hui force Japan to reconstruct its political ties with Taiwan. Before Chen's victory, the ruling parties in Japan had been dealing only with the KMT. Political channels between Japan and Taiwan has diversified, however, as Chen's victory brings in new players such as the DDP and the Democratic Party of Japan (DPJ), the largest opposition party in Japan. In sum, then, Chen Shui-bian's victory has opened up an opportunity for Japan to divorce its relationship with Taiwan from the constraints of Beijing under the 1972 system.

Complexity of the Bilateral Relationship

As the significance of Chen's election for Japan is better understood in a historical context, this section will examine the historical development of the bilateral relationship, which is unique and complex. Japan's relationship with Taiwan has gone through three different phases. It shifted from a colonial relationship (Phase I) to a formal diplomatic relationship (Phase II) to an unofficial relationship (Phase III). The 1972 normalization between Japan and the PRC wedged Japan and Taiwan in a new system. Chen's victory undermines the 1972 system by eliminating two residues of the past: the Chinese civil war and the Japanese colonial legacy. A fourth phase may now be in the process of construction (see Figure 9.1).

Phase I: Colonial Relationship

Taiwan first became a colony of Japan in 1895 as a result of Japan's victory over Qing China in the Sino-Japanese War (1894–1895). Through fifty years of its colonial rule, Japan built Taiwan's economic and social infrastructure. Harbors, roads, and railroads were constructed or modernized. Moreover, the education system and public hygiene were improved. As a result, the Taiwanese living standard rose rapidly. Although Japan lost Taiwan as a territory after its defeat in World War II, people with Japanese colonial experience survived. These people, known as the "Japanese-speaking generation," later advanced to the political front line through democratization and have contributed to the improvement of bilateral ties. When Japan surrendered in 1945, Taiwan was "restored" to the ROC as promised by the Allied Forces in the Cairo Declaration of 1943.[7] But the Chinese civil war, which erupted soon after World War II, complicated Japan's relationship with Taiwan. With the KMT's defeat by the CCP in the civil war, Taiwan was transformed from a colony of Japan to a province of the ROC and then to the de facto ROC within a matter of four years. The civil war and the KMT's withdrawal to Taiwan created a complex social structure on the island. Here was a land with a Taiwanese population, once ruled by the Japanese, that was dominated by a handful of Chinese whom the Japanese fought in World War II. The massacre of 28 February 1947 in which an estimated 28,000 Taiwanese

Figure 9.1 **Japan's Relationship with Taiwan** (1895–2000 and Beyond)

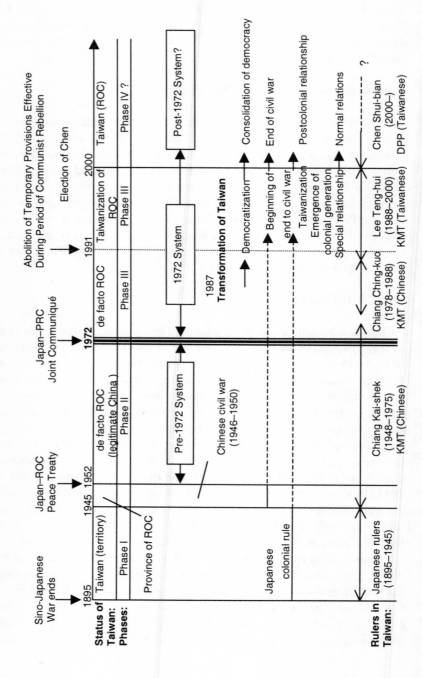

people were slaughtered by the KMT and the nearly three decades of political oppression that followed, created a deep chasm between the Taiwanese and the mainlanders even to this date.

The division of China in 1949 and the beginning of the Cold War in Asia in the following year affected Japan's relationship with China and the fate of Taiwan in the 1951 San Francisco Peace Treaty. Due to disagreement among the Allied Forces, especially the United States and Great Britain who recognized different Chinas as legitimate, neither Taipei nor Beijing was invited as a signatory of the treaty. Therefore, with which China was Japan to conclude the peace treaty? The answer was left to Japan to decide after its independence. The status of Taiwan, which was to be restored to the ROC, was left ambiguous in the treaty. According to the treaty, Japan "renounced" Taiwan but the pact does not specify to which China it returns.

Phase II: Formal Diplomatic Relations Before 1972

During the two decades between 1952 and 1972, the Japan–Taiwan relationship was in fact the Japan–China relationship. The Japanese government concluded a peace treaty with the ROC in April 1952 that recognized Taipei as the sole legal government of China. The issue of whether to choose Taipei or Beijing as the signatory with whom to conclude a peace treaty was controversial in Japan because the ROC no longer controlled the Chinese mainland. There is evidence showing that Japan did not want to rush its decision regarding with which China to conclude the peace treaty. In his memoir, Yoshida Shigeru, the prime minister of Japan at the time, stated that while he wished to develop economic ties and friendly relations with Taipei, he did not want to deny the presence of the Beijing government.[8] Under strong pressure from the United States at the beginning of the Cold War in Asia in 1950, however, Japan had little choice but to choose Taipei over Beijing.

From 1952 to 1972, Japan searched for an equidistant diplomacy between Taipei and Beijing. Although the Japanese government strove to overcome the fiction of "one China," in which Taipei was the sole legal government of China, by developing trade relations with mainland China under the principle of "separation of politics from economics" (*seikei bunri*), it was not easy to walk such a tightrope. As economic and cultural exchanges between Japan and mainland China expanded, the bilateral relationship began to approach the realm of "high politics"—issues pertaining to the substantial question of "one China." In the 1957 trade negotiations, Beijing demanded privileged status for its trade representatives and rights such as freedom of travel and the right to fly the national flag. In consideration of Taipei, Tokyo did not approve such demands. In 1958, an incident in which a Japanese right winger pulled down the PRC national flag at the Chinese commodity exhibition in Nagasaki led Beijing to temporarily suspend all economic and cultural exchanges with Japan after the Japanese government treated the case as a minor offense (exchanges were resumed in 1960). Later, in 1963, Japan and Taiwan faced a diplomatic crisis when Taipei recalled its ambassador to protest Tokyo's decision to extend Export-Import Bank of Japan credit to Nichibo's chemical fiber plant exports to mainland China. Taipei regarded the bank's extension of credit as governmental economic aid to mainland China.

During this period Japan was unable to make a breakthrough in its relationship with Taiwan and mainland China. Indeed, normalization of official ties with both Chinese governments was almost impossible without American assent. As Yoshihide Soeya points out, Japan's "autonomous diplomacy" toward Beijing was only possible within the permissible range of its "cooperative diplomacy" with the United States.[9] After all, the two key decisions in Japan's relationship with Taiwan—the conclusion of the Japan–ROC Peace Treaty in 1952 and the normalization of diplomatic ties with the PRC in 1972—were not the products of Japan's own volition.

Phase III: The 1972 System

When Washington announced President Nixon's forthcoming visit to Beijing in July 1971, demands for diplomatic normalization with the PRC peaked in Japan. Prime Minister Tanaka Kakuei, only two months after his election, flew to Beijing and a joint communiqué was signed between Japan and the PRC in September 1972. Following the signatory ceremony in Shanghai, Foreign Minister Ohira Masayoshi announced: "It is the view of the Japanese government that, following normalization of relations with China, the Japan–ROC Peace Treaty has lost its significance and should be regarded as terminated." In response Taipei immediately severed diplomatic relations with Japan, putting a full stop to two decades of formal diplomatic relations.

The 1972 communiqué is more than an international agreement between Japan and the PRC. It is the frame to a system—the "1972 system"—that characterizes the nature of the relationship among Japan, the PRC, and Taiwan and sets Tokyo's policy toward Taipei and Beijing in the post-1972 era.[10] In the joint communiqué, the Japanese government recognizes the PRC as the sole legal government of China and "understands and respects" Beijing's position that Taiwan is an inseparable part of the PRC and Taiwan is an internal affair of China.[11] Based on the 1972 communiqué, the Japanese government defines its relations with Taiwan to be a nongovernmental working relationship and has maintained exchanges of a private and regional nature. Thus, embassies and consulates in both countries were replaced by the Association of East Asian Relations (Taiwan) and the Interchange Association (Japan)—private institutions authorized by the respective governments to maintain nongovernmental relationship.

Political relations between Japan and Taiwan were not entirely cut off, however. Following Japan's normalization with the PRC, twenty-three pro-Taiwanese Liberal Democratic Party (LDP) politicians promoted the Sino-Japanese Parliamentarian Cordial Association (SJPCA) in March 1973 to repair the damage caused by the severing of diplomatic ties. Since then Tokyo and Taipei have maintained political contact between the LDP and the KMT through the SJPCA.[12] Under the 1972 system, the SJPCA has served as a political channel between Japan and Taiwan in "supplementing the Interchange Association, which lacks the power to resolve issues pertaining to 'high politics.'"[13] For example, when all flights between Japan and Taiwan were interrupted in 1973 for fourteen months as a result of the dispute over the handling of China Airlines, Taiwan's flag carrier, the SJPCA mediated between the two governments. The SJPCA also persuaded the Ministry of Foreign Affairs on elevating Taiwan's status in Japan and promoted Japanese investment to Taiwan in order to alleviate the Taiwanese complaint over its chronic trade deficit with Japan. Moreover, the SJPCA exchanged views with KMT members through occasional visits to Taiwan on National Anniversary Day and other major events.

Under the 1972 system, Japan's relationship with Taiwan is vulnerable to pressure from the PRC because the bilateral relationship is defined solely in the 1972 joint communiqué. There is no other legal basis to institutionalize it. Therefore, Japan's relationship with Taiwan can be politicized at will by Beijing, even in the realm of "low politics." Beijing often insists that Tokyo comply with the spirit as well as the letter of the 1972 communiqué. Japan's relationship with Taiwan is therefore very different from U.S.–Taiwan relations, which are institutionalized by the Taiwan Relations Act (TRA). The TRA authorizes the United States not only to maintain commercial and cultural relations with Taiwan, but also to provide Taiwan with arms to defend itself. It is understood that the TRA, which is a law passed by Congress, supersedes the three communiqués the United States signed with the PRC.[14]

Moreover, under the 1972 system Japan seeks stability in its relationship with Taiwan in the realm of "low politics" and with the PRC in "high politics." Because Japan regards Taiwan's strategic importance secondary to that of China, Tokyo is reluctant to take any action in regard to Taiwan that may disturb its friendship with mainland China. The 1972 system was effective in the late 1970s and early to mid-1980s when Taiwan was focusing on its economic development and the restoration of internal legitimacy, which had been undermined by international isolation in the 1970s, especially the severing of diplomatic ties with the United States in 1979. During this period Japan's relationship with Taiwan never entered the realm of "high politics," except for the Kokaryo Incident of 1987 in which the Osaka High Court ruled in favor of Taiwan regarding the disputed title to property in the student dormitory at Kyoto University.

Expansion of economic and cultural exchanges has created a stable relationship between Japan and Taiwan. Japanese visitors to Taiwan increased from 204,000 in 1972 to 1,012,000 in 1989. Although the number dropped to 914,000 in 1990, it still represented 47 percent of all foreign visitors to Taiwan. Similarly, Taiwanese visitors to Tokyo increased from 47,000 in 1972 to 502,000 in 1989—some 17 percent of all foreign visitors to Japan. Figures on trade were impressive as well. In 1989, Japan's exports to Taiwan amounted to US$16.9 billion and imports reached US$9.5 billion. In comparison to 1972, the year diplomatic ties were severed, exports increased by approximately sixteenfold and imports by almost twenty-six-fold.[15] From 1987 to 1992, total trade between Japan and Taiwan had indeed surpassed that between Japan and the PRC.[16]

The expansion of trade and cultural exchanges has forced Japan to make certain practical adjustments in its relationship with Taiwan. In May 1992, for instance, the representative offices of Taiwan in Japan were renamed the Taipei Economic and Cultural Representative Office (formerly the Association of East Asian Relations). Over the years, staffing has reached pre-1972 levels. On the Japanese side, the position of the Japanese director in Taipei (de facto ambassador) was elevated—a post now assigned by a career diplomat in the Ministry of Foreign Affairs (previously assigned by a noncareer diplomat).[17] Moreover, as a consequence of Taiwan's economic growth, the bilateral relationship formerly confined in the arena of "low politics" began to encroach on "high politics." In January 1993, Japan's Ministry of International Trade and Industry (MITI) sent an official delegation to assist Taiwan's development of industrial technology—Japan's first government mission to Taiwan since the diplomatic rupture of 1972. In May 1993, MITI's director-general visited Taiwan—the first high-ranking government official to visit the island. In November 1993, Japanese Prime Minister Hosokawa Morihiro exchanged a few words with Taiwan's Minister of Economic Affairs, Vincent Siew, at the APEC meeting in Seattle. This marked the first time a Japanese prime minister had contacted a Taiwanese minister since 1972.[18]

Taiwan's Transformation: Challenges to the 1972 System

Besides the practical adjustments due to expansion of economic and cultural exchanges, Taiwan's democratization in the late 1980s and early 1990s has

come to challenge both dimensions of the 1972 system: the bilateral relationship and Japan's Taiwan policy. With the emergence of new political and
social figures in Taiwan, Japan could no longer handle bilateral issues through
the customary political channels with the KMT. Moreover, the appearance
of Lee Teng-hui and the Japanese-speaking generation, along with growing
distrust of the PRC, have changed Japanese attitudes toward Taiwan. Certainly this change has strengthened bilateral ties between Japan and Taiwan.
But it was the new security imperatives in the post–Cold War era that undermined the 1972 system. With the alteration in the nature of the cross-strait
conflict, Japan could no longer depend on peace and stability in the Taiwan
Strait, which is vital to its national interest, simply by relying on Beijing.

Diversification of Players in Taiwan

Democratization brought new players as well as new problems between Japan and Taiwan. Taiwan became a pluralistic democracy with the formation
of new parties such as the DPP and the New Party (splitting from the KMT
in 1993) after martial law was lifted in 1987.[19] Moreover, freedom of the
press and freedom of association allowed Taiwanese to raise their concerns
openly and to mobilize themselves. As a result, unresolved issues of "high
politics" began to surface between Japan and Taiwan, issues such as the territoriality of the Senkaku Islands (Diaoyu Dao in Chinese), war reparations
to former Taiwanese soldiers in the Japanese military, and compensation of
Taiwanese "comfort women." The SJPCA was not very effective in many of
these cases, which were led by opposition parties and interest groups in Taiwan. In fact, Japan's political parties failed to adapt to the new diversifica-
tion of political and social figures. Neither the LDP nor other political parties
developed any channels with the opposition parties in Taiwan.[20]

Changing Images of Taiwan

Democratization changed the characteristics of the bilateral relationship between
Japan and Taiwan with the emergence of Taiwanese people who had experi-
enced Japanese colonial rule. These people, exemplified by Lee Teng-hui, are
fluent in Japanese and have positive feelings toward Japan. Indeed Lee, who
became president in 1986, had studied at Kyoto Imperial University (currently
Kyoto University) and served briefly in the Japanese imperial army during the
Pacific War as a second lieutenant. He does not hesitate to say that he was
Japanese until the age of twenty-two when the Japanese colonial rule ended.
Lee and the Japanese-speaking generation have succeeded in getting Japan's
attention, as well as changing the Japanese image of Taiwan, which was by no

means positive prior to democratization. The image of Taiwan was basically that of an authoritarian government. In general, the Japanese politicians and academics who did associate with Taiwan were either sympathizers of Chiang Kai-shek, right-wing nationalists, or anticommunists—not the mainstream in Japanese society.[21]

President Lee Teng-hui's interview with Shiba Ryotaro, a respected Japanese writer, in March 1994 was a critical event in terms of changing the Japanese image of Taiwan. In his interview, Lee confided his "sorrow of being a Taiwanese" to Shiba: "Taiwan has always been controlled by a foreign government in its history. The KMT is also a foreign government. . . . In the past, people over seventy like us could not rest well at night. I don't want our future generations to have such an experience."[22] This interview, which was conducted in Japanese in one of the country's most popular weekly magazines, gave Japanese citizens a favorable image of the pro-Japan Taiwanese leader and his country. Moreover, to have someone in the mainstream like Shiba interview the president of the ROC seems to have sent a positive signal to the Japanese public. But this same interview, in which Lee compared himself with Moses in the Exodus, offended the Chinese leaders in Beijing and led them to conclude that Lee is a separatist.[23]

Moreover, Taiwan made the headlines in Japanese newspapers in the fall of 1994 when the Olympics Commission in Asia (OCA) invited Lee Teng-hui to attend the opening ceremony of the Asian Games in Hiroshima. According to the OCA charter, the organization's president reserves the right to invite guests from member nations and regions, of which Taiwan is a part. Beijing strongly protested Lee's visit, however, and even threatened to withdraw from the games. In the end, Lee's invitation was canceled but the Japanese government compromised by allowing Hsu Li-te, vice-president of the Executive Yuan, to visit Japan as an alternate. Beijing opposed Hsu's visit, as well, but Tokyo did not yield this time. As a result, Hsu became the highest Taiwanese government official to visit Japan since diplomatic ties were severed in 1972.[24] Many Japanese people felt that Beijing's obstinate resistance to Lee's visit was unreasonable considering this was simply a sporting event.

Japanese images of Taiwan seem to have improved in inverse relation to their views of mainland China in the global context of the end of the Cold War and the collapse of socialist regimes. Previously, Japanese people had generally positive images of the PRC due to Japan's historical and cultural ties with mainland China. Such images were boosted in the late 1970s as the PRC became "free China" and "open China" thanks to Deng Xiaoping's economic reforms. According to a survey conducted by the Japanese government in 1980, 78.6 percent of the respondents said they feel "favorable" toward Chinese while only 14.7 percent answered "don't feel favorable." Throughout the 1980s, Japanese affinity toward the Chinese remained as high as 60 percent or even 70 percent.[25] The Tiananmen massacre of June 1989, however, shattered such favorable images. According to the same polls, Japanese affinity toward China, which reached 68.5 percent in 1988, dropped to 51.6 percent after the massacre, while those who answered "don't feel favorable" climbed from 26.4 percent to 43.1 percent.[26]

The PRC's image deteriorated further in the eyes of the Japanese public along with a series of events: the underground nuclear experiments of 1995, the Taiwan Strait crisis of 1996, and the rapid military buildup of recent years. Among the Japanese public, these incidents have led to a perception of a Chinese threat. According to a public opinion survey by the Japanese government on Japan–China relations, respondents who answered "don't think the bilateral relations are in good shape" outnumbered those who responded "think the bilateral relations are in good shape" for the first time in 1995 and have done so ever since except for the year 1997.[27]

Along with the changing images of Taiwan and the PRC, the ideological boundary between the pro-China faction and the pro-Taiwan faction in Japanese politics began to crumble in the post–Cold War era. This opened up a new avenue for politicians who were no longer necessarily anti-Beijing but simply pro-democratic to develop an interest in Taiwan.[28] Such phenomena coincided with the generation change in Japanese politics. Both pro-Taiwan and pro-China politicians, those who took part in the political battle over normalization with the PRC in 1972, are retiring from the main stage—replaced by younger politicians who are concerned about China's rapid economic growth and military modernization. Unlike the previous generation, they have no residual wartime guilt regarding the Chinese and are willing to express their dissatisfaction with China's persistent criticism of Japan's historical record.

Challenges to Japan's Taiwan Policy

A bigger challenge to the 1972 system concerns Japan's Taiwan policy. Under the 1972 system, Japan sought peace and stability in the Taiwan Strait by relying on Beijing and neglecting Taiwan. Taiwan's transformation and increasing cross-strait tensions, however, have challenged such an approach. President Lee Teng-hui's visit to the United States in June 1995 transformed Beijing's Taiwan policy from a peaceful approach into a coercive one. Since Lee's visit, the PRC has intermittently conducted military exercises, including missile launches in the Taiwan Strait, right up to Taiwan's first direct presidential election in March 1996. Such maneuvers in the Taiwan Strait compelled the United States to dispatch two aircraft carriers to the area—the largest naval movement in the Asia-Pacific region since the Vietnam War.

Instability and a possible military conflict in the Taiwan Strait are great security concerns for Japan. Certainly Japan has a strong interest in the region. The sea-lane through which Japan transports almost 90 percent of its oil supply from the Middle East runs through the waters near Taiwan.[29] It is also in Japan's interest to protect its trade: Mainland China and Taiwan are the second- and third-largest markets for Japanese exports. Moreover, its geographic proximity makes Taiwan a serious security concern for Japan. After all, Yonaguni Island of Okinawa prefecture is only one hundred kilometers distant from Taiwan. During the missile crisis of March 1996, the Chinese missiles, which landed only sixty kilometers from Yonaguni Island, disturbed the life of Japanese citizens in the area. This incident led to unprecedented complaints by the Japanese government to Beijing. The Ministry of Foreign Affairs summoned a Chinese official from the Chinese Embassy and expressed its concern: "Increasing tensions in the Taiwan Strait are not desirable for peace and stability in East Asia. We are deeply concerned about the military exercise."[30]

Japan's security concerns regarding the Taiwan Strait are by no means novel. The revised U.S.–Japan Security Treaty of 1960 guaranteed the United States the use of facilities in Japan for the maintenance of international peace and security in the Far East. At the time, the Japanese government acknowledged Taiwan to be included in the area defined as the "Far East." A stronger commitment to Taiwan's security was expressed by Prime Minister Sato Eisaku in 1969 when he stated that "peace and stability in the Taiwan region are a very important element of Japan's security" in the joint communiqué with the United States. Despite the diplomatic rupture between Japan and Taiwan in 1972, the provisions of the U.S.–Japan Security Treaty remain effective to this date. The security treaty, along with the TRA, is believed to have contributed to peace and stability in the Taiwan Strait.

The missile crisis of 1996, in which the United States intervened by dispatching two aircraft carriers, reaffirmed Taiwan's significant implications for Japan's security. A military conflict in the Taiwan Strait would differ from war on the Korean peninsula. In the Taiwan Strait a conflict could turn into a global war between the United States and China that would inevitably force Japan to make a crucial decision on whether to participate or not. If the United States decided to intervene, Japan would face a dilemma: whether to comply with the provisions of the U.S.–Japan defense guidelines and risk its friendship with the PRC or not comply and jeopardize its alliance with the United States. The latter option seems less feasible since Japan's security relationship with the United States remains the core of its security policy even in the post–Cold War era. Moreover, Tokyo must decide how to react to a military conflict in the Taiwan Strait in case the United States refuses to get involved. This scenario is by no means unthinkable.

There are signs of adjustments, although subtle, in Japan's Taiwan policy in the broad context of Japan's security policy since the 1996 Taiwan missile crisis. In 1997, the Japanese government undertook the revision of the Guidelines for U.S.–Japan Defense Cooperation in order to strengthen its military cooperation with the United States to cope with new security threats in the post–Cold War era. When the defense perimeter in the new guidelines became an issue in the Japanese Diet, Beijing began to pressure the Japanese government to exclude Taiwan from what the new guidelines call the "areas surrounding Japan." Tokyo rejected Beijing's pressure by claiming that "areas surrounding Japan" is situational in nature, not geographical. Japan again demonstrated its firm stance on Taiwan at the summit meeting between Prime Minister Obuchi Keizo and President Jiang Zemin in Tokyo in 1998. Beijing asked Tokyo to endorse the "Three Nos"—no support for Taiwan's independence, no support for Taiwan's membership in international organizations comprised of sovereign states, and no support for "one China, one Taiwan"— in the joint declaration between Japan and the PRC; but the Japanese government refused and simply reiterated its observance of the 1972 joint communiqué.

Implications of Chen's Victory

While the election of Chen Shui-bian did not cause the Japanese government to change its Taiwan policy immediately, it has had two significant implications. First, it sharpened Japan's security concern since stability (or the status quo) in the Taiwan Strait is now based on a fragile foundation. When the KMT was in power, there was a general expectation that the KMT and the CCP would eventually come to an agreement on how to achieve "one China" through negotiations. While both the KMT and the CCP disagreed on who represents "China," they did not deny there was only "one China."[31] But with Chen's victory, a soft-landing scenario is now difficult to imagine. Although they would not dare express it, Chen and the DPP leaders aim to secure Taiwan's independence. For Chen's DPP, unification with mainland China is an option at best.

Second, Chen's victory may challenge Japan's perception of the Taiwan issue. Tokyo has acknowledged since 1972 Beijing's claim that Taiwan is an internal affair of China. Such acknowledgement was based on the premise that the issue derives from the Chinese civil war of 1947 between the KMT and the CCP. With the defeat of the KMT, however, there is now a condition in which one can say that Taiwan is no longer a "Chinese" internal affair. For Chen's DPP is an indigenous political party of Taiwan: It did not come from mainland China nor did it fight a civil war with the communists. In this sense, the election of a non-KMT leader signifies a de facto end to the Chinese civil war dimension of the conflict between Taiwan and mainland China.[32] Such a perceptional change on the Taiwan issue would allow Japan's policy toward Taiwan to be more autonomous from the 1972 system. Such a policy shift would not violate the 1972 joint communiqué since Tokyo never recognized that Taiwan is part of the PRC. It only "understands" and "respects" the PRC's position that "Taiwan is an inalienable part of the PRC." Moreover, Clause 3 of the communiqué states that the Japanese government "firmly maintains its stand under Article 8 of the Postdam Proclamation." Article 8 of the proclamation refers to the Cairo Declaration, which states that "Formosa" (Taiwan) is to be restored to the ROC. This roundabout reference implies that Japan renounced Taiwan but takes no position on its present status.[33]

While this reasoning might be logical, such a shift will not lead to an immediate, conspicuous change in Japan's policy toward Taiwan. After all, the damage it would cause to Japan's relationship with the PRC is evident. From a pragmatic standpoint, today Taiwan is even more so an internal affair of the PRC since the Chinese leaders have adopted nationalism as a new source of internal legitimacy in lieu of communist doctrine in the post–Cold War era. The loss of Taiwan would not only undermine the legitimacy of the communist regime, but could also challenge the territorial integrity of the PRC by inciting regions such as Tibet and Xinjiang to follow suit. Moreover, Japan's interest is peace and stability in the Taiwan Strait, not to support the independence of Taiwan, which Beijing firmly opposes.

But the peace and security that Japan wants in the Taiwan Strait can no longer be sustained by favoring China and neglecting Taiwan. As demonstrated in Lee Teng-hui's "two-state theory" in 1999, Taiwan's words and deeds could trigger tension and conflict in the Taiwan Strait—anathema to Japan's economic as well as security interests. As a result of Chen's victory, therefore, Japan is being urged to take a more active role in constructing a security environment in which Taiwan and mainland China can coexist peacefully. Certainly Japan can promote political dialogue between Taipei and Beijing as well as encourage a Track Two security dialogue among Japan, the United States, the PRC, and Taiwan. Beijing may oppose these efforts as an intervention in China's internal affairs; but it is evident that if a war breaks out in the Taiwan Strait, the Taiwan issue is for Japan no longer a Chinese internal affair.

Toward a Normal Relationship

At the bilateral level, Chen's election marked the retirement of Lee Teng-hui and the defeat of the KMT. Lee Teng-hui's retirement forces Japan to reconstruct its relationship with Taiwan. Lee's contribution to the bilateral relationship, as mentioned earlier, was significant. Since he was fluent in the language and had great knowledge of Japan, President Lee was solely in charge of Taiwan's relations with Japan.[34] Unlike Lee, Chen Shui-bian neither speaks Japanese nor has a special attachment to Japan. This, however, does not mean that the bilateral ties must deteriorate. The role of political leaders is important but not fundamental. After all, it is mutual interests that link nations. Japan and Taiwan both benefit from mutual trade and both share a great interest in maintaining peace and stability in the Taiwan Strait. Lee's retirement, therefore, presents an opportunity for Japan and Taiwan to strengthen their relationship since it inevitably forces them to establish multiple channels. In other words, the weight of the relationship is shifting from individual-based diplomacy to a more diverse approach. Since 1972, political relations between Japan and Taiwan have been maintained solely through the ruling parties. The LDP had formed no relationship with the DPP until its victory in March 2000. Taken by surprise with Chen's victory, the SJPCA sent a delegation to Taipei to meet the new president. Meanwhile, the DPJ is eager to develop political ties with the DPP. Hatoyama Yukio, the DPJ party leader, has had personal ties with President Chen Shui-bian from the days when the DPP was in opposition. The DPJ established the Sino-Japan Friendship Parliamentarian Federation in April 2000 to promote exchanges between the two parties. In May the DPJ sent four legislators to attend Chen's inauguration ceremony and the SJPCA sent twelve. It has been said that Hatoyama and the DPJ are eager to build new relationships with both Beijing and Taipei.

At the same time, the Chen administration is aiming to expand its ties with the DPJ and other parties while maintaining the channel with the LDP.[35] In an interview with the author, the head of the Taipei Economic and Cultural Representative Office in Japan, Lo Fu-chen, said he had met with politicians from all political parties but the Communist Party of Japan since he assumed his current position in May 2000.[36] In sum, then, the exit of Lee Teng-hui and the Japanese-speaking generation marked not only the end of a special relationship between Japan and Taiwan that was based on a Japanese colonial legacy but also the beginning of a new relationship.

Challenges to a New Relationship

Many variables govern the restructuring of the bilateral relationship between Japan and Taiwan. First is the mutual understanding between Japan and the new Taiwan. Earlier I argued that strong mutual interests between Japan and Taiwan supersede the generation gap. Lack of mutual understanding and respect, however, could harm the relationship. Japan should no longer look at Taiwan through the lens of the "Japanese colonial legacy." Such an approach could be problematic with Taiwanese of the postcolonial era. Unlike the previous generation that experienced Japanese rule, Chen's generation has no nostalgic feelings toward Japan. Indeed the postwar generation, which grew up under the KMT's anti-Japanese education, is rather critical of Japan.[37] Former President Lee seems to have a good understanding of the Japanese government's position. Lee did not push too hard on his visit to Japan, for example, and often made comments such as "I do not wish to put Japan in an awkward position" or "I will visit whenever Japan is ready to accept me."

Chen Shui-bian and his staff, by contrast, are more straightforward. When Chang Chun-hsiung, then the secretary general to the president, now the premier, was denied entry to Japan to attend the funeral of the late Prime Minister Obuchi Keizo in June 2000, Chen's new government did not hesitate to express its dissatisfaction. Chang said: "Paying too much attention to political considerations will do nothing to promote friendship and exchanges between the two countries and is not what the Japanese people would like to see."[38] When former President Lee was dissuaded by Tokyo from visiting Japan to attend the Asia Open Forum (an academic conference) in October 2000, President Chen criticized the Japanese government: "Why does Japan always fear Chinese reaction when it is a sovereign nation-state? . . . If Japan still cannot accept Lee's visit even though he is now retired and an ordinary citizen, many Taiwanese people will not understand this."[39] More recently, in March 2001, the popular Japanese cartoonist Kobayashi Yoshinori was temporarily refused entry to Taiwan because of his description of Taiwanese comfort women in his book *On Taiwan*. Although the ban was lifted in three weeks, the incident offered a glimpse of the new bilateral relationship between Japan and Taiwan in the post-Lee era. Contentious issues that lie unresolved between Japan and Taiwan—such as Taiwan's huge trade deficits with Japan, the comfort women issue, and the territorial dispute over the Senkaku Islands—may resurface in the near future.

Meanwhile, the DPP's perception of Japan is also uncertain. Indeed, there are indications that the DPP government is neglecting its relationship with Japan. It has been reported, for example, that Hsiao Mei-chien, international director of the DPP, said: "I focus more on the relationship with the United States than that with Japan. . . . I am dissatisfied with Japan's pro-Beijing policy. . . . Honestly, Japan is neglecting Taiwan. If this continues to be the case, we will review our special relationship and treat Japan like one of the many others."[40] While her frustration with the Japanese government is understandable, the DPP cannot expect from Japan the same support it receives from the United States. Japan does not have the TRA, lacks a powerful legislature like the U.S. Congress, and is more sensitive toward Beijing due to its past history of invasion as well as geographic contiguity.

This does not mean that Japan is not important to Taiwan, however. The U.S.–Japan Security Treaty, which has complemented the TRA as a deterrent to military conflict in the Taiwan Strait, is crucial for Taiwan's security both in peacetime and wartime. Although the treaty is vital to Japan's security, this does not translate to Japan's unconditional cooperation in support of the U.S. military in case of a contingency in the Taiwan Strait. Therefore, it is important for Taipei to maintain close ties with Tokyo. Moreover, Japan's policy toward mainland China is not entirely conciliatory. Certainly the Japanese government did not yield to Beijing's pressure to profess the "Three Nos" in the 1998 joint declaration. At the time, many did not doubt that Japan would bow to Beijing's demand since President Clinton had affirmed the "Three Nos" in August 1998. But the Japanese government denied there was any need for the "Three Nos" and simply reiterated its observance of the 1972 joint communiqué in the joint declaration. If Japan had followed the United States by recognizing the "Three Nos," it would have dashed Taipei's hopes for reentry to the United Nations and other international organizations.

The second variable is Japan's political leadership. Japanese politics is still in transition after the demise of the 1955 system in 1993, which ended thirty-eight years of LDP predominance. Weak political leadership has allowed civil servants to gain greater influence in Japan's foreign policymaking. In general, the bureaucrats are consistent but conservative. Without strong leadership, therefore, Japan's policy toward Taiwan will be governed by a bureaucratic "safety first" (*kotonakare-shugi*) mentality and continue to be restrained by the 1972 system. Moreover, changes in Japan's political landscape could favor Taiwan. The old generation of pro-Taiwanese politicians and pro-China politicians, for example, is retiring. While the new generation acknowledges the importance of Japan's ties with mainland China, they have greater respect for Taiwan's vibrant democratic practices than their predecessors did. At present, the Japanese government goes no further than expressing a desire for the "peaceful resolution" of the Taiwan issue. But as the younger generation gains higher positions in the party and assumes ministerial posts in the future, it may strengthen Japan's democratic commitment to Taiwan by adding a condition that any settlement of Taiwan's future status is expected to be peaceful as well as acceptable to people on both sides of the strait.[41]

The third variable is the challenges from civil society to policymakers at the top. Bilateral interactions at the people-to-people level between Japan and Taiwan have been widening and deepening over the past several years. Despite the limitation of interactions at the government level, Taiwan has vigorously promoted a "metropolitan diplomacy" in strengthening bilateral ties at the regional level. In January 2001, the DPP leader Hsieh Chang-ting (also the mayor of Kaohsiung), paid a visit to Osaka and Yokohama to inspect the development of waterfront cities in Japan. This marked the first visit by the DPP head to Japan.[42] The mayor of Tokyo, Ishihara Shintaro, internationally known as a right-wing politician, attended Chen Shui-bian's inauguration ceremony in May 2000. Ishihara had already visited Taiwan in November 1999 to inspect the aftermath of the September earthquake and met with President Lee Teng-hui to exchange views on the bilateral relationship. When the earthquake struck central Taiwan, causing more than 2,000 deaths, Japan immediately dispatched the largest rescue group, 125 men, to the site. Moreover, significant donations were raised in Japan through charity events by Japanese and Taiwanese celebrities. These events, picked up in the Taiwanese media, did much to enhance Taiwan's image of Japan.

Especially impressive are the subcultural ties between Japan and Taiwan. Japanese pop culture, everything from music to fashion, is extremely popular among Taiwanese teens. In fact, it has become a social phenomenon in Taiwan. The word "*harizu*," a Taiwanese word for Japan mania, has gained wide currency. Taiwan, likewise, has achieved a secure place in the heart of the Japanese people. Taiwanese celebrities such as Vivian Hsu and Kaneshiro Takeshi are famous TV figures in Japan. Taiwan is a popular travel destination for young Japanese. Books on Taiwan occupy a large share of the shelves in Japanese bookstores. While the titles of publications on mainland China are often dreary and formal, those on Taiwan are, by contrast, positive and appealing. One finds many books by Taiwanese authors either praising Japanese culture or inspiring the Japanese people to recover from their war guilt. With the expansion of such ties between people in Japan and Taiwan, it will be difficult for policymakers to ignore public sentiment.

Beyond the 1972 System?

As we have seen, the transformation of Taiwan, of which the election of Chen is the culmination, is making it difficult for the Japanese government to treat Taiwan according to the 1972 system. Taiwan is no longer a mere economic partner for Japan; today it is a significant security issue. The 1996 missile crisis in the context of the post–Cold War era was a turning point. To maintain peace and stability in the Taiwan Strait and secure its national interest, Japan can no longer ignore Taiwan but needs to engage it despite Beijing's pressure. Moreover, the transformation of the bilateral relationship in the post-Lee era and growing public sympathy are forcing Japan to separate its Taiwan policy from the constraints of the 1972 system. This, however, is not to suggest there will be an immediate change. Beijing's insistence that Taiwan is an internal affair of China still prevails. Therefore, any departure from the 1972 system will be subtle and incremental. Japan's decision to grant former President Lee Teng-hui a visa to visit Japan in April 2000 is a sign of change—considering that Beijing vigorously opposed it and Tokyo once acknowledged Beijing's claim that Lee is not an ordinary individual.

Although the changes are subtle, Japan must deliberate what the new Taiwan means to Japan. Taiwan, once a colony of Japan, then a formal diplomatic partner, then a neglected partner, has now become an important partner to Japan through its own democratic transformation. The Japanese-speaking generation, exemplified in Lee Teng-hui, has disappeared from center stage. But Taiwan is important to Japan in three dimensions. Economically, Taiwan today is Japan's third-largest trade partner after the United States and the PRC, ranking third in terms of Japan's exports and fifth in imports.[43] Politically and strategically, peace and stability in the Taiwan Strait cannot be sustained without engaging Taiwan. Finally, Japan and Taiwan have developed strong social and cultural ties. Both are economically advanced, politically democratized, culturally postmodern. With Chen's victory, Japan's relationship with Taiwan is entering a new phase beyond the 1972 system.

Notes

1. Ministry of Foreign Affairs of Japan, "Remarks by Foreign Minister Kono Yohei on the Result of the 'Presidential' Election in Taiwan," 18 March 2000 (www.mofa.go.jp/announce/2000/3/318.html).

2. See Office of the Press Secretary, White House, "President Congratulates Chen Shui-bian on Taiwan Election (New Opportunity for China, Taiwan to Resolve Differences)," 18 March 2000; available from the Public Diplomacy Query website.

3. The understanding between Japan and the PRC in the 1972 joint communiqué became obligatory when the two countries later signed the Treaty of Peace and Friendship in 1978. In the Japan–China joint declaration of 1998, Japan reaffirmed that there is "one China" and pledged to maintain its "exchanges of a private and regional nature with Taiwan."

4. *Sankei Shimbun*, 8 July 2000 (Tokyo Morning Edition, Internet).

5. On 20 April 2001, the Japanese government announced that it will issue former President Lee Teng-hui a visa to visit Japan for a medical checkup. Tokyo explained that the decision is based on a "humanitarian standpoint." See *Sankei Shimbun*, 21 April 2001.

6. Statistical data are from He-yi Yang, *Nihon to Taiwan Kaikyo Ryogan to no Kankei: Tokei Shiryo to Nenpyo* [Relationship between Japan and two sides of the Taiwan Strait: Statistics and chronology] (Tokyo: Taipei Economic and Cultural Representative Office in Japan, 1992), p. 1; and Gaikoku Boeki Gaikyo [Foreign trade outlook], 2000.

7. The statement in the Cairo Declaration reads: "All the territories Japan has stolen from the Chinese, such as Manchuria, Formosa, and the Pescadores, shall be restored to the Republic of China." Formosa and the Pescadores are part of what is known as Taiwan today. See Database of Postwar Japanese Politics and Diplomacy, Basic Documents of Postwar International Politics (http://www.ioc.u-tokyo.ac.jp/~worldjpn/documents/indices/docs/index-ENG.html).

8. Yoshida Shigeru, *Kaiso Junen* [Recollections of ten years], vol. 3 (Tokyo: Shincho-sha, 1957), p. 72.

9. Yoshihide Soeya, *Japan's Economic Diplomacy with China, 1945–1978* (Oxford: Clarendon, 1998), pp. 8 and 12.

10. The term "1972 system" is not my original. Ryosei Kokubun uses the term "72 *nen Taisei*" [72 system] in referring to the structure that has provided stability between Japan and the PRC since 1972. See Ryosei Kokubun, "Reisen Shuketsu-go no Nitchu Kankei—'72–nen Taisei' no Tenkan" [Japan-China relations in the post–Cold War era—transition of the "72 system"], *Kokusai Mondai* 490 (January 2001):42–56.

11. Before the normalization of 1972, Beijing proposed a set of guidelines: (1) There is only one China and the government of the PRC is the sole legal government that represents the Chinese people; (2) Taiwan is a province of China, an inalienable part of the Chinese territory; and (3) therefore the issue of Taiwan is a Chinese internal affair. These "three principles for the restoration of relations" (*fukko san gensoku*) were reaffirmed by the Japanese government in the 1972 joint communiqué. The preamble of the communiqué says that the Japanese government fully understands "the three principles for the restoration of relations put forward by the government of the People's Republic of China."

12. The SJPCA became a nonpartisan organization in 1997 when political parties that split off from the LDP in 1993 agreed to form a consolidated organization. In March 2001 there were about 270 members.

13. Keizo Takemi, "Nittai Kankei" [Japan–Taiwan relationship], in *Taiwan Hyakka* [Everything about Taiwan], ed. Wakabayashi Masahiro, Ryu Jinkei, and Matsunaga Seigi (Tokyo: Taishukan Shoten, 1994), p. 102. Keizo Takemi is a member of the SJPCA and a prominent scholar on Japan–Taiwan relations.

14. For example, according to the East Asian Strategy Report (1998), the U.S.–Taiwan relationship is "*governed* by the Taiwan Relations Act (TRA) and *guided* by the three U.S.–PRC joint communiqués" (emphasis added).

15. Keizo Takemi, "Nittai Kankei: Zeijyaku no naka no Antei" [Japan–Taiwan relations: Stability within vulnerability], *Sekai* (April 1991):60–61.

16. Satoshi Amako, "Nihon kara mita Taiwan Mondai to Tenkanki no Nittai Kankei" [Japanese perspective on the Taiwan problem and Japan–Taiwan relations in transition], *Kokusai Mondai* 488 (November 2000):50.

17. Ryoichi Hamamoto, "Nihon to no Kankei" [Relations with Japan], in *Motto Shiritai Taiwan* [Wanting to know more about Taiwan], 2nd ed., ed. Masahiro Wakabayashi (Tokyo: Kobundo, 1998), p. 285.

18. Ibid., p. 286.

19. The DPP was formed in 1986, a year before the lifting of martial law.

20. Keizo Takemi ascribes the lack of political ties between Japan's political parties and the opposition parties in Taiwan to Japanese politicians' failure to appreciate the extent of democratization in Taiwan. See Keizo Takemi, "Nitchu Nittai Kankei ni okeru Shin chu Shin tai ha no Shuen—Gekido no Niju-isseiki, Nihon ni Motomerareru Gaiko Senryaku to wa" [Termination of pro-China and pro-Taiwan factions in Japan–

China, Japan–Taiwan relations—Searching a strategy for Japan's diplomacy in the turbulent twenty-first century], *Mondai to Kenkyu* (May 1997):61–62.

21. Kokubun, "Reisen Shuketsu-go no Nitchu Kankei," p. 53.

22. Shiba Ryotaro, "Basho no Kurushimi: Taiwanjin ni Umareta Hiai" [Agony of place: A sorrow to be born Taiwanese], *Shukan Asahi*, 6–13 May 1994, p. 46.

23. Suisheng Zhao, "Making Sense of the 1995–96 Crisis in the Taiwan Strait," in *Across the Taiwan Strait: Mainland China, Taiwan, and the 1995–96 Crisis*, ed. Suisheng Zhao (New York: Routledge, 1999), p. 7.

24. Hamamoto, "Nihon to no Kankei," p. 279.

25. Kokubun, "Reisen Shuketsu-go no Nitchu Kankei," pp. 42–43.

26. Ibid.

27. Cabinet Office, Government of Japan, "Gaiko ni kansuru Yoron Chosa" [Public opinion survey on diplomacy], October 2001 (http://www.cao.go.jp/).

28. You Watari, "Taiwan Mondai o Kangaeru: 'Chuka Minkoku zai Taiwan' to iu 'Kuni' ni Sun de" [Living in a "country" called "Republic of China in Taiwan"], *Toa* 378 (December 1998):96; Amako, "Nihon kara mita Taiwan," p. 54.

29. Shigeo Hiramatsu, "Sekiyu, Shokuryo no Seimeisen o mamoru tame ni Nihon wa Taiwan, Kankoku to Renkei su be ki da" [In order to protect the lifeline of oil and food, Japan should ally with Taiwan and South Korea], *Sapio*, 28 June 2000, pp. 14–15.

30. Hamamoto, "Nihon to no Kankei," p. 289.

31. See "The Meaning of 'One China,'" adopted by the National Unification Council, Taipei, 1 August 1992 (www.mac.gov.tw/mlpolicy/chinae.htm).

32. I consider the termination of the temporary provisions (effective during the period of communist rebellion) in 1991 a de jure end to the civil war dimension of the cross-strait conflict.

33. Beijing and Tokyo have different interpretations over Clause 3 of the joint communiqué. Beijing accepted the wordings of Clause 3 since it specifies restoration of Taiwan to the ROC to which it claims succession. For Japan, the Cairo Declaration has no legal obligation regarding Taiwan's status since the final disposal of the territory is determined by the 1952 San Francisco Peace Treaty. See *Tenkanki no Ampo* [U.S.–Japan security treaty in transition], ed. Mainichi Shimbun-sha Seiji-bu (Tokyo: Mainichi Shimbun-sha, 1979), pp. 253–256; Akihiko Tanaka, *Nitchu Kankei: 1945–1990* [Japan–China relations: 1945–1990] (Tokyo: Tokyo Daigaku Shuppankai, 1991), footnote 30, p. 220; *Taiwan no Hoteki chii* [The legal status of Taiwan], ed. Ming-min Peng and Ng Yuzin Chiautong (Tokyo: Tokyo Daigaku Shuppankai, 1976), pp. 202–203 and footnotes 15 and 16.

34. Masahiro Wakabayashi, "Taiwan Chin Sui hen Shin Seiken no Kadai" [Challenges for the new Chen Shui-bian administration], *Toa* 398 (August 2000):79.

35. Katsuhiko Shimizu, "Nittai-kan ni mo Ihen Jimin kara Minshu?" [Changes in Japan–Taiwan relations: From LDP to DPJ?], *Asahi Shimbun Weekly AERA*, 5 March 2001, p. 19; *Sankei Shimbun*, 24 May 2000.

36. Personal interview with Representative Lo Fu-chen, 1 March 2001.

37. The Taiwanese government revised history textbooks in 1997. The new text is less ideological and says that Japanese colonial rule provided the social and human infrastructure for economic development in the postwar period. Influenced by the Japanese pop subculture, teenagers in Taiwan today seem to be pro-Japanese.

38. "Taiwan Regrets Japanese Rejection of Taipei Envoy to Obuchi Funeral," *China Times*, 6 June 2000 (www.chinatimes.com.tw//english/epolitic/8906050.html).

39. *Sankei Shimbun*, 17 September 2000 (Tokyo Morning Edition, Internet).

40. Renho, "Kono mama de ha Hachi nen go no Taiwan Shin Soto wa America Jushi de Nihon wa musi to iu koto ni naru" [Taiwan's new president in eight years will emphasize the U.S. and neglect Japan], *Sapio*, 28 June 2000, pp. 20–21.

41. The U.S. commitment to Taiwan's security has increased in the past few years. The Clinton administration said the differences should be "resolved peacefully" and by the "assent of the Taiwanese people." This stance has been basically adopted by the Bush administration as well. Secretary of State Colin Powell stated in his confirmation testimony: "We expect and demand a peaceful settlement, one acceptable to people on both sides of the Taiwan Strait." See Confirmation Hearing by Colin L. Powell, 17 January 2001 (http://www.state.gov/s/index.cfm?docid=443).

42. "Sha Chotei Minshinto Shuseki ga Honichi" [DPP Chairman Hsieh Chang-ting visits Japan], *Chuka Shuho* [China weekly], 8 February 2001, p. 4.

43. The statistics are from 1998. See *Japan 2000: An International Comparison* (Tokyo: Keizai Koho Center, 1999), p. 60.

APPENDIX A

Taiwan Relations Act

13 STAT.14
PUBLIC LAW 96–8–APR.10, 1979(H.R.2479)

An Act to help maintain peace, security, and stability in the Western Pacific and to promote the foreign policy of the United States by authorizing the continuation of commercial, cultural, and other relations between the people of the United States and the people on Taiwan, and prior for other purpose.

Short Title

Section 1.

This Act may be cited as the "Taiwan Relations Act."

Findings and Declaration of Policy

Section 2.

(A) The President having terminated governmental relations between the United States and the governing authorities on Taiwan recognized by the United States as the Republic of China prior to January 1, 1979, the Congress finds that the enactment of this Act is necessary—
  1. to help maintain peace, security, and stability in the Western Pacific; and
  2. to promote the foreign policy of the United States by authorizing the continuation of commercial, cultural, and other relations between the people of the United States and the people on Taiwan.
(B) It is the policy of the United States—
  1. to preserve and promote extensive, close, and friendly commercial, cultural, and other relations between the people of the United States and the people on Taiwan as well as the people on the China mainland and all other peoples of the Western Pacific area;
  2. to declare that peace and stability in the area are in the political,

security, and economic interests of the United States, and are matters of international concern;

3. to make clear that the United States decision to establish diplomatic relations with the People's Republic of China rests upon
the expectation that the future of Taiwan will be determined by
peaceful means;

4. to consider any effort to determine the future of Taiwan by other
than peaceful means, including by boycotts, or embargoes, a threat
to the peace and security of the Western Pacific area and of grave
concern to the United States;

5. to provide Taiwan with arms of a defensive character; and

6. to maintain the capacity of the United States to resist any resort to
force or other forms of coercion that would jeopardize the security, or the social or economic systems, of the people on Taiwan.

(C) Nothing contained in this Act shall contravene the interest of the United
States in human rights, especially with respect to the human rights of all the
approximately 18 million inhabitants of Taiwan. The preservation and enhancement of the human rights of all the people on Taiwan are hereby reaffirmed as an objective of the United States.

Implementation of United States Policy with Regard to Taiwan

Section 3.

(A) In furtherance of the policy set forth in section 2 of this Act, the United
States will make available to Taiwan such defense articles and defense services in such quantity as may be necessary to enable Taiwan to maintain a
sufficient self-defense capability.

(B) The President and the Congress shall determine the nature and quantity of such defense articles and services based solely upon their judgement
of the needs of Taiwan, in accordance with procedures established by law.
Such determination of Taiwan's defense needs shall include review by United
States military authorities in connection with recommendations to the President and the Congress.

(C) The President is directed to inform the Congress promptly of any
threat to the security or the social or economic system of the people on Taiwan and any danger to the interests of the United States arising therefrom.
The President and the Congress shall determine, in accordance with constitutional processes, appropriate action by the United States in response to any
such danger.

Application of Laws: International Agreements

Section 4.

(A) The absence of diplomatic relations or recognition shall not affect the application of the laws of the United States with respect to Taiwan, and the laws of the United States shall apply with respect to Taiwan in the manner that the laws of the United States applied with respect to Taiwan prior to January 1, 1979.

(B) The application of subsection (a) of this section shall include, but not be limited to, the following:

1. Whenever the laws of the United States refer or relate to foreign countries, nations, states, governments, or similar entitles, such terms shall include and such laws shall apply with respect to Taiwan.

2. Whenever authorized by or pursuant to the laws of the United States to conduct or carry out programs, transactions, or other relations with respect to foreign countries, nations, states, governments, or similar entities, the President or any agency of the United States Government is authorized to conduct and carry out, in accordance with section 6 of this Act, such programs, transactions, and other relations with respect to Taiwan (including, but not limited to, the preformance of services for the United States through contracts with commercial entities on Taiwan), in accordance with the applicable laws of the United States.

3. (a) The absence of diplomatic relations and recognition with respect to Taiwan shall not abrogate, infringe, modify, deny, or otherwise affect in any way any rights or obligations (including but not limited to those involving contracts, debts, or property interests of any kind) under the laws of the United States heretofore or hereafter acquired by or with respect to Taiwan.

3. (b) For all purposes under the laws of the United States, including actions in any court in the United States, recognition of the People's Republic of China shall not affect in any way the ownership of or other rights or interests in properties, tangible and intangible, and other things of value, owned or held on or prior to December 31, 1978, or thereafter acquired or earned by the governing authorities on Taiwan.

4. Whenever the application of the laws of the United States depends upon the law that is or was applicable on Taiwan or compliance therewith, the law applied by the people on Taiwan shall be considered the applicable law for that purpose.

5. Nothing in this Act, nor the facts of the President's action in extending diplomatic recognition to the People's Republic of China, the absence of diplomatic relations between the people on Taiwan and the United States, or the lack of recognition by the United States, and attendant circumstances thereto, shall be construed in any administrative or judicial proceeding as a basis for any United States Government agency, commission, or department to make a finding of fact or determination of law, under the Atomic Energy Act of 1954 and the Nuclear Non-Proliferation Act of 1978, to deny an export license application or to revoke an existing export license for nuclear exports to Taiwan.

6. For purposes of the Immigration and Nationality Act, Taiwan may be treated in the manner specified in the first sentence of section 202(B) of that Act.

7. The capacity of Taiwan to sue and be sued in courts in the United States, in accordance with the laws of the United States, shall not be abrogated, infringed, modified, denied, or otherwise affected in any way by the absence of diplomatic relations or recognition.

8. No requirement, whether expressed or implied, under the laws of the United States with respect to maintenance of diplomatic relations or recognition shall be applicable with respect to Taiwan.

(C) For all purposes, including actions in any court in the United States, the Congress approves the continuation in force of all treaties and other international agreements, including multilateral conventions, entered into by the United States and the governing authorities on Taiwan recognized by the United States as the Republic of China prior to January 1, 1979, and in force between them on December 31, 1978, unless and until terminated in accordance with law.

(D) Nothing in this Act may be construed as a basis for supporting the exclusion or expulsion of Taiwan from continued membership in any international financial institution or any other international organization.

Overseas Private Investment Corporation

Section 5.

(A) During the three-year period beginning on the date of enactment of this Act, the $1,000 per capita income restriction in clause (2) of the second undesignated paragraph of section 231 of the Foreign Assistance Act of 1961 shall not restrict the activities of the Overseas Private Investment Corporation in determining whether to provide any insurance, reinsurance, loans, or guaranties with respect to investment projects on Taiwan.

(B) Except as provided in subsection (A) of this section, in issuing insurance, reinsurance, loans, or guaranties with respect to investment projects on Taiwan, the Overseas Private Insurance Corporation will apply the same criteria as those applicable in other parts of the world.

The American Institute In Taiwan

Section 6.

(A) Programs, transactions, and other relations conducted or carried out by the President or any agency of the United States Government with respect to Taiwan, shall in the manner and to the extent directed by the President, be conducted and carried out by or through—
    1. The American Institute in Taiwan, a nonprofit corporation incorporated under the laws of the District of Columbia, or
    2. such comparable successor nongovernmental entity as the President may designate, (hereafter in this Act referred to as the "Institute").

(B) Whenever the President or any agency of the United States Government is authorized or required by or pursuant to the laws of the United States to enter into, perform, enforce, or have inforce an agreement or transaction relative to Taiwan, such agreement or transaction shall be entered into, performed, and enforced, in the manner and to the extent directed by the President, by or through the Institute.

(C) To the extent that any law, rule, regulation, or ordinance of the District of Columbia, or of any State or political subdivision thereof in which the Institute is incorporated or doing business, impedes or otherwise interferes with the performance of the functions of the Institute pursuant to this Act, such law, rule, regulations, or ordinance shall be deemed to be preempted by this Act.

Services by the Institute to United States Citizens on Taiwan

Section 7.

(A) The Institute may authorize any of its employees on Taiwan—
    1. to administer to or take from any person an oath, affirmation, affidavit, or deposition, and to perform any notarial act which any notary public is required or authorized by law to perform within the United States;
    2. to act as provisional conservator of the personal estates of deceased United States citizens; and

3. to assist and protect the interests of United States persons by performing other acts such as are authorized to be performed outside the United States for consular purposes by such laws of the United States as the President may specify.

(B) Acts performed by authorized employees of the Institute incorporated under this section shall be valid, and of like force and effect within the United States, as if performed by any other person authorized under the laws of the United States to perform such acts.

Tax Exempt Status of the Institute

Section 8.

(A) The institute, its property, and its income are exempt from all taxation now or hereafter imposed by the United States (except to the extent that section 11(A)3 of this Act requires the imposition of taxes imposed under chapter 21 of the Internal Revenue Code of 1954, relating to the Federal Insurance Contributions Act or by any State or local taxing authority of the United States.

(B) For purposes of the Internal Revenue Code of 1954, the Institute shall be treated as an organization described in sections 170(B)(l)(a), 170(C), 2055(A), 2106(A)(2)(a), 2522(A), and 2522(B).

Furnishing Property and Services to and Obtaining Services from the Institute

Section 9.

(A) Any agency of the United States Government is authorized to sell, loan, or lease property (including interests therein) to, and to perform administrative and technical support functions and services for the operations of, the Institute upon such terms and condition as the President may direct. Reimbursements to agencies under this subsection shall be credited to the current applicable appropriation of the agency concerned.

(B) Any agency of the United States Government is authorized to acquire and accept services from the Institute upon such terms and conditions as the President may direct. Whenever the President determines it to be infurtherance of the purposes of this Act, the procurement of services by such agencies from the Institute may be effected without regard to such laws of the United States normally applicable to the acquisition of services by such agencies as the President may specify by Executive order.

(C) Any agency of the United States Government making funds available to the Institute in accordance with this Act shall make arrangements with the Institute for the Comptroller General of the United States to have access to the books and records of the Institute and the opportunity to audit the operations of the Institute.

Taiwan Instrumentality

Section 10.

(A) Whenever the President or any agency of the United States Government is authorized or required by or pursuant to the laws of the United States to render or provide to or to receive or accept from Taiwan, any performance, communication, assurance, undertaking, or other action, such action shall, in the manner and to the extent directed by the President, be rendered or provided to, or received or accepted from, an instrumentality established by Taiwan which the President determines has the necessary authority under the laws applied by the people on Taiwan to provide assurances and take other actions on behalf of Taiwan in accordance with this Act.

(B) The President is requested to extend to the instrumentality established by Taiwan the same number of offices and complement of personnel as were previously operated in the United States by the governing authorities on Taiwan recognized as the Republic of China prior to January 1, 1979.

(C) Upon the granting by Taiwan of comparable privileges and immunities with respect to the Institute and its appropriated personnel, the President is authorized to extend with respect to the Taiwan instrumentality and its appropriate personnel, such privileges and immunities (subject to appropriate conditions and obligations) as may be necessary for the effective performance of their functions.

Separation of Government Personnel for Employment with the Institute

Section 11.

(A)1. Under such terms and conditions as the President may direct, any agency of the United States Government may separate from Government service for a specified period any officer or employee of that agency who accepts employment with the Institute.

 2. An officer or employee separated by an agency under paragraph
  (1) of this subsection for employment with the Institute shall be

entitled upon termination of such employment to reemployment or reinstatement with such agency (or a successor agency) in an appropriate position with the attendant rights, privileges, and benefits with the officer or employee would have had or acquired had he or she not been so separated, subject to such time period and other conditions as the President may prescribe.

3. An officer or employee entitled to reemployment or reinstatement rights under paragraph (2) of this subsection shall, while continuously employed by the Institute with no break in continuity of service, continue to participate in any benefit program in which such officer or employee was participating prior to employment by the Institute, including programs for compensation for job related death, injury, or illness; programs for health and life insurance; programs for annual, sick, and other statutory leave; and programs for retirement under any system established by the laws of the United States; except that employment with the Institute shall be the basis for participation in such programs only to the extent that employee deductions and employer contributions, as required, in payment for such participation for the period of employment with the Institute, are currently deposited in the program's or system's fund or depository. Death or retirement of any such officer or employee during approved service with the Institute and prior to reemployment or reinstatement shall be considered a death in or retirement from Government service for purposes of any employee or survivor benefits acquired by reason of service with an agency of the United States Government.

4. Any officer or employee of an agency of the United States Government who entered into service with the Institute on approved leave of absence without pay prior to the enactment of this Act shall receive the benefits of this section for the period of such service.

(B) Any agency of the United States Government employing alien personnel on Taiwan may transfer such personnel, with accrued allowances, benefits, and rights, to the Institute without a break in service for purposes of retirement and other benefits, including continued participation in any system established by the laws of the United States for the retirement of employees in which the alien was participating prior to the transfer to the Institute, except that employment with the Institute shall be creditable for retirement purposes only to the extent that employee deductions and employer contributions, as required, in payment for such participation for the period for employment with the Institute, are currently deposited in the system's fund or depository.

(C) Employees of the Institute shall not be employees of the United States and, in representing the Institute, shall be exempt from section 207 of title 18, United States Code.

(D)1. For purposes of sections 911 and 913 of the Internal Revenue Code of 1954, amounts paid by the Institute to its employee shall not be treated as earned income. Amounts received by employees of the Institute shall not be included in gross income, and shall be exempt from taxation, to the extent that they are equivalent to amounts received by civilian officers and employees of the Government of the United States as allowances and benefits which are exempt from taxation under section 912 of such Code.

2. Except to the extent required by subsection(a)(3) of this section, service performed in the employ of the Institute shall not constitute employment for purposes of chapter 21 of such Code and title II of the Social Security Act.

Reporting Requirements

Section 12.

(A) The Secretary of State shall transmit to the Congress the text of any agreement to which the Institute is a party. However, any such agreement the immediate public disclosure of which would, in the opinion of the President, be prejudicial to the national security of the United States shall not be so transmitted to the Congress but shall be transmitted to the Committee on Foreign Relations of the Senate and the Committee on Foreign Affairs of the House of Representatives under an appropriate injunction of secrecy to be removed only upon due notice from the President.

(B) For purposes of subsection (a), the term "agreement" includes
1. any agreement entered into between the Institute and the governing authorities on Taiwan or the Instrumentality established by Taiwan; and
2. any agreement entered into between the Institute and an agency of the United States Government.

(C) Agreements and transactions made or to be made by or through the Institute shall be subject to the same congressional notification, review, and approval requirements and procedures as if such agreements and transactions were made by or through the agency of the United States Government on behalf of which the Institute is acting.

(D) During the two-year period beginning on the effective date of this Act, the Secretary of State shall transmit to the Speaker of the House of Representatives and the Committee on Foreign Relations of the Senate, every six months, a report describing and reviewing economic relations between the United States and Taiwan, noting any interference with normal commercial relations.

Rules and Regulations

Section 13.

The President is authorized to prescribe such rules and regulations as he may deem appropriate to carry out the purposes of this Act. During the three-year period beginning on the effective date of this Act, such rules and regulations shall be transmitted promptly to the Speaker of the House of Representatives and to the Committee on Foreign Relations of the Senate. Such action shall not, however, relieve the Institute of the responsibilities placed upon it by this Act.

Congressional Oversight

Section 14.

(A) The Committee on Foreign Affairs of the House of Representatives, the Committee on Foreign Relations of the Senate, and other appropriate committees of the Congress shall monitor—
1. the implementation of the provisions of this Act;
2. the operation and procedures of the Institute;
3. the legal and technical aspects of the continuing relationship between the United States and Taiwan; and
4. the implementation of the policies of the United States concerning security and cooperation in East Asia.

(B) Such committees shall report, as appropriate, to their respective House on the results of their monitoring.

Definitions

Section 15.

For purposes of this Act—
(1) the term "laws of the United States" includes any statute, rule, regulation, ordinance, order, or judicial rule of decision of the United States or any political subdivision thereof; and

(2) the term "Taiwan" includes, as the context may require, the islands of Taiwan and the Pescadores, the people on those islands, corporations and other entities and associations created or organized under the laws applied on those islands, and the governing authorities on Taiwan recognized by the United States as the Republic of China prior to January 1, 1979, and any successor governing authorities (including political subdivisions, agencies, and instrumentalities thereof).

Authorization of Appropriations

Section 16.

In addition to funds otherwise available to carry out the provisions of this Act, there are authorized to be appropriated to the Secretary of State for the fiscal year 1980 such funds as may be necessary to carry out such provisions. Such funds are authorized to remain available until expended.

Severability of Provisions

Section 17.

If any provision of this Act or the application thereof to any person or circumstance is held invalid, the remainder of the Act and the application of such provision to any other person or circumstance shall not be affected thereby.

Effective Date

Section 18.

This Act shall be effective as of January 1, 1979.

Legislative History

HOUSE REPORTS: No. 96–26 (Comm. on Foreign Affairs) and No. 96–71 (Comm. of Conference)
SENATE REPORT: No.96–7 (Comm. on Foreign Relations).
CONGRESSIONAL RECORD, Vol. 125 (1979):
Mar. 8, 13, considered and passed House.
Mar. 7, 8, 12, 13, s. 245 considered and passed Senate.

Mar. 14, proceedings vitiated; H.R. 2479, amended, passed in lieu.

Mar. 28, House agreed to conference report.

Mar. 29, Senate agreed to conference report.

WEEKLY COMPILATION OF PRESIDENTIAL DOCUMENTS, Vol. 15, No. 15:

Apr. 10, Presidential statement.

APPENDIX B

Text of the Joint Communiqué Issued by The United States of America and The People's Republic of China

February 27, 1972 in Shanghai

President Richard Nixon of the United States of America, visited the People's Republic of China at the invitation of Premier Chou En-lai of the People's Republic of China from February 21 to February 28, 1972. Accompanying the President were Mrs. Nixon, U.S. Secretary of State William Rogers, Assistant to the President Dr. Henry Kissinger, and other American officials.

President Nixon met with Chairman Mao Tse-tung of the Communist Party of China on February 21. The two leaders had a serious and frank exchange of views on Sino-U.S. relations and world affairs.

During the visit, extensive, earnest and frank discussions were held between President Nixon and Premier Chou En-lai on the normalization of relations between the United States of America and the People's Republic of China, as well as on other matters of interest to both sides. In addition, Secretary of State William Rogers and Foreign Minister Chi Peng-fei held talks in the same spirit.

President Nixon and his party visited Peking and viewed cultural, industrial and agricultural sites, and they also toured Hang-chow and Shanghai where, continuing discussions with Chinese leaders, they viewed similar places of interest.

The leaders of the People's Republic of China and the United States of America found it beneficial to have this opportunity, after so many years without contact, to present candidly to one another their views on a variety of issues. They reviewed the international situation in which important changes and great upheavals are taking place and expounded their respective positions and attitudes.

The U.S. side stated: Peace in Asia and peace in the world requires efforts both to reduce immediate tensions and to eliminate the basic causes of conflict. The United States will work for a just and secure peace: just, because it fulfills the aspirations of peoples and nations for freedom and progress; secure, because it removes the danger of foreign aggression.

The United States supports individual freedom and social progress for all the peoples of the world, free of outside pressure or intervention.

The United States believes that the effort to reduce tensions is served by improving communication between countries that have different ideologies so as to lessen the risks of confrontation through accident, miscalculation or misunderstanding.

Countries should treat each other with mutual respect and be willing to compete peacefully, letting performance be the ultimate judge. No country should claim infallibility and each country should be prepared to re-examine its own attitudes for the common good.

The United States stressed that the peoples of Indochina should be allowed to determine their destiny without outside intervention; its constant primary objective has been a negotiated solution; the eight point proposal put forward by the Republic of Vietnam and the United States on January 27, 1972, represents a basis for the attainment of that objective; in the absence of a negotiated settlement the United States envisages the ultimate withdrawal of all U.S. forces from the region consistent with the aim of self-determination for each country of Indochina.

The United States will maintain its close ties with and support for the Republic of Korea; the United States will support efforts of the Republic of Korea to seek a relaxation of tension and increased communication in the Korean peninsula.

The United States places the highest value on its friendly relations with Japan; it will continue to develop the existing close bonds.

Consistent with the United Nations Security Council resolution of December 21, 1971, the United States favors the continuation of the ceasefire between India and Pakistan and the withdrawal of all military forces to within their own territories and to their own sides of the ceasefire line in Jammu and Kashmir; the United States supports the right of the people of South Asia to share their own future in peace, free of military threat, and without having the area become the subject of great power rivalry.

The Chinese side stated: Wherever there is oppression, there is resistance. Countries want independence, nations want liberation and the people want revolution—this has become the irresistible trend of history. All nations, big or small, should be equal; big nations should not bully the small and strong nations should not bully the weak.

China will never be a superpower and it opposes hegemony and power politics of any kind. The Chinese side stated that it firmly supports the struggles of all the oppressed people and nations for freedom and liberation and that the people of all countries have the right to choose their social systems according to their own wishes and the right to safeguard the independence, sovereignty and territorial integrity of their own countries and oppose foreign aggression, interference, control and subversion. All foreign troops should be withdrawn to their own countries.

The Chinese side expressed its firm support to the peoples of Vietnam, Laos and Cambodia in their efforts for the attainment of their goal and its firm support to the seven point proposal of the provisional revolutionary government of the Republic of South Vietnam and the elaboration of February this year on the two key problems in the proposal, and to the joint declaration of the summit conference of the Indo-Chinese peoples.

It firmly supports the eight-point program for the peaceful unification of Korea put forward by the Government of the Democratic People's Republic of Korea on April 12, 1971, and the stand for the abolition of the "U.N. Commission for the Unification and Rehabilitation of Korea."

It firmly opposes the revival and outward expansion of Japanese militarism and firmly supports the Japanese people's desire to build an independent, democratic, peaceful and neutral Japan.

It firmly maintains that India and Pakistan should, in accordance with the United Nations resolutions on the India-Pakistan question, immediately withdraw all their forces to their respective territories and to their own sides of the ceasefire line in Jammu and Kashmir and firmly supports the Pakistan government and people in their struggle to preserve their independence and sovereignty and the people of Jammu and Kashmir in their struggle for the right of self-determination.

There are essential differences between China and the United States in their social systems and foreign policies. However, the two sides agreed that countries, regardless of their social systems, should conduct their relations on the principles of respect for the sovereignty and territorial integrity of all states, non-aggression against other states, non-interference in the internal affairs of other states, equality and mutual benefit, and peaceful coexistence. International disputes should be settled on this basis, without resorting to the use of threat of force. The United States and the People's Republic of China are prepared to apply these principles to their mutual relations.

With these principles of international relations in mind the two sides stated that:

—Progress toward the normalization of relations between China and the

United States is in the interests of all countries; both wish to reduce the danger of international military conflict;

—Neither should seek hegemony in the Asia-Pacific region and each is opposed to efforts by any other country or group of countries to establish such hegemony; and

—Neither is prepared to negotiate on behalf of any third party or to enter into agreements or understandings with the other directed at other states.

Both sides are of the view that it would be against the interests of the peoples of the world for any major country to collude with another against other countries, or for major countries to divide up the world into spheres of interest.

The two sides reviewed the long-standing serious disputes between China and the United States. The Chinese side reaffirmed its position: the Taiwan question is the crucial question, obstructing the normalization of relations between China and the United States, the Government of the People's Republic of China is the sole legal government of China; Taiwan is a province of China which has long been returned to the motherland; the liberation of Taiwan is China's internal affair in which no other country has the right to interfere; and all U.S. forces and military installations must be withdrawn from Taiwan. The Chinese government firmly opposes any activities which aim at the creation of "one China, one Taiwan," "one China, two governments," "two Chinas," and "independent Taiwan" or advocate that "the status of Taiwan remains to be determined."

The U.S. side declared: The United States acknowledges that all Chinese on either side of the Taiwan Strait maintain there is but one China and that Taiwan is a part of China. The United States Government does not challenge that position. It reaffirms its interest in a peaceful settlement of the Taiwan question by the Chinese themselves. With this prospect in mind, it affirms the ultimate objective of the withdrawal of all U.S. forces and military installations from Taiwan. In the meantime, it will progressively reduce its forces and military installations on Taiwan as the tension in the area diminishes.

The two sides agreed that it is desirable to broaden the understanding between the two peoples. To this end, they discussed specific areas in such fields as science, technology, culture, sports and journalism, in which people-to-people contacts and exchanges would be mutually beneficial. Each side undertakes to facilitate the further development of such contacts and exchanges.

Both sides view bilateral trade as another area from which mutual benefit can be derived, and agreed that economic relations based on equality and mutual benefit are in the interest of the peoples of the two countries. They agree to facilitate the progressive development of trade between their two countries.

The two sides agreed that they will stay in contact through various channels, including the sending of a senior U.S. representative to Peking from time to time for concrete consultations to further the normalization of relations between the two countries and continue to exchange views on issues of common interest.

The two sides expressed the hope that the gains achieved during this visit would open up new prospects for the relations between the two countries. They believe that the normalization of relations between the two countries is not only in the interest of the Chinese and American peoples but also contributes to the relaxation of tension in Asia and the world.

President Nixon, Mrs. Nixon and the American party expressed their appreciation for the gracious hospitality shown them by the government and people of the People's Republic of China.

APPENDIX C

Joint Communiqué on the Establishment of Diplomatic Relations Between the United States of America and the People's Republic of China

January 1, 1979

The United States of America and the People's Republic of China have agreed to recognize each other and to establish diplomatic relations as of January 1, 1979.

The United States of America recognizes the government of the People's Republic of China as the sole legal government of China. Within this context, the people of the United States will maintain cultural, commercial, and other unofficial relations with the people of Taiwan.

The United States of America and the People's Republic of China reaffirm the principles agreed on by the two sides in the Shanghai Communiqué and emphasize once again that:

—Both wish to reduce the danger of international military conflict.

—Neither should seek hegemony in the Asia-Pacific region or in any other region of the world and each is opposed to efforts by any other country or group of countries to establish such hegemony.

—Neither is prepared to negotiate on behalf of any third party or to enter into agreements or understandings with the other directed at other states.

—The government of the United States of America acknowledges the Chinese position that there is but one China and Taiwan is part of China.

—Both believe that normalization of Sino-American relations is not only in the interest of the Chinese and American peoples but also contributes to the cause of peace in Asia and the world.

The United States of America and the People's Republic of China will exchange ambassadors and establish embassies on March 1, 1979.

APPENDIX D

Text of Joint Communiqué

August 17, 1982

1. In the Joint Communiqué on the establishment of diplomatic relations on January 1, 1979, issued by the government of the United States of America and the government of the People's Republic of China, the United States of America recognized the government of the People's Republic of China as the sole legal government of China, and it acknowledged the Chinese position that there is but one China and Taiwan is part of China. Within that context, the two sides agreed that the people of the United States would continue to maintain cultural, commercial and other unofficial relations with the people of Taiwan. On this basis, relations between the United States and China were normalized.

2. The question of United States arms sales to Taiwan was not settled in the course of negotiations between the two countries on establishing diplomatic relations. The "two sides held differing positions, and the Chinese side stated that it would raise the issue again following normalization. Recognizing that this issue would seriously hamper the development of United States–China relations, they have held further discussions on it, during and since the meetings between President Ronald Reagan and Premier Chao Tsi-yang and between Secretary of State Alexander M. Haig, Jr. and Vice Premier and Foreign Minister Huang Hua in October 1981.

3. Respect for each other's sovereignty and territorial integrity and non-interference in each other's internal affairs constitutes the fundamental principles guiding United States–China relations. These principles were confirmed in the Shanghai Communiqué of February 28, 1972, and reaffirmed in the Joint Communiqué on the establishment of diplomatic relations which came into effect on January 1, 1979. Both sides emphatically state that these principles continue to govern all aspects of their relations.

4. The Chinese government reiterates that the question of Taiwan is China's internal affair. The message of compatriots in Taiwan issued by China on

January 1, 1979, promulgated a fundamental policy of striving for peaceful reunification of the motherland. The nine-point proposal put forward by China on September 30, 1981, represented a further major effort under this fundamental policy to strive for a peaceful solution of the Taiwan question.

5. The United States government attaches great importance to its relations with China, and reiterates that it has no intention of infringing on Chinese sovereignty and territorial integrity, or interfering in China's internal affairs, or pursuing a policy of "two Chinas" or "one China, one Taiwan." The United States understands and appreciates the Chinese policy of striving for a peaceful resolution of the Taiwan question as indicated in China's message to compatriots in Taiwan issued on January 1, 1979, and the nine-point proposal put forward by China on September 30, 1981. The new situation which has emerged with regard to the Taiwan question also provides favorable conditions for the settlement of United States–China differences over the question of United States arms sales to Taiwan.

6. Having in mind the foregoing statements of both sides, the United States government states that it does not seek to carry out a long-term policy of arms sales to Taiwan, that its arms sales to Taiwan will not exceed, either in qualitative or quantitative terms, the level of those supplied in recent years since the establishment of diplomatic relations between the United States and China, and that it intends to reduce gradually its sales of arms to Taiwan, leading over a period of time to a final resolution. In so stating, the United States acknowledges China's consistent position regarding the thorough settlement of this issue.

7. In order to bring about, over a period of time, a final settlement of the question of United States arms sales to Taiwan, which is an issue rooted in history, the two governments will make every effort to adopt measures and create conditions conducive to the thorough settlement of this issue.

8. The development of United States–China relations is not only in the interests of the two peoples but also conducive to peace and stability in the world. The two sides are determined, on the principle of equality and mutual benefit, to strengthen their ties in the economic, cultural, educational, scientific, technological and other fields and make strong, joint efforts for the continued development of relations between the governments and the peoples of the United States and China.

9. In order to bring about the healthy development of United States–China relations, maintain world peace and oppose aggression and expansion, the two governments reaffirm the principles agreed on by the two sides in the Shanghai Communiqué and the Communiqué on the establishment of diplomatic relations. The two sides will maintain contact and hold appropriate consultations on bilateral and international issues of common interest.

Contributors

Muthiah Alagappa is Senior Fellow and Director, East-West Center, Washington. He received a Ph.D. in international affairs from the Fletcher School of Law and Diplomacy at Tufts University. His research interests include international relations theory, international politics in the Asia-Pacific region, and comparative politics in Asia.

Yoshihisa Amae is a Ph.D. candidate in the Department of Political Science, University of Hawai'i at Manoa, and also a Degree Fellow at the East-West Center. He received an M.A. in Political Science from the University of Hawai'i at Manoa in 1998. His areas of research interest include U.S./China/Taiwan relations and regional security in Northeast Asia.

Tain-Jy Chen is professor of economics at National Taiwan University. He received a Ph.D. in economics from Pennsylvania State University. His research interests include international trade and international investment.

C.Y. Cyrus Chu is Distinguished Research Fellow and vice-president, Academia Sinica, Taipei. He received a Ph.D. in economics from the University of Michigan (Ann Arbor). His research interests include public economics, law, and economics.

Yun-han Chu is professor of political science at National Taiwan University and serves concurrently as vice-president of the Chiang Ching-kuo Foundation for International Scholarly Exchange. He received a Ph.D. in political science from the University of Minnesota. His research interests include the politics of Greater China, East Asian political economy, and democratization.

Chua Beng Huat is professor of sociology at the National University of Singapore. He received a Ph.D. in sociology from York University in Toronto, Canada. His major fields of research include comparative politics in Southeast Asia, urban and housing policies, and emerging consumer cultures in Asia.

Larry Diamond is Senior Fellow at the Hoover Institution, Stanford, and coeditor of the *Journal of Democracy*. He received a Ph.D. in sociology from Stanford University. His research interests include democratic consolidation in Taiwan, comparative global trends in democratic development, and public opinion in new democracies.

Bruce J. Dickson is associate professor of political science and international affairs and director of the Sigur Center for Asian Studies at George Washington University. He received a Ph.D. in political science from the University of Michigan. His research interests include political change in China and Taiwan.

Qingguo Jia is professor and associate dean of the School of International Studies of Peking University. He received a Ph.D. in government from Cornell University. His research interests include U.S.–China relations, relations between the Chinese mainland and Taiwan, and Chinese foreign policy as well as Chinese politics.

Alan M. Wachman is assistant professor of international politics at the Fletcher School of Law and Diplomacy at Tufts University. He received a Ph.D. in government from Harvard University. His research interests include Chinese foreign policy, cross-strait relations, and U.S. interaction with East Asia.

Yu-Shan Wu is a professor in the Department of Political Science at National Taiwan University. He received a Ph.D. in political science from the University of California (Berkeley). His research interests include the political and economic transitions of formerly socialist countries (PRC, Russia, Eastern Europe), Taiwan politics, and cross-strait relations.

Index